AN APOLOGY FOR POETRY

୧୨୧୨୧୨୧୨

D0494706

MANCHESTER
1824
Manchester University Press

AN APOLOGY FOR POETRY

or THE DEFENCE OF POESY

Sir Philip Sidney

ↄ℘ↄ℘ↄ℘ↄ℘

edited by GEOFFREY SHEPHERD

*revised & expanded for this
third edition by* R. W. MASLEN

Manchester University Press

MANCHESTER AND NEW YORK

distributed exclusively in the USA by Palgrave

First and second edition © Geoffrey Shepherd 1965, 1973
Revised material for third edition © R. W. Maslen 2002

The right of R. W. Maslen to be identified as the author
of the introduction and notes has been asserted by him
in accordance with the Copyright, Designs and Patents Act 1988.

First edition published 1965 by
Thomas Nelson & Sons Ltd

Second edition published 1973
by Manchester University Press
Reprinted 1977, 1979, 1984, 1989

Third edition published by Manchester University Press
Oxford Road, Manchester M13 9NR, UK
and Room 400, 175 Fifth Avenue, New York, NY 10010, USA
www.manchesteruniversitypress.co.uk

Distributed exclusively in the USA by
Palgrave, 175 Fifth Avenue, New York, NY 10010, USA

Distributed exclusively in Canada by
UBC Press, University of British Columbia, 2029 West Mall,
Vancouver, BC, Canada V6T 1Z2

British Library Cataloguing-in-Publication Data
A catalogue record for this book is available from the British Library
Library of Congress Cataloging-in-Publication Data applied for

ISBN 0 7190 5375 7 *hardback*
ISBN 0 7190 5376 5 *paperback*

Third edition first published 2002

14 13 12 11 10 09 08 07 06   10 9 8 7 6 5 4 3 2

Designed in Abode Garamond fonts by Max Nettleton FCSD
Typeset by SNP Best-set Typesetter Ltd., Hong Kong
Printed in Great Britain
by Bell & Bain Ltd, Glasgow

CONTENTS

ɔɛɔɛɔɛɔɛɔ

ACKNOWLEDGMENTS

e/ɔe/ɔe/ɔe/ɔe/ɔ

My first thanks should go to previous editors of Sidney's *Apology*, especially Jan van Dorsten and Katherine Duncan-Jones, from whose notes I have learned much more than I could put into practice here. My thanks to Professor Gerald Hammond of the University of Manchester, for mentioning my name to Manchester University Press in connection with this project; and to my colleagues in the department of English Literature at the University of Glasgow, especially Professor Willy Maley and Dr Donald Mackenzie, two of the best and most generous scholars a student of the Renaissance could have the good fortune to work with. My greatest debts of gratitude are these: to my colleague Robert Cummings, whose help, constant encouragement, and encyclopaedic knowledge have made a difficult task a little easier and a great deal more pleasant, and whose hand will be found in all the best new notes to this edition; and to my wife Kirsty, who has worked with me on every sentence.

e/ɔ

Geoffrey Shepherd dedicated his edition of the *Apology* to the memory of C. S. Lewis. I would like to dedicate this second version of that edition to the memory of John Fowler, teacher and friend; and to Kirsty and Bethany, with love.

ABBREVIATIONS

ᴄ⁊ᴄ⁊ᴄ⁊ᴄ⁊ᴄ⁊ᴄ⁊

Throughout the Introduction and Notes, books listed in the Bibliography are referred to by the name of the author or editor and the date of publication. For example: Duncan-Jones 1991, 73, refers to Katherine Duncan-Jones, *Sir Philip Sidney: Courtier Poet*, p. 73. Exceptions are listed below.

Ad Her.	*Rhetorica ad Herennium*, ed. Caplan (Loeb Library)
CP	*Classical Philology*
EETS	Early English Text Society Publications
ELH	*Journal of English Literary History*
HLB	*Huntington Library Bulletin*
HLQ	*Huntington Library Quarterly*
JEGP	*Journal of English and Germanic Philology*
JHI	*Journal of the History of Ideas*
JWCI	*Journal of the Warburg and Courtauld Institutes*
Misc. Prose	*Miscellaneous Prose of Sir Philip Sidney*, ed. Katherine Duncan-Jones and Jan van Dorsten
MLN	*Modern Language Notes*
MLQ	*Modern Language Quarterly*
MLR	*Modern Language Review*
MPh	*Modern Philology*
NA	*The Countess of Pembroke's Arcadia (The New Arcadia)*, ed. Victor Skretkowicz
NQ	*Notes and Queries*
OA	*The Old Arcadia*, ed. Katherine Duncan-Jones
OED	Oxford English Dictionary
Olney	Olney's text of the *Apology*
PL	*Patrologia Latina*, ed. Migne (quoted by volume and column)
PMLA	*Publications of the Modern Language Association of America*
Ponsonby	Ponsonby's text of the *Apology*
PQ	*Philological Quarterly*

RES   *Review of English Studies*
SEL   *Studies in English Literature*
SP   *Studies in Philology*
Tilley   M. P. Tilley, *A Dictionary of the Proverbs of England in the 16th and 17th Centuries*

SELECT BIBLIOGRAPHY

୧୨୧୨୧୨୧୨୧୨

Only texts directly relevant to the study of the *Apology* or of general importance for its understanding are listed here. To save space I have not listed articles. The essay collections contain some of the most important of these, others can be found in the notes and bibliographies of books, and several are mentioned in the Notes and Introduction to this edition. There are many modern texts of the *Apology*; I have listed only a few of them.

All Shakespeare citations are taken from the Oxford edition, edited by Gary Taylor and Stanley Wells, listed below under 'Other Primary Texts'. References to classical texts are to the Loeb editions, except where stated. The Loeb translations have in most cases been modified to make the sense clearer.

Editions of Sidney's works

Cook, Albert S. (ed.) *The Defense of Poesy, otherwise known as An Apology for Poetry* (Boston, 1890)

Duncan-Jones, Katherine (ed.) *The Defence of Poesy*, in *Sir Philip Sidney*, Oxford Authors (Oxford, 1989), pp. 212–50

———. *The Old Arcadia*, The World's Classics (Oxford, 1973)

Duncan-Jones, Katherine, and Jan van Dorsten (ed.) *Miscellaneous Prose of Sir Philip Sidney* (Oxford, 1973)

Evans, Maurice (ed.) *The Countess of Pembroke's Arcadia (The New Arcadia)* (Harmondsworth, 1977)

Feuillerat, Albert (ed.) *The Complete Works of Sir Philip Sidney* (4 vols, Cambridge 1912–26; rev. 1962)

Pears, S. A. (ed.) *The Correspondence of Sir Philip Sidney and Hubert Languet* (London, 1845)

Ringler, William (ed.) *The Poems of Sir Philip Sidney* (Oxford, 1962)

Robertson, Jean (ed.) *The Countess of Pembroke's Arcadia (The Old Arcadia)* (Oxford, 1973)

Robinson, Forrest G. (ed.) *An Apology for Poetry* (Indianapolis, 1977)

Shepherd, Geoffrey (ed.) *An Apology for Poetry or The Defence of Poesy* (London, 1965)

Shuckburgh, E. S. (ed.) *The Defence of Poesie* (Cambridge, 1891)

Skretkowicz, Victor (ed.) *The Countess of Pembroke's Arcadia (The New Arcadia)* (Oxford, 1987)

Smith, G. Gregory (ed.) *An Apology for Poetrie*, in *Elizabethan Critical Essays* (2 vols, Oxford, 1904), vol. 1, pp. 148–207

Watson, Elizabeth Porges (ed.) *Defence of Poesie, Astrophil and Stella and Other Writings*, Everyman's Library (London and Rutland, Vermont, 1997)

A Woorke Concerning the Trewnesse of the Christian Religion, by Philip of Mornay, Lord of Plessie Marlie, Begunne to be Translated into English by Sir Philip Sidney and finished by Arthur Golding (London, 1587)

Other primary texts

Agrippa, Henry Cornelius. *Of the Vanitie and Uncertaintie of Artes and Sciences*, trans. J[ames] S[anford] (London, 1569)

Ascham, Roger. *The English Works of Roger Ascham*, ed. W. A. Wright (Cambridge, 1904)

Augustine, St *Of the Citie of God*, trans. John Healey (London, 1610)

Bacon, Francis. *The Advancement of Learning and New Atlantis* (1605 and 1627), ed. Arthur Johnston (Oxford, 1974)

Boccaccio, Giovanni. *Boccaccio on Poetry, being the Preface and the Fourteenth and Fifteenth Books of Boccaccio's Genealogia Deorum Gentilium*, ed. and trans. Charles G. Osgood (Princeton, 1930)

Calvin, John. *Institutes of the Christian Religion*, ed. John T. McNeill, trans. Ford Lewis Battles (2 vols, London 1961)

Castelvetro, Lodovico. *Poetica d'Aristotele vulgarizzata et sposta* (Basel, 1576)

Castiglione, Baldassare. *The Book of the Courtier* (1561), trans. Thomas Hoby, Everyman's Library (London, 1928)

Chapman, George. *The Poems of George Chapman*, ed. P. B. Bartlett (New York and London, 1941)

Daniello, Bernardino. *La poetica* (Venice, 1536)

Elyot, Sir Thomas. *The Boke Named The Governour* (1531), ed. H. H. S. Croft (2 vols, London, 1883)

Erasmus, Desiderius. *Collected Works* 24, *Literary and Educational Writings 2: De copia and De ratione studii*, ed. Craig R. Thompson (Toronto, Buffalo and London, 1978)

——. *The Praise of Folie* (1549), trans. Sir Thomas Chaloner, ed. Clarence H. Miller, EETS (London, 1965)

Fracastorius, G. *Naugerius*, trans. Ruth Kelso, introduction by M. W. Bundy, University of Illinois Studies in Language and Literature, IX, 3 (Urbana, Ill., 1924)

Fraunce, Abraham. *The Arcadian Rhetorike* (1588), ed. Edith Seaton, Luttrell Society Reprints, IX (Oxford, 1950)

Gascoigne, George. *Complete Works*, ed. J. W. Cunliffe (2 vols, Cambridge, 1907–10)

Gilbert, Allan H. (ed.). *Literary Criticism: Plato to Dryden* (New York, 1940)

Gosson, Stephen. *Markets of Bawdrie: The Dramatic Criticism of Stephen Gosson*, ed. Arthur F. Kinney (Salzburg, 1974)

Greville, Fulke. *Poems and Dramas*, ed. G. Bullough (2 vols, London, 1938)

——. *The Prose Works of Fulke Greville, Lord Brooke*, ed. John Gouws (Oxford, 1986)

Hall, John. *The Court of Virtue* (1565), ed. Russell A. Fraser (London, 1961)

Harvey, Gabriel. *Ciceronianus* (1577), ed. Harold S. Wilson and Clarence A. Forbes, University of Nebraska Studies in the Humanities, IV (Lincoln, Neb., 1945)

——. *Gabriel Harvey's Marginalia*, ed. G. C. Moore-Smith (Stratford-upon-Avon, 1913)

Hoskins, Sir John. *Directions for Speech and Style* (c. 1599), ed. H. H. Hudson (Princeton, 1935)

Jonson, Ben. *The Complete Poems*, ed. George Parfitt (Harmondsworth, 1975, rev. 1988)

Lyly, John. *Euphues: The Anatomy of Wit; Euphues and his England* (1578 and 1580), ed. M. W. Croll and H. Clemons (London and New York, 1916)

Meres, Francis. *Poetrie*, ed. Don Cameron Allen, University of Illinois Studies in Language and Literature, XVI, 3–4 (Urbana, Ill., 1933)

Minturno, Antonio. *De poeta libri sex* (Venice, 1559)

——. *L'arte poetica* (Naples, 1725)

The Mirror for Magistrates, ed. Lily B. Campbell (Cambridge, 1938)

Moffet, Thomas. *Nobilis, or A View of the Life and Death of a Sidney*, ed. V. B. Heltzel and H. H. Hudson (San Marino, Cal., 1940)

More, Thomas. *Utopia* (1551), introduction by Richard Marius, trans. Ralph Robinson, Everyman's Library (London, 1985)

Mulcaster, Richard. *The First Part of the Elementarie* (1582), ed. E. T. Campagnac (Oxford, 1925)

North, Thomas. *Plutarch's Lives of the Noble Grecians and Romans* (1579), introd. George Wyndham, The Tudor Translations, VII (5 vols, London, 1895).

Puttenham, George. *The Arte of English Poesie* (1589), ed. Gladys Willcock and Alice Walker (Cambridge, 1936)

Rainolde, Richard. *A Booke Called the Foundacion of Rhetorike* (London, 1563)

Rainolds, John. *Oratio in laudem artis poeticae* (1572), ed. William Ringler, trans. W. Allen, Princeton Studies in English, XX (Princeton, 1940)

Robortello, Francisco. *In librum Aristotelis de arte poetica explicationes* (Florence, 1548)

Salutati, Coluccio. *De laboribus Herculis*, ed. B. L. Ullman (2 vols, Turin, 1951)

Scaliger, Julius Caesar. *Poetices libri septem* (Heidelberg, 1617)

Shakespeare, William. *The Complete Works*, ed. Stanley Wells and Gary Taylor (Oxford, 1986)

Smith, G. Gregory (ed.). *Elizabethan Critical Essays* (2 vols, Oxford, 1904)

Spenser, Edmund. *The Faerie Queene*, ed. A. C. Hamilton (London and New York, 1977, rev. 1980)

——. *The Yale Edition of the Shorter Poems of Edmund Spenser*, ed. William A. Oram *et al.* (New Haven and London, 1989)

Temple, William. *William Temple's Analysis of Sir Philip Sidney's Apology for Poetry: An Edition and Translation*, ed. John Webster (Binghamton, N.Y. 1984)

Vickers, Brian (ed.). *English Renaissance Literary Criticism* (Oxford, 1999)

Vives, Luis. *De tradendis disciplinis* (1531), trans. Foster Watson, *Vives on Education* (Cambridge, 1931)
Wills, Richard. *De re poetica*, ed. A. D. S. Fowler, Luttrell Society Reprints, XVII (Oxford, 1958)
Wilson, Sir Thomas. *The Arte of Rhetorique* (1560), ed. G. H. Mair (Oxford, 1909)

Secondary texts

Abbott, Edwin A. *A Shakespearian Grammar* (London, 1870)
Atkins, J. W. H. *English Literary Criticism: The Renascence* (London, 1940)
Attridge, Derek. *Well-weighed Syllables: Elizabethan Verse in Classical Metres* (London, 1974)
Axton, Marie (ed.). *Three Tudor Interludes* (Cambridge, 1982)
Baldwin, Charles S. *Renaissance Literary Theory and Practice* (New York, 1939)
Baldwin, T. W. *William Shakspere's Small Latine and lesse Greeke* (2 vols, Urbana, Ill., 1944)
Barish, Jonas. *The Antitheatrical Prejudice* (Berkeley, Los Angeles and London, 1981)
Blunt, Sir Anthony. *Artsitic Theory in Italy 1450–1600* (Oxford, 1940)
Bolgar, R. R. *The Classical Heritage and its Beneficiaries* (Cambridge, 1954)
Bronowski, Jacob. *The Poet's Defence* (Cambridge, 1939)
Bundy, Murray W. *The Theory of the Imagination in Classical and Medieval Thought*, University of Illinois Studies in Language and Literature, XII, 2–3 (Urbana, Ill., 1927)
Bush, Douglas. *The Renaissance and English Humanism* (Toronto, 1939)
Buxton, John. *Elizabethan Taste* (London, 1963)
——. *Sir Philip Sidney and the English Renaissance*, rev. ed. (London, 1964)
Campbell, Lily B. *Divine Poetry and Drama in Sixteenth Century England* (Cambridge and Berkeley, 1959)
Cassirer, Ernst. *The Individual and the Cosmos in Renaissance Philosophy* (Oxford, 1965)
Charlton, H. B. *Castelvetro's Theory of Poetry* (Manchester, 1913)
Clark, D. L. *Rhetoric and Poetry in the Renaissance* (New York, 1922)
Clements, Robert J. *Critical Theory and Practice of the Pléiade* (Cambridge, Mass., 1942)
Crane, W. G. *Wit and Rhetoric in the Renaissance* (New York, 1937)
Croft-Murray, Edward. *Decorative Painting in England 1537–1837* (2 vols, London 1962–70)
Curtius, E. R. *European Literature and the Latin Middle Ages*, trans. W. R. Trask (London, 1953)
Doherty, M. J. *The Mistress-Knowledge: Sir Philip Sidney's Defence of Poesie and Literary Architectonics in the English Renaissance* (Nashville, Tenn., 1991)
Doran, Madeleine. *Endeavors of Art* (Madison, Wis., 1954)
Duncan-Jones, Katherine. *Sir Philip Sidney: Courtier Poet* (London, 1991)
Ferguson, Margaret W. *Trials of Desire: Renaissance Defences of Poetry* (New Haven and London, 1983)

Fraser, Russell. *The War Against Poetry* (Princeton, 1970)

Gent, Lucy. *Picture and Poetry 1560–1620* (Leamington Spa, 1981)

Gombrich, E. H. *Art and Illusion* (London, 1960)

Greenblatt, Stephen. *Renaissance Self-fashioning from More to Shakespeare* (Chicago and London, 1980)

Greene, Thomas M. *The Light in Troy: Imitation and Discovery in Renaissance Poetry* (New Haven and London, 1982)

Hadfield, Andrew. *Literature, Politics and National Identity* (Cambridge, 1994)

Hall, Vernon. *Renaissance Literary Criticism: A Study of its Social Content* (New York, 1945)

Hamilton, A. C. *Sir Philip Sidney: A Study of his Life and Works* (Cambridge, 1977)

Hathaway, Baxter. *The Age of Criticism: The Late Renaissance in Italy* (New York, 1962)

Haydn, Hiram C. *The Counter-Reformation* (New York, 1950)

Helgerson, Richard. *The Elizabethan Prodigals* (Berkeley, Los Angeles and London, 1976)

——. *Forms of Nationhood: The Elizabethan Writing of England* (Chicago and London, 1992)

Heninger, S. K. *Sidney and Spenser: The Poet as Maker* (University Park and London, 1989)

Herman, Peter C. *Squitter-wits and Muse-haters: Sidney, Spenser, Milton and Renaissance Antipoetic Sentiment* (Detroit, 1996)

Herrick, Marvin T. *The Fusion of Horatian and Aristotelian Criticism, 1531–1555* (Urbana, Ill., 1946)

Hill, Christopher. *Society and Puritanism in Pre-revolutionary England* (London, 1964)

Howell, Wilbur S. *Logic and Rhetoric in England, 1500–1700* (Princeton, 1956)

Jones, Richard Foster. *The Triumph of the English Language* (Stanford, Cal., 1953)

Kalstone, David. *Sidney's Poetry: Contexts and Interpretations* (Cambridge, Mass., 1965)

Kay, Dennis (ed.). *Sir Philip Sidney: An Anthology of Modern Criticism* (Oxford, 1987)

Kendrick, T. D. *British Antiquity* (London, 1950)

Kinney, Arthur F. (ed.). *Essential Articles for the Study of Sir Philip Sidney* (Hamden, Conn., 1986)

—— (ed.). *Sidney in Retrospect* (Amherst, Mass., 1988)

Kraye, Jill (ed.). *The Cambridge Companion to Renaissance Humanism* (Cambridge, 1996)

Kristeller, Oskar P. *Renaissance Thought: The Classical, Scholastic and Humanistic Strains* (New York, 1961)

Lanham, R. A. *A Handlist of Rhetorical Terms: A Guide for Students of English Literature* (Berkeley, Los Angeles and London, 1968)

Lea, Kathleen M. *Italian Popular Comedy: A Study in the Commedia dell'arte, 1560–1620, with Special Reference to the English Stage* (2 vols, Oxford, 1934)

Levao, Ronald. *Renaissance Minds and their Fictions* (Berkeley and Los Angeles, 1985)

Lewalski, Barbara K. (ed.). *Renaissance Genres: Essays on Theory, History, and Interpretation* (Cambridge, Mass., and London, 1986)

Maslen, R. W. *Elizabethan Fictions: Espionage, Counter-espionage and the Duplicity of Fiction in Early Elizabethan Prose Narratives* (Oxford, 1997)

Matz, Robert. *Defending Literature in Early Modern England: Renaissance Literary Theory in Social Context* (Cambridge, 2000)

Myrick, Kenneth O. *Sir Philip Sidney as a Literary Craftsman* (1935; rev. Lincoln, Neb., 1965)

Norbrook, David. *Poetry and Politics in the English Renaissance* (London, 1984)

Ong, Walter J. *Ramus, Method and the Decay of Dialogue* (Cambridge, Mass., 1958)

Panofsky, E. *Idea: A Concept in Art Theory*, trans. Joseph J. S. Peake (New York and London, 1968)

Patterson, Annabel. *Censorship and Interpretation: The Conditions of Writing and Reading in Early Modern England* (Madison, Wis., 1984)

Pilger, A. *Barockthemen* (2 vols, Budapest and Berlin, 1956)

Rice, Eugene F. *The Renaissance Idea of Wisdom* (Cambridge, Mass., 1958)

Robinson, Forrest G. *The Shape of Things Known: Sidney's Apology in its Philosophical Tradition* (Cambridge, Mass., 1972)

Rubel, Veré L. *Poetic Diction in the English Renaissance from Skelton through Spenser* (New York, 1941)

Sasek, Lawrence A. *The Literary Temper of the English Puritans*, Louisiana State University Studies, Humanities Series, IX (Baton Rouge, 1961)

Spingarn, J. E. *A History of Literary Criticism in the Renaissance* (2nd ed., New York, 1908)

Stewart, Alan. *Close Readers: Humanism and Sodomy in Early Modern England* (Princeton, 1997)

——. *Philip Sidney: A Double Life* (London, 2000)

Sweeting, Elizabeth J. *Studies in Early Tudor Criticism* (Oxford, 1940)

Thaler, Alwin. *Shakespeare and Sir Philip Sidney: The Influence of the Defence of Poesy* (Cambridge, Mass., 1947)

Thompson, John. *The Founding of English Metre* (London, 1961)

Toffanin, Giuseppe. *La fine dell'umanesimo* (Naples, 1933)

Tuve, Rosamund. *Elizabethan and Metaphysical Imagery* (Chicago, 1947)

Van Dorsten, J. A. *Poets, Patrons, and Professors: Sir Philip Sidney, Daniel Rogers, and the Leiden Humanists* (Leiden, 1962)

Waller, Gary F., and Michael D. Moore (eds). *Sir Philip Sidney and the Interpretation of Renaissance Culture* (London and Totawa, N.J., 1984)

Weinberg, Bernard. *A History of Literary Criticism in the Italian Renaissance* (2 vols, Chicago, 1961)

Weiner, Andrew. *Sir Philip Sidney and the Poetics of Protestantism* (Minneapolis, 1978)

Woodward, W. H. *Studies in Education during the Age of the Renaissance* (Cambridge, 1906)

Worden, Blair. *The Sound of Virtue: Philip Sidney's Arcadia and Elizabethan Politics* (New Haven, Conn., 1996)

Woudhuysen, H. R. *Sir Philip Sidney and the Circulation of Manuscripts 1558–1640* (Oxford, 1996)

Yates, Frances A. *The French Academies of the Sixteenth Century*, Studies of the Warburg Institute, XV (London, 1947)

——. *The Art of Memory* (Harmondsworth, 1969)

Zandvoort, R. W. *Sidney's Arcadia* (Amsterdam, 1929)

INTRODUCTION

ɷɷɷɷɷɷ

Introducing *An Apology for Poetry*

Philip Sidney's *An Apology for Poetry* – also known as *The Defence of Poesy* – is the most stylish and seductive work of literary theory written in the Renaissance.[1] According to its own definition of the word, it is a poem in prose, conjuring up the verbal picture of an ideal poetry as imagined by a poet – Sidney himself – and urging, wooing, reasoning and joking with its English readers in an ebullient effort to convince them of poetry's superiority to all other branches of learning. But it is also, unexpectedly, a confession of failure. Sidney tells us he wrote it when the reputation of poetry was at its lowest ebb, and acknowledges that there is good reason for the contempt in which it is currently held. Since ancient times, he claims, poetic practice has rarely lived up to its theoretical potential. With a few honourable exceptions, English poems in particular have always been of poor quality, and they are worse now than ever. Most modern English poets resemble disease-ridden whores, who offer their less than pleasurable commodities for cash to the highest bidder without a thought for the more important social ends they should serve. Sidney himself, he admits, shares their diseases. *An Apology for Poetry*, then, is both a celebration of the limitless capacity of poetry as it might be and a diagnosis of its lamentable condition as it is. And both celebration and diagnosis are couched in terms that vividly evoke the central concerns of late sixteenth-century European politics. It is, among other things, a controversial political document, a daring intervention in international affairs which more or less covertly criticizes the government of the day for its foreign and domestic policies. And in Elizabethan England such criticism carried considerable risks for the critic.

[1] Sidney does not seem to have given his essay a title. The alternative titles by which it is usually known are those of the two first editions, *An Apology for Poetry* published by Henry Olney and *The Defence of Poesy* published by William Ponsonby. Both appeared in 1595.

For Sidney, poetry does not have to be verse, confined to the rules of rhythm or metre, as many of his predecessors insisted it should be. Instead he defines it as fiction: writing, speech, or song which makes no claim to represent things or people that exist or once existed, but which fabricates attractive verbal images or gripping stories that appeal equally to the intellect and the emotions, with the aim of stimulating their recipients to action. As a result poetry crops up everywhere. It manifests itself in the form of anecdotes, fables, and parables which lend persuasiveness and clarity to philosophical arguments, political speeches, or religious teachings. It occurs in history books, in the form of imaginary speeches put into the mouths of historical characters to give substance to a particular version of the past. It invades scientific treatises, in the shape of comparisons or analogies demonstrating the practical application of scientific theories. And it fills the fields and the city streets with song: the hymn, the ballad, the lampoon and the prophecy are all the province of the poet. Poetry is a mode of thought inseparable from the condition of being human, and this, in Sidney's view, is what makes it worth studying.

Above all, the *Apology* argues, poetry is the most efficient persuasive force available to human beings. The poet is the man (in the *Apology*, though not in Sidney's other writings, he is always a man) who exploits the resources of language most freely and fearlessly for what he considers the common good – or for the good of his class or political faction. Poetry, in other words, is useful, and its usefulness makes it dangerous. No text asserts the danger as well as the delight of poetry more eloquently than Sidney's. The reasons for this will I hope become apparent in the course of this introduction.

We do not know exactly when the *Apology* was written.[2] It was probably begun after December 1579, when Edmund Spenser's *The Shepheardes Calender* was printed, since Sidney refers to Spenser's text as one of the few good English poems published in recent years (110/17ff.), and it was presumably finished before Sidney set off to fight in the Netherlands in 1585, the year before his death. Most scholars assume it was written in the earlier part of this period, during the winter of 1579–80. This is largely because of the literary climate at the time. *The Shepheardes Calender* was published along with a detailed commentary by a friend of Spenser's who signed himself E.K.: it was dedicated to Sidney, and it represented the most sustained effort so far in literary history to set up an English poem as worthy of comparison with ancient and modern poetic achievements on the European continent. Earlier in 1579 another important text was published: *The School of Abuse* by Stephen Gosson, which describes itself as 'a pleasaunt inuective against Poets, Pipers, Plaiers,

---

[2] For a full discussion of the date see *Misc. Prose*, 59–63.

Jesters, and such like Caterpillers of a Commonwelth' (Gosson 1974, 69). Gosson's eloquent attack on the malpractices of modern poets and playwrights was dedicated to Sidney, like Spenser's poem, and caused enough of a stir in London to warrant a second edition, three counter-attacks on behalf of the stage, and a defence of the *School* by Gosson before the year was out.[3] It seems reasonable to suppose that Gosson's and Spenser's texts might have stimulated their dedicatee Sidney into writing down his own thoughts on the right and wrong uses of poetry.

As we shall see, *The School of Abuse* in particular seems to be echoed throughout the *Apology*, especially in the section on contemporary English poetry.[4] It shares with Sidney's text a formal rhetorical structure, an often bantering tone, and a refusal to meddle with deep theological issues (it is a *pleasant* rather than a solemn invective). More seriously (and the interplay between wit and seriousness is common to both), Sidney's and Gosson's texts share the conviction that they are being written at a time of crisis in England's national identity, when England stands on the verge of losing its independence either to foreign powers or to foreign cultural values. This conviction would also have been shared by many other Protestant Englishmen in 1579, when Elizabeth I was being courted by the Catholic heir to the throne of France, the Duke of Alençon. One man, Philip Stubbes, had a hand cut off for saying so in print. For all its claims to universal applicability, *An Apology for Poetry* can be read, if we wish, as an oblique response to the immediate threat posed to English nationhood by Elizabeth's projected Catholic marriage.[5] Certainly it is everywhere concerned with the historical circumstances of its own production: and some knowledge of these circumstances is helpful if we are to understand it.

Some knowledge of Sidney's career is helpful, too.[6] From its first sentence the *Apology* declares its intimate involvement with the life of its author. It was written, he tells us, to vindicate what he calls his 'unelected vocation' (81/27) – the poetic career he never intended to pursue – from its many detractors, and it is disarmingly honest about the self-interest that motivated its composition. Every stage of its argument is peppered with phrases that remind us we are reading a writer's biased observations rather than a set of impartial assessments: 'I think', 'I hope', 'I fear me', 'I know'. Such phrases arise, of course, from Sidney's thorough ground-

---

[3] See Gosson 1974, introduction.

[4] For detailed accounts of Gosson's possible influence on the *Apology* see Arthur F. Kinney, 'Parody and its Implications in Sydney's Defense of Poesie', *SEL* 12 (1972), 1–19; Gosson, 1974, introduction; and Herman 1996, chs 1 and 2.

[5] For Sidney's involvement in the Elizabethan project of 'writing England' see Helgerson 1992, introduction, and Hadfield 1994, ch. 5. My discussion in this introduction is especially indebted to the latter.

[6] We are fortunate in having two excellent recent biographies of Sidney: Duncan-Jones 1991 and Stewart 2000.

ing in the art of rhetoric – often defined in the sixteenth century as the art of persuasion – which occupied a central position in the educational curriculum of early modern Europe. Teachers of rhetoric took the spoken word as the model for all written discourse, and so inculcated in their pupils an acute sensitivity to the respective social and ideological positions of writer and reader, speaker and audience: a sensitivity essential to the public performances of lawyers, preachers, and politicians.[7] But Sidney's repeated use of the first person invites us to remain unusually alert, as we read, to the particular prejudices and assumptions that determine the course of his discussion: and a glance at his life may furnish some important clues as to the direction he is coming from.

This is not to say, of course, that the relationship between the *Apology* and Sidney's life is unproblematic. From time to time Sidney's persuasive strategies involve him in self-evident contradictions, some of which were pointed out to him by his secretary, William Temple, in a logical analysis of the *Apology* written in the mid-1580s which remains a remarkable testimony to the skills in close reading cultivated by educated Elizabethans (Temple 1984). And Sidney himself discourages us from taking the *Apology* at face value, or from believing that he understood what he wrote in the *Apology* to be 'true' in any simple sense. Poets like the author of this essay, he explains, do not deal in truths or certainties – indeed, the 'cloudy knowledge of mankind' renders all such dealings dubious (103/11–12) – but only with 'what should or should not be' (103/17), the moral and emotional imperatives to which, the poets claim, their imaginations give them access. Sidney's favourite word is 'truly' (it occurs at least thirty-four times in the *Apology*), but he invariably uses it to signal the contingent status of truth, to announce the approach of a particularly contentious or opinionated utterance: 'Truly, as me seemeth' (89/34), 'truly I imagine' (100/10), 'It is already said (and, as I think, truly said)' (101/24), 'Truly, this is much, if there be much truth in it' (102/32), and, most trickily of all, 'I answer paradoxically, but truly, I think truly, that of all writers under the sun the poet is the least liar' (103/1–2) – a sentence that reaches giddy heights of complexity, especially if we remember that the man who writes this is himself a poet, and therefore scarcely the most trustworthy witness as to the poet's trustworthiness. There is a slippery quality in Sidney's writings which should put us on our guard whenever we are tempted to make grandiose statements about his intentions or convictions. Whether we regard this quality as infuriating or exhilarating will depend on what we expect from our reading. *An Apology for Poetry* offers us an unrivalled opportunity to scrutinize our expectations as readers – perhaps even to revise them.

---

[7] See Brian Vickers, *In Defence of Rhetoric* (Oxford, 1988), especially ch. 5, for a lucid introduction to the Renaissance study of rhetoric in schools and elsewhere.

An Apology for Poetry and the life of Sidney

Sir Philip Sidney never meant to be remembered as a poet. At least, this is what he repeatedly insists. At the beginning of the *Apology* he comments as if in surprise on the stroke of 'mischance' or bad luck which was responsible, 'in these my not old years and idlest times', for his 'having slipped into the title of a poet' (81/25–6); the last phrase suggests that the title of poet, like Sidney's knighthood, was an honour he neither expected nor deserved. In his most celebrated collection of poems, the sonnet-sequence *Astrophil and Stella*, he speaks of his 'toyes' (the word he invariably uses for what we might now call his literary works) as an unwelcome distraction from the serious business for which his education had prepared him.[8] His friend Fulke Greville, who wrote a life of Sidney now known as the *Dedication*, assures us that however brilliant his poetic productions may have been 'yet . . . they were scribbled rather as pamphlets for entertainment of time and friends than any account of himself to the world' (Greville 1986, 11). For Greville, Sidney's actions in his lifetime were more important than his writing. Greville presents his biography as an example to Protestant activists of a career well spent in attempting to intervene in European affairs, at terrible cost to himself, on behalf of the true religion (Protestantism) as it struggled for survival in a hostile environment, hemmed in on every side by Catholic imperialism.[9] Sidney himself, rather than his poetry, was the 'lively picture' which those who survived him should strive to emulate; and if he accomplished less in the political sphere than his qualities might have led his friends to hope, it was 'because his industry, judgement and affections perchance seemed too great for the cautious wisdoms of little Monarchies to be safe in' (Greville, 24) – that is, because Elizabeth I did not trust him.[10]

It is easy to see Sidney's literary works as the products of frustrated political ambition. His career began with enormous promise. His father, Sir Henry Sidney, was three times Lord Deputy of Ireland, the Queen's representative in her most turbulent colony, and no doubt expected Philip to follow in his footsteps. His mother Mary was a member of one of the most powerful Tudor dynasties, the Dudleys – a family that aspired to royal status. One of her brothers had briefly sat on the throne of England thanks to his ill-fated marriage to Lady Jane Grey. Another

---

[8] See *Astrophil and Stella* 18 (Ringler 1962, 173–4). See also K. Duncan-Jones, 'Philip Sidney's Toys', in Kay 1987, 61–80.

[9] The most detailed recent account of Sidney's political activities and their relationship to his writings is that of Blair Worden (Worden 1996).

[10] For Sidney's vexed relationship with his queen, see Norbrook 1984, ch. 4, esp. 98–9; Hamilton 1977, ch. 1; and Maureen Quilligan, 'Sidney and His Queen', in *The Historical Renaissance*, ed. Heather Dubrow and Richard Strier (Chicago and London, 1988), 171–96.

brother, Robert Dudley, Earl of Leicester, entertained the hope of achieving royalty through a still more splendid marriage, to Elizabeth I herself. When Sidney was born in 1554 his godfather was Philip II of Spain – at that time king of England by virtue of his marriage to Mary Tudor – and until about 1580 he was the legal heir to the vast fortunes of his uncle the Earl of Leicester. Philip's education was superb: he went first (with Greville) to one of the best schools in England, Shrewsbury, and afterwards to Christ Church, the most splendid of Oxford colleges. Then, at the age of eighteen, he set out on an astonishing three-year tour of Europe which took him to France, Germany, Italy, Hungary, Poland, Prague, and Vienna. Everywhere he went he met politicians, scholars, artists, printers, and princes, and was received with the respect and attention due to a rising star: a young man who could be expected to play a major role in international politics. Metaphorically at least, from this point in his life Sidney was seen, and possibly saw himself, as a prince in waiting. It is as a prince – Alexander the Great – that the Protestant scholar Théophile de Banos addresses him in a letter;[11] and it is as a 'princely spirit' that Greville describes him in the *Dedication*,[12] and Sir Walter Raleigh remembers him in his epitaph of 1593.[13] He might even have achieved genuine princely status: at one stage William of Orange seems to have wanted him for his son-in-law.[14] But this prince never came into his inheritance. Apart from a single diplomatic mission to Prague in 1577, Sidney was never given a position of political respon-sibility of the kind his education was designed to suit him for – at least, not until his appointment as second-in-command of the English forces in the Netherlands in the last year of his life. Even his knighthood was not his own: he was knighted in 1583 to enable him to act as stand-in for a German prince who was to be awarded the Order of the Garter *in absentia*. He slipped into the title of knight in much the same way as he slipped into the title of poet: by default.

By the time this happened he had slipped out of another, more valu-able title. His uncle the Earl of Leicester had got married secretly in 1578 to the widowed Countess of Essex; and in 1580 or 1581 the birth of Leicester's son Robert ousted Sidney from his position as his uncle's heir apparent. During the period between these two events another episode took place which reminded Sidney of the distance between his 'Great expectation'[15] – the hopes he had of achieving eminence in the political and military spheres – and his actual status. In 1579 a quarrel broke out between him and the Earl of Oxford, who was a member of one of the

[11] Duncan-Jones 1991, 70.
[12] Greville 1986, 38.
[13] Duncan-Jones 1989, 326–7.
[14] See Duncan-Jones 1991, 132ff.
[15] *Astrophil and Stella* 21, line 8 (Ringler 1962, 175).

most ancient noble families in England. The quarrel was perhaps connected to the proposed marriage between Elizabeth I and the Catholic Duke of Alençon. Sidney and Leicester opposed the match; the Earl of Oxford supported it. When Oxford challenged Sidney to a duel, the Queen herself intervened to prevent the matter from being taken any further; and she did so (according to Greville) in terms that put Sidney firmly in his place: 'The Queen . . . like an excellent monarch, lays before him the difference in degree between earls and gentlemen; [and] the respect inferiors ought [i.e. owed] to their superiors' (Greville 1986, 40). The episode seems to have left Sidney unusually touchy about his claims to aristocratic birth: it may have been in response to it that his father and uncle instructed a herald to draw up their family pedigrees, which traced the Sidneys back to the time of Henry II (with the help of four forged documents).[16] When in 1584 a pamphlet was published attacking the Earl of Leicester as an enemy to the state, Sidney replied with a defence which dwelt at length on the noble origins of the Dudley family, and which ended with an offer to fight the author of the libellous pamphlet hand-to-hand 'in any place of Europe' (*Misc. Prose*, 140). As Katherine Duncan-Jones has remarked, the *Defence of Leicester* reads like a self-conscious resumption of the quarrel with Oxford which had broken out on a tennis-court five years before, which had similarly ended with an unanswered challenge, and which perhaps lingered on in Sidney's mind as a piece of humiliating unfinished business.[17]

Sidney's *Apology* or *Defence of Poetry* was, in fact, one of three 'defences' he wrote in the course of his life, and two of the three were defences of his family. The first, known as the *Discourse on Irish Affairs*, was written in 1577 to vindicate his father's policies in Ireland.[18] Sir Henry Sidney had been accused of corruption and financial incompetence in his attempts to impose the 'cess' or land-tax on Irish noble families who claimed exemption from it. The accusations against him were reinforced by the presence at the English Court of his enemy the Earl of Ormond, one of Elizabeth's most favoured courtiers. In the process Sir Henry's authority as 'pro-rex', the Queen's representative in Ireland, was undermined by direct appeal to the Queen herself, and his personal reputation was sullied by claims that he had systematically misinformed the Queen and her council of his proceedings. As it turned out, Sir Henry was exonerated by Elizabeth in a letter she sent him towards the end of the year. But the persistent attacks on him clearly rankled with both father and son. In the *Discourse* Sidney charges Sir Henry's accusers of pursuing a policy enshrined in a familiar proverb: 'backbite apace: for men's nature

[16] See Duncan-Jones 1991, 165.
[17] See Duncan-Jones 1991, 269.
[18] Printed in *Misc. Prose*, 3–12.

is such that though the wound be healed, the scar remains' (*Misc. Prose*, 9). Eight years later he invoked the same proverb in his *Defence of Leicester*, implying that, however ineffectual slanderous assaults on a person's private conduct might be, the scars they left behind remained indelibly inscribed on the defendant's body and mind, serving as a constant reminder of the vulnerability of even the most immaculate reputation (*Misc. Prose*, 130). Long before he died in 1586, as a result of a wound received on a battlefield in the Netherlands, Sidney had learned what it was to feel embattled in the field of Court politics, and had received inward scars of a kind which were particularly difficult to treat.

Fulke Greville seems to have been right in one sense at least, when he said that Sidney did not write his imaginative works to give 'any account of himself to the world'. None of Sidney's poetry or prose was printed before his death,[19] and, although some of his poetry circulated in manuscript from the 1570s onwards, access to his literary texts was seen in his lifetime as a privilege granted only to a fortunate minority of readers. His father's secretary Edmund Molyneux wrote of his prose romance the *Arcadia* that 'few works of like subject hath been either of some more earnestly sought, choicely kept, nor placed in better place, amongst better jewels than that was; so that a special dear friend he should be that could have a sight, but much more dear that could once obtain a copy of it' (Duncan-Jones 1989, 312). The first version of the *Arcadia* – begun perhaps in 1577 and finished in 1580 – survives in eleven early manuscripts, and three more at least are known to have existed; Greville describes it as 'common', that is, widely known (*OA*, vii). By contrast, the *Apology* does not seem to have got much beyond the circle of his immediate family and friends until the mid-1590s.[20] This, at least, is the implication of Henry Olney's preface to his 1595 edition of the *Apology*.[21] Olney tells us that certain 'great ones' – among them presumably Sidney's sister Mary Herbert, Countess of Pembroke – have 'interred this blessed innocent' (that is, the defence of poetry) 'in themselves', and that he expects to be attacked for his presumption in making himself the first 'bewrayer' of the defence to the public, through the medium of print, without their permission. Before 1595, when two editions of the *Apology* were brought out within a few months of each other, the only people we know of who had certainly read the essay were Sidney's sister, his private secretary William Temple, and his friend Sir John Harington, who made use of it in the preface to his translation of *Orlando Furioso* (1591).[22] If the *Apology* is in some sense Sidney's 'account

---

[19] With the possible exception of two sonnets; see Woudhuysen 1996, 210.
[20] See Woudhuysen 1996, 234.
[21] Printed at the beginning of the Notes in this edition.
[22] Woudhuysen speculates that Penelope Rich may also have owned a copy. For all these associations with the *Apology* see Woudhuysen 1996, 234.

of himself', a defence of his reputation to match his defences of his father and uncle, he did not deliver it to the world in general – unlike his defence of Leicester, which he prepared for publication.[23] Sidney seems to have kept a close eye on manuscripts of his defence of poetry, for reasons we can only guess at.

Perhaps it gave him pleasure at this unhappy stage of his career – during the early 1580s – to maintain control over his own literary creations, given the strict limitations of his control over his public affairs. After Sidney's quarrel with Oxford in 1579, Elizabeth I referred to both men as her 'creations' and stressed a monarch's need to keep her subjects under a tight rein (Greville 1986, 40). Sidney's older contemporary George Puttenham developed this notion of the monarch as the poetic 'creator' of her subjects in his treatise *The Arte of English Poesie*, published in 1589. For Puttenham, the Queen of England was the 'most excellent Poet' alive, 'making in maner what ye list, the poore man rich, the lewd well learned, the coward couragious, and vile both noble and valiant' (Puttenham 1936, 4–5). Elizabeth, that is, was able to make anything she liked of the human material she had in front of her. For Sidney, on the other hand, the best of poets was capable of a great deal more. 'Only the poet,' he writes, 'disdaining to be tied to any . . . subjection, lifted up with the vigour of his own invention, doth grow in effect into another nature, in making things either better than Nature bringeth forth, or, quite anew, forms such as never were in Nature . . . Her world is brazen, the poets only deliver a golden' (85/17–27). Elizabeth is part of the sordid brazen world which exists beyond the poet's pages; practitioners of the 'princely' art of poetry disdain to be tied to her subjection. Elizabeth came to be known to her admirers as Astraea, the classical goddess of Justice;[24] but poets are capable of recreating the Golden Age when (according to the Roman poet Ovid) the *real* Astraea lived on earth. Within the confines of the *Apology for Poetry*, at least, Sidney was a *bona fide* prince, with a very much larger territory (and a great deal more power over it) than Elizabeth possessed in England. Elizabeth's was a little monarchy, Sidney's imaginary country was a vast one.

Greville referred to the revised version of Sidney's great romance, now known as the *New Arcadia*, as 'this extraordinary frame of his own commonwealth' (Greville 1986, 10), a rival for the celebrated imaginary commonwealths of Plato (the *Republic*) and Sir Thomas More (*Utopia*, first published in 1516). But the *New Arcadia* is a deeply troubled work, portraying a Greek princedom run by a disastrously over-cautious pacifist:

[23] See *Misc. Prose*, 124.
[24] See Frances A. Yates, *Astraea: The Imperial Theme in the Sixteenth Century* (London, 1975).

a state which, like England, is under constant threat of assault from its neighbours, and which briefly succumbs to assault from within. The claim of being Sidney's 'own commonwealth' might more reasonably be made for the *Apology*, since the text explicitly sets itself up in opposition to the attack on poets in Plato's *Republic* (106/42ff.), and insists that More's *Utopia* is a poetic failure (91/20–5). Indeed, the *Apology* is through much of its length a brilliant fusion of the most important imaginary ideals that were current in the sixteenth century: from the ideal prince, as exemplified in Xenophon's *Cyropaedia*, to the ideal orator, as delineated in Cicero's *De oratore*; from the ideal courtier, a chimera pursued through the pages of Castiglione's *The Courtier* (1528), to the ideal teacher, a figure made familiar in England by Roger Ascham's celebrated treatise on teaching Latin, *The Schoolmaster* (1570). For Sidney, the poet is the only mortal who has imaginative access to all these disparate ideals and who has the power to make them both visible and attractive to his fellow mortals. And he is also the only one capable of making an ideal state for these ideal figures to occupy. Such an imaginary state may not yet exist on paper, but the *idea* of such a state may be entertained by poets, as the example of More's *Utopia* shows: 'for that way of patterning a commonwealth was most absolute, though [More] perchance hath not so absolutely performed it' (91/23–5). Whatever limitations poetry may have had in practice, its theoretical potential is as boundless as the poet's imagination. And this places the poet streets ahead of the cautious rulers whose little monarchies he is condemned to live in.

As if to demonstrate the sheer range of the poet's mind ('the zodiac of his . . . wit', 85/23), Sidney's *Apology* is geographically hugely expansive: it travels as far afield as Sidney had done in the 1570s, and it visits many of the same places. It opens with an anecdote set in Vienna, where Sidney converses in Italian with a famous riding-school teacher; and it goes on to display Sidney's familiarity with modern Italian literature and literary theory, and indicates that he had seen Venice (109/6). It shows an informed interest in Turkish culture which Sidney could have acquired on his visit to Hungary, where the war against the Turks was being waged (83/18–19); and it later refers explicitly to Sidney's Hungarian visit (99/10–13). It parades his familiarity with Italian, French and Spanish (115/38–44), and (somewhat misleadingly) with 'Dutch' (German), which Sidney stubbornly refused to learn on his tour of Europe. It touches on his knowledge of Irish and Welsh poetry, acquired through his father's close connections with those two countries, and the poetry of Scotland – he twice mentions the great Scottish political theorist and dramatist George Buchanan, with whom he had corresponded. And it evinces Sidney's fascination with the New World, which he hoped to visit in future. All these allusions to contemporary cultures are seamlessly woven in with a complex tapestry of allusions to Sidney's extensive reading among the Greek and Latin classics, from the philosophical works of Plato and Plutarch to the prose fictions of Heliodorus and Apuleius, from Cicero's treatises on rhetoric to the histories of Xenophon, Livy, and Quintus Curtius. In the *Apology*, Sidney's remarkable education both in experience and in book-learning, in literature, politics, philosophy, diplomacy, history and military training, found an outlet which it had not yet found in English public life. Contemporary readers confronted with such evidence of Sidney's accomplishments might well have found themselves wondering how on earth such a valuable subject could have found himself ('in these my not old years and idlest times') with the time on his hands to write about poetry, when he ought to have been engaged in more directly political action. And they might have concluded that Sidney's political inertia was a direct result of the state of affairs in Elizabethan England.

Throughout the *Apology* Sidney argues for England's potential to match other nations, from ancient Greece and Rome to modern Italy, in the writing of poetry and in the various forms of action which poetry is uniquely qualified to encourage. The English language is eminently suited to a variety of verse forms and persuasive techniques, and in the past the poetic achievements of England have been more than matched by its military successes: at one point Sidney casually sets the names of English victories at Poitiers and Agincourt alongside the greatest military triumphs of ancient times, the battles of Marathon and Pharsalia (89/21–2). But in his own time, England's immense potential – both military and poetic – remains unfulfilled. Only a few years after Sidney wrote the *Apology*, George Puttenham was to celebrate modern English poetic achievements with enthusiasm in *The Arte of English Poesie*. Sidney, by contrast, is everywhere concerned to play them down. This is not necessarily a matter of objective critical judgment: indeed, Sidney stresses the difficulty, even the impossibility, of arriving at an unbiased judgment of anything. His list of successful English poetry (110/11ff.) is remarkably short: it excludes, for instance, the verse of Sir Thomas Wyatt (1503–42), whose introduction of the sonnet form into England might have recommended him to Sidney the sonneteer, and of George Gascoigne (c. 1539–77), the leading poet of the previous decade, whose accomplishments in poetry, prose and court entertainment anticipate Sidney's.[25] But Sidney is not arguing in this section of the *Apology* that there is no good poetry in England: only that most good English poetry has not yet found its way into print (see 110/22). It is therefore in his interest to exclude all but a few printed poems from his list.

---

[25] He could have read Wyatt's poetry in the book that contained Surrey's: *Tottel's Miscellany* (1557). Gascoigne's had been published in two volumes in the 1570s: *A Hundreth Sundrie Flowres* (1573) and *The Posies of George Gascoigne Esquire* (1575).

The lack of good English poetry in print, he implies, is a direct result of the Elizabethan government's quietist attitude to Catholic Europe: its efforts to placate the Catholic nations, France and Spain, which Sidney and his political associates in the Earl of Leicester's circle considered to be disastrously ill-advised. Now that an 'over-faint quietness' has enveloped England, poetry has lost the good reputation it used to enjoy in times of war (109/4ff.). For the most part, only bad poets 'with servile wits' get published (109/11): and their servility presumably consists of encouraging Englishmen to indulge themselves in the lazy pleasures of peace. Sidney's idleness is forced on him by 'idle England' (109/10), and so is his defence of poetry. If England had been more active it would not have scorned the good poets who, Sidney contends, are the pre-eminent stirrers-up of action, and Sidney would not have had to defend them (for one thing, he would not have had time). He would also, he implies, have been less inclined to leave his poetry in manuscript. Like other good poets of his generation, he chose to circulate his texts in private rather than be identified with the 'base men with servile wits' who found favour with the printers (109/11). Early readers of the *Apology*, then, perusing it in manuscript, might have seen its physical form as evidence of Sidney's refusal to be servile to the petty demands of 'idle England'. And they might have seen the *Apology*, in part at least, as a subtle critique of the architects of Elizabethan foreign policy.

Sidney refers to the period of the *Apology*'s composition as a time of crisis in England's national identity. England and the English language have limitless potential, but the chance to fulfil that potential is being recklessly squandered even as Sidney writes, and his writing is a sign that it is being squandered. But his Elizabethan readers might have surmised something more specific from his discussion of the current state of English poetry. Sidney implies, or so they might have guessed, that it is not just England's passivity that threatens to prevent it from taking its place alongside the other modern nations he mentions, whose poetry and military adventurousness have been fruitfully combined in the preceding century. A still more deadly threat arises from its active negotiations with the Catholic nations: and in particular from Elizabeth's marriage negotiations with the Catholic heir to the throne of France. In 1579 Sidney had written a letter to Elizabeth I warning her of the dangers of marrying Alençon.[26] This letter was probably the text of Sidney's which achieved the widest circulation in his lifetime. In it he argued that the chief danger of the match was that England would be gradually absorbed into France: that it would become no more than a troublesome satellite on the edge of the French dominions, very much like Ireland with relation to Elizabethan England. Alençon's aims would be

[26] Printed in *Misc. Prose*, 33–57.

to make France great and to subject England to the yoke of Catholicism; and the English, having been weakened 'as well by long peace . . . as by the poison of [religious] division' (*Misc. Prose*, 50), would be powerless to stop him attaining those ends. To support his argument Sidney alludes to the troublesome marriage of his godfather Philip II of Spain to the last Catholic Queen of England, Mary Tudor, Elizabeth's sister. In the process he invokes a period of extreme danger both to Elizabeth herself and to the Protestant cause in England: Elizabeth was imprisoned in the Tower of London on a charge of high treason in the year of Mary's marriage. Then as now, England had been on the verge of losing its Protestant princess and its independence both at once – this time to Spain – and only the death of Mary had saved the country from becoming an outpost of Catholic Europe.

The crisis in England's national identity manifests itself in the *Apology* in the question-mark that hangs over the lineage of contemporary English poets. Alone among modern nations, England has disavowed its maternal relationship to its poets: it acts towards them less like a parent than like the stereotypical 'stepmother' (108/25) who resentfully raises another woman's children. The only poets who flourish under these conditions are 'bastard poets', the illegitimate offspring of the Muses, and true poets have retired into obscurity because they are unwilling to have their noble birth contaminated by association with these base-born upstarts (they 'are better content to suppress the outflowing of their wit, than, by publishing them, to be accounted knights of the same order' (109/22–3)). Modern English dramatic poetry is so bad that, 'like an unmannerly daughter showing a bad education', it 'causeth her mother Poesy's honesty to be called in question' (113/15–17). In other words, the English poet's pedigree is in a worse condition than that of Sidney's family. And it would not perhaps have taken much for Sidney's earliest readers to see a connection between the uncertain state of the poets' lineage and the threat posed to the lineage of the English monarchy by Elizabeth's projected marriage to Alençon. The one good reason for such a marriage, Sidney argued in his famous letter, was to furnish the Queen with 'the bliss of children' (*Misc. Prose*, 51) – something which any other husband could do just as well as the Frenchman. And children are a decidedly mixed blessing: 'many princes have lost their crowns, whose own children were manifest successors', and some have had 'their own children used as instruments of their ruin' (54). In addition the letter suggests that although 'in so lineal a monarchy' as the English one, Elizabeth's subjects have imbibed the love of their sovereign along with their mother's milk, 'an odious marriage with a stranger' could only have the effect of turning the bulk of her subjects against her (54–5). What makes Elizabeth 'the most excellent fruit of all your progenitors' (57) is not her royal birth (after all, Elizabeth had twice been declared a bastard, once by her father and once by her sister Mary) but her status as the protector of the Protestant religion: a status which her French husband would place in jeopardy. If England's poets stood in danger of losing their inheritance, the rest of the English nation – including Elizabeth herself – might not be far behind in losing theirs.

As we have seen, one of Sidney's first editors, Henry Olney, regarded the *Apology* as the innocent child of its dead father, snatched from the womb of oblivion by a courageous act of theft. Many literary critics, too, have regarded Sidney's text as innocent: innocent of contamination by contemporary politics, untainted by a polemical purpose, a kind of free-floating testimonial to the essential and unchanging function of poetry. I am suggesting here, as a number of critics have done in recent years, that the *Apology* can be read in a different way, as a text which is very far from innocent of national or European politics.[27] It could be argued, in fact, that Olney's very insistence on its pristine spotlessness indicates his consciousness that it could be read as decidedly 'spotted' or tarnished in one way or another. Perhaps Olney sensed that Sidney's defence, as well as his own temerity in putting it into print, might find itself in need of defending.

Attacks on poetry

English poetry, at least, was in bad need of defending at the beginning of the 1580s. Like the reputation of Sidney's family, the reputation of the poet – his claim to the highest of 'titles' in the state he served – was under attack: and Sidney's defence of the poet resembles his defence of the Earl of Leicester in its insistence on the antiquity and nobility of the true poet's lineage. Indeed, for Sidney poetry's nobility is closely allied with the nobility of the English aristocracy. The few English writers he praises include Sir Thomas Sackville, Earl of Dorset (co-author of *Gorboduc* and the *Mirror for Magistrates*), and Henry Howard, Earl of Surrey, the only English poet he singles out for unqualified approval. Sidney finds in Surrey's lyrics 'many things tasting of a noble birth, and worthy of a noble mind' (110/16–17). His poetry demonstrates the authenticity of his nobility, and his nobility is what makes his poems worth praising.[28]

But Surrey's noble birth was a controversial topic. The Earl was arrested in 1546 on several charges of treason, and beheaded in 1547. One of the charges brought against him was that he laid claim through his

[27] See for example Alan Sinfield, 'The Cultural Politics of the *Defence of Poetry*', in Waller and Moore 1984, 124–43, and Victor Skretkowicz, 'Sidney's *Defence of Poetry*, Henri Estienne, and Huguenot Nationalist Satire', *Sidney Journal* 16 (Spring 1998), no. 1, 3–24.
[28] For further discussion of Sidney's interest in Surrey see Hadfield 1994, ch. 5, esp. 143–8.

lineage to the throne of England (and his son, the Duke of Norfolk, was executed in 1572 for plotting to strengthen his family's claim to the throne by marrying Mary Queen of Scots). Surrey, then, was decidedly not 'servile', as are the 'bastard poets' who print their poems for money. Nor are the other good English poets Sidney mentions. Sackville's tragedy *Gorboduc* (performed in 1562) was written to frighten Elizabeth either into marriage and childbearing or into naming her successor – it graphically describes the consequences of failing to settle a kingdom on a single designated heir to the throne.[29] The *Mirror for Magistrates* (1559), to which Sackville contributed two important poems, was suppressed by the Catholic censors in the reign of Mary Tudor, perhaps because it persistently reminded its readers that the lineage of the English royal family was a fiercely contested one.[30] Sir Thomas More died for defying Henry VIII on the related questions of his marriage to Anne Boleyn (Elizabeth's mother) and the separation of the English church from Rome. At the same time, the *Utopia* could be seen as a fierce attack on corrupt politicians and churchmen in pre-Reformation Europe. Even the less aristocratic English writers Sidney mentions were by no means slavish servants of the crown. Among Protestants in Tudor England, Geoffrey Chaucer was widely regarded as a proto-Protestant satirist of the medieval church; and Edmund Spenser's *Shepheardes Calender* consciously followed in the Protestant satirical tradition which was thought to have been initiated by Chaucer (it has been read by recent commentators as a trenchant critique of the mismanagement of the Elizabethan church and state).[31] For Sidney, the best poetry is written by men who are either involved in or closely concerned with the business of government: and its tone is invariably oppositional, either explicitly or implicitly critical of the ruling authorities.

As I have said, two of the poets Sidney mentions – More and Surrey – were beheaded for their opposition to the crown: and this links them once again to Sidney's family history. Sidney's grandfather, John Dudley, Earl of Northumberland, had been executed for high treason (like Surrey he had sought to claim royalty for his family). So had his great-grandfather Edmund Dudley (like More he was one of Henry VIII's sacrificial victims). In his *Defence of Leicester* Sidney took the extraordinary step of citing the fall of his grandfather as evidence of the greatness of his own ancestry: only the grand scale of his grandfather's aspirations permitted him to be 'so thunder-stricken' (*Misc. Prose*, 139) as to suffer

---

[29] See David Bevington, *Tudor Drama and Politics: A Critical Approach to Topical Meaning* (Cambridge, Mass., 1968), 141–7.

[30] See Andrew Hadfield's excellent discussion of the *Mirror*, Hadfield 1994, ch. 3.

[31] For Chaucer as proto-Protestant and Spenser's place in the Protestant satirical tradition see John N. King, 'Spenser's *Shepheardes Calender* and Protestant Pastoral Satire', in Lewalski 1986, 369–98.

execution, unlike the ancestors of Leicester's accuser, who were never tempted to rise above the mud that engendered them. But Sidney's repeated assertions of his own noble birth were not, I think, designed to prop up a stable, time-honoured social hierarchy. They served instead as reminders of the flexibility of that hierarchy, whose order had been shaken and reversed on so many occasions in history. The story of Sidney's family was the story of England in miniature, where the power-relations between monarchy and aristocracy had undergone innumerable subtle and not-so-subtle alterations. This may have been one reason why Elizabeth (whose claim to the throne was being challenged even as Sidney wrote by the rival claim of Mary Queen of Scots) distrusted Sidney and his uncle. The title of the 1584 attack on Leicester was given in the first printed edition as *Leicester's Commonwealth*, emphasizing the Earl's presumed ambition to control the English state. The imaginary alternative commonwealths Sidney alludes to in the *Apology* had counterparts in the imaginations of his contemporaries: counterparts which might stir their imaginers into action as effectively as poetry stirs its readers in Sidney's text.

The controversial English poets Sidney recommends came from a long line of poetic agitators against real and imagined systems of government. From ancient times poetry had been seen as a potential menace to the social order, and had called forth attacks from the self-appointed custodians of public morality.[32] The first and most influential of these attacks was directed against the threat posed by poets to an imaginary commonwealth: Plato's Republic. For the philosopher Plato, writing in the fourth century B.C., poets were second-rate craftsmen: imitators who had no direct access to or serious interest in the things they mimicked; producers of luxury goods without a recognizable function in a properly run state. He thought that their appeals to the emotions – especially grief, and especially in the theatre – encouraged emotional self-indulgence and even cowardice in their audience. Above all, he disapproved of the fictions they disseminated about the gods. Stories about the vindictiveness and sexual profligacy of divine beings and their semi-divine children could only have a deleterious effect on those who heard them. Plato therefore advocated a strict control over the forms of poetry permissible in the well-ordered republic. Responsible poets should represent only simple images of virtue ('hymns to the gods or praises of good men' (*Republic*, X, 607)), and poets who depicted vice in their poems should not be permitted to live within the bounds of a respectable city.

Subsequent attacks on poetry relied heavily on Plato's perception of

[32] For detailed accounts of the anti-poetic prejudice see Fraser 1970, Barish 1981, and Herman 1996.

the poet as an irresponsible gossip-monger who brought the gods into disrepute, or worse still a traitor, 'one who gives a city over into the hands of villains, and destroys the better citizens' (*Republic*, X, 605). Early Christian apologists such as Tertullian attacked the Roman theatre for fostering pagan beliefs, and in the early fifth century St Augustine summarized their arguments in *The City of God*. Augustine has a strong admiration for the persuasive powers of poetry, even when it is used to promote 'a full wrong divinity' (as Sidney puts it).[33] In his opinion 'the excellency of [man's] capacity maketh the rare goodnesse of his creation apparant, euen then when hee goeth about things that are either superfluous or pernicious' (Augustine 1610, 908). But poetry has proved particularly 'pernicious', especially dramatic poetry. For Augustine, the Roman theatre was the tool of 'most deceitfull and malignant deuils' masquerading as deities, whose 'onely delight was to haue most bestiall and abhominable practises, either published as their true exploits, or faigned of them by poeticall inuentions; these they commanded to be publikely presented in playes and at solemne feastes' (Augustine 1610, 155). Theatres were directly responsible for the sack of Rome during the Punic wars, since they encouraged the Roman people to weaken themselves by imitating the depraved actions of the pagan gods. Augustine also accuses the poets of having been mouthpieces for corrupt human rulers as well as demons: dishonest historians who depicted their mortal masters as divine in order to lend their crimes a spurious authority for future generations. He therefore agrees with Plato that non-religious poets should be expelled from the ideal state, as serious impediments to the ongoing Christian project of establishing the kingdom of God on earth.

Like everything he wrote, Augustine's attack on pagan poetry was highly influential throughout the medieval period; but it found a new and somewhat different place in the sixteenth-century academic curriculum thanks to the commentary added to it by the Spanish scholar Juan Luis Vives, which Sidney might well have known. For Plato and Augustine, poets were the seductive demolishers of cities. For Vives, on the other hand, they were the founders of cities and courageous critics of the crimes of the ruling classes, as well as occasional blasphemers. Vives' passionate endorsement of the poet's productions marks him out as a devotee of the New Learning: the effort to recover ancient Greek and Roman texts and to understand them in their historical context which has come to be known as humanism.[34] The humanist movement began in fourteenth-century Italy, where it quickly set itself up in opposition to the near-monopoly on learning possessed by the medieval

---

[33] See Augustine, *Confessions*, 3.2.2–4.

[34] For useful introductions to humanism see Anthony Grafton and Lisa Jardine, *From Humanism to the Humanities: Education and the Liberal Arts in Fifteenth- and Sixteenth-century Europe* (London, 1986), and Kraye 1996.

church. For the church, there was only one truth which was always and everywhere the same. The pre-Christian peoples did not have it, and after the birth of Christ its only mediators were the authorities approved by the church of Rome: the theologians, grammarians, logicians and philosophers known as scholastics, who sought to articulate truth through the use of highly specialized forms of discourse comprehensible only to the initiated. The humanists, on the other hand, were often sponsored by secular members of the governing classes – princes and their advisers, noble families, wealthy merchants – who were engaged in power-struggles with political and commercial rivals both secular and ecclesiastical. Many humanists were lawyers, notaries, or secretaries rather than clerics, and their interests lay in promoting the discourse of popular communication – rhetoric – which was most valuable in the law-courts, the marketplace and the debating-chamber, rather than logic, the tool of the professional theologian. Poetry was held to be the ultimate form of popular communication, and defences of poetry played a central role in the humanists' theoretical explications of their quest to recover and interpret classical texts from the time of Petrarch onwards.

The most elaborate early humanist defence of poetry is the *Genealogy of the Pagan Gods* by Giovanni Boccaccio, author of the *Decameron* and an important influence on one of Sidney's heroes, Chaucer. Boccaccio accepts Plato's and Augustine's point that the ancient poets had made up or elaborated stories about the pagan gods, but he turns this into a virtue: they told their stories as a means of imparting knowledge.[35] Pagan myths are allegories which encode a number of different kinds of information. On one level they narrate historical events, celebrating the actions of real men or women as if they were the actions of gods. On another level they contain what we would now call scientific observations, figurative accounts of the mysterious forces which govern the physical world. On a third level they convey the half-glimpses of knowledge about the Christian God which were available to enlightened thinkers in pre-Christian times. This conception of poetry as an allegorical 'dark philosophy', a method of delivering valuable information in code from one generation of scholars to another, remained popular with intellectuals in England until well into the seventeenth century. Arthur Golding used it to justify his translation of Ovid's *Metamorphoses* in the 1560s, George Chapman subscribed to it in the 1590s, and Francis Bacon was still producing allegorical readings of ancient myths in the early seventeenth century.[36] For these writers, men such as Boccaccio

---

[35] See Boccaccio 1930, introduction.
[36] See the Preface to Arthur Golding's translation of the *Metamorphoses* (1567); Chapman 1941, introduction; and Bacon's *De Sapientia Veterum* (*Of the Wisdom of the Ancients*) (1609), Preface. Bacon suggests that the most profitable 'sense' of ancient fables or parables need not be related to the original intentions of the men who invented them.

had succeeded in restoring poets to the status of productive members of society, well qualified to take their place alongside theologians, philosophers and historians in any Christian commonwealth. Broadly speaking, medieval theorists thought of poetry as a humble occupation, the province of schoolteachers and itinerant storytellers whose modest skills were well suited to the simple tasks of making up stories and composing verse.[37] The early humanists, by contrast, turned poets into members of the ruling classes similar to the dignitaries they served, and the emblem of their power was the laurel wreath, the crown awarded to poets and victorious military leaders alike.

But with the Reformation the position of poets changed again. Plato's and Augustine's strictures were once more invoked by both loyal Catholics and reformers: the poets, they said, were responsible for spreading lies about religion, and their activities were one of the causes of the split within the church. The Catholic Thomas More accused Protestants of having invented a new religion out of their diseased imaginations, while the Protestant William Tyndale, translator of the Bible into English, accused the Catholics of replacing the scriptures with poetry, and sarcastically congratulated the papacy on choosing the poet More as its spokesman.[38] From that time onwards, the notion that poetry offered a dangerously enticing alternative to the scriptures was often repeated in England. In 1549, for instance, the Protestant poet William Baldwin (editor and co-author of the *Mirror for Magistrates*, which Sidney considered 'meetly furnished of beautiful parts' (110/15–16)) expressed the hope that his English version of the biblical Song of Solomon might replace the songs of secular love which were popular at Court;[39] and in 1565 the Protestant surgeon John Hall published a religious poetry-collection called *The Court of Virtue*, whose title announced its ambition to supplant the popular collection of English love-poems, *The Court of Venus* (c. 1530), in the libraries of devout English subjects.[40] But Protestants were by no means alone in their opposition to secular poetry and fiction. Writing as an anti-Protestant polemicist, Sir Thomas More declared that he would rather Erasmus's *Praise of Folly* and his own *Utopia* were burned than translated into English, when their witty games with political and religious issues would fall into the hands of uneducated readers to the detriment of their spiritual health.[41] And More was as virulent as Tyndale in his condemnation of medieval chivalric romance. For More and Tyndale, stories about knights and their adulterous love-affairs (which remained as popular as

---

[37] See Shepherd 1965, 17–19.
[38] See Greenblatt 1980, ch. 2, esp. 112–13, and Herman 1996, 35.
[39] See *The Canticles or Balades of Salomon* (1549), sig. A3r.
[40] See Hall 1961, introduction.
[41] See Greenblatt 1980, 63.

ever in the sixteenth century) represented all that was corrupt about late medieval society, when the church had encouraged the fabrication of fictions pandering to the nastiest erotic fantasies of its members.[42] Many later writers agreed with them. According to E.K., who wrote the commentary on Spenser's *Shepheardes Calender*, Arthurian literature was written 'by a sort of bald Friers and knavish shavelings' who 'soughte to nousell the comen people in ignorounce, least being once acquainted with the truth of things, they woulde in tyme smell out the untruth of theyr . . . Massepenie religion' (Spenser 1989, 115). Even for defenders of poetry such as E.K., poetry could serve as the ideal instrument for the spreaders of religious fictions, in modern times as in the early years of the Christian church.

During Sidney's lifetime, the view of poetry as a seductive distraction from the religious education of the Christian reader was most fiercely articulated by the eminent humanist Roger Ascham, former tutor to Edward VI and Elizabeth I.[43] Ascham's *The Schoolmaster* is concerned first and foremost with the teaching of Latin, and the teaching method he recommends is that of enticing the young pupil into the classroom by making his studies attractive. In this he sets himself up in opposition to what he claims is the usual practice among Elizabethan schoolmasters, who like to beat their charges into submission. But Ascham's gently persuasive pedagogic project is threatened by the superior attractions of modern poetry. In the course of *The Schoolmaster* he repeatedly sets up secular love-poetry and erotic stories as vicious counterparts of the classical and biblical texts which form the basis of the humanist curriculum. In medieval times, he tells his readers, depraved monks seduced young men away from the scriptures by composing romances like the tales of King Arthur, the pleasure of which 'standeth . . . in open mans slaughter, and bold bawdrye'; 'Yet I know,' he goes on, 'when Gods Bible was banished the Court, and *Morte Arthure* receiued into the Princes chamber' (Ascham 1904, 231). But in recent years a more insidious poetic menace has arisen, in the form of 'bawdie bookes . . . made in Italie, and translated in England' (230–1). What books these are he does not specify, but one assumes they contain Italian poetry and prose fiction, since Ascham later inveighs against readers who 'haue in more reuerence, the triumphes of Petrarche: than

---

[42] See Fraser 1970, 3 and 77. A satisfactory assessment of the popularity of chivalric romance in the sixteenth century has yet to be written. One view of these romances – which is that they achieved new popularity with the translation of *Amadis de Gaule* into French and English in the late sixteenth century – is voiced by Paul Salzman, with bibliographic references, in his *English Prose Fiction 1558–1700: A Critical History* (Oxford, 1985), 5.
[43] See Maslen 1997, introduction, and ch. 1, 41–51.

the Genesis of Moses . . . a tale in *Bocace* [i.e. Boccaccio], than a storie of the Bible' (232). Italian books, Ascham argues, have been more effective than teams of Catholic infiltrators in undermining the Protestant integrity of England. 'They open,' he writes, 'not fond and common wayes to vice, but such subtle, cunnyng, new, and diuerse shiftes, to cary yong willes to vanitie, and yong wittes to mischief . . . as the simple head of an English man is not hable to inuent, nor neuer was hard of in England before, yea when Papistrie ouerflowed all'. Italians are subtle, the heads of Englishmen are simple, and the 'mery bookes of *Italie*' (230), which appeal with equal force to the intellect and the emotions, the 'wit' and the 'will', would seem to be the most effective method of substituting Italian sophistication for the English qualities of directness, honesty, and familiarity with the biblical word of God. After this preparatory process of substitution has been accomplished, Ascham argues, it will take only another step or two to convert England to Catholicism.

Ascham was by no means averse to poetry as such. He had a high regard for the Greek and Roman tragedians and epic poets, urged English versifiers to adopt classical metres in their vernacular compositions, and wrote verses on the death of one of his favourite pupils, John Whitney, which he included in the second part of *The Schoolmaster* (Ascham 1904, 241–2). But this was the poetry of *amicitia* or friendship between men; we know this because Ascham tells us that Whitney and he studied Cicero's dialogue *De amicitia* together a little before the young man's death.[44] The poetry he disapproves of would seem to be verse and prose fiction concerning *amor*, the love between men and women: these, he says, 'be the inchauntements of *Circes*' (229) – Circe being the female magician who transformed the companions of Ulysses into beasts in Homer's epic poem, the *Odyssey*. Ascham's most important successor in the war against corrupt forms of poetry, Stephen Gosson, took his arguments a few steps further.[45] The title of Gosson's invective, *The School of Abuse* (1579), proclaims its debt to *The Schoolmaster*; and in it Gosson argues that poets, playwrights 'and such like Caterpillers of the Commonwelth' (Gosson 1974, 69) have set up an informal school of their own to rival the official humanist curriculum taught by responsible pedagogues in English schools and universities: a school, that is, of abuse or corruption, where the enchantress Circe and her poetic acolytes instruct their young charges in the pleasures not of books but of the bed. The effect of this abominable alternative education will be to admit not only foreign ideologies, but eventually foreign

---

[44] See Stewart 1997, ch. 4, esp. 148–60.
[45] See Maslen 1997, ch. 1, 51–67.

powers, on to English soil. 'There was neuer fort so strong,' writes Gosson, 'but it might be battered, neuer ground so fruitful, but it might be barren: neuer countrie so populous, but it might be wast: neuer Monarch so mighty, but he might be weakened: neuer Realme so large, but it might be lessened: neuer kingdom so florishing, but it might bee decayed' (106–7). England's enemies are merely waiting for the debilitating influence of poets and players to take hold of the youth of England before pouring in through the breaches in the island's defensive system.

Gosson's primary target, like Ascham's, is 'amarous Poets', who offer their young readers 'the Cuppes of *Circes*, that turne reasonable Creatures into brute Beastes' (76–7). He describes them as teachers of lessons in erotic self-gratification, and commends Plato for expelling them from his ideal state. The worst of their productions are plays, and he sees the modern theatre as the perfect vehicle for smuggling Italian values into England: 'Compare *London* to *Rome*, and *England* to *Italy*, you shall finde the Theaters of the one, the abuses of the other, to be rife among vs' (91). And like Ascham, Gosson believes that one of the most dangerous aspects of modern poetry is its moral complexity: its tendency to encourage writers to produce indiscriminate mixtures of good and evil, virtue and vice in their efforts to entertain their audiences. Gosson considers variety – the inventive yoking together of many different elements – to be what makes writing attractive, and confesses that poets are the wittiest exponents of verbal variety; but 'notwithstanding', he adds, 'that wit is dearly bought: where hony and gall are mixed, it will be hard to seuer the one from the other' (77). Moral lessons, he argues, should be clear and simple, since the human mind is simple; there can therefore be no justification for communicating the truth through a web of falsehoods, as the poets claim to do when they state that their fictions convey valuable lessons to their readers. Poetry is the product of idleness and encourages only idleness in its recipients. It is therefore both the symptom and the cause of the unhealthy condition of modern England – what Gosson sees as its rapid decline into effeminacy. Gosson ends his argument with an appeal to the Lord Mayor of London to exercise his powers of censorship over the plays performed in the city, and a clarion call to the women of London to shun the theatres. The wheel has come full circle: for Gosson as for Plato, poets are traitors to the nation, preparing the ground for England's surrender to its hostile neighbours. In a later publication, *Playes Confuted in Five Actions* (1582), he again follows Plato in advocating the expulsion of all unauthorized forms of imaginative writing from the purlieus of the besieged English commonwealth. When Sidney wrote his *Apology*, the irresponsible poet or playwright was in some writers' eyes among the most dangerous domestic enemies of the Elizabethan state.

Sidney and the prodigal poet

One of the strangest things about the early Elizabethan poets for a modern reader is the extent to which they seem to concur with Gosson's assessment of poetry. Gosson himself was a playwright whose plays were still on stage when he wrote his attack on the contemporary theatre. He was not, as he has frequently been called, a 'Puritan' – a radical reformer who felt that the contemporary church had not gone far enough in expelling Catholic practices and who wanted an end to the episcopal system. He ended his days, as his modern editor points out, with something of a reputation as an anti-Puritan controversialist.[46] He had studied in the same schools as the poets, attended Oxford along with Sidney and other men who later became prominent writers of imaginative fiction, and wrote in a style that was highly fashionable with Elizabethan novelists (in fact, *The School of Abuse* ends with an advertisement for a novel he had just completed). He was a member, in fact, of what Richard Helgerson has described as a generation of 'prodigals' among Elizabethan poets: male writers active from the 1570s to the late 1580s who identified themselves with the biblical figure of the Prodigal Son.[47] This is the young man in one of Christ's parables who demands his inheritance from his father, leaves home and spends all his money in the pursuit of the pleasures of the flesh, then returns to his father in penitent mood to ask his forgiveness.[48] Gosson adopts the stance of the penitent prodigal mid-way through his *School* when he confesses that he is a reformed poet: 'I haue sinned, and am sorry for my fault: hee runnes farre that neuer turnes, better late then neuer' (Gosson 1974, 96). And an astonishing number of other writers of poetry and imaginative fiction in the decade leading up to the writing of Sidney's *Apology* chose to present their careers as following – or having the potential to follow – the pattern established by Christ's parable. George Gascoigne, George Whetstone, George Pettie, John Lyly – all printed their poetry or prose fiction with a kind of health warning attached, acknowledging that their romantic stories and love-lyrics are the products of a wasted youth, that the reader should avoid doing the things that are described in their pages, and that the writer is now ready to enter the next phase of his career as prodigal by returning to the paternal embrace of the Elizabethan authorities. Gascoigne, Whetstone, and the rest have developed their verbal talents among the fleshpots of erotic literature, and are prepared now to turn them to more legitimate uses if anyone is willing to give them employment.

Implicit in the stance of the prodigal poets is the assumption that

---

[46] See Gosson 1974, introduction.
[47] See Helgerson 1976.
[48] Luke 15:11–32.

the centuries-old attack on poetry was at least partly justified.[49] For the early Elizabethan poets as for the poet-haters, erotic fictions and amorous verses are the products of idleness; they awaken unhealthy sexual appetites in their young readers, and are essentially un-English in character, self-conscious imitations of the diabolical Italian books condemned by Ascham, and just as able to seduce their English audience into an acceptance of perverse Italian values: atheism, republicanism, intellectual sophistication, and freedom of speech. Why, then, did these poets write poetry? And more importantly, why did they print it? One answer might be that they fully intended their readers to recognize the dangers young men courted when writing erotic verse and prose: the danger of wasting their considerable talents on the composition of worthless texts, and of seducing their youthful audiences into enrolling in the 'school of abuse' where women and poets were the principal teachers.[50] For other writers as for Sidney, the fact that they were writing poetry at all showed that they were idle: that they had been offered no better employment, and that their education was restlessly searching for an outlet. Followers of Ascham might well have suspected that writing poetry was merely a prelude to producing still more controversial texts – such as propaganda for England's enemies. The poets of the 1570s were effectively engaging in a form of blackmail: give us work, they warned the Elizabethan government, or somebody else will: and the work for which we are best suited is that of undermining the moral fibre of nations.

The potentially harmful effects of erotic poetry were certainly taken seriously by the Elizabethan censors. The most celebrated poet of the 1570s, George Gascoigne, had at least one collection of poetry withdrawn from circulation by the ecclesiastical High Commission, the body responsible for vetting printed texts.[51] This may well have been reason enough for Sidney to have avoided mentioning him in the *Apology*. And one of the young poets who wrote a reply to Gosson's *School of Abuse*, Thomas Lodge, had his *Defence of Poetry* (1579) suppressed as soon as it was printed.[52] Lodge responded in his next published book, *An Alarum against Usurers* (1584), by presenting himself as yet another penitent prodigal, eager to make up for his earlier rashness by using his talents in a more socially acceptable manner – that is, by joining Gosson in satirizing contemporary social abuses. In his *Defence of Poetry* Lodge makes much of the point that Gosson bears a close resemblance to the poets

---

[49] See Herman 1996.
[50] See Maslen 1997, introduction.
[51] See C. T. Prouty, *George Gascoigne: Elizabethan Courtier, Soldier, and Poet* (New York, 1942). For a more recent account of the censorship of Gascoigne's work see Cyndia Susan Clegg, *Press Censorship in Elizabethan England* (Cambridge, 1997), ch. 5.
[52] See Smith 1904, I, 61, and Helgerson 1977, ch. 6, esp. 108–9.

he despises: 'You say that Poets are subtil; if so, you haue learned that poynt of them; you can well glose on a trifeling text' (Smith 1904, I, 65). Because of this resemblance, Lodge hopes it will be easy to effect Gosson's conversion from poet-hater to lover of the Muses;[53] but, as it turns out, he found it more expedient to convert himself (temporarily at least) into a second Gosson. And this was a course followed by a number of his contemporaries.

Lodge's *Defence of Poetry* does not look to modern eyes a particularly controversial work; yet he himself seems to have had a premonition that it would be taken as such by the Elizabethan authorities, especially in the section defending the stage. 'I must now search my wits,' he announces:

> I see this shall passe throughe many seuere sensors handling; I must aduise me what I write, and write that I would wysh. I way wel the seriousnes of the cause, and regarde very much the iudges of my endeuor, whom, if I could, I would perswade that I woulde not nourish abuse, nether mayntaine that which should be an vniuersall discomoditye. I hope they wil not iudge before they read, nether condemne without occasion.
>
> (Smith 1904, I, 79)

Lodge's acute sense of the seriousness of the case against him stems from his wholehearted agreement with parts of Gosson's attack on the con-temporary theatre. 'I praise your reprehension in that,' he tells Gosson at one point, 'you did well in discommending the abuse, and surely I wysh that that folly wer disclaymed; it is not to be admitted, it maks those sinne, whiche perhaps, if it were not, would haue binne present at a good sermon' (84). And in *An Alarum against Usurers* – which is dedicated to Sidney – Lodge concedes that Gosson had 'a good cause' for his objections to the Elizabethan stage and 'a good pen' with which to articulate them. Despite his willingness to take up the opposite 'cause' in the dispute about poetry – and university students were taught to argue *in utramque partem* (on both sides) in any debate – Lodge seems to have shared some of Gosson's opinions on the current state of English poetry. And there is reason to suppose that Sidney, too, found much to agree with in Gosson's polemic.[54]

Like Lodge's *Alarum against Usurers*, *The School of Abuse* was dedi-cated to Sidney, and it has often been argued that the *Apology* was written as an answer to Gosson. It has also been assumed that Sidney was implacably hostile to Gosson's position. This assumption would seem to be borne out by a comment in a letter from the poet Edmund Spenser to the Cambridge scholar Gabriel Harvey, published by Harvey in 1580. After mentioning a recent conversation with Sidney, Spenser

[53] See Smith 1904, I, 72–3.
[54] See Herman 1996, ch. 2.

goes on: 'Newe Bookes I heare of none, but only of one, that writing a certaine Booke, called *The Schoole of Abuse*, and dedicating it to Maister *Sidney*, was for hys labor scorned, if at leaste it be in the goodnesse of that nature to scorne' (Smith 1904, I, 89). Spenser does not tell us what, if anything, Sidney 'scorned' about *The School of Abuse* – or how Spenser knew he scorned it. Perhaps Sidney objected to the style of the treatise, since Gosson writes in the elaborately patterned manner which has come to be known as Euphuism, and which is dismissed in the *Apology* as 'a most tedious prattling' (114/30–1). But there is no evidence in Spenser's letter that Sidney found fault with Gosson's *reasoning*: it was his *dedication* that he is supposed to have resented. Spenser tells this story to show that it is the height of folly 'not to regarde aforehande the inclination and qualitie of him to whome wee dedicate oure Bookes', and thus to explain his hesitation over whether to dedicate his own writings ('my *Slomber* and the other pamphlets') to Sidney. Spenser evidently felt he had as much chance as Gosson of being scorned for his presumption in seeking Sidney's patronage without permission. Besides, Gosson does not seem to have fallen out of favour with his scornful dedicatee. He dedicated his second book to Sidney,[55] despite the fact that it contained a spirited defence of *The School of Abuse*, and this suggests that Gosson had received at least some sort of reward or encouragement for his earlier dedication. Sidney must have had an exceptionally 'noble nature' if he went on permitting a writer he despised to associate him with his publications.

But Sidney shares many of Gosson's views – or seems to accept them at various crucial points in his argument. Like Gosson (and like Plato before him) he argues that the ideal poetry should be simple and easily understood, and that it should not encourage its readers to confuse good with evil: 'If the poet do his part aright, he will show you in Tantalus, Atreus, and such like, nothing that is not to be shunned; in Cyrus, Aeneas, Ulysses, each thing to be followed' (92/34–6). But the pregnant 'if' that begins this sentence – one of the many conditionals that fill the *Apology* – indicates that Sidney can offer no guarantees that the poet *will* 'do his part aright'. In fact, poets very often do the opposite. The comic genre, for instance, has been brought into disrepute by 'naughty play-makers and stage-keepers' (98/2–3), especially in the Elizabethan theatre (112/11ff.). As we have seen, Sidney agrees with Gosson that the wrong sort of poetry is dominant in his own country, and that bad poets have been complicit with the recent decline of England as a military power. Sidney, in fact, is prepared to acknowledge that much modern poetry 'abuseth men's wit, training it to wanton sinfulness and lustful love' (103/44); and his frequent use of the term 'abuse' at this important

---

[55] *The Ephemerides of Phialo* (1579).

stage in his discussion, together with many other verbal echoes of Gosson's and Ascham's texts, brings him perilously close to accepting their strictures. He reverses Gosson's claim that 'Poetry abuseth man's wit' and proposes instead that 'man's wit abuseth Poetry' (104/16–17); but he goes on to echo Gosson's assessment of the dire consequences of such abuse: 'I yield that Poesy may not only be abused, but that being abused, by the reason of his sweet charming force, it can do more hurt than any other *army* of words' (104/27–9, my emphasis). This is no argument for banning poetry from the state, he adds, since 'whatsoever, being abused, doth most harm, being rightly used . . . doth most good' (104/31–3). Nevertheless, the drift of Sidney's reasoning here is that poetry may serve as the deadliest of verbal weapons, the soldier's most prized intellectual possession, and that its services are as readily available to a nation's enemies – domestic as well as foreign – as to its defenders: 'With a sword thou mayest kill thy father, and with a sword thou mayest defend thy prince and country' (104/41–2). And within a few pages he is confessing that poetry in England is in no fit state to defend its prince and country. The implication is that the nations where poetry is highly regarded are in a very much stronger position than England when it comes to emulating the military successes of the Macedonian conqueror Alexander or the 'triumphant captains' of ancient Rome. Poetry is a 'fit soil for praise to dwell upon' (108/9); and nations whose 'soil' is inimical to poetry (and the only such nation on earth, Sidney tells us, is England (108/42)) are in danger of having the poets' weapons turned against them.

Sidney also agrees with some of Gosson's more specific criticisms of current English poetry. Gosson argued that 'in all our recreations we shoulde haue an instructer at our elbowes to feede the soule' (Gosson 1974, 88–9), and condemned the English stage for failing to act as such a spiritual instructor. Sidney says something similar. Like the mythical youth Icarus, who ignored the instructions of his father Daedalus and died as a result, English poets pay no attention to the rules and patterns which would help them to perfect their art (109/39ff.). Sidney's reference to Daedalus leaves his readers in no doubt as to the calamitous consequences for the poet of ignoring one's instructors – Icarus's dismissal of his father's guidance was frequently used as an analogue for the disobedience of the prodigal son. For Sidney as for Gosson, England is a nation of prodigal sons, willing to do anything to satisfy their cravings for money and status, yet arrogantly self-reliant and contemptuous of even the best authorities when it comes to seeking models for their compositions. Most English poetry has no logical structure (it is 'a confused mass of words'), and the theatre in particular offends against the rules of 'honest civility' as well as of 'skilful Poetry' (110/29); in other words, it threatens to reintroduce barbarism on to English soil. Like Gosson,

Sidney considers that English plays lack a sense either of place or of history (110/41ff.); and, in a text which lays heavy emphasis on the antiquity of poetry and its long association with the English nation, such geographical and historical negligence is unforgivable, even in plays that deal with a fictitious past. In addition, English plays violate the rules of decorum or 'decency': the notion, derived from the Roman poet Horace, that each social class should be represented by poets in a language and poetic genre suitable to its position in the social hierarchy. As the playwright George Whetstone put it in the dedication to his play *Promos and Cassandra* (1578):

> Manye tymes (to make mirthe) they [i.e. the playwrights] make a Clowne companion with a Kinge; in theyr graue Counsels they allow the aduise of fooles; yea, they vse one order of speach for all persons: a grose *Indecorum*, for a Crowe wyll yll counterfet the Nightingale's sweete voice; euen so affected speeche doth misbecome a Clowne.
>
> (Smith 1904, I, 59–60)

In Sidney's opinion, too, the London playwrights indiscriminately mix 'kings and clowns' (112/2) – monarchs and peasants – in the interest of making their audiences laugh at 'sinful things' (113/1); a breach of decorum which many Elizabethan commentators held to jeopardize the stability of the state itself by encouraging insubordination. Finally, English poets struggle so hard to make their language look attractive that they deck it out like a foreign 'courtesan' or whore, using 'so far-fetched words, [that] they may seem monsters, but must seem strangers, to any poor Englishman' (113/36ff.). In other words, they have sullied the reputation both of their 'mother Poesy' (113/16–17) and of their mother tongue. For Sidney as well as for Gosson, English poetry suffers from a 'common infection' – a textually transmitted disease – imported from abroad, and Sidney himself is 'sick among the rest' (115/9).

The *Apology* presents itself as a cure for England's poetic sickness. Through its exposure of the symptoms of the national infection, Sidney hopes that English poets, by 'acknowledging ourselves somewhat awry ... may bend to the right use both of matter and manner' (115/11–12). At the same time, by characterizing these poets as the descendants of Icarus, the classical equivalent of the prodigal son, he offers little hope that conventional pedagogic methods will heal or convert them. In Elizabethan versions of Christ's parable, the young man is always subjected to a lengthy moral diatribe from a representative of the older generation before he sets out on his sexual adventures. And the young man always ignores the advice he is given. Only bitter experience finally convinces him that his patriarchal counsellor was right all along; only the pain of going 'awry' can lend authority to a teacher's theories. But Sidney's *Apology* is not the advice of an elderly teacher. Sidney is a young man 'sick among the rest', enrolled in the school of abuse like the poets and playwrights he castigates: as prodigal, as self-absorbed, as idle and as sexually irresponsible as the rest of his generation.[56] It is not for nothing that Sidney recommends the parable of the 'lost child and the gracious father' as an ideal subject for poets (91/37ff.), and as having a particular imaginative hold on Sidney himself ('Truly, for myself, me seems I see before my eyes the lost child's disdainful prodigality, turned to envy a swine's dinner'). Sidney is not, as he has often been presented, a lone genius who dissociates himself from the poetic practices of his less distinguished fellow-countrymen. The advantages of his education and his class may have given him a wider intellectual frame of reference than that of mere gentleman-poets such as Gascoigne, Whetstone, and Lodge; but he was taught along similar lines, his concerns were often identical, and he presented himself as an author using the same scriptural paradigm: that of the rebellious young man who spurns the advice of his elders and nearly loses everything in the process. Sidney casts himself as a prodigal. But the vital difference between him and his non-aristocratic contemporaries is that he does not cast himself as a *penitent* prodigal.

The form his prodigality takes in his poetic works would have been instantly recognizable to readers of Ascham's *Schoolmaster*. Like the Italianate young men in the English Court, and like the young men Ascham describes as 'quick wits' – masters of verbal improvisation, rapid assimilators of information, always ready with a clever but superficial response to any question – Sidney the poet is obsessed with sexual desire. Both versions of the *Arcadia* and his sonnet-sequence *Astrophil and Stella* take love as their subject. All three texts are based (among other things) on Italian books: the pastoral romance *Arcadia* (1485) by Jacopo Sannazzaro, and the sonnets of the fourteenth-century humanist Petrarch. The first version of the *Arcadia* (completed c. 1580) – known as the *Old Arcadia* – describes a young prince, Pyrocles, breaking away from his conventional education and succumbing instead to the irresistible attractions of what Sidney calls the 'school of affection' (*OA*, 276). And the influence of this school is very much as Ascham and Gosson predicted: it transforms Pyrocles into a woman (he dons a female disguise to get close to the princess he loves), transforms his speech from rational discourse to the metaphor-laden discourse of poetry, and diverts all his intellectual energies into formulating elaborate plots to distract his superiors while he gets into bed with his royal mistress. The political consequences of Pyrocles's transformation are as disastrous as the poet-haters could have imagined. Rebellion breaks out in the Greek state of Arcadia as a direct result of Pyrocles's machinations – the rebels are afraid that Basilius, their ruler, is being governed by the strange woman who has insinuated herself into his household. By the last part of the book

[56] See Helgerson 1976, ch. 7.

Basilius is seemingly dead, poisoned by his own wife; his daughters are in prison under suspicion of collaborating with foreign spies; the Arcadian throne is occupied by a neighbouring monarch; and Pyrocles and his friend Musidorus are awaiting execution for rape and murder. The combined effects of erotic poetry as Plato and his successors saw them – treachery, intellectual oversophistication, youthful disobedience, the feminizing of young men by their attraction to women, and the rest – could hardly have been more graphically illustrated, it seems, than in the dramatic finale of the *Old Arcadia*. And the direct link between truancy and high treason could hardly have been more convincingly traced.

Astrophil and Stella, too, explicitly declares its affiliation with the literature of truancy. The famous opening sonnet depicts the poet Astrophil discarding all the 'artificial rules' and 'imitative patterns' made available to him by his education and by the writings of others, in an effort to find words to express his desire for a woman:

> But words came halting forth, wanting Invention's stay,
> Invention, Nature's child, fled step-dame Studie's blowes,
> And others' feete still seem'd but strangers in my way.
> Thus great with child to speake, and helplesse in my throwes,
> Biting my trewand pen, beating my selfe for spite,
> 'Foole,' said my Muse to me, 'look in thy heart and write.'
> (Ringler 1962, 166)

The poem announces Astrophil as a student in the 'school of affection' – fleeing the blows of an aggressive educational system, like the pupils of Eton college in the anecdote that opens Ascham's *Schoolmaster*, who ran away for fear of a beating.[57] Much of *Astrophil and Stella* is taken up with metaphors of the schoolroom, and Astrophil's neglect of the lessons taught by schoolmasters, churchmen (as in sonnet 5), and friendly advisers (sonnets 14 and 21) is a consequence of his preoccupation with lessons taught by Cupid, by his mistress Stella, and by a kiss, which he calls 'schoolmaster of delight' (sonnet 79). Unlike previous Elizabethan prodigals, however, Astrophil makes no final apology for his truancy from his conventional schooling. The lessons he learns at Stella's hands are as difficult to master as the complexities of grammar, translation and political theory as taught in an Elizabethan university – indeed, he never fully masters them. And his acceptance of Stella both as his schoolmistress and eventually as his 'Queene' (sonnet 107) remains unchanged at the end of the sequence. This truant never loses his regard for the woman, the passion, and the system of values for which he committed truancy. In the same way, despite all the disasters they have

---

[57] See Ascham 1904, 175ff.

brought on themselves and their mistresses, the princes Pyrocles and Musidorus in the *Old Arcadia* remain proudly impenitent as they languish in prison awaiting trial in the final 'Book or Act' of the narrative. 'We have lived,' one of them tells the other, 'and have lived to be good to ourselves and others' (*OA*, 321). If Astrophil and the princes end up in a dark place, it is not because they make the wrong choices, but because the stars, and the older generation who lay claim to ownership of the stars and the destinies they govern, are ranged against them.

According to his biographer Katherine Duncan-Jones, Sidney's own life was marked by repeated acts of truancy: from his efforts to avoid the attentions of his self-appointed mentor, the political theorist Hubert Languet, in the early 1570s, to his prolonged absences from Court at the end of the decade, which Languet regarded as detrimental to the young man's political career.[58] In the penultimate year of his life Sidney made elaborate preparations for a particularly dramatic flight from his domestic responsibilities to both wife and country, when he arranged to accompany Sir Francis Drake on an expedition to the West Indies without the permission of the Queen or his father-in-law.[59] His flight (Greville tells us) was prevented only by a last-minute intervention by the Queen herself. Truancy, then – the minor act of rebellion whereby the pupil takes the reins of his education into his own hands, in protest (according to Roger Ascham) against the pedagogic methods of inadequate schoolmasters – remained a course of action Sidney was always willing to contemplate as a mark of his distaste for the prescriptions of his elders. And *An Apology for Poetry* marks itself out as a peculiarly thoughtful act of truancy from its first page.

The structure of *An Apology for Poetry*

Before going on to examine Sidney's text as the work of a politically sophisticated prodigal, we need to consider the rhetorical form Sidney gave it. Sidney's early readers would have been trained from childhood in the art of composing and analysing persuasive discourse, using models provided by textbooks on rhetoric such as Quintilian's *Institutio oratoria* or the anonymous *Rhetorica ad Herennium*. Since the work of Kenneth Myrick in the 1930s it has been generally recognized that the *Apology* is organized along the lines of a classical oration or formal speech: specifically, a judicial or forensic oration of the kind that would have been used by the counsel for the defence in a criminal trial.[60] This supports the notion that Sidney wrote it as a response to a specific attack

---

[58] See Duncan-Jones 1991, 71ff.
[59] See Duncan-Jones 1991, 273–4, and Stewart 2000, 265–74.
[60] See Myrick 1965, ch. 2.

or set of attacks such as Gosson's *School of Abuse*. Geoffrey Shepherd sees it as falling into seven parts, along the lines recommended by Sidney's acquaintance Thomas Wilson in his celebrated handbook *The Art of Rhetorique* (1553).[61] The parts may be construed as follows:

1 INTRODUCTION or EXORDIUM (81/1–82/4)
Sidney adopts what the author of the *Rhetorica ad Herennium* calls a 'subtle approach' to the case – an approach to be used when the audience is assumed to be prejudiced against the client (in this case, poetry). He uses a humorous anecdote to establish a genial relationship between himself and his audience, and establishes his concern with the theory and practice of the art he is defending.

2 STATEMENT OF FACTS or NARRATION (82/5–86/16)
Sidney presents the facts which give dignity to poetry, such as its antiquity, its universality, and the etymological meanings of the various words for poet in Latin, Greek, and English. He makes a preliminary statement about what makes poetry superior to the other arts: it is not constrained by the laws of the material universe.

3 PROPOSITION (86/17–20)
This summarizes the argument of the *Apology*. Poetry is to be valued for what it is: imitation which aims 'to teach and delight' its recipients.

4 DIVISION (86/21–87/44)
Divides up poetry into its different kinds, in order to clarify the definition he gave of it in the PROPOSITION, and to form the basis for his ensuing demonstration of its value.

5 PROOF or CONFIRMATION (88/1–100/14)
Argues for poetry's superiority to its rival disciplines, philosophy and history, by showing that it is more effective in persuading people to virtuous action. Analyses the functions of the different kinds of poetry.

[The proof is followed by a SUMMARY of the whole argument up to this point (100/15–35). The summary concludes that poetry is the best of all disciplines.]

6 REFUTATION (100/36–108/11)
Demolishes the case that has been made against poetry by its antagonists.

[Again the REFUTATION is followed by a SUMMARY of this part of Sidney's argument (108/12–21), which turns the inade-

---

[61] See Shepherd 1965, 11ff.

quacy of the case against poetry into further PROOF of its excellence.]

[DIGRESSION (108/22–116/14)
Discusses the current state of poetry in England, and shows how it fails to meet the standards of ideal poetry as they have been laid out in parts 2 to 6. The digression takes the form of an oration within an oration, and can be divided into five parts:

i. STATEMENT OF FACTS or NARRATION, which describes the situation: that poetry was once highly valued in England, but is now despised and badly practised (108/22–109/23).

ii. PROPOSITION, that poets need to recognize their own mistakes if they are to write good poetry (109/24–33).

iii. DIVISION. This identifies three prerequisites for the writing of good poetry: theory, imitation, and practice; and divides poetic practice into 'two principal parts – matter to be expressed by words and words to express our matter' (109/33–110/10).

iv. PROOF or CONFIRMATION that poetry is badly practised in England. The evidence is arranged under the two headings established in the DIVISION, 'matter' and 'words' (subject matter and style). Under the first he deals with defects in past practice of poetry in England, then with defects in contemporary drama and verse (110/11–113/34). Under the second he deals with various kinds of verbal and stylistic affectation, and concludes with a commendation of the English language for its rich vocabulary and metrical versatility (113/35–116/14).

v. CONCLUSION of DIGRESSION (16/15–20). This leads into]

7   CONCLUSION or PERORATION of the whole *Apology*
(116/20 to the end)

It will be clear, I hope, from what I have said so far, that I regard the 'Digression' – the oration-within-an oration which deals with the state of poetry in contemporary England – as the core of the *Apology*, its *raison d'être*. From beginning to end the *Apology* is concerned with the vexed relationship between theory and practice, between the imaginary ideal of poetry and the extant poetic texts which have never – or very rarely – met that ideal. It would seem inevitable that an essay written in English which takes poetry as its subject, and which stresses the value of 'virtuous action', of practising what responsible poet-teachers preach, should reach its culmination in an analysis

of the poetic art as it is currently practised in England.[62] But if the
'Digression' is the most important section of the *Apology*, why call it a
digression?

The answer is that Sidney himself encourages his readers to treat this
section as an appendix, the work of a man who has been carried away
by enthusiasm into areas extraneous to his initial project, which was to
defend poetry *in general* rather than as the product of any particular
culture. 'But since I have run so long a career in this matter', the section
begins, 'methinks, before I give my pen a full stop, it shall be *but a little
more lost time* to inquire' why England has abandoned its former passion
for imaginative writing (108/22ff., my emphasis). Later he apologizes for
'straying' from matters relevant to poetry into a discussion of style which
might have been better suited to a teacher of rhetoric (115/5). The section
ends with another apology: 'much more . . . might be said, but that I
find already the triflingness of this discourse is much too much enlarged'
(116/12–14). The section on English poetry, we are told, is a waste of
time, an unwarranted turning aside from the strict topic of the essay, a
trifle which threatens to confirm the 'triflingness' of the *Apology* as a
whole.

But this last remark should alert us to the ironic tone of Sidney's
apologies for his Digression. The *Apology* has made claims for poetry
that are very far from trifling, and has supported these claims with
weighty authorities, from the gods of the humanist intellect – Aristotle,
Plato, Plutarch – to the Bible itself. The Digression is trifling only if the
rest of Sidney's argument may be easily dismissed, and his case has been
too strongly argued for that. The apparently marginal status of his discussion of English poetry within his essay reflects the marginal status of
poetry in Elizabethan England: and by the time we reach this discussion Sidney might reasonably expect us to be convinced – or at least to
be convinced that he is convinced – that marginalizing poetry is a
mistake. He might also expect us to have remembered that a light treatment of a subject need not imply that the subject is unimportant. In
his 'Refutation' he recalls the humanist tradition of handling serious subjects lightly, mentioning as examples two serio-comic humanist treatises
which were hugely influential in his time: *The Praise of Folly*, by the great
educationalist Erasmus, and *Of the Vanitie of the Artes and Sciences* by
the magician-scientist Cornelius Agrippa. Erasmus and Agrippa, he tells
us, 'had another foundation, than the superficial part would promise'

---

[62] In saying so I am taking issue with O. B. Hardison, whose influential essay 'The
Two Voices of Sidney's *Apology*', in Kinney 1988, 45–61, argues that the *Apology* was written
in two stages, beginning life as a response to Gosson's *School of Abuse*, and later partly
revised as a neo-classical tract. The Digression, Hardison argues, incorporates Sidney's revi-
sions, and its argument cannot be reconciled with the rest of the *Apology*. See Hadfield
1994, ch. 5, for a convincing refutation of Hardison's thesis.

(101/15–16) – that is, their apparently facetious texts had serious points to make. Both were critiques, written by progressive intellectuals, of the educational, political and religious shortcomings of the early sixteenth-century European authorities in all three areas; both made extensive and elaborate use of many kinds of irony; and Sidney draws on both texts in his essay. Bearing this in mind, it would not be unreasonable to suppose that the 'foundation' of the *Apology* might lie in its most professedly irrelevant section: the Digression. The supposition may be strengthened if we also bear in mind that no essay written in England before the *Apology* had gone into much detail about the state of English verse, fiction or drama – with a few notable exceptions, such as Gosson's *School of Abuse* and E. K.'s notes on *The Shepheardes Calender*. The Latin *Oration in Praise of the Poetic Art* by John Rainolds,[63] the treatise *De re poetica* by Richard Wills (Wills 1958), even Lodge's reply to Gosson, say little or nothing about anything written in English. Sidney's contemporaries could be expected to pay particular attention to the part of his work that dealt with a topic that had hardly been touched on in the past. And this section has been carefully prepared for in the sections leading up to it.

The *Apology* opens with a statement of the situation which has 'provoked' Sidney to write in defence of poetry: that 'from almost the highest estimation of learning' the poetic art has 'fallen to be the laughing-stock of children' (81/31ff.). The hostile readers responsible for this situation are clearly his English contemporaries, those men of his own nation who 'inveigh against Poetry' in spite of their learning (82/5–6). In fact, Sidney's implied readers are always English. He assumes they share a common interest in 'our mother tongue' (82/29), a common contempt for 'our neighbour country Ireland' (83/19), and a common awareness of the Welsh as 'the true remnant of the ancient Britons' (83/28). They are likely to be offended by his application to the scriptures of a term – poetry – 'which is *among us* thrown down to so ridiculous an estimation' (84/29–30, my emphasis), and are equally likely to be impressed by the happy coincidence that 'we Englishmen', like the Greeks, refer to the poet as a 'maker' (84/37–8). And the poet-haters are particularly concerned with what they take to be the decline in military standards 'both in other nations and *in ours*, before poets did soften us' (102/27–8, my emphasis). These and other allusions to the collective Englishness of the *Apology*'s writer and his readers suggest that both parties will have a considerable stake in the section relating to poetry in contemporary England.

---

[63] Ascribed by J. W. Binns to Henry Dethick: see Binns, 'Henry Dethick in Praise of Poetry: the First Appearance in Print of an Elizabethan Treatise', *Library* 30 (1975), 199–216.

The shape of the *Apology*, too, implies that an analysis of the situation in England will form the climax of its argument. A fall has taken place: poetry has 'fallen' or been 'thrown down' from its once lofty place in the nation's estimation, and has reached its nadir in the present day; and the *Apology* neatly replicates this plunge in poetry's fortunes. A simplified analysis of the essay's structure might note (as Shepherd notes)[64] that it arranges itself in three broad sections: first a commendation of poetry as the best of all arts and sciences, then a refutation of the case against it, and finally a summary of the problems and potential of poetry written in English. Broadly speaking, the trajectory of the three sections is downwards: the first deals with poetry as it ought to be, the second with poetry as it is imagined by its enemies, the third with the current poetic practices that confirm the worst of these hostile imaginings. The *Apology*, then, might be said to re-enact the biblical Fall of Man, from the perfect Edenic state – which Sidney conflates with the classical Golden Age described by Hesiod and Ovid – when poetry assisted at the birth of civilization; through the Iron Ages of ancient Greece and Rome, when heroic poets such as Xenophon and Virgil reminded their readers of the ideals they had lost;[65] to the degenerate Elizabethan state, when the poet has been reduced to an object of derision. According to this analysis, the Digression forms an integral part of the *Apology*'s admirably inclusive account of literary history. The narrowing of its focus, from poetry in general to poetry in a specific place and time, mimicks the narrowing concerns of the poet as he responds to the pressures of an increasingly timid national regime.

But the fact that poetry has followed in its history the inexorable decline that sixteenth-century historians traced in the successive generations of humankind does not rob it of its preeminence among the arts. All other fields of human endeavour have undergone a similar falling-off, from the military discipline to the academic studies of history and philosophy. The final end of all learning, Sidney tells us, 'is to lead and draw us to as high a perfection as our degenerate souls, made worse by their clayey lodgings, can be capable of' (88/7–9). And the only branch of learning that takes the fallen nature of mankind into due consideration – that recognizes both in theory and practice the degeneracy, as well as the supreme possibilities, of the human mind and soul – is poetry. Far from undermining Sidney's case, then, the *Apology*'s re-enactment of the Fall reinforces his argument for the value of this most despised of human arts. Poetry may have declined and fallen like the nations that have practised it, but it still provides the firmest foundation – or the most fruitful soil, to use another of Sidney's metaphors

---

[64] See Shepherd 1965, 12.
[65] Sidney describes Xenophon's *Cyropaedia* as 'an absolute heroical poem'; see 87/31–2.

– for moral and national regeneration. And the nation that stands to benefit most from this regeneration is the nation whose language is best suited to the metrical and lexical needs of poetry. It should hardly come as a surprise when Sidney announces at the end of the Digression that this nation is England.

Poetry and the Fall

Sidney's theory of poetry is famously eclectic. He draws on an immense range of theoretical texts, poetic and philosophical, political, educational, and historical, and mentions the names of many thinkers ancient and modern to whom he is more or less indebted, among them Agrippa, Aristotle, Erasmus, Horace, Landino, More, Plato, Plutarch, Scaliger, and Xenophon. He does not mention by name a great many more with whom he was undoubtedly familiar, such as Amyot, Ascham, Castiglione, Gosson, Elyot, Minturno, Ramus, and Ronsard. Scholarly opinion is sharply divided as to exactly how well he knew these writers' works and how important they were to him. How well, for instance, did he know the Italian poetic theories to which his own bears so many similarities? He had plenty of opportunity to get to know them, since he had travelled in Italy and spoke Italian – but some similarities could as easily have arisen from conversation or even coincidence as from first-hand acquaintance.[66] He refers to Dante's *Divine Comedy* twice (93/29 and 117/1), and this has led some scholars to assume that he had read the greatest of medieval poems, but if so one might also assume that he would have had a great deal more to say about it than he does. In the analysis of the *Apology* that follows, I shall concentrate on explaining what I take to be Sidney's argument, and shall make little attempt to indicate the many points at which it intersects with other contemporary theories except where this seems helpful to elucidate his meaning. The notes to this edition indicate his possible debts in detail. At this stage it is merely necessary to point out that Sidney's originality lies not in the individual points he makes but in the way he weaves them together.

If the overall structure of the *Apology* is that of a judicial oration in seven parts, its metaphorical structure is closer to that of a poem, an interlaced romance such as Ariosto's *Orlando Furioso* or Sidney's own *New Arcadia*.[67] Sequences of metaphors run through the text from start

[66] Shepherd's contention, for instance, that Sidney had 'a direct knowledge of advanced contemporary theorising on art' – meaning the theories of the Italian Mannerists (Shepherd 1965, 64–6) – is challenged by D. H. Craig in his essay 'A Hybrid Growth: Sidney's Theory of Poetry in *An Apology for Poetry*', in Kinney 1988, 62–80.
[67] For a discussion of the *Apology* as poem, see Catherine Barnes, 'The Hidden Persuader: the Complex Speaking Voice of Sidney's *Defence of Poetry*', in Kinney 1986, 155–65.

to finish, surfacing and resurfacing like coloured threads in a tapestry – the 'rich tapestry', perhaps, to which he compares poetry itself (85/24) – and lend a continuity to his discussion over and above its sometimes ambiguously worded argument.[68] Many of the scholarly disagreements over Sidney's meaning arise from the intensely figurative means by which he expresses himself. But close examination of these metaphors can help to identify the consistent set of concerns which lies at the heart of his efforts to rehabilitate his craft. And such an examination can also help to remind us that the *Apology* is a brilliant exemplar of the best kind of early modern poetry as well as a defence of it.

For Sidney, poetry is the art of the fallen world.[69] The point is worth repeating because it is fundamental to his argument: humanity has suffered at some point in its past an appalling calamity which left it flawed, damaged, unhinged – capable, at best, of recalling mentally the state of perfection from which it has been precipitated, but unable to reproduce more than an occasional dim shadow of that perfection in its daily activities. This was a view of history shared by both the Christian and the classical religious traditions. The former mourned the loss of the special relationship between God and human beings that obtained in the Garden of Eden; the latter lamented the happy society of the Golden Age, when the genial craftsman-god Saturn ruled the universe, when gods and people and beasts lived in harmony together and the fruits of the earth were distributed equally among its inhabitants. According to both traditions, the human memory of perfection was growing dimmer as the passing years carried the species ever further from its origins. Human beings were growing more selfish, more violent and devious in pursuit of their own interests, less willing to subject their private desires to the impartial test of reason. And, according to Sidney, the only human activity capable of bringing a substantial proportion of the species some way back along the road to its fortunate past was poetry, because of its equal appeal to the two warring components of the human constitution, reason and passion.

From the beginning, the *Apology* emphasizes the sheer difficulty of making its case in this fallen world, where both the apologist and his readers are locked in their own peculiar brands of passionate self-obsession. It opens with an anecdote about one of Sidney's teachers, the master horseman Pugliano, an irascible Italian who one day waxed so eloquent in praise of his discipline – horsemanship – 'that if I had not been a piece of a logician before I came to him, I think he would have

---

[68] For a discussion of one such group of metaphors – military ones – see Edward Berry, 'The Poet as Warrior in Sidney's *Defence of Poetry*', *SEL* 29 (1989), 21–34.

[69] For Sidney's handling of the Fall in the *Apology* see Frank B. Evans, 'The Concept of the Fall in Sidney's *Apologie*', *Renaissance Papers* (1969), 9–14, and Craig, 'A Hybrid Growth', in Kinney 1988, 62–80.

persuaded me to have wished myself a horse' (81/18–20). The incident taught Sidney a valuable lesson: 'that self-love is better than any gilding to make that seem gorgeous wherein ourselves are parties' (81/21–2). Everyone in the *Apology* is equally addicted to self-love – the text is populated with Puglianos – and the first third of the essay stresses this repeatedly. It presents itself as a competition between the arts or sciences, a sort of intellectual Olympic games in which poetry pits itself against its rivals among the academic disciplines in a bid to establish itself as the best of all forms of knowledge available to humanity. Poetry, of course, emerges victorious, but Sidney has warned us from the start that this is inevitable. Like Pugliano's his defence is driven by 'strong affection' for his subject, like Pugliano he may at times use 'weak arguments' but will end by convincing himself (if nobody else) more firmly than ever (81/23). And like Pugliano he addresses an audience which is equally driven by 'strong affection' – that is, by their emotional attachment to poetry's rival disciplines.

At each stage he reminds us of ways in which the 'judgment' – his favourite word for the power of rational assessment – is contaminated by the passions or emotions. When he claims that parts of the Bible may be described as poetry, he announces at once his fear that the claim will horrify some of his readers, and begs them to consider the point 'with quiet judgments' (84/30). This suggests that many readers' judgments are very far from quiet (that is, disinterested), and that they will be prone to articulate their private opinions and prejudices noisily and aggressively if Sidney fails to calm them down. Later he accuses those who despise 'philosophical' poetry of having had their reason distorted by some sort of illness, as a sick man's appetite is warped by his condition: 'the fault is in their judgments quite out of taste, and not in the sweet food of sweetly uttered knowledge' (86/38–40). This in turn suggests that there should be some universal standard by which the validity of a person's judgment may be measured. But there is little agreement as to what this standard may be. Astronomers, scientists, musicians and mathematicians passionately cleave to the notion that their own supremely rational disciplines offer the most direct pathway to 'perfection' – and betray their personal failings in their efforts to prove it (88/4ff.). Philosophers and historians, the poet's chief rivals in the competition between the arts, become enraged before they have even begun to make a case for the supremacy of their respective disciplines: the philosophers get 'angry with any man in whom they see the foul fault of anger' (88/40–1), the historian denies 'in a great chafe, that any man . . . is comparable to him' (89/16). Enemies of heroic poetry are 'prejudiced with a prejudicating humour' (100/6–7). If we conceive of the *Apology* as an intervention for the defence in an imaginary trial, with poetry in the dock, the final 'sentence' or legal judgment (88/4) looks as though it will be hopelessly compromised by the sheer weight of hostile emotions ranged against the accused.

We might well be reminded of the trial of the princes at the end of the *Old Arcadia*. In the fifth and final book of Sidney's prose fiction the heroes of the book, Pyrocles and his friend Musidorus, are charged with treason, rape and regicide, and find themselves vilified by a vindictive prosecutor whose sense of justice has been perverted by his rage and grief over the apparent murder of his late master, Duke Basilius of Arcadia. In his eagerness to see Basilius avenged, the prosecutor is even willing to go to the length of suppressing vital evidence for the defence – letters from the Duke's two daughters exonerating the princes – so as to obtain the sentence he requires. But however 'overgone with rage' he may be (*OA*, 345), the prosecutor is no more than an extreme case of the susceptibility to overblown emotion and prejudice that characterizes all human beings. The judge himself recognizes this when he instructs the Arcadians to 'remember I am a man; that is to say, a creature whose reason is often darkened with error' (315). And the structure of the *Old Arcadia* resembles that of the *Apology* in its recognition of the original cause of this tendency to 'error' in men and women. The fourth book of the narrative – the book that immediately precedes the trial – is full of references to falls: from the comic fall of a girl out of a tree at its opening (232) – a witty pastiche of the Fall of Eve – to the lament of the Duke's wife when she thinks she has killed her husband: 'O bottomless pit of sorrow in which I cannot contain myself . . . still falling and yet by the infiniteness of it never fallen!' (242); from the suicide attempt of Pyrocles, the noise of whose 'fall' awakens his lover Philoclea (253), to the 'falling down' of her sister Pamela as she pleads for the life of Musidorus (268).[70] The sequence of falls culminates (if that is the right word) in the collapse into confusion of the Arcadian state as news spreads of the Duke's death. The crowd of distraught Arcadians who receive the news resembles, the narrator tells us, 'a falling steeple, the parts whereof (as windows, stones, and pinnacles) were well, but the whole mass ruinous' (277). The trial begins, then, at the point in the narrative when we have been made most conscious of the effects of the Fall: both on the individual, whose judgment in each case is swayed by passion, and on the body politic, where the administration of justice will presumably be guided by the emotions of fear and greed that have almost torn it apart.

The princes in *Arcadia* are accused by their prosecutor of having subjected his nation to all the vagaries of a poetic narrative – of having brought it to the brink of ruin by subjecting its ruling family to the laws

---

[70] Additional references occur on pp. 235, 238, 239, 242, 245, 246, 252, 253, 254, 255, 266, 269, 272, etc. The word 'fall' often occurs several times on one page.

of poetry. They have involved Basilius and his dependants, he says, in 'such changes and traverses as a quiet poet could scarce fill a poem withal' (337), with the result that the weaknesses of the monarchic system have been disastrously exposed.[71] The prosecutor does not exaggerate: as consternation spreads through Arcadia after the princes' arrest, the narrator comments that this offers 'a notable example of how great dissipations monarchal governments are subject unto; for now their prince and guide had left them, they had not experience to rule, and had not whom to obey' (277). In the *Apology* poetry is no less politically potent than the Arcadian prosecutor suggests, and its effects may be no less explosive. But it is also capable, if properly applied, of subjecting rulers and governments to *positive* transformations, of reversing the plunge from grace that is carrying the human race, and the English nation in particular, on its cataclysmic downward course. Poetic 'changes and traverses' may work to a nation's advantage as well as to its detriment, if national prejudices and opinions may be changed, or exploited to work change. And poetry is the art that is best suited to changing things in a postlapsarian context.

This transformative power is implicit in Sidney's account of poetry's origins. After its anecdotal Introduction comes the Statement of Facts or Narration, and in it the apologist asserts, like all early modern defenders of learned disciplines, the antiquity of the art he celebrates. Poetry has its roots at the beginning of recorded time. Indeed, it is responsible for recording the most ancient of times: poets were the first masters of the art of writing, the first men who 'made pens deliverers of their knowledge to their posterity' in the shape of versified history and moral philosophy (82/17). They were also the first to draw primitive people together into civil societies. From the beginning, then, poets specialized in resisting the lapses into savagery which the degenerate condition of humanity makes inevitable. Above all, they specialized in transforming bands of savages into nations: coherent social units with histories, legal constitutions, geographical possessions and languages of their own. The ancient poet Amphion founded Thebes; Dante, Petrarch, and Boccaccio made the Italian language 'a treasure-house of science'; the English poets Chaucer and Gower moulded their mother tongue into a supremely versatile medium for intellectual communication. And this poetic work of cultivating the human inward wilderness, of preparing the ground for national efflorescence, is still going on as Sidney writes. The most barbarous nations, as Sidney sees them, both within and beyond the limits of the Tudor domains – the Irish, the Welsh, the Turks,

---

[71] Philanax later describes Pyrocles in strikingly Gossonian terms, as 'the arrantest strumpet in luxuriousness, the cunningest forger in falsehood; a player in disguising, a tiger in cruelty, a dragon in ungratefulness' (*OA*, 338).

the 'simple Indians' – revere their poets, and it is the poets of these nations who give them the potential to raise themselves to a higher cultural level by instilling in them 'a pleasure in the exercises of the mind' (83/26). Conversely, we might infer that the nations who fail to cultivate poetry – and the references to the Irish and the Welsh bring the English to mind – may be putting themselves in danger of relapsing into mindless barbarism. Already Sidney is anticipating his contention, in the Digression, that the decline of English poetry is inseparable from the decline of the English nation.

The heroically persuasive poets who founded civilization closely resemble the rhetoricians so beloved of the humanists, who vigorously ply their 'delightful vein' to charm their audiences into the reception of 'highest knowledge' (82/35–6). But in the *Apology* Sidney is concerned to show that poets are distinct from, and superior to, the practitioners of other disciplines, including rhetoric. The classical terms for poet offer the first clues to their distinctiveness. The Latin term was *vates*, prophet, and Sidney points out that the Bible itself supports the idea that poets could predict the future: the biblical King David incorporated prophecies into his 'divine poem', the psalms (84/16). But the Greek term 'poet', meaning maker, expresses more precisely the poet's role in the fallen world. It implies that the poet is in a profound sense radical: not only does he make things, but he makes things happen. All other branches of learning (with the notable exception of divinity) study Nature: the composition of the material universe and its inhabitants as they have existed since the loss of Eden. 'The lawyer saith what men have determined,' Sidney reminds us, 'the historian what men have done' (85/8–9). Even the rhetorician is preoccupied only with persuading fallen men of the validity of his positions in the interests of furthering his immediate purpose – he does nothing to bring his hearers closer to an understanding of what it would be like *not* to be fallen. But the poet takes the fallen world merely as his starting point, his imaginative springboard to higher things. He can create other worlds, other states, other people – even entirely new beings – which are better than those we have. 'Nature never set forth the earth in so rich tapestry as divers poets have done,' Sidney declares in his most famously effusive passage, 'neither with pleasant rivers, fruitful trees, sweet-smelling flowers, nor whatsoever else may make the too much loved earth more lovely. Her world is brazen, the poets only deliver a golden' (85/24–7). The poet is able both to imagine prelapsarian perfection and, crucially, to represent that perfection in such a way as to make his readers both desire it and desire to imitate it. Like other thinkers he can summon up a mental picture – the '*Idea* or fore-conceit' (85/35) – of his ideal world, or man, or state, but unlike the rest he can convey that picture through vivid words into the hearts and heads of others, thus bringing it closer to material existence. Imagining, for instance, a perfect prince such as Cyrus, he can 'bestow a Cyrus upon the world to make many Cyruses, if they [i.e. his readers] will learn aright why and how that maker made him' (85/41–3). The poet, then, is not just a fabricator of imaginary objects but a shaper of people, who works on his readers' minds and through these on the societies they inhabit.

It is here that Sidney introduces his first direct reference to the Fall. Aware that some might think him 'saucy' for comparing the poet's creative powers with 'the efficacy of Nature' (85/44ff.), he deflects this criticism by attributing the poet's powers to God, who made man (alone among his creations) capable of envisaging perfection. Human beings even resemble God in their ability to bring forth 'with the force of a divine breath' – that is, through words – things far superior to Nature's workmanship (86/5). But humanity is also a fundamentally divided species, torn between contradictory impulses. On the one hand we possess an 'erected wit', the intellectual faculty that can elevate or 'erect' us to a mental plane far above the lowly level to which we have fallen (86/7). This is the faculty that enables the poet to envisage perfection. On the other hand we are possessed by an 'infected will' (86/8), an overwhelming desire for the contents of the 'too much loved earth' which constantly diverts us from our potential upward course. This diversion, Sidney tells us, provides 'no small argument . . . of that first accursed fall of Adam' (86/6–7). The highest achievements of the poets, in other words, proclaim both the immense potential of humanity and the immense distance that lies between our current state and the fulfilment of this potential. The *Apology* is partly dedicated to the problem of identifying the propulsive force that will bridge the distance: a force that poetry dispenses more than any other discipline. But Sidney is equally committed to demonstrating that poetry is the only art that ministers to the dual nature of humanity, its unique fusion of the spiritual with the physical, of boundless mental agility with a congenital infection that misdirects its mental powers.

The poet's ministration to our dual nature is implicit in the tension between two major groups of metaphors Sidney uses to describe his discipline. On the one hand the poet is master of infinite space, vaulting from earth to heaven with the aid of his 'high flying liberty of conceit' (84/13), evading the physical and historical constraints that govern other disciplines and 'freely ranging only within the zodiac of his own wit' (85/23). On the other hand he is a kind of second Adam, tending an imaginative earthly garden to rival Eden. Sidney's practical interest in gardening is attested by his correspondence with the eminent French botanist Charles de l'Ecluse, whom he met in Vienna;[72] and

---

[72] See Duncan-Jones 1991, 65.

horticultural metaphors abound alongside metaphors of flight throughout the *Apology*: from the garden of Apollo, which the philosopher Plato
raids for the poetic 'flowers' that decorate his philosophical dialogues
(83/3), to the garden of the poet's golden world adorned with 'pleasant
rivers, fruitful trees, sweet-smelling flowers'; from the 'fair vineyard'
which the poet plants to entice his readers into his fictional dominions
(95/12) to the many references to the moral and intellectual 'fruit' borne
by poetry.[73] Like all the best intellectual disciplines, poetry works to
'plant goodness even in the secretest cabinet of our souls' (90/5–6) – the
tiniest and most private inward chambers of the mind become alive and
productive at its touch. But unlike the other disciplines, poetry offers
its adherents a place to *live in* rather than to visit. Philosophy, history,
and the rest build schoolrooms to occupy our working hours; they
ignore, repudiate, and attempt to police the hours of leisure and the
pursuit of pleasure which take up the rest of our daily schedule. Poetry,
on the other hand, offers its devotees accommodation fit for all uses,
with rooms and grounds for every function, and the endless potential
for constructing more.

This is the implication of one of the most celebrated phrases in the
Apology: the statement that poetry serves as 'an imaginative ground-plot
of a profitable invention' (103/31–2). A ground-plot was a piece of land
ripe for development, either as a garden or as the foundation of a building. Sidney elaborates on the phrase at the end of the Refutation, when
he transmutes the poetic art into an Edenic landscape which has not yet
been fully developed for human habitation (108/9ff.). Poetry, he says, is
'a fit soil for praise to dwell upon', a soil on which he urges us to 'plant
more laurels for to engarland our poets' heads', watered (as Eden was)
by 'clear springs' and unencumbered by serpents: objections to poetry
may be 'trodden down' as easily as the snake whose head was to be
bruised by Eve's descendants after the biblical Fall. For all its libertarian
high soaring, then, poetry for Sidney is firmly based on the earth – hence
the rather startling metaphorical juxtaposition midway through the digression, when he insists that 'as the fertilest ground must be manured,
so must the highest-flying wit have a Daedalus to guide him' (109/
39–40). The meeting of the two sets of metaphors may here look
awkward, perhaps even contradictory, but it is what lends the *Apology*
the dual quality of solidity combined with energy, of pragmatism combined with vision, which best serves its ultimate political purpose. The
poet's inventive cultivation of the intellectual soil is a *manifestation* of
his high-flying liberty, and both aspects of his personality must be
brought to bear if he is to accomplish the task Sidney has set him, which
is to reform (or replant, or rebuild) the English nation.

---

[73] See e.g. 83/27; 86/32; 90/20–1; 94/34; 100/7; 102/41; 113/20.

The poet and his rivals

Sidney's commitment to the task of national regeneration means that he is reluctant to discuss certain kinds of poetry at any length in the *Apology*. 'Divine' poetry, for instance – the most high-flying variety of all – is simply not relevant to his present concerns. Thus, when he comes to define poetry in his Proposition (he tells us it is an art of imitation, 'with this end, to teach and delight' (86/19–20)), he speaks with all due respect of poets such as David who 'did imitate the inconceivable excellencies of God' (86/22–3), but excludes them from his defence on the grounds that nobody 'that hath the Holy Ghost in due holy reverence' could possibly find them objectionable (86/27–8). These grounds for their exclusion are scarcely convincing, since he includes in the category of divine poets the pagan poet-prophets Orpheus, Amphion, and Homer, who wrote 'in a full wrong divinity' (86/28) and who were therefore among the principal targets of attack by Christian poet-haters from Tertullian to Gosson. The real reason for excepting theological matters from his essay is given later on, when he tells us that the divine has its scope 'as far beyond any of these as eternity exceedeth a moment' (89/40–1). Eternity occupies a different dimension from the one we inhabit, and Sidney is fundamentally concerned with the space we live in: the earth, the nation, the household. An art that deals only with things spiritual leaves too much of our dual nature unacknowledged and unsatisfied.

He also excludes from consideration a second kind of poet, 'them that deal with matters philosophical' (86/35). By this he means those who represent things as they are, confining themselves to moral, scientific, or historical topics drawn from the study of their own and other people's experience or researches. The scope of this second kind of poets is too narrow to be useful to his argument, just as the first was too vast. By concerning themselves only with what has been and what is, they render themselves incapable of instituting change, and changing things is what Sidney wants poetry to do. The vocabulary he uses to describe them is that of stifling confinement: they are 'wrapped within the fold of the proposed subject' as a baby is tightly bound in linen (86/41–2), and this infantile condition robs them of the liberty that enables 'right poets' to choose their own 'course'.

These 'right poets' (86/44), the poets with whom the *Apology* concerns itself, produce only fictions. He describes them in exuberantly energetic terms: they 'imitate to teach and delight, and to imitate borrow nothing of what is, hath been, or shall be; but range, only reined with learned discretion, into the divine consideration of what may be and should be' (87/8–11). Sidney's subject is the poet as maker, not the poet as prophet or servant; and the reason for his very specific choice of subject is now becoming clearer. The 'right poets' intervene in earthly affairs, but do so with a freedom of movement which resembles that of God himself. Since they concern themselves exclusively with 'the *divine* consideration of what may be and should be', their creative imitations are independent of all earthly powers. They 'borrow nothing', and therefore owe nothing, to any extant regime or faction; their only fealty is to the divine. This freedom from political subjection, as well as the youthful energy with which they exercise that freedom, distinguishes them from the practitioners of every other discipline.

The phrase that best describes what Sidney does *not* want poetry to be is the one he uses to describe the rival disciplines of astronomy, music, mathematics, and 'natural and supernatural' philosophy (88/14) – the study of the material world and the non-human forces that govern it. These, he tells us, are no more than 'serving sciences' (88/23), humble domestics in the entourage of more exalted branches of learning. By this he means that they accumulate material which may be useful but is not essential to 'the highest end' of knowledge, 'which stands' (Sidney thinks) 'in the knowledge of a man's self' and in the 'virtuous action' to which such knowledge gives rise (88/24–33). The 'serving sciences' contribute towards this ultimate purpose, he tells us, in much the same way as a saddler supplies the needs of a more elevated discipline, horsemanship, or as horsemanship serves the more socially and politically urgent requirements of military action. This analogy, recalling the opening anecdote about the equestrian Pugliano, shifts the notion of 'serving sciences' from the intellectual sphere to the military or political. As well as serving other disciplines, Sidney implies, the 'serving sciences' occupy the lower ranks in a strictly hierarchical chain of command, at the highest level of which stand the disciplines which have a direct bearing on the way human beings organize their personal, social and political lives. The topmost level is occupied by the most exalted public servant of all, the figure who directs every action undertaken by the state: the prince. The *Apology* is designed to demonstrate that poets 'have a most just title to be princes over all the rest' (88/32–3), and that they have been toppled from their deserved pre-eminence by an act of moral and intellectual treason. And one of Sidney's chief arguments for the poet's pre-eminence is that he need serve no earthly princes.

In this, we learn in the next section of the essay, the 'right poet' is quite different from his chief rivals among the teachers of academic disciplines, the moral philosopher and the historian. The historian in particular has his pedagogic efforts seriously hampered by his 'servile' status. He claims to teach 'virtuous action' by offering real examples of such actions from the past; but these examples are profoundly problematic. In the first place, their claim to authenticity is questionable. Not only are the reputed facts 'built upon the notable foundation of hearsay' (89/11), but they suffer too from the various forms of political bias which make it next to impossible for the historian to 'pick truth out of partiality' (89/12). In the second place, even the most truthful historian is forced by the nature of his discipline into complicity with tyranny. He is a 'tyrant in table-talk' (89/16), dominating dinnerparties with his obsessive concern for accuracy; but he also gives his support to less amiable forms of despotism. Being 'captived to the truth of a foolish world', his exemplary narratives are 'many times a terror from well-doing, and an encouragement to unbridled wickedness' (94/1–2). And the wickedness he most encourages is that of the tyrant – the man of power who imprisons or kills his enemies. The historical narrative is repeatedly forced to mimic acts of tyrannical injustice, leaving the 'valiant Miltiades' to 'rot in his fetters', putting to death 'the accomplished Socrates', driving the 'virtuous Cato' to kill himself while 'rebel Caesar' – the man who brought an end to Roman republicanism – bestows his name like an honorific on succeeding generations of despots (94/3ff.). The poet, by contrast, is free to punish tyrants as he wishes in his fictions (94/13–14), or to fashion ideal princes without seeking the support of the current government, or to dismiss princes from office altogether, as Plato and More did in their imaginary republics (91/21–5). The historian is locked into a cycle of atrocities from which he cannot escape. The poet's 'high flying liberty of conceit', on the other hand, looks increasingly like a specifically political liberty as the *Apology* unfolds.

The historian, with his encouragement of 'unbridled wickedness', is a hopeless horseman compared to the poet, who knows how to 'rein' his imagination with 'learned discretion'. The poet's other chief rival – the moral philosopher, who devotes his life to teaching his pupils the difference between right and wrong – is an equally hopeless gardener. His subject matter is not limited to the recalcitrant set of facts relayed by the historian; he can discuss the universal principles of virtue and vice as freely as the poet. But his ability to 'plant goodness' in his pupils is severely curtailed by his teaching method. He deals with theory, not practice – with precepts, not examples – and this concentration on abstract principles renders his work at best unattractive, at worst incomprehensible. His use of 'thorny argument', 'hard of utterance' and 'misty to be conceived' (90/12–13), makes the intellectual territory he occupies sound like a boggy moorland, vastly less fruitful than the gardens and vineyards of the poet. The 'infallible grounds of wisdom' with which moral philosophy stocks the memory 'lie dark before the imaginative and judging power', an obscurity which suggests that they will not yield much in the way of moral or intellectual nourishment ('fruit') to those who are not already wise (90/40–1). And his brash interference in political matters renders him as vulnerable to tyranny as the historian. The philosopher teaches virtue, Sidney tells us, 'by making known his enemy, vice, which must be destroyed, and his cumbersome servant, passion, which must be mastered' (89/2–4). Such pedagogic belligerence – conveyed in the vocabulary of mastery and destruction – is likely to raise the hackles of masterful and destructive men, especially rulers. The philosopher's directness betrays, in fact, a catastrophic lack of tact. He is prepared to risk his personal safety 'by plain setting down' how virtue 'extendeth itself out of the limits of a man's own little world to the government of families, and maintaining of public societies' (89/5–7). And his outspoken interference in public and private affairs is always getting him into trouble. Sidney mentions the philosopher Socrates, forced to commit suicide by a hostile Athenian state (94/4). Later he points out that Alexander the Great put the philosopher Callisthenes to death 'for his seeming philosophical, indeed mutinous, stubbornness' (105/38–9), and later still that 'many cities banished philosophers as not fit members to live among them' (106/30–1). Plato himself was helpless against tyranny: he 'could do so little' with the tyrant Dionysius 'that he himself of a philosopher was made a slave' (106/36–7). Philosophers, in other words, are as much 'captived to the truth of a foolish world' as historians – in a quite literal sense: they are vulnerable to imprisonment, enslavement, execution. As More pointed out in the *Utopia*, the philosopher's problem is that he is incompetent in the arts of persuasion and flattery which are essential prerequisites for those who wish their voices to be heard by corrupt politicians.[74] The poet's expertise in these arts, by contrast, not only makes him welcome among politicians, courtiers, and soldiers but gives him a quasi-monarchic power over them unmatched by that of any other teacher.

So what is the source of the poet's matchless persuasive power? The metaphor of the poet as gardener suggests that he 'plants' the image of goodness in his readers' minds (95/39), where it can grow and fructify without further interference from the poet. But how is this plantation accomplished? The answer lies in the most famous metaphor in the *Apology*, that of the poem as 'speaking picture' (86/19).[75] This is the metaphor that most neatly illustrates the poet's ability to negotiate the gap between the universal principles studied by the philosopher and the particular examples provided by the historian, between mind and body. And it also offers the best clue to poetry's attractiveness.

Sidney's interest in and familiarity with the rich diversity of visual arts in early modern Europe is well documented.[76] Greville tells us that

---

[74] See More 1985, 47.

[75] The fullest (and most contentious) account of the place of this metaphor in the *Apology* is Robinson 1972. See also S. F. Heninger, 'Speaking Pictures: Sidney's Rapprochement between Poetry and Painting', in Waller and Moore 1984, 3–16.

[76] See K. Duncan-Jones, 'Sidney and Titian', in *English Renaissance Studies Presented to Dame Helen Gardner in Honour of her Seventieth Birthday*, ed. John Carey (Oxford 1980), 1–11; Gent 1981, 26–7 and 29; Duncan-Jones 1991, 75–6.

he sought out and patronized 'cunning painters' in his continental travels (Greville 1986, 21). He had his portrait done at least three times in the early 1570s, once by the portrait medallist Antonio Abondio, once by Paolo Veronese and once by an unknown artist, perhaps Cornelius Ketel; and this is not so much a sign of Sidney's vanity as of his acute awareness of the practical applications of the pictorial arts. He shared with his contemporaries the conviction that visual representations served a number of social and political functions, and that their aesthetic appeal was of importance only as it supported or undermined these functions. A portrait, for instance, might be used to announce the sitter's ambitions (Duncan-Jones reads the anonymous portrait as a personal manifesto),[77] or to strengthen friendships (Hubert Languet hung Veronese's picture of him 'in full view' in his house),[78] or to signal the availability of eligible young aristocrats on the marriage market (Pyrocles in the *Arcadia* falls in love with Philoclea on seeing her portrait). Book illustrations offered visual commentaries on written texts: both Sannazzaro's *Arcadia* and Spenser's *Shepheardes Calender* were extensively illustrated. And the walls of wealthy Elizabethan homes were richly adorned with tapestries, painted cloths, and murals on a range of improving subjects.[79] The stories of Dives and Lazarus and the prodigal son were perennial favourites (see **91/34–43**), and Sidney lists further suitable themes for domestic pictures in the Refutation: 'Abraham sacrificing his son Isaac, Judith killing Holofernes, David fighting with Goliath' (**104/23–4**). But as the example of Pyrocles shows, painting was not solely associated with moral instruction. It was thought to be uniquely capable of bringing things to life, of operating in a quasi-miraculous way on the viewer's senses, and through these on his or her intellect and emotions, and this capacity could be deployed to many ends, not all of them moral.[80] In his most extended discussion of a picture's effect on 'the powers of the mind' Sidney describes the visual experience produced by poems and paintings as a form of physical assault: they 'strike', 'pierce', and 'possess the sight of the soul' like an invading army or a rapist (**90/27–8**). Painters and poets operate on the body as well as the mind. This is what links them, and this is what distinguishes them from the practitioners of rival disciplines.

Its intense physicality is at once the glory and the shame of poetry. If the 'final end' of learning is 'to lead and draw us to as high a perfection as our degenerate souls, made worse by their clayey lodgings, can be capable of' (**88/7–9**), then due account must be taken both of the

---

[77] Duncan-Jones 1991, 114.
[78] Stewart 2000, 126.
[79] See Croft-Murray 1962–70, I, 28. For an example of a wall-painting depicting a biblical scene (the prodigal son) see plate 38.
[80] See Gent 1981, ch. 3.

soul and of the 'clayey lodgings' it inhabits. Poetry exploits those clayey lodgings as its chief means of drawing its readers towards the beauty of virtue – or not, as the case may be. And its exploitation of the body goes far beyond anything achieved by the painter. It woos, titillates, allures its recipients by simulating bodies, objects or actions which 'satisfy' all the senses, not just the sense of sight (90/33). In Elizabethan times the most celebrated myth of painterly verisimilitude was the story of the Greek artist Zeuxis, who painted a bunch of grapes so lifelike that wild birds came to peck at it.[81] Sidney does not mention the story, but he does suggest that poets entice their readers into their texts, as Zeuxis did, by tempting their bodily appetites, presenting them 'at the first' with 'a cluster of grapes, that full of that taste, you may long to pass further' (95/12–13). Poets, then, have an advantage over Zeuxis, who tricked the birds' eyesight but failed to gratify their tastebuds. Like expert cooks they offer 'food for the tenderest stomachs' (92/3–4): a 'medicine of cherries' for the distempered appetite (96/10), or a fable about eating to suppress a rebellion (96/13ff.). Their metrical music (and music, Sidney tells us, is 'the most divine striker of the senses', 101/35) offers us the authentic 'sound of virtue' (92/7) and stirs the heart 'more than with a trumpet' (99/7). And their pictorial imaginations, through which 'all virtues, vices, and passions' are 'laid to the view', offer us a range of 'familiar insights' into the workings of the mind through their depiction of bodies in extremity (91/6ff.): the eyeless Oedipus representing 'remorse of conscience', Atreus who served up his wife's bastards at a banquet as an instance of 'self-devouring cruelty', Medea's murder of her own children signifying 'the sour-sweetness of revenge'. These feeling, vociferous pictures 'inhabit both the memory and judgment' as the philosopher's abstract generalizations and the historian's pedantic specificities cannot. Like tapestries or murals they bedeck the walls of our minds, shining, illuminating and resonating through our corporeal houses. They occupy all the spaces in which we live, from the most public to the most secret. None of the other arts can boast the same intimacy with the labyrinths of the human anatomy. And this intimacy is as problematic as it is pedagogically convenient.

Sidney first develops the notion of the poem as 'speaking picture' in his account of the 'right poet', who resembles, he tells us, the best sort of painters: those 'who having no law but wit, bestow that in colours upon you which is fittest for the eye to see: as the constant though lamenting look of Lucretia, when she punished in herself another's fault; wherein he painteth not Lucretia whom he never saw, but painteth the outward beauty of such a virtue' (87/3–7). Like the best painters, poets make verbal imitations of the ideal pictures they conceive in their 'wits',

---

[81] See Gent 1981, 34. The anecdote comes from Pliny, *Natural History*, XXXV.

pictures which represent particular examples of universal virtues. These creative imitations endow us with a 'true lively knowledge' of their subjects, enabling us to 'grow', like a plant or a child, 'to a judicial comprehending' of them (90/36–7). In addition, speaking pictures are as delightful as they are instructive, and their delightfulness is what makes them instructive. They 'move men', arouse their emotions and desires, as strongly as they appeal to their rational understanding of what constitutes goodness (87/15–7). By moving men they stir them to action. And the sort of action they encourage is hinted at by Sidney's choice of Lucretia as the subject for an exemplary painting or poem.

The painter who sets out to represent Lucretia must be guided, Sidney tells us, by 'no law but wit' if he is to make her an accurate representation of virtue. He must share, in other words, the courageous independence of the poet, his 'liberty of conceit', his free ranging within the uncircumscribed zodiac of the mind. And here as elsewhere the painter and his companion artist the poet would seem to be proponents of a specifically political conception of liberty. The suicide of Lucretia was an act of resistance to tyranny: she killed herself after being raped by a relative of the corrupt Roman monarch, Tarquinius Superbus, and her death sparked off the revolution that brought an end to monarchic rule in Rome and led to the establishment of the Roman republic. This is only the first and most dramatic instance in the *Apology* of poetry's hostility to despotism. At his most aggressive, the poet 'deviseth new punishments in hell for tyrants' (94/13–14), but he is also capable, as the caustic philosopher is not, of finding more obliquely persuasive means to reform despotic monarchs. In the Bible, Nathan the prophet deploys a simple poetic fiction to 'do the tenderest office of a friend' – and the most dangerous office of a counsellor – when he draws King David's attention to his crimes of adultery and murder by means of a fable (96/29ff.). The pastoral genre 'can show the misery of people under hard lords or ravening soldiers' (97/17–18), while the tragic 'maketh kings fear to be tyrants, and tyrants manifest their tyrannical humours' (98/27–8). The Digression offers as an example of a good tragic theme the story of Hecuba, who avenged herself 'most cruelly' on the tyrant Polymnestor (111/34ff.). So successful are these poetic interventions in politics that 'Certain poets', Sidney tells us, 'so prevailed with Hiero the First, that of a tyrant they made him a just king' (106/34–6). By choosing the picture of Lucretia as his first example of a 'speaking picture' Sidney suggests not only that some of the virtues poets depict are political ones but that their depictions of political actions are likely to be as effective as Lucretia's carefully staged self-punishment.

But this first example is also suggestive in another sense. Early modern paintings of Lucretia invariably depict her as an object of erotic desire for the male spectator as much as for her princely rapist.[82] She is usually naked, often alone – in the original story told by Livy her death was witnessed by her husband and his allies, whereas the painters place her in a state of intimate isolation with the viewer – and she frequently seems to be in a state of mournful ecstasy. Sidney's familiarity with such representations is implied, perhaps, by his description of her 'constant though lamenting look . . . when she punished in herself another's fault' (87/4–6); but, whether he was thinking of any particular picture or not, he could have found no more potent expression of the fusion of the political with the erotic in art than a painting of Lucretia. The delight by which the poet attracts his audience, then, is a stimulation of the senses, an arousal of the appetite, which includes the provocation of sexual desire as a legitimate part of its *modus operandi*. When Sidney goes on to offer further instances of successful poetic 'speaking pictures', he chooses Xenophon's *Cyropaedia* and Heliodorus's *Theagenes and Chariclea* as his second and third examples, the former a political text, 'the portraiture of a just empire', the latter a 'picture of love' (87/30–3). Neither of these ambitious word-paintings is privileged over the other, and Sidney's own prose poem, the *Arcadia*, fuses the political with the erotic – taking hints from both Xenophon and Heliodorus – to often unnerving effect.

As the *Apology* proceeds, the moral and political instructions offered by poetry become increasingly entangled with the vocabulary of desire. In the Psalms, Sidney tells us early in the essay, David shows himself 'a passionate lover of that unspeakable and everlasting beauty to be seen by the eyes of the mind, only cleared by faith' (84/26–8). Later we learn that poetry 'ever setteth virtue so out in her best colours . . . that one must needs be enamoured of her' (93/37–9), and later still he repeats the point again: 'if the saying of Plato and Tully be true, that who could see virtue would be wonderfully ravished with the love of her beauty – [the poet] sets her out to make her more lovely in her holiday apparel' (99/32–5). Lyric poetry strives to 'awake the thoughts from the sleep of idleness, to *embrace* honourable enterprises' (99/24–5), while 'the lofty image' of the epic heroes '*inflameth the mind with desire* to be worthy' (99/40–1, my emphases). Seductive clothing rivals vivid painting as a metaphor for poetry's appeal to the senses. The poets chose rhyme as the 'fittest raiment' for their fictions (87/40), and 'mistress Philosophy' must borrow the 'masking raiment of Poesy' when she wishes to allure her adherents (96/2–3). The 'apparel' of the simplest lyric would be immeasurably improved if 'trimmed in the gorgeous eloquence of Pindar' (99/10); the poet 'bringeth his own stuff' or cloth to make up

---

[82] For a detailed account of Renaissance representations of Lucretia see Ian Donaldson, *The Rapes of Lucretia: A Myth and its Transformations* (Oxford, 1982).

his compositions (100/22–3); and Plutarch trims the 'garments' of history and philosophy with 'guards' or decorative borders of poetry (108/7). At one point Sidney even transforms poetry into an essential cosmetic aid for the woman who wishes to 'fashion her countenance to the best grace' – that is, to master the art of make-up (92/30–3).[83] Masks, disguises, and all the ingenious tricks of flirtatious concealment are the stock-in-trade of the poet, who combines the functions of the tailor, the fashion guru, and the pimp with his more exalted role of imitating virtue.

This emphasis on the physicality of poetry's effects on its readers is an impudent rhetorical tactic for Sidney to have adopted in the context of the Elizabethan critical debate. As we have seen, the opponents of modern imaginative writing – Ascham and Gosson in particular – saw the appeal of erotic poetry to the senses as a debilitating influence on the vulnerable young, encouraging idleness, effeminacy, deviousness, and the insidious erosion of English Protestant values. But Sidney's erotic metaphors are so woven in with poetic examples of political, military and patriotic virtues – Cyrus, Aeneas, Ulysses, Achilles, Hercules, Turnus – that he makes those virtues inseparable from the intensely physical means by which they are made attractive. As a result, any attempt to sunder virtue from physicality makes the attempter look out of touch, academically cloistered, naive. And this is just how Sidney portrays the poet's 'principal challengers' among the academic disciplines (88/35ff.). The verbal portraits he paints of poetry's competitors, the moral philosopher and the historian, show them as pedants rather than activists, caricatures of the hidebound academics or pedagogues who were the butt of endless humanist jokes. In his own words, they are the 'self-wise-seeming school-masters' who are an ideal subject for comedy (113/9). The moral philosophers are mocked for a lack of self-knowledge and social grace which is embodied in what they wear: they are 'rudely clothed for to witness outwardly their contempt of outward things' (88/38–9). The historians are hopelessly behind the times: they carry 'old mouse-eaten records', are 'better acquainted with a thousand years ago than with the present age', 'curious for antiquities', 'a wonder to young folks', and cherish an exaggerated respect for 'Old-aged experience' (89/8ff.). Worse still, both parties lack certain intellectual limbs: the philosopher teaches only theory, the historian records only what has been practised, but 'both, not having both, do both halt' – that is, hobble on their one sound leg (90/10–11). Under the circumstances, their claims to supremacy in the field of leading men to action seem absurd. Both scholars are impotent, physically as well as intellectually; neither young men nor young women

---

[83] For Elizabethan hostility to cosmetics, and its association with the art of painting, see Gent 1981, 7 note.

will be attracted to them; and the subsequent, more serious investigation into their claims as teachers is overlaid by this initial comic exposure of their bodily inadequacies, like a schoolboy's crude anatomical sketch on the cover of a dull textbook.

The poet, on the other hand, is young and athletic, with a 'presence full of majesty and beauty' (97/4). His delight in the physical is an effect of his youth, which must be harnessed, not suppressed – after all, sexual energy is a prerequisite for the very existence of families and nations. He is a courtier and soldier as well as a scholar – and the first two are represented in Elizabethan texts as distinctively young men's occupations. He is, in fact, a version of the Philip Sidney who writes in his defence. From one point of view, the *Apology* consists of an elaborately fictionalized self-portrait which invites comparison with the less flattering portraits of poetry's 'principal challengers'. And as the essay unfolds, as the 'parts' of the poet are more narrowly scrutinized for a possible 'blemish' (97/5), the function of this portrait becomes increasingly apparent.

Productive truancy in the *Apology*

From its opening *An Apology for Poetry* announces itself as a young man's book, written by an aristocrat of 'not old years' in his 'idlest times' (81/25). As such it risks instant rejection by professional scholars like the historian or the philosopher, who regarded youth as a period of anarchic waywardness to be left behind as quickly as possible, and whose one ambition was to turn the young generation into faithful copies of themselves. According to Sidney's contemporary Geoffrey Fenton, 'if a man be younge . . . the readynge [of history] will make hym old, not in yeares, wich the most parte cold be content to shyfte of and forgo, but in experience and wisedom'.[84] Sidney proposes that there is no need either to become old or to study 'old-aged experience' to know and practise virtue. For one thing, as Fenton acknowledges, immaturity is not so much a condition of a person's age as a state of mind; and Sidney suggests, like Erasmus in *The Praise of Folly*, that we are all subject to it.[85] Most men, he tells us, are 'childish in the best things, till they be cradled in their graves' (95/24–5). This is why the early poets were forced to act as wetnurses to humanity, 'whose milk by little and little enabled them to feed afterwards of tougher knowledges' (82/9–10). Most men, too, are as implacably hostile to being 'brought to school again' as the most obstinate juvenile delinquent (95/29). By adopting the stance of an appeal by the young to the young, then, the *Apology* addresses itself to the

[84] *Certain Tragical Discourses of Bandello*, introd. R. L. Douglas (2 vols, London, 1898), I, 3. The passage occurs in the Dedication to Sidney's mother.
[85] See Erasmus 1965, 16–22.

widest possible audience, in terms that will tempt the truant as well as the good pupil, the childishly old as well as the child. 'With a tale forsooth he cometh unto you,' we learn, 'with a tale which holdeth children from play, and old men from the chimney corner' (95/17–19). Sidney's text is the very opposite of a schoolbook, and as such sets itself up in friendly rivalry with the most celebrated schoolbook written in English at the time: Roger Ascham's *The Schoolmaster*.

This rivalry is evident as early as the Introduction. The *Apology* begins by wittily investing the equerry Pugliano with the status of Sidney's principal teacher, an improbable substitute for the enlightened schoolmaster whom Ascham sets at the centre of his pedagogic system. Young Sidney found himself provoked, he says, by the Italian's eloquent defence of horsemanship to write something in defence of poetry, 'which if I handle with more good will than good reasons, bear with me, since the scholar is to be pardoned that followeth in the steps of his master' (81/27–9). Sidney's debt to his equestrian 'master' manifests itself throughout the *Apology* in its occasional references to horsemanship: in the comparison of the 'serving sciences' to the craft of the saddler, for instance, or the allusion to the poet's course 'reined only with learned discretion'; in the description of Sidney's argument as a 'career' (108/22) – a horse-race or tilt; in his mocking allusion to bad Elizabethan poets as mounted on 'post-horses' or 'Pacolet's horse' instead of the winged steed Pegasus, the ancient metaphor for poetic inspiration (109/19, 111/28); or in his apology for 'straying' into the Digression like an ill-trained colt. These manifestations of an equestrian obsession are not without classical precedent. If Sidney acknowledges a riding instructor as his master he is merely following the example of the ancient Greeks, 'who set those toys at so high a price that Philip of Macedon' – Sidney's namesake, whose name means 'lover of horses' – 'reckoned a horserace won at Olympus among his three fearful felicities' (99/21–3). And if he rejects the older men whom the humanists considered the best of teachers, he is merely imitating Philip's son, young Alexander the Great, who 'left his schoolmaster, living Aristotle, behind him, but took dead Homer with him' when he went to conquer Asia (105/36–7).

For readers familiar with Ascham's *Schoolmaster*, Philip's high regard for horsemanship and Alexander's decision to abandon his tutor were as closely related as father to son. Ascham complains in his treatise that among the contemporary English aristocracy 'more care is had, yea and that emonges verie wise men, to finde out rather a cunnynge man for their horse, than a cunnyng man for their children' (Ascham 1904, 193). Horsemanship, Ascham believes, is in a better condition than school-teaching in Elizabethan England;[86] and Sidney's 'learner-like admiration'

---

[86] See also Ascham 1904, 193 and 195.

for Pugliano (81/9) might have confirmed Ascham's suspicion that the children of the English aristocracy were more interested in sports than in Latin. The *Apology* occupies the premises to which, Ascham tells us, the truants from the Elizabethan schoolroom are driven by the aggressive teaching practices of 'fond [i.e. foolish] scholemasters', who seek to drive learning into their pupils by violence instead of by the gentle methods Ascham recommends. The beatings these men administer are 'the onelie cause,' Ascham opines, 'that commonly, the yong ientlemen of England, go so vnwillinglie to schole, and run so fast to the stable: For in verie deede fond scholemasters, by feare, do beate into them, the hatred of learning, and wise riders, by ientle allurements, do breed vp in them, the loue of riding. They finde feare, and bondage in scholes, They feele libertie and freedome in stables: which causeth them, vtterlie to abhore the one, and most gladlie to haunt the other' (Ascham 1904, 198–9). By Ascham's own confession, the practitioners of Pugliano's craft offer a better pedagogic example than most Elizabethan teachers. We are by now well acquainted with Sidney's passion for 'libertie and freedome'; so we should hardly be surprised if he represents escape from the 'bondage' of the traditional Tudor schoolroom as a particularly productive form of truancy.

But even Ascham's more kindly schoolroom, where children are allured to a deep pleasure in knowledge through a 'deepe knowledge of pleasure' (201), is too restrictive for Sidney's exuberant young poet-aristocrat. Sidney shows this most openly, perhaps, when he comments that 'honest King Arthur' will 'never displease a soldier' (105/26): as we have seen, Ascham waxed eloquent on the harmful effect on young men of reading chivalric romances, especially Arthurian ones. When Sidney confesses his own 'barbarousness' in admiring the 'old song of Percy and Douglas' (99/5–6), he uses a term Ascham throws out repeatedly when inveighing against the practice of writing rhymed verse in English (Ascham 1904, 289ff.) – a practice which the old scholar abhors but which Sidney considers the equal of classical metres in 'sweetness' and 'majesty' (115/36–7). In the course of his invective, Ascham tells us that Cicero ascribed 'mere barbariousnes' to 'poore England' for its lack of learning (Ascham 1904, 292–3), so that in embracing rhyme Sidney delivers a calculated snub to 'diligent imitators' of Cicero such as Ascham himself (see 114/3). Similarly, Sidney's admiring references to Italian poets such as Petrarch, Boccaccio, Dante, and Sannazzaro fly in the face of Ascham's famous attack on Italian books; his allusions to the fine clothes with which poetry beautifies virtue read like a mocking retaliation to Ascham's complaints about the absurd apparel worn at the English Court;[87] and his passage on love in modern poetry makes

---

[87] See Ascham 1904, 208.

Ascham's strictures on Italian love-poems and love-stories sound thoroughly ungracious. Most strikingly, perhaps, Ascham prefers the qualities of the 'hard' wit in a pupil – the steady plodder – to the qualities of the volatile 'quick wits' who 'commonlie may proue the best Poetes, but not the wisest Orators' (Ascham 1904, 188ff.). Sidney, by contrast, thinks that 'hard dull wits' need to be raised to their full potential by the attractive powers of poetry (83/24–5). His ideal poet is the 'highest-flying wit' (109/40), who soars, gallops, trumpets, seduces, assaults, and generally engages in a flurry of activity which might have thrown Ascham into paroxysms of anxiety. He is prepared to acknowledge, with Ascham, that the wit or intellect is a two-edged sword: on the one hand, the 'erected wit' offers human beings a glimpse of perfection, on the other, 'man's wit' when applied exclusively to sexual scurrility 'abuseth' both poetry and its eager young readers (104/17).[88] But this is only to say that poetry is the most powerful tool of the intellect, which can do the most good in the right hands as well as the most harm in the wrong ones: 'with a sword thou mayest kill thy father, and with a sword thou mayest defend thy prince and country' (104/41–2). In stressing only the worst aspects of poetic 'quick wits', Ascham is rejecting what might be the most effective means of defending England against its enemies. In intellectual as well as military terms Ascham and his fellow schoolmasters have only a very tenuous grasp of strategy.

Sidney's most brazen act of impudence is to invert the relationship between poets and other teachers which Ascham and his fellow pedants took for granted. Replying to those 'poet-haters' (100/41) who adopt Plato's attack on poets in the *Republic* as the basis of their case against poetry, Sidney accuses Plato, the greatest of philosophical instructors, of having treacherously turned against the men who educated him. 'For indeed,' he observes,

> after the philosophers had picked out of the sweet mysteries of Poetry the right discerning true points of knowledge, they forthwith, putting it in method, and making a school-art of that which the poets did only teach by a divine delightfulness, beginning to spurn at their guides, like ungrateful prentices, were not content to set up shops for themselves, but sought by all means to discredit their masters; which by the force of delight being barred them, the less they could overthrow them, the more they hated them.
>
> (106/21–9)

In the *Apology* the poets are the erstwhile 'masters' of the philosophers and other purveyors of 'school arts'. But their historical priority means that they are also their more aristocratic forebears. The essay begins, as we have seen, by arguing that poetry is the most ancient form of learning and that the ancient poets were 'fathers' of all other thinkers (82/19,

[88] For a full discussion of Renaissance views on wit see Crane 1937.

and compare 100/16). If this is the case, then philosophers, schoolmasters and similar poet-haters – the 'ungrateful prentices' who seek 'to discredit their masters', the brood of vipers who devour their parents (82/11–12) – are in a worse moral position than the young prodigals they wish to reform. Attacks on poetry, Sidney tells us with deceptive glibness, bring with them 'great danger of civil war among the Muses' (82/4) – a mutually destructive combat between the forces of competing disciplines on the soil of the country they share. If, as he has argued, poets 'have a most just title to be princes over all the rest' (88/32–3), then the poet-haters are the traitors and rebels, not the poets. Sidney's saucy defection from the educational programme offered by his elders is no act of truancy but a return to the ancient practices that established his country's identity.

By the time we reach the Refutation, where Sidney meets one by one the principal charges brought against poetry by its enemies, the inversion of the roles of poet and poet-hater has become explicit. The poet-haters 'do *prodigally* spend a great many wandering words in quips and scoffs' (101/1, my emphasis), like Ascham's prodigal quick wits who are 'readie scoffers, priuie mockers, and euer ouer light and merry' (Ascham 1904, 189). The poets, by contrast, are not only 'of most fatherly antiquity' (100/16) but encourage the utmost respect for fathers: 'Who readeth Aeneas carrying old Anchises on his back, that wisheth not it were his fortune to perform so excellent an act?' (95/36–8). The poet, in other words, carries the older generation towards a brighter future as Aeneas carried his old father away from the flames of Troy towards the founding of a new nation. This is the final 'speaking picture' with which Sidney leaves us at the close of the Proof or Confirmation: Aeneas the heroic soldier-adventurer, an invention of the poets (Sidney contrasts Virgil's ideal 'feigned' Aeneas with the treacherous 'right' Aeneas as represented in the work of the historian Dares Phrygius, 92/29–30), whose struggles to lead his party of wandering Trojan exiles to fully fledged nationhood deserve to be 'worn in the tablet of your memory' as a model for the emerging nations of Europe (99/42). And if we do indeed bear Aeneas in mind as we read the rest of the *Apology*, we will emerge with a clear perception of the complex relationship between poetry and nationhood as Sidney sees it.

According to many Tudor historians, Aeneas was the great grandfather of the founder of Britain, Brutus, who gave his name to the island of Albion after purging it of its original inhabitants – an aggressive race of giants – and establishing a neo-Trojan dynasty in their place.[89] From

---

[89] For a full account of this tradition see Kendrick 1950. A convenient summary is provided in Graham Parry, *The Trophies of Time: English Antiquarians of the Seventeenth Century* (Oxford and New York, 1995), 26–9.

one point of view, then, Virgil's Aeneas gave the impetus for the founding of the English nation. Sidney's interest in the early history of England and her neighbours is as well attested as his interest in painting.[90] It manifests itself in his letters to Languet, where he discusses the strengths and weaknesses of a history of ancient Britain written by his father's protégé Humphrey Lhuyd, and it emerges in the *Apology* when he refers to the Welsh as the 'true remnant of the ancient Britons' (83/28).[91] He would have been well aware of the myth of Brutus, and conscious too that its authenticity was as fiercely contested as the authenticity of Virgil's representation of Aeneas.[92] But as we have seen, Sidney sees the notion of historical authenticity as of limited value: the false Aeneas of Virgil is more useful as a stimulant to virtuous action than the 'historical' Aeneas of Dares Phyrgius. In a letter to his brother Robert he points out that even the fact-obsessed historian makes himself 'a poet sometimes, for ornament' (Duncan-Jones 1989, 292), lending substance to his true examples of virtue and vice with the aid of poetry – that is, of carefully disguised fictions. These intrusions of fiction into history help to explain the impact on populations of events whose actual impact is unknown, and the explanations they offer deserve to be carefully noted: 'for though perchance they were not so, yet it is enough they might be so'. He says much the same thing in the *Apology*; the historian must often 'tell events whereof he can yield no cause; or, if he do, it must be poetical' (93/7–8). At crucial moments in any historical narrative, then, the responsible historian's claim to authenticity must subordinate itself to his role as a moral and political instructor; and this point lies at the core of Sidney's attack on poet-haters in the Refutation.

The poet-haters represent themselves as the exclusive custodians of the truth about poetry and its place in the history of the English nation. But their claim to historical authenticity is as poetic as the purely imaginative writing they condemn. They specialize in distorting the judgment (instead of 'enabling' it as teachers should) by 'carping and taunting at each thing which, by stirring the spleen, may *stay the brain from a through-beholding* the worthiness of the subject' (101/2–3, my emphasis). Their preferred targets are things of 'sacred . . . majesty' (101/5), and they forfeit all their pretensions to moral or historical

---

[90] For his interest in history generally, see F. J. Levy, 'Sir Philip Sidney and the Idea of History', *Bibliothèque d'Humanisme et Renaissance* 26 (1964), 608–17, and Elizabeth Story Donno, 'Old Mouse-eaten Records: History in Sidney's *Apology*', in Kay 1987, 147–67.

[91] See Duncan-Jones 1991, 72–3; Sidney's antiquarian poem, 'The 7 Wonders of Wilton', Ringler 1962, 149–51; and his commendation of Polydore Vergil and Holinshed to his friend Edward Denny, Duncan-Jones 1989, 289. Sidney could have met the historian William Camden at Oxford (see Duncan-Jones 1991, 40, and Stewart 2000, 55); Camden published his account of ancient British history, *Britannia*, in 1586.

[92] See Hadfield 1994, 140.

gravitas by their 'scoffing' argumentative methods, 'so as the best title in true English they get with their merriments is to be called good fools, for so have our grave forefathers ever termed that humorous kind of jesters' (101/19–22). This final sentence is one of Sidney's most brilliant rhetorical inversions. The poet supplants the poet-hater as the custodian of the wisdom of 'our grave [English] forefathers'. Indeed, the poet-hater's command of the English language itself would seem to be faulty – Sidney the poet speaks 'true English' where his opponents speak only a tangle of thought-inhibiting falsehoods. And the poet-hater who loves to mock 'majesty' is exposed as the least majestic of English subjects, with no claim to any hereditary 'title' except the humiliating one of a professional fool. In this first phase of the Refutation, then, the poet-haters' version of history – where poets are mendacious upstarts and their opponents are the bastions of truth – is turned on its head. And in the process the definition of truth itself is called into question.

It is in the Refutation that the *Apology's* extraordinary barrage of allusions to truth reaches its climax, as Sidney concludes the list of charges against poetry with the wry observation, 'Truly, this is much, if there be much truth in it' (102/32). Sidney's term 'truly', as I pointed out at the beginning of this introduction, invariably occurs at moments when he is at his most controversial, when the truth of his claims is self-evidently in dispute. The most striking instance of this usage comes in his response to the first really grave charge against poetry, 'that it is the mother of lies' (102/23). To this Sidney replies with an extraordinary blend of assertiveness and caution: 'I answer paradoxically, but truly, I think truly, that of all writers under the sun the poet is the least liar, and, though he would, as a poet can scarcely be a liar' (103/1–3). The reason is, of course, that the poet 'nothing affirms, and therefore never lieth' (103/8–9); he makes no claim to historical accuracy, unlike the historian, who 'affirming many things, can, in the cloudy knowledge of mankind, hardly escape from many lies' (103/11–12). In a world where the best information is enveloped in uncertainty, where apparent facts are merely probabilities (or as Sidney calls them, 'conjectured likelihoods', 93/3), the only honest way to state an opinion about the truth is to qualify one's statement, as Sidney does, with a modest disclaimer: 'I think'.

Sidney's wittiest illustration of the contingent status of truth in a fallen world occurs earlier in his argument, when he is comparing the relative merits of fictional examples and historical ones as aids to moral guidance. To facilitate the comparison he selects one example 'wherein a poet and a historian do concur' of a story with a seemingly straightforward moral application (93/9ff.). The historian's version of the story, as Herodotus and Justin tell it, concerns a faithful servant of King Darius who pretended to desert to his master's Babylonian enemies in order to 'find means to deliver them over to Darius'. To make his pretence more convincing, the servant cut off his ears and nose, so that the Babylonians accepted him into their camp without question. The prose poet Xenophon, Sidney claims, tells the same story about Abradatas, the faithful ally of King Cyrus.[93] In this case, he goes on, the poet's feigned example is clearly as effective as the historian's in teaching its reader how to 'serve your prince by such an honest dissimulation'; indeed ('truly') it is better, since Abradatas only cut off his ears, so that in imitating him 'you shall save your nose by the bargain'. But the real wit of the passage lies in the fact that both versions of the story are designed to teach their readers how to lie. The service of princes demands 'dissimulation', and it is reasonable to suppose that poetry would have more to teach us on the duplicitous art of 'feigning' than history, which prides itself on its commitment to 'truth'. Besides, in both versions of the story the definition of 'truth' depends on which side you happen to favour. Abradatas's 'feigning' demonstrates his 'truth' to Cyrus, just as the servant's proves his loyalty to Darius; but in each case one must assume that the enemies they duped would have seen their dissimulations in quite another light. Truth here, as elsewhere in the *Apology*, is a fiercely contested concept, whose ownership is claimed with equal conviction by opposing parties in any ideological quarrel, and whose nature is rendered problematic by the 'cloudy knowledge of mankind' as to what exactly constitutes 'virtuous action'.

This cloudiness similarly enfolds the 'principal, if not the only, abuse' Sidney concedes to have been practised by the poets: that they have 'abused men's wit' by 'training it to wanton sinfulness and lustful love' (103/44ff.). The passage in the Refutation where he makes this concession marks a crucial turning-point in the *Apology*. Up to this moment Sidney has been mounting a powerful defence of the ideal poet, punctuated by reminders that he is speaking about poetry as it should be rather than as it is. Now he states openly what he has been hinting at throughout the essay: that the practice of contemporary poetry has somehow detached itself from the ideals he has been proposing. 'Now swarm', he told us early in the argument, 'many versifiers that need never answer to the name of poets' (87/28–9). The comic genre, he told us later, has been 'justly made odious' by 'naughty play-makers and stage-keepers', and he promised at that point to respond to the 'argument of abuse' at a yet later stage in his discussion (98/2–4). With the discussion of love in the Refutation he begins to deal with this 'argument of

---

[93] I share Margaret Ferguson's suspicion that Sidney was fully aware that he had invented this example (Ferguson 1983, 144, and 229, note 22); 'the feigned example of Abradatas' superior feigning', as she puts it, 'is not to be found in Xenophon at all'. See 93/20 note.

abuse' – that poetry corrupts its readers by subjecting them to 'wanton shows of better hidden matters' (104/25–6). If poetry's aim is to teach delightfully, the poet-haters claim that modern poets privilege delight over pedagogy; that the erotic desire which Sidney has situated at the heart of poetry's power over its readers has overwhelmed its instructive purpose. Still worse, they claim that poetry instructs its readers not in 'virtuous action' but in the pursuit of desire; that comedies, for instance, 'rather teach than reprehend amorous conceits', that 'the Lyric is larded with passionate sonnets, the Elegiac weeps the want of his mistress, and that even to the Heroical Cupid hath ambitiously climbed' (104/2–5). In the sentences that follow, the Refutation transforms itself into a series of further concessions to poetry's enemies. One by one Sidney grants 'whatsoever they will have granted, that not only love, but lust, but vanity, but (if they list) scurrility, possesseth many leaves of the poets' books' (104/13–15). The ideal poetry he has so carefully delineated in the course of his essay seems to vanish before these admissions like a nebulous mirage, a castle in the air, a lie detected.

But Sidney's response to the poet-haters' 'argument of abuse' is in fact wonderfully ambivalent. For one thing, we have already seen that he thinks a good deal more highly of 'amorous conceits' than most schoolmasters do. This was evident from the moment he praised the 'sugared invention of that picture of love' in a romance by Heliodorus at the beginning of the essay (87/32–3), and he now reminds us of his opinion in parenthetical asides: 'grant love of beauty to be a beastly fault (although it be very hard, since only man, and no beast, hath that gift to discern beauty); grant that lovely name of Love to deserve all hateful reproaches (although even some of my masters the philosophers spent a good deal of their lamp-oil in setting forth the excellency of it)' (104/8–12). At a later stage in his argument, when addressing once again the issue of the abuse of comedy in the contemporary theatre, he draws a careful distinction between 'scurrility, unworthy of any chaste ears' and the 'delight' with which men are ravished when they see a fair woman (112/11–40). To confuse 'love of beauty' and 'that lovely name of Love' with scurrility is a sign not just of bad manners but of ignorance in the poet-haters.

Manners are, however, an important indication of the difference between the princely poet and his schoolmasterly antagonists. The poet-haters' objection to the abuse of poetry, he points out, is scarcely adequate as an objection to poetry as such, since they are objecting only to poetry's subject, not to its techniques – so that if they are honest 'they will find their sentence may *with good manners* put the last words foremost, and not say that Poetry abuseth man's wit, but that man's wit abuseth Poetry' (104/15–17). If, then, the poet-haters refuse to reverse their judgment they will merely expose their own lack of breeding, and hence their ignoble origins, by attacking Poetry for something that is not her fault. More seriously, they will expose their willingness to mis-interpret history by obscuring the real relationship between poetry and its cultural and historical context. Throughout the *Apology* Sidney has stressed the fact that the concept of ideal poetry exists quite separately from poetry's practitioner, the poet, who is subject like all men to the vagaries of corrupt ideologies and tyrannical regimes. The discussion of Abradatas closes with the admission that, if very few poets besides Xenophon have exploited their art to effective political or military ends, 'yet say I and say again, I speak of the art, and not of the artificer' (93/31–2). Pindar's failure to write lyrics on serious themes was, Sidney insists, 'the fault of the poet, and not of the poetry' (99/20), and the failings of More's *Utopia* were 'the fault of the man and not of the poet' (91/22–3). Poetry's status as the art of the fallen world means that its practice inevitably falls short of what it should be; but Sidney represents its shortcomings as the effect of pernicious outside influences, injected into the poetic art by individual poets as a result of the historical or national conditions under which they write. Pindar was adversely affected by 'the time and custom of the Greeks' (99/21); the ancient poets who told pornographic stories about the gods 'did not induce such opinions, but did imitate those opinions already induced' (107/11–13); Chaucer wrote with miraculous farsightedness in a 'misty time' of intel-lectual and doctrinal ignorance (110/13). And Sidney makes the same claim about the love-poetry that dominates the Elizabethan age. If it is true that every poetic genre in the present age has been infected by love as if by a disease, then poetry has been infected from outside, and the art itself is not responsible for its current tendency 'to infect the fancy with unworthy objects' (104/20–1). The whole drift of Sidney's argu-ment tends towards the conclusion that if the poet-haters think there is something wrong with poetic practice, they should look beyond poetry for an explanation. And the explanation Sidney offers in the last part of the *Apology* is a decidedly controversial one.

Poetry and the betrayal of Elizabethan England

The poet-haters' unmannerly misreporting of history – their insistence that poetry has abused man's wit instead of the other way round – would seem to be a habitual practice of theirs. 'They allege', Sidney tells us,

> that before poets began to be in price our nation hath set their hearts' delight upon action, and not upon imagination, rather doing things worthy to be written, than writing things fit to be done. What that beforetime was, I think scarcely Sphinx can tell, since no memory is so ancient that hath the prece-dence of Poetry. And certain it is that, in our plainest homeliness, yet never was the Albion nation without poetry.
>
> (105/1–7)

The poet-haters' version of English history is here exposed as imaginary, a myth like that of the riddling Sphinx in the story of Oedipus, a piece of pure poetry, in fact, of the sort they profess to detest. The most prominent Elizabethan exponent of this myth was Gosson, who argued in *The School of Abuse* that poetry, playgoing, and piping were responsible for the loss of what he calls 'the olde discipline of England':

> *Dion* sayth, that english men could suffer watching and labor, hunger & thirst, and beare of al stormes with hed and shoulders, they vsed slender weapons, went naked, and were good soldiours, they fed vppon rootes and barkes of trees, they would stand vp to the chin many dayes in marishes without victualles . . . But the exercise that is nowe among vs, is banqueting, playing, pipyng, and dauncing, and all suche delightes as may win vs to pleasure, or rocke us a sleepe.
>
> (Gosson 1974, 91)

Gosson substantiates this claim for a time when Englishmen 'set their hearts' delight upon action, and not upon imagination' by reference to the ancient British queen Bunduica, whose resistance to the invading forces of Rome was cited by Tudor historians as a prototype of English nationalism. Bunduica derided the Roman invaders as 'vnwoorthy the name of men, or title of Souldiers, because they were smoothly appareled, soft lodged, daintely feasted, bathed in warme waters, rubbed with sweet oyntments, strewd with fine poulders, wine swillers, singers, Dauncers, and Players' (95). Poets and players were the men responsible for reducing the Romans to this state of luxuriant effeminacy, and Gosson implies that the proliferation of poets and players in modern England has reduced its people to the same degenerate condition. 'God hath now blessed *England* with a Queene,' he claims, who resembles Bunduica in her qualities as leader; but 'wee vnworthy seruants of so mild a Mistresse, vnnatural children of so good a mother, vnthankful subiects of so louing a prince, wound her royall hart with abusing her lenitie' (95–6). Like most Elizabethan social commentators Gosson lays the blame for the collapse of good relations between the authorities and their subjects – or the good mother and her unnatural children – squarely on the subject. And the most disastrous consequence of this social and moral collapse is that it has turned the once courageous Englishmen into a bunch of lascivious women.

Sidney's response is to question Gosson's credentials as a historian. 'Certain it is', he says – and the phrase emphasizes the uncertainty that surrounds Gosson's assertions – 'that, in our plainest homeliness, yet never was the Albion nation without poetry' (105/6–7). Gosson anachronistically refers to Bunduica as 'Queene of Englande' in an effort to underline her resemblance to Elizabeth I; Sidney quietly corrects the anachronism by using the most ancient of names for Britain, Albion. And he goes on to point out the folly of the view that to repudiate learning, of which poetry is a branch, gives nations a military advantage over their civilized neighbours. 'This indeed,' he scoffs, 'is the ordinary doctrine of ignorance', a form of teaching worthy of the barbaric Goths who destroyed Rome (105/16). Gosson's championing of cultural vandalism shows that texts like the *School* are designed not to propagate knowledge but to stifle it, not to enhance the cultural status of the English but to encourage their regression to the condition of naked root-eating marsh-dwellers. *The School of Abuse* is no better than 'a chainshot against all learning' (105/8), including the history which it exploits to make its case against poetry.

Even as Sidney develops this reasoned response to Gosson, the military metaphors he uses accumulate, undermining the poet-haters' argument that 'before poets did soften us' the English nation was 'full of courage, given to martial exercises, the pillars of manlike liberty' (102/28–9). Sidney's admission that poetry may be used as an incitement to sexual transgression is transformed, as he makes it, into evidence of the quasi-martial forcefulness of his discipline. Being misused, 'by the reason of his sweet charming force, [poetry] can do more hurt than any other army of words' (104/28–9); it is a sword which can be used in defence of the poet's country as effectively as in offence against it (104/41–2); and in the triumphant climax to the Refutation he concludes that 'Poetry is the companion of camps' (105/25), an appropriate ally for conquerors such as Alexander the Great, 'the phoenix of warlike princes' (105/35). By the end of this sequence of statements the 'sweet charming force' of poetry is not merely not antagonistic to militarism; it has become at once the most ancient and the most effective stimulus to military action. The sentence in which Sidney makes this pronouncement again brilliantly underlines the contingent status of all historical assertions. 'And if to a slight conjecture a conjecture may be opposed,' it begins – the 'slight conjecture' being that poetry has feminized the English nation – 'truly it may seem, that as by him [i.e. the poet] their learned men took almost their first light of knowledge, so their active men received their first motions of courage' (105/29–32). Poetry is as inextricably a part of military history as it is of the history of ideas – Homer's poetry accompanied Alexander in his conquests – and historiography itself relies heavily on poetic 'conjecture' to construct its narratives, including the narrative that takes poetry to be the ruin of a nation's martial aspirations.

The last part of the Refutation, where Sidney answers the charge that the philosopher Plato expelled poets from his ideal republic, returns to his earlier strategy of depicting philosophers as impractical academics, useless in the battlefield ('the quiddity of *ens* and *prima materia* will hardly agree with a corslet', 105/24–5), useless as political advisers (Plato was made a slave by the tyrant he tried to reform), and more inclined to encourage 'effeminate wantonness' than any reputable poet (Plato himself championed 'abominable filthiness' – that is, homoerotic love – and 'community' of women, 106/41–4). The poets expelled by Plato from his republic were those who contaminated the ancient Greek religion with 'wrong opinions' and 'light tales' (107/9). Yet the religion Plato sought to purify has since been exposed by Christianity as a mesh of superstitious 'dreams'; and in the *Ion* Plato makes it plain that he thought as superstitiously of poets as the poets did of the gods: 'he attributeth unto Poesy more than myself do, namely, to be a very inspiring of a divine force, far above man's wit' (107/36–8). Plato, in other words – who is 'of all philosophers . . . , the most poetical' (106/17–18) – is subject to the very same charges that have been laid against the poets. Evidently Sidney could act the 'playing wit' as nimbly as his enemies, 'carping and taunting' at the worthiest subjects – such as the supreme philosopher – with all the iconoclastic impudence of the poet-haters themselves. The difference is that Sidney's aristocratic manners remain impeccable even as he challenges the poet-haters' assumption that Plato is one of their number. 'I had much rather,' he concludes, '(since truly I may do it) show their mistaking of Plato . . . than go about to overthrow his authority' (107/32–5). His response to the appeal to Plato ends by enlisting him as 'our patron and not our adversary', one who gave 'due honour' to the poet's discipline and who deserves to be held in 'admiration' when he is not misusing his philosophical genius (107/30–6). With infinite courtesy Plato's abuse has been turned into commendation, the sentence he gave against poets in the *Republic* has been reversed, and the greatest of poetry's traditional enemies has been shown to be her son, the poet's brother, suffering from nothing more serious than a severe case of sibling rivalry.

The Refutation, then, substantiates what the Proof or Confirmation taught us: that history depends on poetic conjecture, that soldiership is encouraged rather than disabled by the 'sweet charming force' of poetry, and that the philosopher is the poet's close relative, with all his faults and little of his charm – like the disgruntled brother of the Prodigal Son. Poetry, in other words, is bound up with every human discipline, linked both by blood and by family resemblance with the most distinguished exponents of every art, nourished by and nourishing the physical and intellectual impulses that stimulate every kind of action, good or bad. To reject it is artificially to drive a wedge through a close-knit familial community, and by extension through the national community of which the family is both the model and the chief component. This is precisely what the poet-haters have done in Elizabethan England, and the Digression presents us with the plot of the absorbing national drama that has been engendered by their unwarranted hostility to fiction.

The drama is the exact obverse of the drama of England as Gosson represented it, in which poets were the 'unnatural children' of their 'good mother' Elizabeth, rejecting the ancient moral and cultural values of their country in favour of continental lasciviousness and effeminacy. Sidney's drama opens not with children who reject their mother but with a mother who rejects her children: 'it shall be but a little more lost time to inquire why England (the mother of excellent minds) should be grown so hard a stepmother to poets' (108/23–5); and, although the reasons for the mother's rejection of her offspring are not given at this stage, we might assume that it arises, at least in part, from an unconditional acceptance of the Gossonian version of literary history. The effects of this abandonment of the maternal role on the part of England are made plain at once. They are first of all implied in a passing allusion to the *Aeneid* (108/28), a Latin quotation ('O Muse! the causes and the crimes relate; / What goddess was provok'd, and whence her hate') which reminds us of the relentless persecution of Aeneas, founder of Rome and ancestor of the founder of Britain, by Juno, mother of the gods. The dismissal of poetry, it is implied, is tantamount to a turning aside from the mission of establishing a great European nation fit to rival ancient Rome, the nation founded by Aeneas. And it is a policy which sets England radically at odds with her European rivals. All of England's neighbours, from Italy to France, from Germany to Scotland, have 'embraced' the poets like favourite children (108/32–8); only England has given them a 'hard welcome' (108/42). We might read in this passage a rueful allusion to Sidney's own 'hard welcome' at the court of Elizabeth, which contrasted so starkly with the warm embraces he had received at the hands of every other prince in Europe. But the passage suggests also that the poet-haters have alienated England from the policy of her own ancestors: 'For heretofore poets have in England also flourished, and, which is to be noted, even in those times when the trumpet of Mars did sound loudest' (109/2–4). And this detachment of the modern English nation from its heroic past unleashes a bewildering sequence of allusions to acts of sexual transgression. In the course of the Digression Elizabethan England emerges as a land where the relations between parents and children, and the distinction between the offspring of legitimate and illegitimate sexual unions, have broken down altogether: a land in need of a radical cultural overhaul if it is to achieve the international status Sidney has ambitiously claimed for it in the earlier parts of the *Apology*.

Above all, it is a land that has succumbed to indolence, an 'overfaint quietness' (109/4–5) which spurns any kind of action, from writing (England 'now can scarce endure the pain of a pen', 109/10–11) to warfare (Mars's trumpet has fallen silent). This is an atmosphere inimical to poets, who, we learn, 'like Venus (but to better purpose) hath rather be troubled in the net with Mars than enjoy the homely quiet of Vulcan' (109/7–9) – would rather, that is, be engaged in vigorous activity, however illicit, than plunged in domestic torpor. The reference to Venus, the classical goddess of love who cuckolded her husband Vulcan with Mars, the god of war, is another of Sidney's masterpieces of impudence in his self-defence against the poet-haters. This is exactly the sort of scurrilous story or 'light tale' about the gods that led Plato to bar poets from his ideal republic (indeed, Plato includes it in his list of such stories in *Republic*, III); yet it is here being cited as something that 'giveth great praise to Poesy' (109/7), since it confirms the link between poetry and martial action which was one of the key themes of the Refutation. Sexual transgression, Sidney suggests, is not inherently objectionable; it is rendered either vile or praiseworthy by its worse or better purpose. And in the past the poets have invariably 'exercised their delightful vein' in the service of national military glory, which is the best purpose of all – at least, in the eyes of an impertinent young aristocrat like Sidney.

In the 'idle England' of Elizabeth (109/10), by contrast, poetry has given itself over to less noble forms of sexual transgression. Its practitioners have become lazy self-seeking time-servers: 'base men with servile wits undertake it, who think it enough if they can be rewarded of the printer' (109/11–12). Poetry has simultaneously lost its aristocratic status and its championship of liberty; it has become a 'serving science' like all the rest, dependent for its topics on the demands of its paymasters. The 'servile wits' of its Elizabethan practitioners furnish irrefutable proof of their illegitimacy, their base birth: they are the products of the indiscriminate sexual promiscuity which is encouraged (according to Elizabethan tradition) by the vice of idleness, and their publications populate the city bookstalls 'as if all the Muses were got with child to bring forth bastard poets' (109/17). Under these conditions the best poets – the 'right poets' of the Confirmation, the legitimate princes or monarchs of the liberal arts – are hard pressed to distinguish themselves from their base-born rivals. Reluctant to bring their legitimacy into doubt by appearing in print alongside men of doubtful cultural or familial status they are 'better content to suppress the outflowing of their wit, than, by publishing them, to be accounted knights of the same order' (109/22–3). Their works, that is, have been driven into obscurity, lurking in manuscripts like the one that contains the *Apology* itself, reserved for the furtive perusal of a select coterie of its author's fellow spirits.

At the same time, the distinction between the good Elizabethan poets and the bad ones, between the best English poetry in manuscript and its debased counterpart in print, is not as clear as the princely 'right poets' might like to think. Sidney himself confesses that he has been 'admitted into the company of the paper-blurrers' (109/24–5), and the phrase recalls the process of admitting new members into city gilds, such as the Company of Stationers to which all the authorized London printers belonged. He does not necessarily mean that some of his verse has appeared in print (although he might mean this), but he certainly implies that his writing is not so very far removed from that of the 'bastard poets' who write only 'to be rewarded of the printer'; that it belongs, in fact, to the same social and literary class. And as a member of the mixed 'company' of English poets Sidney goes on to admit that 'the very true cause of our wanting estimation is want of desert', and that like his fellow Englishmen he has 'neglected the means' to deserve the 'title' of poet (109/25–9). There is an old saying, he reminds us, that a poet is born, not made (*orator fit, poeta nascitur*, 109/38–9), but for Sidney being born a poet is not enough; one must work to cultivate one's poetic status, just as aristocrats must work to make themselves worthy of their aristocratic 'title' or inheritance. It is in this matter of work, of the labour to refine their gifts through 'Art, Imitation, and Exercise' (109/42–3), that the Elizabethan poets have fallen short, and their collective negligence has made them complicit with the culture of idleness that has cut the English off from their noble ancestry. All have given birth to intellectual bastards: 'so is our brain delivered of much matter which never was begotten by knowledge' (110/3–4). Their lineage has been compromised, their family shamed. Sidney lists a few exceptions – writers from Chaucer to Spenser who are distinguished by their lack of political servility – and the best of these, the Earl of Surrey, is conspicuous for his fusion of 'noble birth' with a 'noble mind' (110/17). But 'Besides these,' Sidney tells us, 'do I not remember to have seen but few (to speak boldly) printed, that have poetical sinews in them' (110/21–2). The body of work produced in print by Elizabethan writers betrays its own illegitimacy by its poor physical condition, the feebleness of its 'sinews'. Put most of this verse into prose, Sidney suggests (a school exercise which Ascham calls *metaphrasis*)[94] and it will quickly become apparent that 'one verse did but beget another, without ordering at the first what should be at the last' (110/24–5). The *Apology* itself only escapes this genealogical attrition by its status as a text designed for circulation in manuscript, not print.

The other public face of Elizabethan poetry, the theatre, is equally vulnerable to the charge of having compromised its noble ancestry. 'Our Tragedies and Comedies', Sidney declares, observe 'rules neither of honest civility nor of skilful Poetry' (110/28–9); with the partial exception of *Gorboduc*, they have abandoned the role of civilising nations which was assigned to poets at the beginning of the *Apology*. Sidney's choice of *Gorboduc* as the sole exception to this rule may not be solely a matter of aesthetic judgment. Like Shakespeare's *King Lear* the tragedy draws on material from ancient British history; it was performed before Elizabeth I as a lesson in the necessity for her to name a successor to the

---

[94] See Ascham 1904, 253ff.

English throne if she wished to avert the bloody civil conflicts it depicts; and it was written by two young aristocrats who went on to take an active part in the public life of the nation. By contrast, Sidney describes a typical Elizabethan tragedy as a hopeless historical muddle, with no sense of place or national identity ('you shall have Asia of the one side, and Afric of the other', 110/41–2), and still less awareness of the need to control theatrical time. In such a tragedy, he tells us, the narrative invariably runs like this: 'two young princes fall in love. After many traverses, she is got with child, delivered of a fair boy, he is lost, groweth a man, falls in love, and is ready to get another child, and all this in two hours' space' (111/9–12). Where *Gorboduc* dealt seriously with the problem of succession, this romantic fantasy reduces the dynastic perplexities of hereditary monarchy to a succession of farcical coincidences which resolve themselves entirely by chance. Only a few pages earlier Sidney had described true tragedy as a serious intervention in high politics, 'that maketh kings fear to be tyrants, and tyrants manifest their tyrannical humours' (98/27–8). Contemporary English tragedy forfeits its pretensions to seriousness by disregarding the class system altogether, 'mingling kings and clowns ... with neither decency nor discretion' (112/2–4). And once again, it is the erotic aspect of modern tragedy that most effectively demonstrates its political frivolity. Whenever comedy intervenes in an Elizabethan tragedy 'we have nothing but scurrility, unworthy of any chaste ears' (112/12–13), exactly as the Gossonian anti-theatrical lobby had complained. The theatre as a whole, then – the most popular form of poetry in England – offers the most dramatic instance of the detachment of the English nation from its noble forebears. 'Like an unmannerly daughter showing a bad education,' Sidney sums up, the modern English theatre 'causeth her mother Poesy's honesty to be called in question' (113/15–17). But he has already proved that 'mother Poesy' is honest: in the Refutation, for instance, he repudiated the suggestion that she was the 'mother of lies', and earlier he recalled her ancient role as the conscientious wetnurse of nations. The real culprit for the 'bad education' of the Elizabethan poets and their theatrical offspring is their 'hard ... Stepmother, England'. And amid all this talk of mothers it is hard to resist the inference that Sidney is offering an oblique criticism of the 'mother' of the English nation, Elizabeth I, whose placatory foreign policy has rendered her children idle.

Sidney's allusions to the aristocratic ancestry of the poet and the princeliness of his qualities have often been taken simply as an expression of his own class interests – a carefully rationalized snobbery. But I have already suggested at the beginning of this introduction that there may have been a more specific political agenda behind these allusions. Sidney's own lineage had been called in question in the famous tennis-court quarrel with the Earl of Oxford, which ended with Elizabeth reminding him that his social status was inferior to Oxford's, and thus delivering an implicit snub to the militant Protestant party to which Sidney belonged, the party headed by Sidney's powerful uncle Robert Dudley, Earl of Leicester. I suggested that Sidney's defence of the 'title' of the poet, his lineage and political status, might be read as another intervention in this quarrel. In this defence Sidney seeks to illustrate his own credentials as a serious contender for public office, first by tracing his unofficial ancestry as a poet, and then by showing how poets had been illegitimately unseated from their deserved pre-eminence in English culture. The Digression's demonstration of the confusion over social hierarchy in contemporary England – accurately mimicked in the lack of decorum in the English theatre, where monarchs and clowns contend for domination of the stage – takes this argument a stage further. The proper relationship between nobles and the people and between monarchs and the nobility was often taken by Tudor thinkers to have originated as a meritocracy: true nobility displayed itself in noble manners and noble actions. One of Sidney's favourite authors, the humanist Sir Thomas Elyot, described the origins of nobility like this:

> in the begynnyng, whan priuate possessions and dignitie were gyuen by the consent of the people, who than had all thinge in commune, and equalitie in degree and condition, vndoubtedly they gaue the one and the other to him at whose vertue they meruailed, and by whose labour and industrie they receiued a commune benefite, as of a commune father that with equall affection loued them . . . where vertue ioyned with great possessions or dignitie hath longe continued in the bloode or house of a gentilman, as it were an inheritaunce, there nobilitie is moost shewed, and these noble men be most to be honored . . . Thus I conclude that nobilitie is nat after the vulgare opinion of men, but is only the praise and surname of vertue; whiche the lenger it continueth in a name or lignage, the more is nobilitie extolled and meruailed at.
>
> (Elyot 1883, II, 27–38)

The doubts Sidney expresses in the Digression over both the 'virtue' of contemporary poets and their 'name and lineage' indicates that true nobility has been ousted from its proper estimation in England. The entire identity of the nobility is in crisis, its genealogy uncertain, the legitimacy of its offspring questioned. And, as we saw at the beginning of this Introduction, the event in recent years that had thrown most doubt over the identity and future of England and her governing classes was the proposed marriage between Elizabeth and the Catholic Duc d'Alençon. The source of the current crisis lay at its head, and the elevation of 'base men' to undeserved 'titles' might be seen as an outcome of the same poor judgment that proposed the Frenchman as a suitable match for the English Queen.

The same might be said of the suppression of the martial qualities that have distinguished Englishmen in the past, when poetry accompanied the English camps at Poitiers and Agincourt (battles in which the English defeated the French as Leicester's faction hoped to defeat the proposed marriage with a Frenchman). In the Elizabethan theatre, Sidney explains at one point in the Digression, the evocation of 'delight' by which poetry ought to stimulate learning has been supplanted by an appeal to a baser reaction in the audience, that of 'loud laughter' (112/14). Delight, he says, arises from the poet's imitation of 'things that have a conveniency to ourselves or the general nature' (112/22) – actions or people that please or attract his readers by arousing their sympathy or desire: a 'fair woman', 'good chances', 'the happiness of our friends, or country' (112/25–30). Laughter is produced by things we hold in contempt, from which we desire to) distance ourselves – 'deformed creatures', 'a matter quite mistaken' (112/27–31). If laughter is all that the modern English stage can produce we must infer that it alienates the bulk of its audience, and that its contribution to 'the happiness of our friends, or country' is altogether negligible. Sidney closes this discussion by suggesting a topic which would arouse both laughter and delight, a speaking picture well suited to the modern stage whose 'delightful teaching' would justify its unusual fusion of the two responses. 'Yet deny I not,' he says,

> but that they may go well together: for as in Alexander's picture well set out we delight without laughter, and in twenty mad antics we laugh without delight; so in Hercules, painted with his great beard and furious countenance, in woman's attire, spinning at Omphale's commandment, it breedeth both delight and laughter. For the representing of so strange a power in love procureth delight: and the scornfulness of the action stirreth laughter.
>
> (112/34–40)

In the Refutation, Alexander was the 'phoenix of warlike princes', and the juxtaposition of his portrait here with the sort of pictorial spectacle privileged in Elizabethan England ('mad antics', decorative paintings representing monstrous beasts and grotesque human figures) is embarrassing enough. But the sight of Hercules 'in woman's attire' is not merely embarrassing: it is also instructive. The 'tales of Hercules, Achilles, Cyrus, and Aeneas' were earlier invoked as examples of poetry's ability to furnish 'the right description of wisdom, valour, and justice' (95/26–8). Here, on the other hand, one of the chief representatives of the 'male' virtues has been set to the most humiliating of 'female' domestic tasks at the behest of a tyrannical queen. This is not so much an instance of poetry feminizing its male readers as an imaginative portrayal of the means by which poetry's readers have been feminized: their subjection to a woman's whimsy which has transformed them into a generation of starry-eyed transvestites.

By the time he wrote this passage Sidney had already painted a poetic speaking picture very similar to the picture of Hercules in drag. The 'strange power of love' manifests itself in the *Old Arcadia* when the young prince Pyrocles dons a female disguise in order to get close to the woman he loves, Philoclea, daughter of Duke Basilius. He is driven to these lengths by the Duke's cowardly withdrawal from public affairs, and his refusal to allow his daughter to be courted by conventional means. Pyrocles is feminized, in fact, not by love but by Basilius. His 'masculine' prowess remains intact despite his disguise; at the end of the first book he kills a lion single-handed, as Hercules did, but for different reasons: to protect and impress the woman he loves. And the parallel with Hercules does not escape unnoticed. Gynecia, Basilius's wife, 'sware she saw the very face of young Hercules killing the Nemean lion' as she witnessed the incident, 'and all, with a grateful assent, confirmed the same praises' (*OA*, 48). It is one of the rare moments in the book when Pyrocles gets an opportunity to behave like a classical hero. The English poets, by contrast, have no outlets for displays of Herculean energy, or even of poetic 'forcibleness or *energia*' (113/32). They are content instead to remain silent, or to 'stir laughter in sinful things' as they write for the theatre (113/1), or to neglect the best function of lyric poetry – that of 'singing the praises of the immortal beauty' of God (113/21) – in favour of writing insipid love-poems, many of which, Sidney declares, 'if I were a mistress, would never persuade me they were in love' (113/26–7). Sidney's willingness here to transform himself imaginatively into a 'mistress' demonstrates the extent to which he, too, has been feminized by the atrophy of English political life.

The very diction of modern poets has undergone a humiliating metamorphosis. Where in the earlier parts of the *Apology* poetic language was metaphorically associated with gorgeous clothing, in the Digression it has lost all sense of style – 'So is that honey-flowing matron eloquence apparelled, or rather disguised, in a courtesan-like painted affectation' (113/37). This is another of Sidney's witty inversions of the poet-haters' position. Ascham complained about the outrageous apparel cultivated by young men at court and took it as yet another sign of their irresponsible prodigality.[95] Sidney reverses the charge and complains that the learned teachers in the universities have adopted linguistic clothes as excessive as any in the writings of the poets. The 'courtesan-like painted affectation' cultivated by modern English writers consists of an excessive use of 'far-fetched' or foreign words and of elaborate rhetorical 'figures and flowers'; but these faults are by no means 'only peculiar to versifiers' (113/38–42). They have their origins in the universities and churches, among the scholars and preachers who have charge over the guidance of Elizabethan youth; who train them up to be 'diligent

[95] Ascham 1904, 208, 221.

imitators' of the ancient rhetoricians and supply them with 'Nizolian paper-books' full of elegant phrases to be slavishly copied (114/4–5). These authoritarian pedagogues, priding themselves on their cultivation of the classical virtues of Cicero and Demosthenes, unwittingly preside over the relapse of English culture into the barbarism to which it ostensibly opposes itself: their lack of stylistic good taste makes them resemble 'those Indians, not content to wear earrings at the fit and natural place of the ears, but they will thrust jewels through their nose and lips, because they will be sure to be fine' (114/7–10). Good English style, linguistically as well as sartorially speaking, resides in the place from which Ascham claimed it had been banished: among the aristocracy. 'Undoubtedly,' says Sidney, 'I have found in divers smally learned courtiers a more sound style than in some professors of learning' (114/42–4). It is in the refusal of these English nobles to be stylistically servile – no matter how politically servile their status as courtiers forces them to be – that the best hope lies of liberating the Herculean qualities of England from their current comic concealment.

England's future

The bulk of the *Apology* functions as a sort of 'speaking picture' representing the ideal poetry in order to stimulate its English readers into heroically virtuous poetic action, and into the political and military action by which poetry is sustained. The Digression, on the other hand, serves as a sort of satirical mirror – like the mirrors provided by tragedy, comedy, satire, and the pastoral – in which those same English readers are forced to confront the dire condition of their national culture. This mirror makes it clear that the English pedagogic and political authorities have betrayed their nation, and that the state of English poetry is merely a reflection of this betrayal. At the beginning of the *Apology* Sidney told us that poetry in his time 'is fallen to be the laughing-stock of children' (82/1); but by the end it is the nation's leaders who are the laughing-stock, with their pompous display of their own intellectual barbarism, their contempt for the cultural and martial values that might raise their country to the same level as the rest of Europe. And the worst thing is that this state of affairs is quite unnecessary.

The last part of the Digression is given over to a celebration of the limitless potential of the English tongue. It is a 'mingled language' (115/14), combining the metrical properties of all the languages in Europe – Italian, German, French, and Spanish – and outstripping them all in the breadth of its vocabulary. It is 'subject' to none of their defects (115/44), a phrase which suggests that it is perfectly adapted to the resistance of political as well as linguistic forms of tyranny. Sidney is even prepared to hint that it might be capable of resisting the most disastrous linguistic effects of the Fall, the confusion of tongues which first divided the earth into nations in the days of the Tower of Babel (or 'Babylon', as Sidney calls it). The Tower was built at a time when all humanity spoke a common language, and was intended to stretch to heaven; but the project foundered when God punished the builders for their ambition by making them mutually incomprehensible and scattering them abroad across the face of the earth. The English language promises to undo this punishment because of its grammatical simplicity; it is 'void of those cumbersome differences of cases, genders, moods, and tenses, which I think was a piece of the Tower of Babylon's curse, that a man should be put to school to learn his mother-tongue' (115/18–20). There is no need to turn to the schoolmasters to learn English; Englishmen are capable of 'uttering sweetly and properly the conceits of the mind' (115/21) without recourse to the classroom bickerings that have dethroned the poet, and without falling into the misunderstandings and differences of opinion to which the misuse of language has given rise throughout the *Apology*. The English tongue, especially as it is practised by courtiers – whose evasion of academic influence is not, as Ascham claimed, a mark of intellectual degeneracy, since it frees them from the abuses of art practised in the schoolroom – has the potential to become the new dominant tongue of Europe.

If this seems an over-optimistic note to end on, Sidney shows a disarming awareness of its extravagance in the final sentences of his essay. The Conclusion opens with a series of hyperbolic claims for poetry, some of which Sidney has either not mentioned or has effectively repudiated in the course of his argument: that poetry contains 'many mysteries', for instance, 'which of purpose were written darkly, lest by profane wits it should be abused' (116/32–4); or that whatever poets write 'proceeds of a divine fury' (116/35) (he told us earlier that Plato took this view but that he, Sidney, did not). He cites an impressive list of names both ancient and modern in support of these claims – Aristotle, Pietro Bembo, Scaliger, Cristoforo Landino – but mixes these with gestures of self-deprecation (the *Apology* is merely 'an ink-wasting toy', 116/21) and jokes (his reference to 'the reverent title of a rhymer' is a particularly witty bit of bathos, 116/24). And the entire passage is governed by his acknowledgment that it is uttered 'in the name of the nine Muses' (116/21–2) – in other words, that it is a piece of fine rhetorical invention. The poet, Sidney previously insisted, 'nothing affirms, and therefore never lieth'; he 'never maketh any circles about your imagination, to conjure you to believe for true what he writes . . . but even for his entry calleth the sweet Muses to inspire into him a good invention' (103/13–16). When Sidney tells us, then, to 'believe' a series of grandiose affirmations about poetry (116/24ff.), we should take him with a pinch of salt. This is not a serious encomium; or rather, its serious foundations (like the foundations of Erasmus's praise of folly) lie else-where: above all, I have suggested, in its revelation of the condition of Elizabethan England in Europe.

The *Apology* ends with a cheerful pastiche of one of the dedicatory epistles that had been addressed to Sidney himself 'in certain printed discourses', including those of the poet-hater Stephen Gosson.[96] Those who choose unconditionally to 'believe' the assertions Sidney has just made will find themselves abruptly transplanted into the absurd world of contemporary poetry in print: 'Thus doing, your name shall flourish in the printers' shops; thus doing, you shall be of kin to many a poeti-cal preface; thus doing, you shall be most fair, most rich, most wise, most all; you shall dwell upon superlatives' (116/40–1). Printed prefaces fashion an alternative genealogy to replace the devalued genealogy of the English nobility and the noble poet. It is a patently false genealogy and a rather silly one (the children of slaves will become '*Herculea proles*', the offspring of Hercules himself, 116/42), but it is better than the alter-native, which is the complacent acceptance of one's base condition. 'But if' (Sidney concludes) 'you have so earth-creeping a mind that it cannot lift itself up to look to the sky of Poetry', your 'rustical disdain' – a con-tempt that implies, if it does not demonstrate, your peasant origins – will cut you off from all hope of founding a dynasty of your own: 'thus much curse I must send you, in the behalf of all poets, that while you live, you live in love, and never get favour for lacking skill of a sonnet, and, when you die, your memory die from the earth for want of an epitaph' (117/9–12). At the end of the *Apology*, as at the beginning, Sidney is harping on the problem of lineage: his own, the poet's, the reader's, perhaps even that of his queen. Nobility is not so much a matter of birth (although as Elyot confessed, birth helps) as of attitude: a will-ingness to cherish personal ambitions and to support ambitious national enterprises. If England is to regain its nobility – or to become a fruitful soil, or a fertile mother – it must begin by reading texts like the *Apology* with respect.

Sidney's own hope (if he had one) of establishing a dynasty was cut off short when he died of an infected wound while pursuing the heroic enterprises on the continent that had characterized his English forebears. The battle of Zutphen in which he got his wound failed to achieve its military objectives. But his quasi-prophetic utterances about the theo-retical potential of English poetry, and the practical example of his own poetic writings, bore abundant fruit in later generations. And none of his texts has proved more enduring than the *Apology for Poetry*, the

---

[96] On the embarrassment given Sidney by one of these dedications, see Stewart 2000, 139–40. This was not the dedication of a 'poetical' work; but any dedication might be read as poetical, by Sidney's definition of the term, if it gives exorbitant praise to its dedicatee.

'blessed innocent' which its printer claimed to have 'delivered from Oblivion's womb'. If the text is less innocent than Olney claims, this will hardly make it less attractive to its readers in the twenty-first century.

A note on this edition

This is not a scholarly edition: that is, it does not record variants between different sixteenth-century versions of the *Apology* in print and manuscript. The only scholarly edition of the text published to date is that of Jan van Dorsten, and this should be consulted by any serious student of Sidney's work. Geoffrey Shepherd explains his procedure in this edition as follows:

> Sidney died in 1586. In 1595 Henry Olney of St Paul's Churchyard published *An Apologie for Poetrie* by the right noble, vertuous, and learned Sir Phillip Sidney, Knight (see title-page). In the same year, perhaps a little earlier, appeared THE DEFENCE of Poesie, by Sir Phillip Sidney, Knight, LONDON Printed for *William Ponsonby* 1595.
>
> The circumstances of publication suggest an amicable rivalry between two parties of Sidney's friends, each in possession of a MS of the *Apology*. Both Olney's text and Ponsonby's are good, carefully printed texts, independently intelligible. The fairly numerous minor variations between them rarely affect the general meaning and seem often to depend upon small changes in emphasis or rhythm, some perhaps rather the results of over-carefulness than of carelessness in preparing MSS of the *Apology*. At Penshurst there is a MS text of the *Apology* in a late sixteenth-century hand, again with its own minor variants, but often agreeing with Olney's text. No doubt several handwritten texts were in fairly wide circulation before publication. The *Apology* was frequently reprinted during the seventeenth century in Sidney's collected works, but none of the trivial variants in these texts of the *Apology* seems to have any authority.
>
> In this edition an attempt is made to present a text which will make the sense of the *Apology* as apparent as possible. In general it is based on Olney's text. Olney's punctuation is rhetorical and his paragraphing designed to show as much the flow as the stages of argument. In this edition the punctuation and paragraphing have been modified and the spelling modernised. Textual variants of any interest or substance are recorded in the Notes.

Shepherd's account should be supplemented with van Dorsten's in his edition (which makes use of an additional sixteenth-century manuscript) and with Henry Woudhuysen's in *Sir Philip Sidney and the Circulation of Manuscripts*.[97] Woudhuysen suggests that the rivalry between the parties of friends who published the early editions of Sidney's works was a good deal less 'amicable' than Shepherd claims. He also suggests that manuscripts of the *Apology* were *not* widely circulated in Sidney's

---

[97] See *Misc. Prose*, 59–72, and Woudhuysen 1996, 232–5.

lifetime. It is, however, true that the variants between sixteenth-century editions and manuscripts are mostly minor ones. I have therefore chosen to reprint Shepherd's text of the *Apology* without alteration, apart from two corrections to Henry Olney's epistle 'To the Reader', which is printed in the notes.

Geoffrey Shepherd's edition of *An Apology for Poetry* is one of the great editions of the twentieth century. Its notes are perhaps its chief splendour; they may be read as an index to classical, medieval, and early modern thinking on poetry and its related disciplines. I have tried not to interfere with them too rashly. In places they have been changed to make their meaning a little clearer, and at times this has involved some simplification; I hope this will not be found to have diminished their value. Here or there my reading of certain phrases or passages differs from Shepherd's. He regarded the influence of Gosson's *School of Abuse* on Sidney's text as negligible, and it will be clear from this introduction that I consider the *School's* influence to be all-pervasive, especially in the Refutation; many of the notes I have added are designed to substantiate this conviction. I have similarly tried to demonstrate that Sidney is likely to have read Ascham's *Schoolmaster* with close attention. The bulk of my other additions consist of suggested readings of words and phrases Shepherd left unglossed, and explanations of classical allusions with which he assumed his readers to be familiar.

Finally, it should be said that the longer I have worked on this new introduction the more I have grown to respect Shepherd's. It is a masterly survey of Western poetic theory from ancient times to the sixteenth century, and I am acutely conscious that the close reading of the *Apology* I have offered in its place constitutes a drastic narrowing of focus. My aim has been to excite the reader's interest in the text and to suggest a few ways of understanding it, most of them stemming from critical developments of the three and a half decades since Shepherd first published his edition. But Shepherd remains the Daedalus at my elbow, and, if I have ignored his example as foolishly as Icarus ignored the advice of his brilliant father, I can only tender his memory an apology, though hardly a defence.

AN
APOLOGIE
for Poetrie.

Written by the right noble, vertu-
ous, and learned, Sir Phillip
Sidney, *Knight*.

Odi profanum vulgus, et arceo.

AT LONDON,
Printed for *Henry Olney*, and are to be sold at
his shop in Paules Church-yard, at the signe
of the George, neere to Cheap-gate.
Anno. 1595.

When the right virtuous Edward Wotton and I were at the Emperor's
court together, we gave ourselves to learn horsemanship of John Pietro
Pugliano, one that with great commendation had the place of an esquire
in his stable. And he, according to the fertileness of the Italian wit, did
not only afford us the demonstration of his practice, but sought to 5
enrich our minds with the contemplations therein which he thought
most precious. But with none I remember mine ears were at any time
more loaden, than when (either angered with slow payment, or moved
with our learner-like admiration) he exercised his speech in the praise
of his faculty. He said soldiers were the noblest estate of mankind, and 10
horsemen the noblest of soldiers. He said they were the masters of war
and ornaments of peace, speedy goers and strong abiders, triumphers
both in camps and courts. Nay, to so unbelieved a point he proceeded,
as that no earthly thing bred such wonder to a prince as to be a good
horseman. Skill of government was but a *pedanteria* in comparison. 15
Then would he add certain praises, by telling what a peerless beast a
horse was, the only serviceable courtier without flattery, the beast of
most beauty, faithfulness, courage, and such more, that if I had not been
a piece of a logician before I came to him, I think he would have persuaded me to have wished myself a horse. But thus much at least with 20
his no few words he drave into me, that self-love is better than any
gilding to make that seem gorgeous wherein ourselves are parties.

Wherein, if Pugliano's strong affection and weak arguments will not
satisfy you, I will give you a nearer example of myself, who (I know not
by what mischance) in these my not old years and idlest times having 25
slipped into the title of a poet, am provoked to say something unto you
in the defence of that my unelected vocation, which if I handle with
more good will than good reasons, bear with me, since the scholar is to
be pardoned that followeth the steps of his master. And yet I must
say that, as I have just cause to make a pitiful defence of poor Poetry, 30
which from almost the highest estimation of learning is fallen to be the

laughing-stock of children, so have I need to bring some more available proofs, since the former is by no man barred of his deserved credit, the silly latter hath had even the names of philosophers used to the defacing of it, with great danger of civil war among the Muses.

5   And first, truly, to all them that, professing learning, inveigh against Poetry, may justly be objected that they go very near to ungratefulness, to seek to deface that which, in the noblest nations and languages that are known, hath been the first light-giver to ignorance, and first nurse, whose milk by little and little enabled them to feed afterwards of tougher

10   knowledges. And will they now play the hedgehog that, being received into the den, drave out his host? Or rather the vipers, that with their birth kill their parents? Let learned Greece in any of her manifold sciences be able to show me one book before Musaeus, Homer, and Hesiod, all three nothing else but poets. Nay, let any history be brought

15   that can say any writers were there before them, if they were not men of the same skill, as Orpheus, Linus, and some other are named, who, having been the first of that country that made pens deliverers of their knowledge to their posterity, may justly challenge to be called their fathers in learning: for not only in time they had this priority (although

20   in itself antiquity be venerable) but went before them, as causes to draw with their charming sweetness the wild untamed wits to an admiration of knowledge. So, as Amphion was said to move stones with his poetry to build Thebes, and Orpheus to be listened to by beasts – indeed stony and beastly people – so among the Romans were Livius Andronicus, and

25   Ennius. So in the Italian language the first that made it aspire to be a treasure-house of science were the poets Dante, Boccaccio, and Petrarch. So in our English were Gower and Chaucer, after whom, encouraged and delighted with their excellent fore-going, others have followed, to beautify our mother tongue, as well in the same kind as in other arts.

30   This did so notably show itself, that the philosophers of Greece durst not a long time appear to the world but under the masks of poets. So Thales, Empedocles, and Parmenides sang their natural philosophy in verses; so did Pythagoras and Phocylides their moral counsels; so did Tyrtaeus in war matters, and Solon in matters of policy: or rather they,

35   being poets, did exercise their delightful vein in those points of highest knowledge, which before them lay hid to the world. For that wise Solon was directly a poet it is manifest, having written in verse the notable fable of the Atlantic Island, which was continued by Plato.

And truly even Plato whosoever well considereth shall find that in

40   the body of his work, though the inside and strength were Philosophy, the skin as it were and beauty depended most of Poetry: for all standeth upon dialogues wherein he feigneth many honest burgesses of Athens to speak of such matters, that, if they had been set on the rack, they would never have confessed them; besides his poetical describing the cir-

cumstances of their meetings, as the well ordering of a banquet, the delicacy of a walk, with interlacing mere tales, as Gyges' Ring, and others, which who knoweth not to be flowers of poetry did never walk into Apollo's garden.

And even historiographers (although their lips sound of things done, 5 and verity be written in their foreheads) have been glad to borrow both fashion and perchance weight of poets. So Herodotus entitled his History by the name of the nine Muses; and both he and all the rest that followed him either stole or usurped of Poetry their passionate describing of passions, the many particularities of battles, which no man 10 could affirm, or, if that be denied me, long orations put in the mouths of great kings and captains, which it is certain they never pronounced.

So that truly neither philosopher nor historiographer could at the first have entered into the gates of popular judgments, if they had not taken a great passport of Poetry, which in all nations at this day, where 15 learning flourisheth not, is plain to be seen; in all which they have some feeling of Poetry.

In Turkey, besides their law-giving divines, they have no other writers but poets. In our neighbour country Ireland, where truly learning goeth very bare, yet are their poets held in a devout reverence. Even among the 20 most barbarous and simple Indians where no writing is, yet have they their poets who make and sing songs, which they call *areytos*, both of their ancestors' deeds and praises of their gods – a sufficient probability that, if ever learning come among them, it must be by having their hard dull wits softened and sharpened with the sweet delights of Poetry; for 25 until they find a pleasure in the exercises of the mind, great promises of much knowledge will little persuade them that know not the fruits of knowledge. In Wales, the true remnant of the ancient Britons, as there are good authorities to show the long time they had poets, which they called *bards*, so through all the conquests of Romans, Saxons, Danes, and 30 Normans, some of whom did seek to ruin all memory of learning from among them, yet do their poets even to this day last; so as it is not more notable in soon beginning than in long continuing.

But since the authors of most of our sciences were the Romans, and before them the Greeks, let us a little stand upon their authorities, but 35 even so far as to see what names they have given unto this now scorned skill.

Among the Romans a poet was called *vates*, which is as much as a diviner, foreseer, or prophet, as by his conjoined words *vaticinium* and *vaticinari* is manifest: so heavenly a title did that excellent people bestow 40 upon this heart-ravishing knowledge. And so far were they carried into the admiration thereof, that they thought in the chanceable hitting upon any such verses great foretokens of their following fortunes were placed. Whereupon grew the word of *Sortes Virgilianae*, when by sudden opening Virgil's book they lighted upon any verse of his making as it is reported by many: whereof the Histories of the Emperors' Lives are full, as of Albinus, the governor of our island, who in his childhood met with this verse,

5   *Arma amens capio nec sat rationis in armis;*

and in his age performed it: which, although it were a very vain and godless superstition, as also it was to think that spirits were commanded by such verses – whereupon this word charms, derived of *carmina*, cometh – so yet serveth it to show the great reverence those wits were
10 held in. And altogether not without ground, since both the oracles of Delphos and Sibylla's prophecies were wholly delivered in verses. For that same exquisite observing of number and measure in words, and that high flying liberty of conceit proper to the poet, did seem to have some divine force in it.
15   And may not I presume a little further, to show the reasonableness of this word *vates*, and say that the holy David's Psalms are a divine poem? If I do, I shall not do it without the testimony of great learned men, both ancient and modern. But even the name psalms will speak for me, which being interpreted, is nothing but songs; then, that it is
20 fully written in metre, as all learned hebricians agree, although the rules be not yet fully found; lastly and principally, his handling his prophecy, which is merely poetical. For what else is the awaking his musical instruments, the often and free changing of persons, his notable *prosopopeias*, when he maketh you, as it were, see God coming in His majesty, his
25 telling of the beasts' joyfulness, and hills leaping, but a heavenly poesy, wherein almost he showeth himself a passionate lover of that unspeakable and everlasting beauty to be seen by the eyes of the mind, only cleared by faith? But truly now having named him, I fear me I seem to profane that holy name, applying it to Poetry, which is among us thrown
30 down to so ridiculous an estimation. But they that with quiet judgments will look a little deeper into it, shall find the end and working of it such as, being rightly applied, deserveth not to be scourged out of the Church of God.
        But now let us see how the Greeks named it, and how they deemed
35 of it. The Greeks called him 'a poet', which name hath, as the most excellent, gone through other languages. It cometh of this word *poiein*, which is 'to make': wherein I know not whether by luck or wisdom, we Englishmen have met with the Greeks in calling him 'a maker': which name, how high and incomparable a title it is, I had rather were known
40 by marking the scope of other sciences than by my partial allegation.
        There is no art delivered to mankind that hath not the works of Nature for his principal object, without which they could not consist, and on which they so depend, as they become actors and players, as it

were, of what Nature will have set forth. So doth the astronomer look upon the stars, and, by that he seeth, setteth down what order Nature hath taken therein. So do the geometrician and arithmetician in their diverse sorts of quantities. So doth the musician in times tell you which by nature agree, which not. The natural philosopher thereon hath his 5 name, and the moral philosopher standeth upon the natural virtues, vices, and passions of man; and 'follow Nature' (saith he) 'therein, and thou shalt not err'. The lawyer saith what men have determined; the historian what men have done. The grammarian speaketh only of the rules of speech; and the rhetorician and logician, considering what in Nature 10 will soonest prove and persuade, thereon give artificial rules, which still are compassed within the circle of a question according to the proposed matter. The physician weigheth the nature of a man's body, and the nature of things helpful or hurtful unto it. And the metaphysic, though it be in the second and abstract notions, and therefore be counted super- 15 natural, yet doth he indeed build upon the depth of Nature.

Only the poet, disdaining to be tied to any such subjection, lifted up with the vigour of his own invention, doth grow in effect into another nature, in making things either better than Nature bringeth forth, or, quite anew, forms such as never were in Nature, as the Heroes, 20 Demigods, Cyclops, Chimeras, Furies, and such like: so as he goeth hand in hand with Nature, not enclosed within the narrow warrant of her gifts, but freely ranging only within the zodiac of his own wit.

Nature never set forth the earth in so rich tapestry as divers poets have done; neither with pleasant rivers, fruitful trees, sweet-smelling 25 flowers, nor whatsoever else may make the too much loved earth more lovely. Her world is brazen, the poets only deliver a golden.

But let those things alone, and go to man – for whom as the other things are, so it seemeth in him her uttermost cunning is employed – and know whether she have brought forth so true a lover as Theagenes, 30 so constant a friend as Pylades, so valiant a man as Orlando, so right a prince as Xenophon's Cyrus, so excellent a man every way as Virgil's Aeneas. Neither let this be jestingly conceived, because the works of the one be essential, the other in imitation or fiction; for any understanding knoweth the skill of the artificer standeth in that *Idea* or fore-conceit 35 of the work, and not in the work itself. And that the poet hath that *Idea* is manifest, by delivering them forth in such excellency as he hath imagined them. Which delivering forth also is not wholly imaginative, as we are wont to say by them that build castles in the air; but so far substantially it worketh, not only to make a Cyrus, which had been but a 40 particular excellency as Nature might have done, but to bestow a Cyrus upon the world to make many Cyruses, if they will learn aright why and how that maker made him.

Neither let it be deemed too saucy a comparison to balance the

highest point of man's wit with the efficacy of Nature; but rather give
right honour to the heavenly Maker of that maker, who having made
man to His own likeness, set him beyond and over all the works of that
second nature: which in nothing he showeth so much as in Poetry, when
5 with the force of a divine breath he bringeth things forth far surpassing
her doings, with no small argument to the incredulous of that first
accursed fall of Adam: since our erected wit maketh us know what perfection is, and yet our infected will keepeth us from reaching unto it.
But these arguments will by few be understood, and by fewer granted.
10 Thus much (I hope) will be given me, that the Greeks with some probability of reason gave him the name above all names of learning.

Now let us go to a more ordinary opening of him, that the truth may
be more palpable: and so I hope, though we get not so unmatched a
praise as the etymology of his names will grant, yet his very description,
15 which no man will deny, shall not justly be barred from a principal
commendation.

Poesy therefore is an art of imitation, for so Aristotle termeth it in
his word *mimesis*, that is to say, a representing, counterfeiting, or figuring forth – to speak metaphorically, a speaking picture – with this end,
20 to teach and delight.

Of this have been three several kinds. The chief, both in antiquity
and excellency, were they that did imitate the inconceivable excellencies
of God. Such were David in his Psalms; Solomon in his Song of Songs,
in his Ecclesiastes, and Proverbs; Moses and Deborah in their Hymns;
25 and the writer of Job: which, beside other, the learned Emanuel Tremellius and Franciscus Junius do entitle the poetical part of the Scripture.
Against these none will speak that hath the Holy Ghost in due holy reverence. In this kind, though in a full wrong divinity, were Orpheus,
Amphion, Homer in his Hymns, and many other, both Greeks and
30 Romans. And this poesy must be used by whosoever will follow St
James's counsel in singing psalms when they are merry, and I know is
used with the fruit of comfort by some, when, in sorrowful pangs of
their death-bringing sins, they find the consolation of the never-leaving
goodness.

35 The second kind is of them that deal with matters philosophical:
either moral, as Tyrtaeus, Phocylides, and Cato; or natural, as Lucretius
and Virgil's Georgics; or astronomical, as Manilius and Pontanus; or historical, as Lucan: which who mislike, the fault is in their judgments
quite out of taste, and not in the sweet food of sweetly uttered
40 knowledge.

But because this second sort is wrapped within the fold of the proposed subject, and takes not the course of his own invention, whether
they properly be poets or no let grammarians dispute, and go to the
third, indeed right poets, of whom chiefly this question ariseth. Betwixt

whom and these second is such a kind of difference as betwixt the
meaner sort of painters, who counterfeit only such faces as are set before
them, and the more excellent, who having no law but wit, bestow that
in colours upon you which is fittest for the eye to see: as the constant
though lamenting look of Lucretia, when she punished in herself 5
another's fault; wherein he painteth not Lucretia whom he never saw,
but painteth the outward beauty of such a virtue. For these third be they
which most properly do imitate to teach and delight, and to imitate
borrow nothing of what is, hath been, or shall be; but range, only reined
with learned discretion, into the divine consideration of what may be 10
and should be. These be they that, as the first and most noble sort may
justly be termed *vates*, so these are waited on in the excellentest languages and best understandings, with the foredescribed name of poets;
for these indeed do merely make to imitate, and imitate both to delight
and teach: and delight to move men to take that goodness in hand, 15
which without delight they would fly as from a stranger, and teach, to
make them know that goodness whereunto they are moved: which being
the noblest scope to which ever any learning was directed, yet want there
not idle tongues to bark at them.

These be subdivided into sundry more special denominations. The 20
most notable be the Heroic, Lyric, Tragic, Comic, Satiric, Iambic,
Elegiac, Pastoral, and certain others, some of these being termed according to the matter they deal with, some by the sorts of verses they liked
best to write in; for indeed the greatest part of poets have apparelled
their poetical inventions in that numbrous kind of writing which is 25
called verse – indeed but apparelled, verse being but an ornament and
no cause to Poetry, since there have been many most excellent poets that
never versified, and now swarm many versifiers that need never answer
to the name of poets. For Xenophon, who did imitate so excellently as
to give us *effigiem justi imperii,* 'the portraiture of a just empire', under 30
the name of Cyrus (as Cicero saith of him), made therein an absolute
heroical poem. So did Heliodorus in his sugared invention of that
picture of love in Theagenes and Chariclea; and yet both these writ in
prose: which I speak to show that it is not rhyming and versing that
maketh a poet – no more than a long gown maketh an advocate, who 35
though he pleaded in armour should be an advocate and no soldier. But
it is that feigning notable images of virtues, vices, or what else, with that
delightful teaching, which must be the right describing note to know a
poet by, although indeed the senate of poets hath chosen verse as their
fittest raiment, meaning, as in matter they passed all in all, so in manner 40
to go beyond them: not speaking (table talk fashion or like men in a
dream) words as they chanceably fall from the mouth, but peizing each
syllable of each word by just proportion according to the dignity of the
subject.

Now therefore it shall not be amiss first to weigh this latter sort of Poetry by his works, and then by his parts, and if in neither of these anatomies he be condemnable, I hope we shall obtain a more favourable sentence. This purifying of wit, this enriching of memory, enabling of
5 judgment, and enlarging of conceit, which commonly we call learning, under what name soever it come forth, or to what immediate end soever it be directed, the final end is to lead and draw us to as high a perfection as our degenerate souls, made worse by their clayey lodgings, can be capable of. This, according to the inclination of the man, bred many
10 formed impressions. For some that thought this felicity principally to be gotten by knowledge, and no knowledge to be so high and heavenly as acquaintance with the stars, gave themselves to Astronomy; others, persuading themselves to be demi-gods if they knew the causes of things, became natural and supernatural philosophers; some an admirable
15 delight drew to Music; and some the certainty of demonstration to the Mathematics. But all, one and other, having this scope – to know, and by knowledge to lift up the mind from the dungeon of the body to the enjoying his own divine essence. But when by the balance of experience it was found that the astronomer looking to the stars might fall into a
20 ditch, that the inquiring philosopher might be blind in himself, and the mathematician might draw forth a straight line with a crooked heart, then lo, did proof, the overruler of opinions, make manifest that all these are but serving sciences, which, as they have each a private end in themselves, so yet are they all directed to the highest end of the mistress-
25 knowledge, by the Greeks called *architectonike*, which stands (as I think) in the knowledge of a man's self, in the ethic and politic consideration, with the end of well-doing and not of well-knowing only: even as the saddler's next end is to make a good saddle, but his farther end to serve a nobler faculty, which is horsemanship; so the horseman's to soldiery,
30 and the soldier not only to have the skill, but to perform the practice of a soldier. So that, the ending end of all earthly learning being virtuous action, those skills, that most serve to bring forth that, have a most just title to be princes over all the rest.

Wherein if we can, show we the poet's nobleness, by setting him
35 before his other competitors, among whom as principal challengers step forth the moral philosophers, whom, me thinketh, I see coming towards me with a sullen gravity, as though they could not abide vice by daylight, rudely clothed for to witness outwardly their contempt of outward things, with books in their hands against glory, whereto they set their
40 names, sophistically speaking against subtlety, and angry with any man in whom they see the foul fault of anger. These men casting largesse as they go of definitions, divisions, and distinctions, with a scornful interrogative do soberly ask whether it be possible to find any path so ready to lead a man to virtue as that which teacheth what virtue is – and tea-

cheth it not only by delivering forth his very being, his causes, and effects, but also by making known his enemy, vice, which must be destroyed, and his cumbersome servant, passion, which must be mastered, by showing the generalities that containeth it, and the specialities that are derived from it; lastly, by plain setting down, how it extendeth 5 itself out of the limits of a man's own little world to the government of families, and maintaining of public societies.

The historian scarcely giveth leisure to the moralist to say so much, but that he, loaden with old mouse-eaten records, authorizing himself (for the most part) upon other histories, whose greatest authorities are 10 built upon the notable foundation of hearsay; having much ado to accord differing writers and to pick truth out of partiality; better acquainted with a thousand years ago than with the present age, and yet better knowing how this world goeth than how his own wit runneth; curious for antiquities and inquisitive of novelties; a wonder to young 15 folks and a tyrant in table talk, denieth, in a great chafe, that any man for teaching of virtue, and virtuous actions is comparable to him. 'I am *testis temporum, lux veritatis, vita memoriae, magistra vitae, nuncia vetustatis.* The philosopher', saith he, 'teacheth a disputative virtue, but I do an active. His virtue is excellent in the dangerless Academy of Plato, but 20 mine showeth forth her honourable face in the battles of Marathon, Pharsalia, Poitiers, and Agincourt. He teacheth virtue by certain abstract considerations, but I only bid you follow the footing of them that have gone before you. Old-aged experience goeth beyond the fine-witted philosopher, but I give the experience of many ages. Lastly, if he make 25 the song-book, I put the learner's hand to the lute; and if he be the guide, I am the light.'

Then would he allege you innumerable examples, conferring story by story, how much the wisest senators and princes have been directed by the credit of history, as Brutus, Alphonsus of Aragon, and who not, 30 if need be? At length the long line of their disputation maketh a point in this, that the one giveth the precept, and the other the example.

Now whom shall we find (since the question standeth for the highest form in the school of learning) to be moderator? Truly, as me seemeth, the poet; and if not a moderator, even the man that ought to carry the 35 title from them both, and much more from all other serving sciences. Therefore compare we the poet with the historian and with the moral philosopher; and if he go beyond them both, no other human skill can match him. For as for the divine, with all reverence it is ever to be excepted, not only for having his scope as far beyond any of these as 40 eternity exceedeth a moment, but even for passing each of these in themselves. And for the lawyer, though *jus* be the daughter of justice, and justice the chief of virtues, yet because he seeketh to make men good rather *formidine poenae* than *virtutis amore*; or, to say righter, doth not endeavour to make men good, but that their evil hurt not others; having no care, so he be a good citizen, how bad a man he be: therefore as our wickedness maketh him necessary, and necessity maketh him honourable, so is he not in the deepest truth to stand in rank with these 5 who all endeavour to take naughtiness away and plant goodness even in the secretest cabinet of our souls. And these four are all that any way deal in that consideration of men's manners, which being the supreme knowledge, they that best breed it deserve the best commendation.

The philosopher therefore and the historian are they which would 10 win the goal, the one by precept, the other by example. But both, not having both, do both halt. For the philosopher, setting down with thorny argument the bare rule, is so hard of utterance and so misty to be conceived, that one that hath no other guide but him shall wade in him till he be old before he shall find sufficient cause to be honest. For 15 his knowledge standeth so upon the abstract and general, that happy is that man who may understand him, and more happy that can apply what he doth understand. On the other side, the historian, wanting the precept, is so tied, not to what should be but to what is, to the particular truth of things and not to the general reason of things, that his 20 example draweth no necessary consequence, and therefore a less fruitful doctrine.

Now doth the peerless poet perform both: for whatsoever the philosopher saith should be done, he giveth a perfect picture of it in some one by whom he presupposeth it was done, so as he coupleth the general 25 notion with the particular example. A perfect picture I say, for he yieldeth to the powers of the mind an image of that whereof the philosopher bestoweth but a wordish description, which doth neither strike, pierce, nor possess the sight of the soul so much as that other doth.

For as in outward things, to a man that had never seen an elephant 30 or a rhinoceros, who should tell him most exquisitely all their shapes, colour, bigness, and particular marks; or of a gorgeous palace, the architecture, with declaring the full beauties might well make the hearer able to repeat, as it were by rote, all he had heard, yet should never satisfy his inward conceits with being witness to itself of a true lively knowledge; 35 but the same man, as soon as he might see those beasts well painted, or the house well in model, should straightways grow, without need of any description, to a judicial comprehending of them: so no doubt the philosopher with his learned definition — be it of virtue, vices, matters of public policy or private government — replenisheth the memory with 40 many infallible grounds of wisdom, which, notwithstanding, lie dark before the imaginative and judging power, if they be not illuminated or figured forth by the speaking picture of poesy.

Tully taketh much pains, and many times not without poetical helps, to make us know the force love of our country hath in us. Let us but

hear old Anchises speaking in the midst of Troy's flames, or see Ulysses
in the fullness of all Calypso's delights bewail his absence from barren
and beggarly Ithaca. Anger, the Stoics say, was a short madness: let but
Sophocles bring you Ajax on a stage, killing and whipping sheep and
oxen, thinking them the army of Greeks, with their chieftains Agamem- 5
non and Menelaus, and tell me if you have not a more familiar insight
into anger than finding in the schoolmen his genus and difference. See
whether wisdom and temperance in Ulysses and Diomedes, valour in
Achilles, friendship in Nisus and Euryalus, even to an ignorant man
carry not an apparent shining; and, contrarily, the remorse of conscience 10
in Oedipus, the soon repenting pride of Agamemnon, the self-
devouring cruelty in his father Atreus, the violence of ambition in the
two Theban brothers, the sour-sweetness of revenge in Medea; and, to
fall lower, the Terentian Gnatho and our Chaucer's Pandar so expressed
that we now use their names to signify their trades; and finally, all 15
virtues, vices, and passions so in their own natural seats laid to the view,
that we seem not to hear of them, but clearly to see through them.

But even in the most excellent determination of goodness, what
philosopher's counsel can so readily direct a prince, as the feigned Cyrus
in Xenophon; or a virtuous man in all fortunes, as Aeneas in Virgil; or 20
a whole commonwealth, as the way of Sir Thomas More's *Utopia*? I say
the way, because where Sir Thomas More erred, it was the fault of the
man and not of the poet, for that way of patterning a commonwealth
was most absolute, though he perchance hath not so absolutely performed it. For the question is, whether the feigned image of poesy or 25
the regular instruction of philosophy hath the more force in teaching:
wherein if the philosophers have more rightly showed themselves
philosophers than the poets have attained to the high top of their profession, as in truth,

Mediocribus esse poetis,   30
Non dii, non homines, non concessere columnae;

it is, I say again, not the fault of the art, but that by few men that art
can be accomplished.

Certainly, even our Saviour Christ could as well have given the moral
commonplaces of uncharitableness and humbleness as the divine narra- 35
tion of Dives and Lazarus; or of disobedience and mercy, as that heavenly discourse of the lost child and the gracious father; but that His
through-searching wisdom knew the estate of Dives burning in hell, and
of Lazarus being in Abraham's bosom, would more constantly (as it
were) inhabit both the memory and judgment. Truly, for myself, me 40
seems I see before my eyes the lost child's disdainful prodigality, turned
to envy a swine's dinner: which by the learned divines are thought not
historical acts, but instructing parables.

For conclusion, I say the philosopher teacheth, but he teacheth obscurely, so as the learned only can understand him; that is to say, he teacheth them that are already taught. But the poet is the food for the tenderest stomachs, the poet is indeed the right popular philosopher, whereof Aesop's tales give good proof; whose pretty allegories, stealing under the formal tales of beasts, make many, more beastly than beasts, begin to hear the sound of virtue from these dumb speakers.

But now may it be alleged that if this imagining of matters be so fit for the imagination, then must the historian needs surpass, who bringeth you images of true matters, such as indeed were done, and not such as fantastically or falsely may be suggested to have been done. Truly, Aristotle himself, in his discourse of poesy, plainly determineth this question, saying that Poetry is *philosophoteron* and *spoudaioteron*, that is to say, it is more philosophical and more studiously serious than history. His reason is, because poesy dealeth with *katholou*, that is to say, with the universal consideration, and the history with *kathekaston*, the particular: 'now', saith he, 'the universal weighs what is fit to be said or done, either in likelihood or necessity (which the poesy considereth in his imposed names), and the particular only marks whether Alcibiades did, or suffered, this or that.' Thus far Aristotle: which reason of his (as all his) is most full of reason.

For indeed, if the question were whether it were better to have a particular act truly or falsely set down, there is no doubt which is to be chosen, no more than whether you had rather have Vespasian's picture right as he was, or, at the painter's pleasure, nothing resembling. But if the question be for your own use and learning, whether it be better to have it set down as it should be, or as it was, then certainly is more doctrinable the feigned Cyrus of Xenophon than the true Cyrus in Justin, and the feigned Aeneas in Virgil than the right Aeneas in Dares Phrygius: as to a lady that desired to fashion her countenance to the best grace, a painter should more benefit her to portray a most sweet face, writing Canidia upon it, than to paint Canidia as she was, who, Horace sweareth, was foul and ill favoured.

If the poet do his part aright, he will show you in Tantalus, Atreus, and such like, nothing that is not to be shunned; in Cyrus, Aeneas, Ulysses, each thing to be followed; where the historian, bound to tell things as things were, cannot be liberal (without he will be poetical) of a perfect pattern, but, as in Alexander or Scipio himself, show doings, some to be liked, some to be misliked. And then how will you discern what to follow but by your own discretion, which you had without reading Quintus Curtius? And whereas a man may say, though in universal consideration of doctrine the poet prevaileth, yet that the history, in his saying such a thing was done, doth warrant a man more in that he shall follow – the answer is manifest: that if he stand upon that *was*

– as if he should argue, because it rained yesterday, therefore it should rain today – then indeed it hath some advantage to a gross conceit; but if he know an example only informs a conjectured likelihood, and so go by reason, the poet doth so far exceed him as he is to frame his example to that which is most reasonable, be it in warlike, politic, or private 5 matters; where the historian in his bare *was* hath many times that which we call fortune to overrule the best wisdom. Many times he must tell events whereof he can yield no cause; or, if he do, it must be poetical.

For that a feigned example hath as much force to teach as a true example (for as for to move, it is clear, since the feigned may be tuned 10 to the highest key of passion), let us take one example wherein a poet and a historian do concur. Herodotus and Justin do both testify that Zopyrus, King Darius' faithful servant, seeing his master long resisted by the rebellious Babylonians, feigned himself in extreme disgrace of his king: for verifying of which , he caused his own nose and ears to be cut 15 off, and so flying to the Babylonians, was received, and for his known valour so far credited, that he did find means to deliver them over to Darius. Much like matter doth Livy record of Tarquinius and his son. Xenophon excellently feigneth such another stratagem performed by Abradatas in Cyrus' behalf. Now would I fain know, if occasion be pre- 20 sented unto you to serve your prince by such an honest dissimulation, why you do not as well learn it of Xenophon's fiction as of the other's verity? And truly so much the better, as you shall save your nose by the bargain; for Abradatas did not counterfeit so far. So then the best of the historian is subject to the poet; for whatsoever action, or faction, what- 25 soever counsel, policy, or war stratagem the historian is bound to recite, that may the poet (if he list) with his imitation make his own, beauti-fying it both for further teaching, and more delighting, as it pleaseth him: having all, from Dante's heaven to his hell, under the authority of his pen. Which if I be asked what poets have done so, as I might well 30 name some, yet say I and say again, I speak of the art, and not of the artificer.

Now, to that which commonly is attributed to the praise of histo-ries, in respect of the notable learning is gotten by marking the success, as though therein a man should see virtue exalted and vice punished – 35 truly that commendation is peculiar to Poetry, and far off from history. For indeed Poetry ever setteth virtue so out in her best colours, making Fortune her well-waiting handmaid, that one must needs be enamoured of her. Well may you see Ulysses in a storm, and in other hard plights; but they are but exercises of patience and magnanimity, to make them 40 shine the more in the near-following prosperity. And of the contrary part, if evil men come to the stage, they ever go out (as the tragedy writer answered to one that misliked the show of such persons) so manacled as they little animate folks to follow them. But the historian, being captived to the truth of a foolish world, is many times a terror from well-doing, and an encouragement to unbridled wickedness.

For see we not valiant Miltiades rot in his fetters? the just Phocion and the accomplished Socrates put to death like traitors? the cruel
5 Severus live prosperously? the excellent Severus miserably murdered? Sylla and Marius dying in their beds? Pompey and Cicero slain then when they would have thought exile a happiness? See we not virtuous Cato driven to kill himself, and rebel Caesar so advanced that his name yet, after 1600 years, lasteth in the highest honour? And mark but even
10 Caesar's own words of the forenamed Sylla (who in that only did honestly, to put down his dishonest tyranny), *literas nescivit*, as if want of learning caused him to do well. He meant it not by Poetry, which, not content with earthly plagues, deviseth new punishments in hell for tyrants, nor yet by Philosophy, which teacheth *occidendos esse*; but no
15 doubt by skill in History, for that indeed can afford your Cypselus, Periander, Phalaris, Dionysius, and I know not how many more of the same kennel, that speed well enough in their abominable injustice or usurpation. I conclude therefore, that he excelleth History, not only in furnishing the mind with knowledge, but in setting it forward to that
20 which deserveth to be called and accounted good: which setting forward, and moving to well-doing, indeed setteth the laurel crown upon the poet as victorious, not only of the historian, but over the philosopher, howsoever in teaching it may be questionable.

For suppose it be granted (that which I suppose with great reason
25 may be denied) that the philosopher, in respect of his methodical proceeding, doth teach more perfectly than the poet, yet do I think that no man is so much *philophilosophos* as to compare the philosopher in moving with the poet.

And that moving is of a higher degree than teaching, it may by this
30 appear, that it is well nigh the cause and the effect of teaching. For who will be taught, if he be not moved with desire to be taught? and what so much good doth that teaching bring forth (I speak still of moral doctrine) as that it moveth one to do that which it doth teach? For, as Aristotle saith, it is not *gnosis* but *praxis* must be the fruit. And how
35 *praxis* cannot be, without being moved to practise, it is no hard matter to consider.

The philosopher showeth you the way, he informeth you of the particularities, as well of the tediousness of the way, as of the pleasant lodging you shall have when your journey is ended, as of the many by-turnings
40 that may divert you from your way. But this is to no man but to him that will read him, and read him with attentive studious painfulness; which constant desire whosoever hath in him, hath already passed half the hardness of the way, and therefore is beholding to the philosopher but for the other half. Nay truly, learned men have learnedly thought

that where once reason hath so much overmastered passion as that the mind hath a free desire to do well, the inward light each mind hath in itself is as good as a philosopher's book; seeing in Nature we know it is well to do well, and what is well and what is evil, although not in the words of art which philosophers bestow upon us; for out of natural 5 conceit the philosophers drew it. But to be moved to do that which we know, or to be moved with desire to know, *hoc opus, hic labor est.*

Now therein of all sciences (I speak still of human, and according to the human conceits) is our poet the monarch. For he doth not only show the way, but giveth so sweet a prospect into the way, as will entice any 10 man to enter into it. Nay, he doth, as if your journey should lie through a fair vineyard, at the first give you a cluster of grapes, that full of that taste, you may long to pass further. He beginneth not with obscure definitions, which must blur the margent with interpretations, and load the memory with doubtfulness; but he cometh to you with words set in 15 delightful proportion, either accompanied with, or prepared for, the well enchanting skill of music; and with a tale forsooth he cometh unto you, with a tale which holdeth children from play, and old men from the chimney corner. And, pretending no more, doth intend the winning of the mind from wickedness to virtue: even as the child is often brought 20 to take most wholesome things by hiding them in such other as have a pleasant taste: which, if one should begin to tell them the nature of aloes or rhubarb they should receive, would sooner take their physic at their ears than at their mouth. So is it in men (most of which are childish in the best things, till they be cradled in their graves): glad they will be 25 to hear the tales of Hercules, Achilles, Cyrus, and Aeneas; and, hearing them, must needs hear the right description of wisdom, valour, and justice; which, if they had been barely, that is to say philosophically, set out, they would swear they be brought to school again.

That imitation whereof Poetry is, hath the most conveniency to 30 Nature of all other, insomuch that, as Aristotle saith, those things which in themselves are horrible, as cruel battles, unnatural monsters, are made in poetical imitation delightful. Truly, I have known men, that even with reading *Amadis de Gaule* (which God knoweth wanteth much of a perfect poesy) have found their hearts moved to the exercise of cour- 35 tesy, liberality, and especially courage. Who readeth Aeneas carrying old Anchises on his back, that wisheth not it were his fortune to perform so excellent an act? Whom do not the words of Turnus move, the tale of Turnus having planted his image in the imagination?

> *Fugientem haec terra videbit?*   40
> *Usque adeone mori miserum est?*

Where the philosophers, as they scorn to delight, so must they be content little to move – saving wrangling whether virtue be the chief or

the only good, whether the contemplative or the active life do excel – which Plato and Boethius well knew, and therefore made mistress Philosophy very often borrow the masking raiment of Poesy. For even those hard-hearted evil men who think virtue a school name, and know no
5 other good but *indulgere genio*, and therefore despise the austere admonitions of the philosopher, and feel not the inward reason they stand upon, yet will be content to be delighted – which is all the good-fellow poet seemeth to promise – and so steal to see the form of goodness (which seen they cannot but love) ere themselves be aware, as if they
10 took a medicine of cherries.

Infinite proofs of the strange effects of this poetical invention might be alleged; only two shall serve, which are so often remembered as I think all men know them. The one of Menenius Agrippa, who, when the whole people of Rome had resolutely divided themselves from the
15 senate, with apparent show of utter ruin, though he were (for that time) an excellent orator, came not among them upon trust of figurative speeches or cunning insinuations, and much less with farfetched maxims of Philosophy, which (especially if they were Platonic) they must have learned geometry before they could well have conceived; but forsooth
20 he behaves himself like a homely and familiar poet. He telleth them a tale, that there was a time when all the parts of the body made a mutinous conspiracy against the belly, which they thought devoured the fruits of each other's labour: they concluded they would let so unprofitable a spender starve. In the end, to be short (for the tale is notorious,
25 and as notorious that it was a tale), with punishing the belly they plagued themselves. This applied by him wrought such effect in the people, as I never read that ever words brought forth but then so sudden and so good an alteration; for upon reasonable conditions a perfect reconcilement ensued. The other is of Nathan the prophet, who, when the
30 holy David had so far forsaken God as to confirm adultery with murder, when he was to do the tenderest office of a friend, in laying his own shame before his eyes, sent by God to call again so chosen a servant, how doth he it but by telling of a man whose beloved lamb was ungratefully taken from his bosom? – the application most divinely true, but
35 the discourse itself feigned; which made David (I speak of the second and instrumental cause) as in a glass to see his own filthiness, as that heavenly psalm of mercy well testifieth.

By these, therefore, examples and reasons, I think it may be manifest that the poet, with that same hand of delight, doth draw the mind
40 more effectually than any other art doth. And so a conclusion not unfitly ensueth: that, as virtue is the most excellent resting place for all worldly learning to make his end of, so Poetry, being the most familiar to teach it, and most princely to move towards it, in the most excellent work is the most excellent workman.

But I am content not only to decipher him by his works (although works in commendation or dispraise must ever hold an high authority), but more narrowly will examine his parts; so that, as in a man, though all together may carry a presence full of majesty and beauty, perchance in some one defectious piece we may find a blemish. Now in his 5 parts, kinds, or species (as you list to term them), it is to be noted that some poesies have coupled together two or three kinds, as tragical and comical, whereupon is risen the tragi-comical. Some, in the like manner, have mingled prose and verse, as Sannazzaro and Boethius. Some have mingled matters heroical and pastoral. But that cometh all to one in this 10 question, for, if severed they be good, the conjunction cannot be hurtful. Therefore, perchance forgetting some and leaving some as needless to be remembered, it shall not be amiss in a word to cite the special kinds, to see what faults may be found in the right use of them.

Is it then the Pastoral poem which is misliked? For perchance where 15 the hedge is lowest they will soonest leap over. Is the poor pipe disdained, which sometime out of Meliboeus' mouth can show the misery of people under hard lords or ravening soldiers? And again, by Tityrus, what blessedness is derived to them that lie lowest from the goodness of them that sit highest; sometimes, under the pretty tales of wolves 20 and sheep, can include the whole considerations of wrong-doing and patience; sometimes show that contention for trifles can get but a trifling victory: where perchance a man may see that even Alexander and Darius, when they strave who should be cock of this world's dunghill, the benefit they got was that the afterlivers may say, 25

Haec memini et victum frustra contendere Thirsin:
Ex illo Corydon, Corydon est tempore nobis.

Or is it the lamenting Elegiac? which in a kind heart would move rather pity than blame, who bewails with the great philosopher Heraclitus the weakness of mankind and the wretchedness of the world; 30 who surely is to be praised, either for compassionate accompanying just causes of lamentation, or for rightly painting out how weak be the passions of woefulness. Is it the bitter but wholesome Iambic? which rubs the galled mind, in making shame the trumpet of villainy with bold and open crying out against naughtiness. Or the Satiric? who 35

Omne vafer vitium ridenti tangit amico;

who sportingly never leaveth until he make a man laugh at folly, and at length ashamed to laugh at himself, which he cannot avoid, without avoiding the folly; who, while

circum praecordia ludit, 40

giveth us to feel how many headaches a passionate life bringeth us to; how, when all is done,

Est Ulubris, animus si nos non deficit aequus.

No, perchance it is the Comic, whom naughty play-makers and stage-
keepers have justly made odious. To the argument of abuse I will answer
after. Only thus much now is to be said, that the Comedy is an imitation of the common errors of our life, which he representeth in the most
5 ridiculous and scornful sort that may be, so as it is impossible that any
beholder can be content to be such a one.

Now, as in geometry the oblique must be known as well as the right,
and in arithmetic the odd as well as the even, so in the actions of
our life who seeth not the filthiness of evil wanteth a great foil to per-
10 ceive the beauty of virtue. This doth the Comedy handle so in our
private and domestical matters, as with hearing it we get as it were an
experience, what is to be looked for of a niggardly Demea, of a crafty
Davus, of a flattering Gnatho, of a vainglorious Thraso; and not only
to know what effects are to be expected, but to know who be such, by
15 the signifying badge given them by the comedian. And little reason hath
any man to say that men learn evil by seeing it so set out; since, as I
said before, there is no man living but, by the force truth hath in
Nature, no sooner seeth these men play their parts, but wisheth them
in pistrinum; although perchance the sack of his own faults lie so behind
20 his back that he seeth not himself dance the same measure; whereto yet
nothing can more open his eyes than to find his own actions con-
temptibly set forth.

So that the right use of Comedy will (I think) by nobody be blamed,
and much less of the high and excellent Tragedy, that openeth the great-
25 est wounds, and showeth forth the ulcers that are covered with tissue;
that maketh kings fear to be tyrants, and tyrants manifest their tyrannical humours; that, with stirring the affects of admiration and commiseration, teacheth the uncertainty of this world, and upon how weak
foundations gilden roofs are builded; that maketh us know,
30

Qui sceptra saevus duro imperio regit,
Timet timentes, metus in auctorem redit.

But how much it can move, Plutarch yieldeth a notable testimony
of the abominable tyrant Alexander Phereaus, from whose eyes a tragedy,
35 well made and represented, drew abundance of tears, who without all
pity had murdered infinite numbers, and some of his own blood; so as
he that was not ashamed to make matters for tragedies, yet could not
resist the sweet violence of a tragedy. And if it wrought no further good
in him, it was that he, in despite of himself, withdrew himself from hear-
40 kening to that which might mollify his hardened heart. But it is not the
Tragedy they do mislike; for it were too absurd to cast out so excellent
a representation of whatsoever is most worthy to be learned.

Is it the Lyric that most displeaseth? who with his tuned lyre and well-accorded voice, giveth praise, the reward of virtue, to virtuous acts; who gives moral precepts, and natural problems; who sometimes raiseth up his voice to the height of the heavens, in singing the lauds of the immortal God. Certainly, I must confess my own barbarousness, I never 5 heard the old song of Percy and Douglas that I found not my heart moved more than with a trumpet; and yet is it sung but by some blind crowder, with no rougher voice than rude style; which, being so evil apparelled in the dust and cobwebs of that uncivil age, what would it work, trimmed in the gorgeous eloquence of Pindar? In Hungary I have 10 seen it the manner at all feasts, and other such meetings, to have songs of their ancestors' valour, which that right soldierlike nation think the chiefest kindlers of brave courage. The incomparable Lacedemonians did not only carry that kind of music ever with them to the field, but even at home, as such songs were made, so were they all content to be 15 the singers of them; when the lusty men were to tell what they did, the old men what they had done, and the young men what they would do. And where a man may say that Pindar many times praiseth highly victories of small moment, matters rather of sport than virtue; as it may be answered, it was the fault of the poet, and not of the poetry, so indeed 20 the chief fault was in the time and custom of the Greeks, who set those toys at so high a price that Philip of Macedon reckoned a horserace won at Olympus among his three fearful felicities. But as the inimitable Pindar often did, so is that kind most capable and most fit to awake the thoughts from the sleep of idleness, to embrace honourable enterprises. 25

There rests the Heroical, whose very name (I think) should daunt all backbiters; for by what conceit can a tongue be directed to speak evil of that which draweth with it no less champions than Achilles, Cyrus, Aeneas, Turnus, Tydeus, and Rinaldo? who doth not only teach and move to a truth, but teacheth and moveth to the most high and excel- 30 lent truth; who maketh magnanimity and justice shine throughout all misty fearfulness and foggy desires; who, if the saying of Plato and Tully be true, that who could see virtue would be wonderfully ravished with the love of her beauty – this man sets her out to make her more lovely in her holiday apparel, to the eye of any that will deign not to disdain 35 until they understand. But if anything be already said in the defence of sweet Poetry, all concurreth to the maintaining the Heroical, which is not only a kind, but the best and most accomplished kind of Poetry. For as the image of each action stirreth and instructeth the mind, so the lofty image of such worthies most inflameth the mind with desire to be 40 worthy, and informs with counsel how to be worthy. Only let Aeneas be worn in the tablet of your memory, how he governeth himself in the ruin of his country; in the preserving his old father, and carrying away his religious ceremonies; in obeying the god's commandment to leave

Dido, though not only all passionate kindness, but even the human consideration of virtuous gratefulness, would have craved other of him; how
in storms, how in sports, how in war, how in peace, how a fugitive, how
victorious, how besieged, how besieging, how to strangers, how to allies,
5 how to enemies, how to his own; lastly, how in his inward self, and how
in his outward government; and I think, in a mind not prejudiced with
a prejudicating humour, he will be found in excellency fruitful, yea, even
as Horace saith,

melius Chrysippo et Crantore.

10 But truly I imagine it falleth out with these poet-whippers, as with
some good women, who often are sick, but in faith they cannot tell
where. So the name of Poetry is odious to them, but neither his cause
nor effects, neither the sum that contains him, nor the particularities
descending from him, give any fast handle to their carping disraise.
15 Since then Poetry is of all human learning the most ancient and of
most fatherly antiquity, as from whence other learnings have taken their
beginnings; since it is so universal that no learned nation doth despise it, nor no barbarous nation is without it; since both Roman and
Greek gave divine names unto it, the one of 'prophesying', the other of
20 'making', and that indeed that name of 'making' is fit for him, considering that whereas other arts retain themselves within their subject, and
receive, as it were, their being from it, the poet only bringeth his own
stuff, and doth not learn a conceit out of a matter, but maketh matter
for a conceit; since neither his description nor his end containeth any
25 evil, the thing described cannot be evil; since his effects be so good as
to teach goodness and to delight the learners; since therein (namely
in moral doctrine, the chief of all knowledges) he doth not only far
pass the historian, but, for instructing, is well nigh comparable to the
philosopher, and, for moving, leaves him behind him; since the Holy
30 Scripture (wherein there is no uncleanness) hath whole parts in it
poetical, and that even our Saviour Christ vouchsafed to use the flowers
of it; since all his kinds are not only in their united forms but in
their severed dissections fully commendable; I think (and think I
think rightly) the laurel crown appointed for triumphing captains doth
35 worthily (of all other learnings) honour the poet's triumph.

But because we have ears as well as tongues, and that the lightest
reasons that may be will seem to weigh greatly, if nothing be put in the
counterbalance, let us hear, and, as well as we can, ponder, what objections may be made against this art, which may be worthy either of yield-
40 ing or answering.

First, truly I note not only in these *mysomousoi*, poet-haters, but in
all that kind of people who seek a praise by dispraising others, that they

do prodigally spend a great many wandering words in quips and scoffs, carping and taunting at each thing which, by stirring the spleen, may stay the brain from a through-beholding the worthiness of the subject. Those kind of objections, as they are full of very idle easiness, since there is nothing of so sacred a majesty but that an itching tongue may rub 5 itself upon it, so deserve they no other answer, but, instead of laughing at the jest, to laugh at the jester. We know a playing wit can praise the discretion of an ass, the comfortableness of being in debt, and the jolly commodity of being sick of the plague. So of the contrary side, if we will turn Ovid's verse, 10

Ut lateat virtus proximitate mali,

that 'good lie hid in nearness of the evil', Agrippa will be as merry in showing the vanity of science as Erasmus was in commending of folly. Neither shall any man or matter escape some touch of these smiling railers. But for Erasmus and Agrippa, they had another foundation, than 15 the superficial part would promise. Marry, these other pleasant fault-finders, who will correct the verb before they understand the noun, and confute others' knowledge before they confirm their own, I would have them only remember that scoffing cometh not of wisdom; so as the best title in true English they get with their merriments is to be called good 20 fools, for so have our grave forefathers ever termed that humorous kind of jesters.

But that which giveth greatest scope to their scorning humours is rhyming and versing. It is already said (and, as I think, truly said) it is not rhyming and versing that maketh poesy. One may be a poet without 25 versing, and a versifier without poetry. But yet presuppose it were inseparable (as indeed it seemeth Scaliger judgeth) truly it were an inseparable commendation. For if *oratio* next to *ratio*, speech next to reason, be the greatest gift bestowed upon mortality, that cannot be praiseless which doth most polish that blessing of speech; which considers each 30 word, not only (as a man may say) by his forcible quality, but by his best measured quantity, carrying even in themselves a harmony – without, perchance, number, measure, order, proportion be in our time grown odious. But lay aside the just praise it hath, by being the only fit speech for Music (Music, I say, the most divine striker of the senses), 35 thus much is undoubtedly true, that if reading be foolish without remembering, memory being the only treasurer of knowledge, those words which are fittest for memory are likewise most convenient for knowledge.

Now, that verse far exceedeth prose in the knitting up of the memory, 40 the reason is manifest: the words (besides their delight, which hath a great affinity to memory) being so set as one word cannot be lost but the whole work fails; which accuseth itself, calleth the remembrance

back to itself, and so most strongly confirmeth it. Besides, one word so, as it were, begetting another, as, be it in rhyme or measured verse, by the former a man shall have a near guess to the follower. Lastly, even they that have taught the art of memory have showed nothing so apt
5 for it as a certain room divided into many places well and thoroughly known. Now, that hath the verse in effect perfectly, every word having his natural seat, which seat must needs make the words remembered. But what needeth more in a thing so known to all men? Who is it that ever was a scholar that doth not carry away some verses of Virgil, Horace,
10 or Cato, which in his youth he learned, and even to his old age serve him for hourly lessons?: as

Percontatorem fugito, nam garrulus idem est.

Dum sibi quisque placet, credula turba sumus.

But the fitness it hath for memory is notably proved by all delivery of
15 arts: wherein for the most part, from Grammar to Logic, Mathematic, Physic, and the rest, the rules chiefly necessary to be borne away are compiled in verses. So that verse being in itself sweet and orderly, and being best for memory, the only handle of knowledge, it must be in jest that any man can speak against it.
20 Now then go we to the most important imputations laid to the poor poets. For aught I can yet learn, they are these. First, that there being many other more fruitful knowledges, a man might better spend his time in them than in this. Secondly, that it is the mother of lies. Thirdly, that it is the nurse of abuse, infecting us with many pestilent desires,
25 with a siren's sweetness drawing the mind to the serpent's tale of sinful fancy – and herein, especially, comedies give the largest field to ear (as Chaucer saith); how both in other nations and in ours, before poets did soften us, we were full of courage, given to martial exercises, the pillars of manlike liberty, and not lulled asleep in shady idleness with poets'
30 pastimes. And lastly, and chiefly, they cry out with an open mouth as if they outshot Robin Hood, that Plato banished them out of his commonwealth. Truly, this is much, if there be much truth in it.
First, to the first, that a man might better spend his time is a reason indeed; but it doth (as they say) but *petere principium*: for if it be, as I
35 affirm, that no learning is so good as that which teacheth and moveth to virtue, and that none can both teach and move thereto so much as Poetry, then is the conclusion manifest that ink and paper cannot be to a more profitable purpose employed. And certainly, though a man should grant their first assumption, it should follow (methinks) very
40 unwillingly, that good is not good because better is better. But I still and utterly deny that there is sprung out of earth a more fruitful knowledge.
To the second therefore, that they should be the principal liars, I

answer paradoxically, but truly, I think truly, that of all writers under the sun the poet is the least liar, and, though he would, as a poet can scarcely be a liar. The astronomer, with his cousin the geometrician, can hardly escape, when they take upon them to measure the height of the stars. How often, think you, do the physicians lie, when they aver things 5 good for sicknesses, which afterwards send Charon a great number of souls drowned in a potion before they come to his ferry? And no less of the rest, which take upon them to affirm. Now for the poet, he nothing affirms, and therefore never lieth. For, as I take it, to lie is to affirm that to be true which is false; so as the other artists, and especially the 10 historian, affirming many things, can, in the cloudy knowledge of mankind, hardly escape from many lies. But the poet (as I said before) never affirmeth. The poet never maketh any circles about your imagination, to conjure you to believe for true what he writes. He citeth not authorities of other histories, but even for his entry calleth the sweet 15 Muses to inspire into him a good invention; in truth, not labouring to tell you what is or is not, but what should or should not be. And therefore, though he recount things not true, yet because he telleth them not for true, he lieth not – without we will say that Nathan lied in his speech before-alleged to David; which as a wicked man durst scarce say, so think 20 I none so simple would say that Aesop lied in the tales of his beasts; for who thinks that Aesop writ it for actually true were well worthy to have his name chronicled among the beasts he writeth of. What child is there that, coming to a play, and seeing *Thebes* written in great letters upon an old door, doth believe that it is Thebes? If then a man can arrive, at 25 that child's age, to know that the poet's persons and doings are but pictures what should be, and not stories what have been, they will never give the lie to things not affirmatively but allegorically and figuratively written. And therefore, as in History looking for truth, they go away full fraught with falsehood, so in Poesy looking but for fiction, they shall 30 use the narration but as an imaginative ground-plot of a profitable invention.

But hereto is replied, that the poets give names to men they write of, which argueth a conceit of an actual truth, and so, not being true, proves a falsehood. And doth the lawyer lie then, when under the names 35 of 'John a Stile' and 'John a Noakes' he puts his case? But that is easily answered. Their naming of men is but to make their picture the more lively, and not to build any history: painting men, they cannot leave men nameless. We see we cannot play at chess but that we must give names to our chessmen; and yet, methinks, he were a very partial cham- 40 pion of truth that would say we lied for giving a piece of wood the reverend title of a bishop. The poet nameth Cyrus or Aeneas no other way than to show what men of their fames, fortunes, and estates should do.

Their third is, how much it abuseth men's wit, training it to wanton

sinfulness and lustful love: for indeed that is the principal, if not the
only, abuse I can hear alleged. They say the Comedies rather teach than
reprehend amorous conceits. They say the Lyric is larded with passionate sonnets, the Elegiac weeps the want of his mistress, and that even to
5 the Heroical Cupid hath ambitiously climbed. Alas, Love, I would thou
couldst as well defend thyself as thou canst offend others. I would those
on whom thou dost attend could either put thee away, or yield good
reason why they keep thee. But grant love of beauty to be a beastly fault
(although it be very hard, since only man, and no beast, hath that gift
10 to discern beauty); grant that lovely name of Love to deserve all hateful
reproaches (although even some of my masters the philosophers spent
a good deal of their lamp-oil in setting forth the excellency of it); grant,
I say, whatsoever they will have granted, that not only love, but lust, but
vanity, but (if they list) scurrility, possesseth many leaves of the poets'
15 books; yet think I, when this is granted, they will find their sentence
may with good manners put the last words foremost, and not say that
Poetry abuseth man's wit, but that man's wit abuseth Poetry.

For I will not deny but that man's wit may make Poesy, which should
be *eikastike*, which some learned have defined, 'figuring forth good
20 things', to be *phantastike*, which doth contrariwise infect the fancy with
unworthy objects; as the painter, that should give to the eye either some
excellent perspective, or some fine picture, fit for building or fortification, or containing in it some notable example, as Abraham sacrificing
his son Isaac, Judith killing Holofernes, David fighting with Goliath,
25 may leave those, and please an ill-pleased eye with wanton shows of
better hidden matters. But what, shall the abuse of a thing make the
right use odious? Nay truly, though I yield that Poesy may not only be
abused, but that being abused, by the reason of his sweet charming force,
it can do more hurt than any other army of words, yet shall it be so far
30 from concluding that the abuse should give reproach to the abused, that
contrariwise it is a good reason, that whatsoever, being abused, doth
most harm, being rightly used (and upon the right use each thing con-
ceiveth his title), doth most good.

Do we not see the skill of Physic (the best rampire to our often-
35 assaulted bodies), being abused, teach poison, the most violent destroyer? Doth not knowledge of Law, whose end is to even and right all
things, being abused, grow the crooked fosterer of horrible injuries?
Doth not (to go to the highest) God's word abused breed heresy, and His
name abused become blasphemy? Truly a needle cannot do much hurt,
40 and as truly (with leave of ladies be it spoken) it cannot do much good.
With a sword thou mayest kill thy father, and with a sword thou mayest
defend thy prince and country. So that, as in their calling poets the fathers
of lies they say nothing, so in this their argument of abuse they prove
the commendation.

They allege herewith, that before poets began to be in price our nation hath set their hearts' delight upon action, and not upon imagination, rather doing things worthy to be written, than writing things fit to be done. What that beforetime was, I think scarcely Sphinx can tell, since no memory is so ancient that hath the precedence of Poetry. And 5 certain it is that, in our plainest homeliness, yet never was the Albion nation without poetry. Marry, this argument, though it be levelled against poetry, yet is it indeed a chainshot against all learning, or bookishness, as they commonly term it. Of such mind were certain Goths, of whom it is written that, having in the spoil of a famous city taken a 10 fair library, one hangman (belike fit to execute the fruits of their wits who had murdered a great number of bodies), would have set fire on it. 'No,' said another very gravely, 'take heed what you do, for while they are busy about these toys, we shall with more leisure conquer their countries.' 15

This indeed is the ordinary doctrine of ignorance, and many words sometimes I have heard spent in it; but because this reason is generally against all learning, as well as Poetry, or rather, all learning but Poetry; because it were too large a digression to handle, or at least too superfluous (since it is manifest that all government of action is to be gotten 20 by knowledge, and knowledge best by gathering many knowledges, which is reading), I only, with Horace, to him that is of that opinion,

jubeo stultum esse libenter;

for as for Poetry itself, it is the freest from this objection.

For Poetry is the companion of the camps. I dare undertake, Orlando 25 Furioso, or honest King Arthur, will never displease a soldier: but the quiddity of *ens* and *prima materia* will hardly agree with a corslet. And therefore, as I said in the beginning, even Turks and Tartars are delighted with poets. Homer, a Greek, flourished before Greece flourished. And if to a slight conjecture a conjecture may be opposed, truly it may seem, 30 that as by him their learned men took almost their first light of knowledge, so their active men received their first motions of courage. Only Alexander's example may serve, who by Plutarch is accounted of such virtue, that Fortune was not his guide but his footstool; whose acts speak for him, though Plutarch did not, – indeed the phoenix of warlike 35 princes. This Alexander left his schoolmaster, living Aristotle, behind him, but took dead Homer with him. He put the philosopher Callisthenes to death for his seeming philosophical, indeed mutinous, stubbornness, but the chief thing he ever was heard to wish for was that Homer had been alive. He well found he received more bravery of mind 40 by the pattern of Achilles than by hearing the definition of fortitude. And therefore, if Cato misliked Fulvius for carrying Ennius with him to the field, it may be answered that, if Cato misliked it, the noble

Fulvius liked it, or else he had not done it: for it was not the excellent
Cato Uticensis (whose authority I would much more have reverenced),
but it was the former, in truth a bitter punisher of faults, but else a man
that had never well sacrificed to the graces. He misliked and cried out
5 upon all Greek learning, and yet, being four score years old, began to
learn it, belike fearing that Pluto understood not Latin. Indeed, the
Roman laws allowed no person to be carried to the wars but he that was
in the soldiers' roll, and therefore, though Cato misliked his unmustered
person, he misliked not his work. And if he had, Scipio Nasica, judged
10 by common consent the best Roman, loved him. Both the other Scipio
brothers, who had by their virtues no less surnames than of Asia and
Afric, so loved him that they caused his body to be buried in their sepul-
chre. So as Cato's authority being but against his person, and that
answered with so far greater than himself, is herein of no validity.
15   But now indeed my burden is great; now Plato's name is laid upon
me, whom, I must confess, of all philosophers I have ever esteemed most
worthy of reverence, and with great reason: since of all philosophers he
is the most poetical. Yet if he will defile the fountain out of which his
flowing streams have proceeded, let us boldly examine with what reasons
20 he did it. First, truly a man might maliciously object that Plato, being
a philosopher, was a natural enemy of poets. For indeed, after the
philosophers had picked out of the sweet mysteries of Poetry the right
discerning true points of knowledge, they forthwith, putting it in
method, and making a school-art of that which the poets did only teach
25 by a divine delightfulness, beginning to spurn at their guides, like
ungrateful prentices, were not content to set up shops for themselves,
but sought by all means to discredit their masters; which by the force
of delight being barred them, the less they could overthrow them, the
more they hated them. For indeed, they found for Homer seven cities
30 strave who should have him for their citizen; where many cities banished philosophers as not fit members to live among them. For only
repeating certain of Euripides' verses, many Athenians had their lives
saved of the Syracusans, when the Athenians themselves thought many
philosophers unworthy to live. Certain poets, as Simonides and Pindar,
35 had so prevailed with Hiero the First, that of a tyrant they made him a
just king; where Plato could do so little with Dionysius, that he himself
of a philosopher was made a slave. But who should do thus, I confess,
should requite the objections made against poets with like cavillation
against philosophers; as likewise one should do that should bid one read
40 *Phaedrus* or *Symposium* in Plato, or the discourse of love in Plutarch,
and see whether any poet do authorize abominable filthiness, as they do.
Again, a man might ask out of what commonwealth Plato did banish
them. In sooth, thence where he himself alloweth community of
women. So as belike this banishment grew not for effeminate wanton-

ness, since little should poetical sonnets be hurtful when a man might
have what woman he listed. But I honour philosophical instructions,
and bless the wits which bred them: so as they be not abused, which is
likewise stretched to Poetry.

St Paul himself (who yet, for the credit of poets, allegeth twice two 5
poets, and one of them by the name of a prophet), setteth a watchword
upon Philosophy, – indeed upon the abuse. So doth Plato upon the
abuse, not upon Poetry. Plato found fault that the poets of his time filled
the world with wrong opinions of the gods, making light tales of that
unspotted essence, and therefore would not have the youth depraved 10
with such opinions. Herein may much be said; let this suffice: the poets
did not induce such opinions, but did imitate those opinions already
induced. For all the Greek stories can well testify that the very religion
of that time stood upon many and many-fashioned gods, not taught so
by the poets, but followed according to their nature of imitation. Who 15
list may read in Plutarch the discourses of Isis and Osiris, of the cause
why oracles ceased, of the divine providence, and see whether the theology of that nation stood not upon such dreams which the poets indeed
superstitiously observed and truly (since they had not the light of Christ)
did much better in it than the philosophers, who, shaking off supersti- 20
tion, brought in atheism. Plato therefore (whose authority I had much
rather justly construe than unjustly resist) meant not in general of poets,
in those words of which Julius Scaliger saith, *Qua authoritate barbari
quidam atque hispidi abuti velint ad poetas e republica exigendos*; but only
meant to drive out those wrong opinions of the Deity (whereof now, 25
without further law, Christianity hath taken away all the hurtful belief),
perchance (as he thought) nourished by the then esteemed poets. And
a man need go no further than to Plato himself to know his meaning:
who, in his dialogue called *Ion*, giveth high and rightly divine commendation to Poetry. So as Plato, banishing the abuse, not the thing – 30
not banishing it, but giving due honour unto it – shall be our patron
and not our adversary. For indeed I had much rather (since truly I may
do it) show their mistaking of Plato (under whose lion's skin they would
make an ass-like braying against Poesy) than go about to overthrow his
authority; whom, the wiser a man is, the more just cause he shall find 35
to have in admiration; especially since he attributeth unto Poesy more
than myself do, namely, to be a very inspiring of a divine force, far above
man's wit, as in the afore-named dialogue is apparent.

Of the other side, who would show the honours have been by the
best sort of judgments granted them, a whole sea of examples would 40
present themselves: Alexanders, Caesars, Scipios, all favourers of poets;
Laelius, called the Roman Socrates, himself a poet, so as part of *Heautontimorumenos* in Terence was supposed to be made by him; and even
the Greek Socrates, whom Apollo confirmed to be the only wise man,

is said to have spent part of his old time in putting Aesop's fables into verses. And therefore, full evil should it become his scholar Plato to put such words in his master's mouth against poets. But what need more? Aristotle writes the Art of Poesy: and why, if it should not be written? 5 Plutarch teacheth the use to be gathered of them, and how, if they should not be read? And who reads Plutarch's either history or philosophy, shall find he trimmeth both their garments with guards of Poesy. But I list not to defend Poesy with the help of her underling Historiography. Let it suffice that it is a fit soil for praise to dwell upon; 10 and what dispraise may set upon it, is either easily overcome, or transformed into just commendation.

So that, since the excellencies of it may be so easily and so justly confirmed, and the low-creeping objections so soon trodden down: it not being an art of lies, but of true doctrine; not of effeminateness, but of 15 notable stirring of courage; not of abusing man's wit, but of strengthening man's wit; not banished, but honoured by Plato; let us rather plant more laurels for to engarland our poet's heads (which honour of being laureate, as besides them only triumphant captains wear, is a sufficient authority to show the price they ought to be had in) than suffer the ill-20 favouring breath of such wrong-speakers once to blow upon the clear springs of Poesy.

But since I have run so long a career in this matter, methinks, before I give my pen a full stop, it shall be but a little more lost time to inquire why England (the mother of excellent minds) should be grown so hard 25 a stepmother to poets, who certainly in wit ought to pass all other, since all only proceedeth from their wit, being indeed makers of themselves, not takers of others. How can I but exclaim,

Musa, mihi causas memora, quo numine laeso?

Sweet Poesy, that hath anciently had kings, emperors, senators, great 30 captains, such as, besides a thousand others, David, Adrian, Sophocles, Germanicus, not only to favour poets, but to be poets; and of our nearer times can present for her patrons a Robert, king of Sicily, the great King Francis of France, King James of Scotland; such cardinals as Bembus and Bibbiena: such famous preachers and teachers as Beza and 35 Melanchthon; so learned philosophers as Fracastorius and Scaliger; so great orators as Pontanus and Muretus; so piercing wits as George Buchanan; so grave counsellors as, besides many, but before all, that Hospital of France, than whom (I think) that realm never brought forth a more accomplished judgment, more firmly builded upon virtue – I 40 say these, with numbers of others, not only to read others' poesies, but to poetize for others' reading – that Poesy, thus embraced in all other places, should only find in our time a hard welcome in England, I think the very earth lamenteth it, and therefore decketh our soil with fewer laurels than it was accustomed. For heretofore poets have in England also flourished, and, which is to be noted, even in those times when the trumpet of Mars did sound loudest. And now that an overfaint quiet- ness should seem to strew the house for poets, they are almost in as good 5 reputation as the mountebanks at Venice. Truly even that, as of the one side it giveth great praise to Poesy, which like Venus (but to better purpose) hath rather be troubled in the net with Mars than enjoy the homely quiet of Vulcan; so serves it for a piece of a reason why they are less grateful to idle England, which now can scarce endure the pain of 10 a pen. Upon this necessarily followeth, that base men with servile wits undertake it, who think it enough if they can be rewarded of the printer. And so as Epaminondas is said, with the honour of his virtue to have made an office, by his exercising it, which before was contemptible, to become highly respected, so these, no more but setting their names to 15 it, by their own disgracefulness disgrace the most graceful Poesy. For now, as if all the Muses were got with child to bring forth bastard poets, without any commission they do post over the banks of Helicon, till they make the readers more weary than post-horses; while, in the mean- time, they,   20

Queis meliore luto finxit praecordia Titan,

are better content to suppress the outflowing of their wit, than, by pub- lishing them, to be accounted knights of the same order.

But I that, before ever I durst aspire unto the dignity, am admitted into the company of the paper-blurrers, do find the very true cause of 25 our wanting estimation is want of desert, taking upon us to be poets in despite of Pallas. Now wherein we want desert were a thankworthy labour to express; but if I knew, I should have mended myself. But I, as I never desired the title, so have I neglected the means to come by it. Only, overmastered by some thoughts, I yielded an inky tribute unto 30 them. Marry, they that delight in Poesy itself should seek to know what they do, and how they do; and especially look themselves in an unflat- tering glass of reason, if they be inclinable unto it. For Poesy must not be drawn by the ears; it must be gently led, or rather it must lead; which was partly the cause that made the ancient-learned affirm it was a divine 35 gift, and no human skill: since all other knowledges lie ready for any that hath strength of wit; a poet no industry can make, if his own genius be not carried unto it; and therefore is it an old proverb, *orator fit, poeta nascitur.* Yet confess I always that as the fertilest ground must be manured, so must the highest-flying wit have a Daedalus to guide him. 40 That Daedalus, they say, both in this and in other, hath three wings to bear itself up into the air of due commendation: that is, Art, Imitation, and Exercise. But these, neither artificial rules nor imitative patterns, we

much cumber ourselves withal. Exercise indeed we do, but that very fore-backwardly: for where we should exercise to know, we exercise as having known; and so is our brain delivered of much matter which never was begotten by knowledge. For there being two principal parts – matter
5 to be expressed by words and words to express the matter – in neither we use Art or Imitation rightly. Our matter is *quodlibet* indeed, though wrongly performing Ovid's verse,

Quicquid conabor dicere, versus erit:

never marshalling it into an assured rank, that almost the readers cannot
10 tell where to find themselves.

Chaucer, undoubtedly, did excellently in his *Troilus and Criseyde*; of whom, truly, I know not whether to marvel more, either that he in that misty time could see so clearly, or that we in this clear age walk so stumblingly after him. Yet had he great wants, fit to be forgiven in so
15 reverent antiquity. I account the *Mirror of Magistrates* meetly furnished of beautiful parts, and in the Earl of Surrey's lyrics many things tasting of a noble birth, and worthy of a noble mind. The *Shepherd's Calendar* hath much poetry in his eclogues, indeed worthy the reading, if I be not deceived. That same framing of his style to an old rustic language I dare
20 not allow, since neither Theocritus in Greek, Virgil in Latin, nor San-nazzaro in Italian did affect it. Besides these, do I not remember to have seen but few (to speak boldly) printed, that have poetical sinews in them: for proof whereof, let but most of the verses be put in prose, and then ask the meaning, and it will be found that one verse did but beget
25 another, without ordering at the first what should be at the last; which becomes a confused mass of words, with a tingling sound of rhyme, barely accompanied with reason.

Our Tragedies and Comedies (not without cause cried out against), observing rules neither of honest civility nor of skilful Poetry, excepting
30 *Gorboduc* (again, I say, of those that I have seen), which notwithstand-ing, as it is full of stately speeches and well-sounding phrases, climbing to the height of Seneca's style, and as full of notable morality, which it doth most delightfully teach, and so obtain the very end of Poesy, yet in truth it is very defectious in the circumstances, which grieveth me,
35 because it might not remain as an exact model of all tragedies. For it is faulty both in place and time, the two necessary companions of all cor-poral actions. For where the stage should always represent but one place, and the uttermost time presupposed in it should be, both by Aristotle's precept and common reason, but one day, there is both many days, and
40 many places, inartificially imagined.

But if it be so in *Gorboduc*, how much more in all the rest? where you shall have Asia of the one side, and Afric of the other, and so many other under-kingdoms, that the player, when he cometh in, must ever begin

with telling where he is, or else the tale will not be conceived. Now ye
shall have three ladies walk to gather flowers and then we must believe
the stage to be a garden. By and by we hear news of shipwreck in the
same place, and then we are to blame if we accept it not for a rock. Upon
the back of that comes out a hideous monster with fire and smoke, and 5
then the miserable beholders are bound to take it for a cave. While in
the meantime two armies fly in, represented with four swords and buck-
lers, and then what hard heart will not receive it for a pitched field?

Now of time they are much more liberal, for ordinary it is that two
young princes fall in love. After many traverses, she is got with child, 10
delivered of a fair boy, he is lost, groweth a man, falls in love, and is
ready to get another child, and all this in two hours' space: which, how
absurd it is in sense, even sense may imagine, and Art hath taught, and
all ancient examples justified, and at this day, the ordinary players in
Italy will not err in. Yet will some bring in an example of *Eunuchus* in 15
Terence, that containeth matter of two days, yet far short of twenty
years. True it is, and so was it to be played in two days, and so fitted to
the time it set forth. And though Plautus hath in one place done amiss,
let us hit with him, and not miss with him. But they will say, How then
shall we set forth a story, which containeth both many places and many 20
times? And do they not know that a tragedy is tied to the laws of Poesy,
and not of History; not bound to follow the story, but, having liberty,
either to feign a quite new matter, or to frame the history to the most
tragical conveniency? Again, many things may be told which cannot be
showed, if they know the difference betwixt reporting and representing. 25
As, for example, I may speak (though I am here) of Peru, and in speech
digress from that to the description of Calicut; but in action I cannot
represent it without Pacolet's horse. And so was the manner the ancients
took, by some *nuncius* to recount things done in former time or other
place. 30

Lastly, if they will represent an history, they must not (as Horace
saith) begin *ab ovo*, but they must come to the principal point of that
one action which they will represent. By example this will be best
expressed. I have a story of young Polydorus, delivered for safety's sake,
with great riches, by his father Priam to Polymnestor, king of Thrace, 35
in the Trojan war time. He, after some years, hearing the overthrow of
Priam, for to make the treasure his own, murdereth the child. The body
of the child is taken up by Hecuba. She, the same day, findeth a sleight
to be revenged most cruelly of the tyrant. Where now would one of our
tragedy writers begin, but with the delivery of the child? Then should 40
he sail over into Thrace, and so spend I know not how many years, and
travel numbers of places. But where doth Euripides? Even with the
finding of the body, leaving the rest to be told by the spirit of Polydorus.
This need no further to be enlarged; the dullest wit may conceive it.

But besides these gross absurdities, how all their plays be neither right
tragedies, nor right comedies, mingling kings and clowns, not because
the matter so carrieth it, but thrust in clowns by head and shoulders, to
play a part in majestical matters, with neither decency nor discretion,
5 so as neither the admiration and commiseration, nor the right sportfulness, is by their mongrel tragi-comedy obtained. I know Apuleius did
somewhat so, but that is a thing recounted with space of time, not represented in one moment; and I know the ancients have one or two examples of tragi-comedies, as Plautus hath *Amphitrio*. But, if we mark them
10 well, we shall find, that they never, or very daintily, match hornpipes
and funerals. So falleth it out that, having indeed no right comedy,
in that comical part of our tragedy, we have nothing but scurrility,
unworthy of any chaste ears, or some extreme show of doltishness,
indeed fit to lift up a loud laughter, and nothing else: where the whole
15 tract of a comedy should be full of delight, as the tragedy should be
still maintained in a well-raised admiration.

But our comedians think there is no delight without laughter; which
is very wrong, for though laughter may come with delight, yet cometh
it not of delight, as though delight should be the cause of laughter; but
20 well may one thing breed both together. Nay, rather in themselves they
have, as it were, a kind of contrariety: for delight we scarcely do but in
things that have a conveniency to ourselves or to the general nature;
laughter almost ever cometh of things most disproportioned to ourselves and nature. Delight hath a joy in it, either permanent or present.
25 Laughter hath only a scornful tickling. For example, we are ravished
with delight to see a fair woman, and yet are far from being moved to
laughter. We laugh at deformed creatures, wherein certainly we cannot
delight. We delight in good chances, we laugh at mischances; we delight
to hear the happiness of our friends, or country, at which he were worthy
30 to be laughed at that would laugh. We shall, contrarily, laugh sometimes
to find a matter quite mistaken and go down the hill against the bias,
in the mouth of some such men, as for the respect of them one shall be
heartily sorry, yet he cannot choose but laugh; and so is rather pained
than delighted with laughter. Yet deny I not but that they may go well
35 together: for as in Alexander's picture well set out we delight without
laughter, and in twenty mad antics we laugh without delight; so in Hercules, painted with his great beard and furious countenance, in woman's
attire, spinning at Omphale's commandment, it breedeth both delight
and laughter. For the representing of so strange a power in love pro-
40 cureth delight: and the scornfulness of the action stirreth laughter.

But I speak to this purpose, that all the end of the comical part be
not upon such scornful matters as stirreth laughter only, but, mixed with
it, that delightful teaching which is the end of Poesy. And the great fault
even in that point of laughter, and forbidden plainly by Aristotle, is that

they stir laughter in sinful things, which are rather execrable than ridiculous; or in miserable, which are rather to be pitied than scorned. For what is it to make folks gape at a wretched beggar, or a beggarly clown; or, against law of hospitality, to jest at strangers, because they speak not English so well as we do? What do we learn? since it is certain 5

> Nil habet infelix paupertas durius in se,
> Quam quod ridiculos homines facit.

But rather a busy loving courtier; a heartless threatening Thraso; a self-wise-seeming schoolmaster; an awry-transformed traveller: these if we saw walk in stage names, which we play naturally, therein were 10 delightful laughter, and teaching delightfulness: as in the other, the tragedies of Buchanan do justly bring forth a divine admiration. But I have lavished out too many words of this play matter. I do it because, as they are excelling parts of Poesy, so is there none so much used in England, and none can be more pitifully abused; which, like an 15 unmannerly daughter showing a bad education, causeth her mother Poesy's honesty to be called in question.

Other sorts of Poetry almost have we none, but that lyrical kind of songs and sonnets: which, Lord, if He gave us so good minds, how well it might be employed, and with how heavenly fruit, both private and 20 public, in singing the praises of the immortal beauty, the immortal goodness of that God who giveth us hands to write and wits to conceive; of which we might well want words, but never matter; of which we could turn our eyes to nothing, but we should ever have new-budding occasions. But truly many of such writings as come under the banner of 25 unresistible love; if I were a mistress, would never persuade me they were in love; so coldly they apply fiery speeches, as men that had rather read lovers' writings (and so caught up certain swelling phrases which hang together like a man which once told me the wind was at north-west and by south, because he would be sure to name winds enough), than that 30 in truth they feel those passions, which easily (as I think) may be betrayed by that same forcibleness or *energia* (as the Greeks call it) of the writer. But let this be a sufficient though short note, that we miss the right use of the material point of Poesy.

Now, for the outside of it, which is words, or (as I may term it) 35 diction, it is even well worse. So is that honey-flowing matron eloquence apparelled, or rather disguised, in a courtesan-like painted affectation: one time with so far-fetched words, they may seem monsters, but must seem strangers, to any poor Englishman; another time with coursing of a letter, as if they were bound to follow the method of a dictionary; 40 another time with figures and flowers extremely winter-starved. But I would this fault were only peculiar to versifiers, and had not as large possession among prose-printers, and (which is to be marvelled) among

many scholars, and (which is to be pitied) among some preachers. Truly I could wish, if at least I might be so bold to wish in a thing beyond the reach of my capacity, the diligent imitators of Tully and Demosthenes (most worthy to be imitated) did not so much keep Nizolian
5 paper-books of their figures and phrases, as by attentive translation (as it were) devour them whole, and make them wholly theirs. For now they cast sugar and spice upon every dish that is served to the table, like those Indians, not content to wear earrings at the fit and natural place of the ears, but they will thrust jewels through their nose and lips, because they
10 will be sure to be fine.

Tully, when he was to drive out Catiline, as it were with a thunderbolt of eloquence, often used that figure of repetition, *Vivit. Vivit? Imo vero etiam in senatum venit*, &c. Indeed, inflamed with a well-grounded rage, he would have his words (as it were) double out of his mouth, and
15 so do that artificially which we see men do in choler naturally. And we, having noted the grace of those words, hale them in sometime to a familiar epistle, when it were too too much choler to be choleric. How well store of *similiter cadences* doth sound with the gravity of the pulpit, I would but invoke Demosthenes' soul to tell, who with a rare daintiness
20 useth them. Truly they have made me think of the sophister that with too much sublety would prove two eggs three, and though he might be counted a sophister, had none for his labour. So these men bringing in such a kind of eloquence, well may they obtain an opinion of a seeming fineness, but persuade few – which should be the end of their fineness.
25   Now for similitudes in certain printed discourses, I think all herbarists, all stories of beasts, fowls, and fishes are rifled up, that they come in multitudes to wait upon any of our conceits; which certainly is as absurd a surfeit to the ears as is possible: for the force of a similitude not being to prove anything to a contrary disputer, but only to explain
30 to a willing hearer; when that is done, the rest is a most tedious prattling, rather over-swaying the memory from the purpose whereto they were applied, than any whit informing the judgment, already either satisfied, or by similitudes not to be satisfied. For my part, I do not doubt, when Antonius and Crassus, the great forefathers of Cicero in eloquence,
35 the one (as Cicero testifieth of them) pretended not to know art, the other not to set by it, because with a plain sensibleness they might win credit of popular ears; which credit is the nearest step to persuasion; which persuasion is the chief mark of Oratory – I do not doubt (I say) but that they used these tracks very sparingly; which, who doth gener-
40 ally use, any man may see doth dance to his own music, and so be noted by the audience more careful to speak curiously than to speak truly.

Undoubtedly (at least to my opinion undoubtedly) I have found in divers smally learned courtiers a more sound style than in some professors of learning; of which I can guess no other cause, but that the courtier, following that which by practice he findeth fittest to nature, therein (though he know it not) doth according to art, though not by art: where the other, using art to show art, and not to hide art (as in these cases he should do), flieth from nature, and indeed abuseth art.

But what? methinks I deserve to be pounded for straying from Poetry 5 to Oratory: but both have such an affinity in this wordish consideration, that I think this digression will make my meaning receive the fuller understanding – which is not to take upon me to teach poets how they should do, but only, finding myself sick among the rest, to show some one or two spots of the common infection grown among the most part 10 of writers; that, acknowledging ourselves somewhat awry, we may bend to the right use both of matter and manner: whereto our language giveth us great occasion, being indeed capable of any excellent exercising of it. I know some will say it is a mingled language. And why not so much the better, taking the best of both the other? Another will say it wanteth 15 grammar. Nay truly, it hath that praise, that it wanteth not grammar: for grammar it might have, but it needs it not; being so easy of itself, and so void of those cumbersome differences of cases, genders, moods, and tenses, which I think was a piece of the Tower of Babylon's curse, that a man should be put to school to learn his mother-tongue. But for 20 the uttering sweetly and properly the conceits of the mind, which is the end of speech, that hath it equally with any other tongue in the world; and is particularly happy in compositions of two or three words together, near the Greek, far beyond the Latin: which is one of the greatest beauties can be in a language. 25

Now of versifying there are two sorts, the one ancient, the other modern: the ancient marked the quantity of each syllable, and according to that framed his verse; the modern observing only number (with some regard of the accent), the chief life of it standeth in that like sounding of the words, which we call rhyme. Whether of these be the most 30 excellent, would bear many speeches: the ancient (no doubt) more fit for music, both words and time observing quantity, and more fit lively to express divers passions, by the low or lofty sound of the well-weighed syllable. The latter likewise, with his rhyme, striketh a certain music to the ear; and, in fine, since it doth delight, though by another way, it 35 obtains the same purpose: there being in either sweetness, and wanting in neither majesty. Truly the English, before any other vulgar language I know, is fit for both sorts: for, for the ancient, the Italian is so full of vowels that it must ever be cumbered with elisions; the Dutch so, of the other side, with consonants, that they cannot yield the sweet sliding fit 40 for a verse; the French in his whole language hath not one word that hath his accent in the last syllable saving two, called *antepenultima*; and little more hath the Spanish, and therefore very gracelessly may they use dactyls. The English is subject to none of these defects.

Now for the rhyme, though we do not observe quantity, yet we observe the accent very precisely, which other languages either cannot do, or will not do so absolutely. That *caesura*, or breathing place in the midst of the verse, neither Italian nor Spanish have, the French and we
5 never almost fail of. Lastly, even the very rhyme itself the Italian cannot put in the last syllable, by the French named the masculine rhyme, but still in the next to the last, which the French call the female, or the next before that, which the Italians term *sdrucciola*. The example of the former is *buono: suono*, of the *sdrucciola*, *femina: semina*. The French, of
10 the other side, hath both the male, as *bon: son*, and the female, as *plaise: taise*, but the *sdrucciola* he hath not: where the English hath all three, as *due: true, father: rather, motion: potion*; with much more which might be said, but that I find already the triflingness of this discourse is much too much enlarged.

15 So that since the ever-praiseworthy Poesy is full of virtue-breeding delightfulness, and void of no gift that ought to be in the noble name of learning; since the blames laid against it are either false or feeble; since the cause why it is not esteemed in England is the fault of poet-apes, not poets; since, lastly, our tongue is most fit to honour Poesy,
20 and to be honored by Poesy; I conjure you all that have had the evil luck to read this ink-wasting toy of mine, even in the name of the Nine Muses, no more to scorn the sacred mysteries of Poesy, no more to laugh at the name of poets, as though they were next inheritors to fools, no more to jest at the reverent title of a rhymer; but to believe, with
25 Aristotle, that they were the ancient treasurers of the Grecians' divinity; to believe, with Bembus, that they were first bringers-in of all civility; to believe, with Scaliger, that no philosopher's precepts can sooner make you an honest man than the reading of Virgil; to believe, with Clauserus, the translator of Cornutus, that it pleased the heavenly Deity,
30 by Hesiod and Homer, under the veil of fables, to give us all knowl-edge, Logic, Rhetoric, Philosophy natural and moral, and *quid non*?; to believe, with me, that there are many mysteries contained in Poetry, which of purpose were written darkly, lest by profane wits it should be abused; to believe, with Landino, that they are so beloved of the
35 gods that whatsoever they write proceeds of a divine fury; lastly, to believe themselves, when they tell you they will make you immortal by their verses.

Thus doing, your name shall flourish in the printer's shops; thus doing, you shall be of kin to many a poetical preface; thus doing, you
40 shall be most fair, most rich, most wise, most all; you shall dwell upon superlatives. Thus doing, though you be *libertino patre natus*, you shall suddenly grow *Herculea proles*,

Si quid mea carmina possunt.

Thus doing, your soul shall be placed with Dante's Beatrix, or Virgil's Anchises. But if (fie of such a but) you be born so near the dull-making cataract of Nilus that you cannot hear the planet-like music of Poetry, if you have so earth-creeping a mind that it cannot lift itself up to look to the sky of Poetry, or rather, by a certain rustical disdain, will become 5 such a mome as to be a Momus of Poetry; then, though I will not wish unto you the ass's ears of Midas, nor to be driven by a poet's verses (as Bubonax was) to hang himself, nor to be rhymed to death, as is said to be done in Ireland; yet thus much curse I must send you, in the behalf of all poets, that while you live, you live in love, and never get favour 10 for lacking skill of a sonnet, and, when you die, your memory die from the earth for want of an epitaph.

NOTES

Olney's edition begins with 'Four Sonnets written by Henry Constable to Sir Philip Sidney's soul'. These are reprinted in *The Poems of Henry Constable*, ed. Joan Grundy (Liverpool, 1960), 167–9. An address to the reader follows:

To the Reader

The stormy winter (dear children of the Muses), which hath so long held back the glorious sunshine of divine Poesy, is here by the sacred pen-breathing words of divine Sir Philip Sidney, not only chased from our fame-inviting clime, but utterly for ever banished eternity. Then graciously regreet the perpetual spring of ever-growing invention, and like kind babes, either enabled by wit or power, help to support me poor midwife, whose daring adventure hath delivered from Oblivion's womb this ever-to-be-admired wit's miracle. Those great ones, who in themselves have interred this blessed innocent, will with Aesculapius condemn me as a detractor from their deities: those who prophet-like have but heard presage of his coming, will (if they will do well) not only defend, but praise me, as the first public bewrayer of Poesy's Messiah. Those who neither have seen, thereby to inter, nor heard, by which they might be inflamed with desire to see, let them (of duty) plead to be my champions, sith both their sight and hearing by mine incurring blame is seasoned. Excellent Poesy (so created by this apology), be thou my defendress; and if any wound me, let thy beauty (my soul's adamant) recure me: if any commend mine endeavoured hardiment, to them commend thy most divinest fury as a winged encouragement: so shalt thou have devoted to thee, and to them obliged

Henry Olney.

p. 81/1   **Edward Wotton**] courtier and diplomat (1548–1626), half-brother of the diplomat and poet Sir Henry Wotton (1568–1639). Sidney got to know him in 1574–5 in Vienna, where Wotton was secretary to the English embassy at the court of the Holy Roman Emperor Maximilian II. Wotton was a beneficiary under Sidney's will and a pall-bearer at his funeral. Sidney's use of the phrase 'right virtuous' to describe him was recalled by George Chapman in the title of a sonnet addressed to Wotton (Chapman 1941, 404–5).

2   **to learn horsemanship**] Sidney unexpectedly opens his defence of poetry with an account of his training as a horseman. It is tempting to see this as a response to the influential treatise on teaching Latin, *The Schoolmaster* (1570) by Roger Ascham (1515–68). Ascham complains that among the

Elizabethan nobility 'commonlie, more care is had . . . to finde out rather a cunnynge man for their horse, than a cunnyng man for their children', and that 'Yong Ientlemen, be wiselier taught to ryde, by common ryders, than to learne, by common Scholemasters' (Ascham 1904, 193 and 198).

2–3 **John Pietro Pugliano**] teacher at the Imperial Riding School in Vienna, founded in 1572.

3 **commendation**] credit.

esquire] In the courts of the sixteenth century the esquire or equerry (officer in charge of the royal stables) was a man of importance. See *OED s.* equerry, 2 and esquire, 1.c.

4 **the fertileness of the Italian wit**] Sidney explained to his brother Robert: 'although indeed some [Italians] be excellently learned, yet are they all given so to counterfeit learning, as a man shall learn among them more false grounds of things than in any place else that I know. For from a tapster upward they are all discoursers [see Sidney's definition of this term, Duncan-Jones 1989, 292]. In certain qualities, as horsemanship, weapons, vaulting and such, are better there than in the other countries; but for the other matters, as well, if not better, you shall have them in those nearer places' (Duncan-Jones 1989, 286–7). The best-known Elizabethan account of the dangerous persuasiveness of the fertile Italian wit is that of Roger Ascham in *The Schoolmaster* (Ascham 1904, 223–30).

6 **contemplations**] theories, as opposed to 'his practice' (5). Sidney, himself a fine horseman, advised his brother Robert: 'At horsemanship, read Grison, Claudio, and a book that is called *La gloria del cavallo* withal, that you may join the thorough contemplation of it with the exercise' (Duncan-Jones 1989, 293). He refers here to three textbooks on horsemanship: Federico Grisone, *Ordini di cavalcare* (Naples, 1550; trans. Thomas Blundeville, 1560); Claudio Corte, *Il cavalerizzo* (Venice, 1573; trans. Bedingfield, 1584); and Pasquale Caracciolo, *La gloria del cavallo* (Venice, 1566). For Sidney's interest in the theory of horsemanship see *NA*, xxii–xxiv.

8 **loaden**] burdened.

slow payment] i.e. of Pugliano's bills for his services. William Temple, Sidney's secretary, who wrote a logical analysis of the *Apology* in the 1580s, loyally supposes that Pugliano was angry at other students' slow payment of their bills (Temple 1984, 63).

9 **admiration**] wonder, astonishment.

10 **faculty**] branch of learning.

estate] class.

12 **strong abiders**] good at holding a position.

13 **to so unbelieved a point he proceeded**] he went to such incredible lengths.

15 *pedanteria*] (Italian) pedantic trifle. Sidney is 'quoting' his Italian tutor Pugliano.

16–17 **what a peerless beast a horse was**] Praise of the horse was recommended as a school exercise by the sixth-century grammarian Priscian in *Praeexercita-*

mina (*Rhetores Latini Minores*, ed. Karl Halm (Leipzig, 1863), 556). See Baldwin 1944, II, 187. Compare G. Buchanan, *Silva*, vi, *Opera* (ed. Ruddiman, 1725), II, 340; Shakespeare, *Venus and Adonis*, 259ff., and *Henry V*, III.vii.1–79.

17 **serviceable**] useful (rather than merely ornamental, as most courtiers are).

18 **such more**] so much more.

19 **a piece of a logician**] a bit of a logician (compare 109/9 and 115/19). Sidney shared with his protégé Abraham Fraunce a lifelong interest in the work of the Protestant logician Peter Ramus (1515–72). A contemporary of Sidney's at Oxford, the poet Richard Carew, claims that Sidney was already well known for his skills in logical disputation as an undergraduate (*The Survey of Cornwall* (1602), fol. 102v). At Oxford he would have become familiar with Aristotelian logic (see M. H. Curtius, *Studies in the Renaissance* 5 (1958), 111–20). In 1574 he may also have heard at Padua the lectures of Zabarelli (teaching there 1564–89), who followed the system of Averroes and treated poetry as part of logic. Many words and phrases in the *Apology* show Sidney's interest in logic: see notes on 20; 85/9–10, 12; 88/42; 91/7; 93/2; 96/35–6; 99/3; 102/34; 105/27; 110/2–4; 114/20–2, 25–33.

20 **wished myself a horse**] One of Crato's pupils in logic expresses a similar wish in *De disciplina scholarium*, *PL* 64, col. 1230 (a favourite medieval text long attributed to the philosopher Boethius (c. 480–524) but probably written in the thirteenth century). Sidney may have seen himself as peculiarly susceptible to Pugliano's arguments, since his first name derives from the Greek for 'horse-lover'. In *Astrophil and Stella*, sonnet 49, Astrophil describes himself transformed into a horse by love (Ringler 1962, 189); and both the *Old* and *New Arcadia* are filled with equestrian metaphors applied to men and women. *Homo* (man) and *equus* (horse) were used as fixed terms in the syllogisms of medieval logic.

21 **self-love**] Compare Erasmus's *Praise of Folly*: 'To this order [i.e. the poets] more than to any other, bothe Selfloue, and Adulacion [flattery] are annexed familiarly' (Erasmus 1965, 73).

22 **wherein ourselves are parties**] in which we have a stake.

23 **Wherein**] of which (i.e. of the power of self-love).
affection] prejudice.

25–6 **having slipped into the title of a poet**] Sidney's poetry – including the *Old Arcadia* and poems from *Certain Sonnets* – was circulating in manuscript among a select circle of his friends and relations while he was writing the *Apology*. See Woudhuysen 1996, part 2. See also *Astrophil and Stella* 90 (Ringler 1962, 224).

27 **unelected**] not chosen by me. The phrase **unelected vocation** conjures up one of the central doctrines of Calvinism: that all men have a vocation or calling – that is, a social function – assigned to them by God, and that straying from this vocation will result in actions which will be 'rejected before God's throne'. See Calvin, *Institutes of the Christian Religion*, III, x, 6. Sidney's playful acknowledgment that his poetic vocation is not his true one suggests

that the social hierarchy of his world has been 'turned topsy-turvy' through human 'stupidity and rashness'.

28–9   **the scholar . . . his master**] i.e. Sidney is to be forgiven for following in the steps of Pugliano. See Matthew 10:25: 'It is enough for the disciple that he be as his master, and the servant as his lord'. See also Castiglione, *The Courtier*. 'He therefore that will bee a good scholler, beside the practising of good thinges must evermore set all his diligence to be like his maister, and (if it were possible) chaung him selfe into him' (Castiglione 1928, 45). Castiglione takes a teacher of horsemanship as his example of an excellent 'maister'.

30   **pitiful**] may mean either that he is defending poetry out of pity or that his defence is a wretched one.

31–82/4   **from almost the highest . . . among the Muses**] In lamenting the status of poetry Sidney is reproducing a humanist commonplace which contrasted contemporary disrespect for letters with the exalted position of poetry in an idealized past. Compare Boccaccio 1930, 117; Salutati 1951, I, i; Fracastorius 1924, 54; and Spenser 1989, October Eclogue, Argument. Sir Thomas Elyot (c. 1490–1546) reiterates the commonplace in a passage which Sidney seems to have known well: 'For the name of a poete, wherat nowe (specially in this realme), men haue suche indignation, that they vse onely poetes and poetry in the contempte of eloquence, was in auncient tyme in hygh estimation: in so moche that all wysdome was supposed to be therein included, and poetry was the first philosophy that euer was knowen: wherby men from their child-hode were brought to the raison howe to lyue well, lernynge therby nat onely maners and naturall affections, but also the wonderfull werkes of nature, mixting serious mater with thynges that were pleasaunt: as it shall be mani-fest to them that shall be so fortunate to rede the noble warkes of Plato and Aristotle, wherin he shall fynde the autoritie of poetes frequently alleged: ye and that more is, in poetes was supposed to be science misticall and inspired, and therfore in latine they were called *Vates*, which worde signifyeth as moche as prophetes' (Elyot 1883, I, 120–2). Compare Puttenham 1936, 16–23. In France the group of poets known as the Pléiade considered that the world grossly undervalued poetry, and worked this judgment into their poetic theory in order to justify the esoteric character of their writing (see Clements 1942, 51–77). There are traces of this theory in the *Apology* (see 116/32–3 note).

31   **fallen to be**] declined so far as to become.

p. 82/1   **available**] powerful.

2   **the former**] i.e. horsemanship.

    his] its (i.e. horsemanship's). The form 'its' was not widely used in written English until after 1600; Sidney invariably uses 'his' as the possessive form of 'it'.

3   **silly**] innocent, defenceless.

3–4   **to the defacing of it**] to put it down.

4 **civil war among the Muses**] The nine Muses of Greek mythology were goddesses of learning and the arts. They were therefore the divine patrons both
of poets and of philosophers.

6 **ungratefulness**] ingratitude.

8–10 **first nurse . . . knowledges**] In Sir John Harington's preface to his translation of *Orlando Furioso* (1591) poetry is described as 'the verie first nurse
and ancient grandmother of all learning' (Smith 1904, II, 194). The idea
that the first poets were the earliest philosophers came to the Renaissance
from ancient times. Cicero, *Tusculan Disputations*, I, iii, was taken up by
John Rainolds (Rainolds 1940, 42), and by Thomas Lodge (Smith 1904, I,
77). Compare Agrippa 1569, ch. 49, fol. 63v–64r, and Puttenham 1936, bk
I, ch. 4, 'How the Poets were the first Philosophers'. Sidney's comparison of
poets to nurses, which is a Renaissance commonplace, ultimately derives
from the Greek writer and traveller Strabo (c. 64 B.C.–A.D. 19), who in *Geo-
graphica*, I, 1 and 2, rebutted Eratosthenes's prejudice against the learning of
the ancient poets. Compare Robortello 1548, 4: '[Strabo] makes it clear that
poetry was formerly a kind of philosophy which through its fables gradually
suckled and nurtured men until the time they would be more capable of
understanding matters in philosophy which are most difficult'. On Strabo's
importance in sixteenth-century critical thinking see Spingarn 1908, 24. For
further references see the index to Weinberg 1961, II, 1180; and compare Wills
1958, 76.

10 **the hedgehog**] A fable of the snake and the hedgehog seems to have appeared
for the first time in the fable collection of Lorenzo Astemio, *Hecatomythium*
(1495). It was included in later Aesopic collections such as the popular schoolbook by J. Camerarius, *Fabellae Aesopicae* (Leipzig, 1564), and William Bullokar's *Aesops Fablz* (see *The Works of William Bullokar*, IV, ed. J. R. Turner
(Leeds, 1969), 184–5). Compare **92/5** note.

11–12 **the vipers . . . parents**] A favourite Elizabethan metaphor for ingratitude.
Pliny describes the birth of the viper's brood as follows: 'On the third day
the viper hatches its young . . . and then pushes them out, one a day to the
number of twenty. The last ones become so impatient of their confinement
that they force a way through the sides of the mother and so kill her' (*Natural
History*, X, lxxxii, 2). See also Aristotle, *History of Animals*, V, 34; Plutarch,
Concerning Talkativeness, 12; etc. Allusions to the murderous birth of vipers
were common in the sixteenth century: compare Wilson 1909, 125; Gosson
1974, 103; Daniel (Smith 1904, II, 373); Greville 1938, I, 179; and see Smith
1904, I, 383 note.

12–13 **sciences**] branches of learning.

13–23 **Musaeus . . . Orpheus**] A full account of the ancient poets listed in this
passage was given by Luis Vives in his notes on St Augustine's *Of the Citie
of God* (Augustine 1610, 687ff.). The belief that poetry preceded all other
forms of writing was handed down from ancient times (by e.g. Strabo; see
above note 8–10, and Plutarch, *The Oracles at Delphi No Longer Given in
Verse*), through the Middle Ages (by e.g. Isidore of Seville, *Etymologies*, VIII,
308, 317–18) to the Renaissance, when eulogists of poetry often supplied lists

of ancient poets similar to this one of Sidney's. See Minturno 1559, fol. 13ff.; Scaliger 1617, I, ii, 10 (see below, 31–6 note); Rainolds 1940, 42ff.; and Wills 1958, 56.

13 **Musaeus**] Thought by the Elizabethans to be one of the most ancient Greek poets, a pupil of Orpheus. A body of poems and oracles associated with the Greek cult of Orphism was attributed to him, as was the poem *Hero and Leander* (written in the fourth or fifth century A.D. by a later Musaeus; Marlowe's version of it was published in 1598, and Chapman's translation in 1616).

Homer] remains the most celebrated of ancient Greek poets. His date of birth is unknown: Herodotus thought he lived in the ninth century B.C. Compare Josephus, *Against Apion*, I, 2: 'There is not any writing which the Greeks agree to be genuine among them ancienter than Homer's poems'.

14 **Hesiod**] of Ascra in Boeotia (eighth century B.C.) wrote the *Theogony* (the first surviving account of the origins of the Greek gods) and *Works and Days* (a treatise on agriculture).

15–16 **any writers . . . same skill**] i.e. any writers existed before them who were not also poets.

16 **Orpheus**] legendary Greek poet, to whom a body of 'Orphic writings' were attributed, although they were in fact of a much later date. In classical times he was said to be the son of a Muse, the servant of Apollo, a teacher of the religion of Dionysus and a revealer of sacred mysteries. He became a potent figure in Renaissance thought; see D. P. Walker, *JWCI* 16 (1953), 100–20.

Linus] the teacher of Orpheus, according to Homer (*Iliad*, XVIII, 570). Other legend makes him the son of a Muse by Apollo.

other] plural; the form without -s was common in the sixteenth century.

17 **deliverers**] transmitters.

18 **challenge**] claim.

19 **fathers in learning**] Compare Plato, *Lysis*, 214; Wills 1958, 78.

20 **went before them**] surpassed them.

21 **charming**] influencing by magic; bewitching (compare 84/8 note).

untamed wits] uneducated minds.

21–2 **admiration of**] wonder at.

22 **Amphion**] Said to have built the city of Thebes by moving stones into place through the power of his music. He was 'Jove's son by Antiope', as Vives explains in his notes to Augustine's *Of the Citie of God* (Augustine 1610, 684). 'Pliny saith he inuented Music . . . Amphion built Thebes (saith Solinus), not that his Harp fetched the stones thither, for that is not likely, but he brought the mountaineers, and highland-men vnto ciuility, and to help in that work.'

23 **Orpheus**] Said to be able to mesmerize beasts by playing the lyre. Amphion was often coupled with Orpheus to illustrate the power of music and poetry. See Daniello 1536, 11ff.; Minturno 1559, 15; Wilson 1909, 47; Rainolds 1940,

76 (and see note); Puttenham 1936, 6; Sidney's Third Song in *Astrophil and Stella* (Ringler 1962, 208). The pairing of Amphion and Orpheus best known to sixteenth-century readers was Horace, *Art of Poetry*, 391ff.:

> Orpheus, a priest, and speaker for the gods,
> First frighted men, that wildly lived, at odds,
> From slaughters, and foul life; and for the same
> Was tigers said, and lions fierce, to tame.
> Amphion, too, that built the Theban towers,
> Was said to move the stones, by his lute's powers,
> And lead them with soft songs, where that he would.
> This was the wisdom, that they had of old,
> Things sacred, from profane to separate;
> The public, from the private; to abate
> Wild raging lusts; prescribe the marriage good;
> Build towns, and carve the laws in leaves of wood.
> And thus, at first, an honour, and a name
> To divine poets, and their verses came.
> Next these great Homer and Tyrtaeus set
> On edge the masculine spirits, and did whet
> Their minds to wars[.]
>
> (Jonson 1988, 366–7)

This passage from Horace was also important in suggesting a method of classifying poets adopted by Scaliger (Scaliger 1617, I, ii; see below, 31–6 note).

23–4 **indeed stony and beastly people**] Erasmus, too, suggests that the supposed powers of Amphion and Orpheus over stones and trees referred to their power over 'stony, woodden, and rude men' (Erasmus 1965, 34).

24–5 **Livius Andronicus, and Ennius**] mentioned by Scaliger (Scaliger 1617, I, ii, 10–11) and Horace (*Epistles* II, i, 50–62). Livius Andronicus (c. 284–204 B.C.) was thought to be the first Latin poet, who wrote both tragedies and comedies and made other adaptations from the Greek. Ennius (239–169 B.C.), the greatest of the early Latin poets, was a teacher and a friend of the Scipios (see **105/42ff.** note). Only fragments survive of his work, which included an epic *Annales* on the history of Rome.

26 **science**] knowledge, learning.

26–9 **Dante . . . other arts**] Sidney refers to **Dante** (1265–1321), **Boccaccio** (1313–75), and **Petrarch** (1304–74) as didactic poets and the founders of Italian literature. But he also refers to them as the authors of works of learning (e.g. Dante with *De monarchia*, Boccaccio as commentator and encyclopaedist, Petrarch in his religious and philosophical tracts). He represents the English poets in the same way: Chaucer was highly regarded by the Elizabethans as a moralist, while Gower introduced his *Confessio amantis* (c. 1386) as a work which 'to Wisdom all belongeth'.

28 **fore-going**] precedent.

29 **as well . . . other arts**] both in poetry and in other branches of learning.

30–1 **philosophers . . . under the masks of poets**] See note on lines 8–10 above. The poet's ability to make complex philosophical ideas both comprehensible and attractive was often adduced in Renaissance criticism as providing the ultimate justification for poetry. See Minturno 1559, 13ff., Puttenham 1936, 8–9, and Boccaccio 1930.

durst not a long time] did not dare for a long time.

31 **the masks of poets]** Masks were used by classical actors to indicate the type of character they were representing on stage (see **98/16** note), and may occasionally have been used on the Tudor stage (see Axton 1982, 32). Compare **96/3** note.

31–6 **So Thales . . . hid to the world]** Thales, Empedocles, Parmenides, Pythagoras, Phocylides, Tyrtaeus and Solon were all early Greek thinkers who wrote poetry. In choosing these examples Sidney seems to be following Scaliger's classification of poets (see notes on **82/23** and **86/21ff**.). Scaliger distinguishes (1) 'scientific' poets, such as Empedocles, Nicander, Aratus, Lucretius; (2) poets of moral philosophy, concerned either with politics, such as Solon and Tyrtaeus, or with economics, such as Hesiod; (3) poets concerned with ethics, such as Phocylides, Theognis, Pythagoras (Scaliger 1617, I, ii); compare Minturno 1559, 15. Sidney confines his selection to the 'philosophers of Greece' (**82/30**), who are thought of now as little more than reputations associated with fragmentary passages of early Greek verse. But in the sixteenth century a substantial body of philosophical verse was ascribed to them, collected by Sidney's friend the scholar-printer Henri Estienne in his *Poesis philosophica* (1573). The praise of poetry in Estienne's preface may have influenced Sidney's *Apology* (see *Misc. Prose*, 74.27ff. note). On Estienne's friendship with Sidney, see Duncan-Jones 1991, 77–8, 233.

32 **Thales]** of Miletus (*fl.* 585 B.C.), of whom some anecdotes but no writings survive, was said to have founded the first Greek school of philosophy, and to have composed poems on *Nautical Astronomy* and on *First Causes.*

Empedocles] of Acragas (*fl.* 450 B.C.): philosopher and scientist. Fragments survive of his poems *On Nature* and *Purifications.*

Parmenides] of Elea (*fl.* 475 B.C.): founder of the Eleatic school of philosophy, who handed down his teaching in the form of an epic poem, which survives in fragments.

natural] of the natural world; scientific.

33 **Pythagoras]** of Samos (*fl.* 530 B.C.), highly influential in the fields of mathematics, geometry, and astronomy. Sidney no doubt had in mind a set of moral verses ascribed to Pythagoras, known as the Golden Sayings. But the philosopher seems to have left nothing in writing and to have insisted on secrecy, although his disciples are associated with the composition of the Orphic poetry (see **82/16** note).

Phocylides] of Miletus (*fl.* 560 B.C.): a poet who wrote gnomic couplets which embodied moral 'counsels' or precepts.

34 **Tyrtaeus]** of Aphidnae (*fl.* 670 B.C.): an Athenian (and, according to later tradition, a lame schoolmaster) who inspired the Spartans to victory through his verses.

Solon] famous Athenian legislator and poet (*fl.* 600 B.C.).

policy] politics, statecraft.

35–6 **did exercise . . . highest knowledge**] i.e. used their ability to produce delight in their readers to communicate the most valuable items of knowledge.

36–8 **Solon . . . Atlantic Island**] Solon was said by Plato in the *Timaeus* to have written an epic about the lost continent of Atlantis.

38 **Plato**] (c. 427–348 B.C.), with Aristotle the most respected of the ancient Greek philosophers. He founded the philosophy of idealism, which posited the existence of an invisible eternal world of 'ideas' (see 85/34–43 note) behind the constantly changing and illusory world perceived by the senses. The only access human beings have to the world of ideas is through reason. He wrote down his philosophy in the form of dialogues. Many philosophers of the fifteenth and sixteenth centuries – prominent among them the Florentine Neoplatonists Marcilio Ficino (1433–99) and Pico della Mirandola (1463–94) – considered themselves his disciples.

39–83/4 **And truly . . . Apollo's garden**] That Plato, who condemned poetry, was himself a poet was often maintained by Renaissance writers (see 106/15ff.). See Daniello 1536, 22: 'Plato . . . is esteemed as a poet by all who understand him. There is not one of his Dialogues . . . in which he does not express his conceptions under a fabulous veil'. Compare Minturno 1559, 16; Scaliger, *Poemata* (Geneva, 1591), I, 13. This view of Plato went back to antiquity: see Quintilian, *Institutes*, V, xi, 39; X, i, 81: and compare Rainolds 1940, 74 note. Scaliger's *Poetices* contains a brief, learned account of dialogue as a poetic form (Scaliger 1617, I, iii, 12–13). Plato usually gave some sort of social setting to the philosophical discussions in his dialogues, and this example was followed by the humanists in their use of dialogue form. Plato's *Symposium* has a banquet for its setting (see 83/1), and *Phaedrus* begins with a country walk.

39 **whosoever well considereth**] whoever considers his work carefully.

41–2 **standeth upon**] depends on.

42 **burgesses**] citizens.

43 **rack**] instrument of torture.

44 **poetical describing**] imaginative descriptions of.

p. 83/1 **as**] such as.

2 **delicacy**] delight, pleasantness.

with interlacing mere tales] as well as weaving obvious fictions (into his dialogues).

Gyges' Ring] In Plato's *Republic*, II, 359, Glaucon tells the story of a shepherd called Gyges, who descends into the Underworld, steals a ring which enables him to become invisible, and uses it to win a kingdom. Plato makes a number of references to the ring and its owner, notably in *Phaedrus*, 230B. Sixteenth-century readers would have been familiar with the tale through Cicero, *De officiis*, III, 9.

4   **Apollo's garden]** Sidney may be thinking of the garden of the Muses, who are Apollo's servants in his capacity as god of poetry. The garden is referred to in Plato's *Ion*, 534, as the location of the 'honey-flowing fountains' of poetic inspiration.

5   **historiographers]** historians.

their lips sound of things done] i.e. they speak of actual events.

6   **verity be written in their foreheads]** i.e. truth is (figuratively) written on their foreheads as an advertisement of their honesty. Sidney is using a common idiom ironically (see Tilley, F 590). He may also have in mind the Remmian law of ancient Rome (mentioned by Cicero, *Pro Sexto Roscio Amerino*, XIX, 55), which dealt with the offence of calumny – bringing a charge against anyone while knowing it to be false. One of the punishments for this offence was for the culprit to be branded on the forehead with the letter K (for *Kalumnia*).

7   **fashion and perchance weight of]** form and perhaps substance from.

7–8   **Herodotus . . . Muses]** The *History* of Herodotus of Halicarnassus (484 – c. 406 B.C.), 'the father of history', was divided by later scholars of Alexandria into nine Books, each named after (**entitled . . . by the name of**) one of the Muses.

9–10   **passionate describing of passions]** Sidney frequently uses this rhetorical figure (called paregmenon or polyptoton, meaning 'employment of the same word in various cases') in *Arcadia*, and less frequently in the *Apology*. Compare 85/26–7; 86/19, 39; 88/38; 92/6, 8–9; 94/44; 95/19; 96/43–4; 100/6–7; 102/32; 104/10; 109/16; and 114/6. In writing and commenting on histories, humanists before Jean Bodin made extensive use of evocative description and **long orations** (11).

10   **particularities]** details.

11–12   **long orations . . . never pronounced]** Scaliger suggests that the Roman historian Livy could be described as a poet, since 'Livy and Thucydides insert orations which were never recognized by those to whom they were attributed' (Scaliger 1617, I, ii).

14   **entered into the gates of popular judgments]** i.e. made themselves attractive or comprehensible to the ordinary reader.

15   **passport]** either (1) a written document permitting a person to travel safely to and from a particular country, or (2) a spoken password allowing entry to a restricted area.

15–17   **which in all nations . . . feeling of Poetry]** Cicero observed that 'even barbarians do not dishonour the name of poet' (*Pro Archia poeta*, IX, 18–19), and many sixteenth-century writers develop this theme. See Scaliger 1617, I, ii, 8; Minturno 1559, 9ff.; Spenser 1989, Argument to October. Puttenham notes that 'the American, the Perusine & the very Canniball' use poetry for 'their highest and holiest matters' (Puttenham 1936, 10).

18–19   **In Turkey . . . poets]** Like other sixteenth-century Europeans Sidney took a keen interest in the Turks, whose Ottoman Empire reached as far as Cyprus and Hungary (Sidney visited Hungary in 1573; see Duncan-Jones 1991, 65). Sidney and Languet discussed Turkish affairs in their correspondence, and T. Washington dedicated his *Travels into Turkey* (1585, but probably completed by 1581) to Sidney and his father. The Turks were considered proficient in the arts of war and deficient in all other arts; compare Montaigne, *Essays*, I, xxiv (see also 105/9–15 note). Sidney expresses his admiration for Turkish military discipline in a letter of 1579 to his brother Robert (Pears 1845, 197). For an account of English interest in Turkish affairs at this time see Samuel Chew, *The Crescent and the Rose: Islam and England During the Renaissance* (New York, 1937).

18 **law-giving divines**] an accurate description of Muslim muftis.

19–20 **Ireland . . . devout reverence**] Sidney's father, Sir Henry Sidney, was Vice-Treasurer in Ireland from 1556 to 1559 and held the office of Lord Deputy Governor of Ireland for three terms beginning in 1565. From his childhood onwards Sidney therefore heard a good deal about conditions in Ireland, which he visited in 1576. The powers of the Irish poets were considered dangerous by the English authorities; see John Derricke, *The Image of Ireland* (1581, dedicated to Sidney), fol. 2r–v, and Duncan-Jones 1991, 110. Spenser gives an account of Irish poetry in *A View of the Present State of Ireland*, ed. Andrew Hadfield and Willy Maley (Oxford, 1997): 'no monument remains of her beginning and first inhabiting; especially having been in those times without letters, but only bare traditions of times and remembrances of Bardes' (46). But yet 'it is certaine, that Ireland hath had the use of letters very anciently, and long before England' (47). The bards still flourish, 'whose profession is to set foorth the praises or dispraises of men in their poems or rymes, the which are had in so high regard and estimation amongst them, that none dare displease them . . . For their verses are taken up with a generall applause, and usually sung at all feasts and meetings' (75).

learning goeth very bare] refers (perhaps) both to the poverty of Irish scholars and to the common English description of the Irish as 'bare-arsed rebels'. See Duncan-Jones 1991, 108–9.

20–3 **Even among . . . their gods**] Sidney concerned himself directly with the voyages of English adventurers to the Americas, invested in them, and almost took part in them (see Duncan-Jones 1991, 273–4). His information here comes from Peter Martyr's account of American culture in *Decades*, III, vii, a translation of which was included in Richard Eden's *The Decades of the Newe Worlde* (1555), fol. 125r–v: 'They gyue them selves chieflye to two thynges: As generally to lerne thoriginall and successe of thynges: And particularlye to reherse the noble factes of their graundefathers . . . and aunces-tours aswell in peace as in warre. These two thynges they haue of owlde tyme composed in certeyne myters and ballettes in their language. These rhymes or ballettes they caule *Areitos*. And as owre mynstrelles are accustomed too synge to the harpe or lute, so doo they in lyke maner synge these songes and daunce to the same.' Cook tells us that *areyto* derives 'from Arawack *aririn*, "rehearse", "repeat"' (Cook 1890, 67).

21 **Indians**] inhabitants of the West Indies.

22 **areytos**] see above, 20–3 note.

23 **probability**] probable proof. See **86/10–11** note.

24–5 **their hard dull wits softened and sharpened**] The action of pleasurable learning on the wits or wit (here meaning something like 'natural intelligence') is described in similar terms by Roger Ascham in *The Schoolmaster*: 'a witte in youth, that is not ouer dulle, heauie, knottie and lumpishe, but hard, rough, and . . . somwhat staffishe . . . such a witte I say, if it be, at the first well handled by the mother, and rightlie smothed and wrought as it should . . . proueth alwaies the best' (Ascham 1904, 190–1).

28–33 **In Wales . . . long continuing**] The Sidney family had many Welsh connections. Sidney's father Sir Henry was Lord President of the Marches of Wales from 1559, and his sister Mary married the Earl of Pembroke, so that Sidney had plenty of opportunity to learn about the poetry of the Welsh. He shared an interest in Welsh history with his father, who supported David Powell in his completion of the antiquarian Humphrey Lhuyd's *Commentarioli Britannicae* (*The Historie of Cambria* (1584), dedicated to Sidney). Languet and Sidney discussed Lhuyd's *Britanniae descriptionis fragmentum* (Cologne, 1572; trans. Thomas Twyne as *Breviary of Britaine* (1573)) in their correspondence (Feuillerat 1912–26, III, 85). John Caius (*De antiquitate Cantabrigiensis Academiae* (1568), 21ff.) praises the early British kings for their learning and patronage of the arts.

28 **the true remnant of the ancient Britons**] The Welsh Tudors strengthened their tenuous claim to the throne by claiming descent from the ancient British kings, themselves descendants of the Trojan founder of Britain, Brutus. See Kendrick 1950, esp. ch. 3.

34 **authors**] originators.

35 **stand upon**] appeal to.

35–6 **but even**] only.

38–41 **Among the Romans . . . knowledge**] The classical association of prophecy with poetry was well known in the Renaissance. See Elyot 1883, I, 122, quoted above, note **81/31–82/4**; Minturno 1559, 15; Wills 1958, 54; Puttenham 1936, 7; and Harington (Smith 1904, II, 205), who follows Sidney.

39 **his**] its.

conjoined] associated.

vaticinium] (Latin) a prophecy.

40 *vaticinari*] (Latin) to prophesy.

41 **heart-ravishing**] Sidney coins an epithet which alludes to the false etymology of *vates* as from *vi mentis*, 'with violence of mind'. See Isidore, *Etymologies*, VIII, vii, 3 (*PL* 82, col. 308).

42–3 **chanceable hitting upon**] random selection of.

43 **foretokens**] omens.

44 **Whereupon grew the word of**] from which the phrase . . . is derived.

Sortes Virgilianae] Refers to the custom of opening a copy of Virgil's works at random and applying the passage on which the eye first fell to the particular circumstances of the inquirer. The practice developed in imperial Roman times. See examples in *Sex scriptores historiae Augustae: Life of Emperor Hadrian*, II, 8, *Life of Alexander Severus*, XIV, 5, and *Life of Clodius Albinus*.

p. 84/2 **the Histories of the Emperors' Lives**] Probably refers to the third volume of *Varii historiae Romanae scriptores*, published by Henri Estienne in 1568 (see 82/31–6), which included the *scriptores historiae Augustae* (see 83/44 note). Sidney recommended this volume to his friend Edward Denny in a letter of 1580 (Duncan-Jones 1989, 287–90). See Robert H. F. Carver, 'Sidney's Emperors', *NQ* 239, no. 1 (March 1994), 29–30.

3 **Albinus**] The *Life of Clodius Albinus* by Julius Capitolinus tells how Albinus, brought up in Africa, became governor of Britain. Acclaimed Emperor by his troops in A.D. 193, he was defeated and killed by Septimius Severus at Lyon in 197.

met with] came across.

5 *Arma . . . armis*] A line from the *Aeneid*, II, 314, translated by Surrey as 'Then, as distraught, I did my armure on, / Ne could I tell yet whereto armes availde' (*Poems*, ed. Emrys Jones (Oxford, 1964), 45). According to Julius Capitolinus, Clodius Albinus often used to repeat this line to the other children at school – a sign of his early attraction to war (*Life of Clodius Albinus*, V, 2).

6–7 **a very vain and godless superstition**] Prophecies were regarded with suspicion by the Tudor authorities, and particularly as incitements to sedition. Agrippa discusses the various kinds of prophecy in *Of the Vanitie . . . of Artes and Sciences*; for references, see Hall 1961, 398–400. A prophecy in verse leads to the withdrawal of Duke Basilius from public life in the *Old Arcadia*, with disastrous results (*OA*, 5ff.).

8 **charms, derived of *carmina***] Sidney's derivation is correct. Besides its familiar meaning of 'song', *carmen* (Latin; *carmina* is the plural form) can also mean 'incantation' – a chant with magical power.

9 **those wits**] i.e. the poets.

11 **Delphos**] Delphi, a town in a ravine on Mount Parnassus in Greece, was the site of the most famous temple of Apollo, where the priestess (Pythia) uttered prophecies which were then set down in hexameter verse (the oracular verses at the beginning of the *Old Arcadia* are Delphic: see above, 6–7 note).

Sibylla's prophecies] The original Sibyl was a prophet in early Greek tradition, and the so-called Sibylline oracles formed a large collection of prophetic writings acquired by Rome early in its history, which were often revised and augmented until their destruction in the reign of Augustus. But prophetic materials from various sources, Jewish, Egyptian, and Christian, continued to be accumulated as Sibylline prophecies during the Middle Ages. Among these were the verses on Judgment Day cited in Augustine, *City of God*, XVIII, 23. Allusions are often made to sacred 'oracles . . . in verses' by writers exalting poetry. See Horace, *Art*, 400ff.; Minturno 1725, 31; Rainolds 1940, 42; Puttenham 1936, 7; Lodge, *Defence* (Smith 1904, I, 71).

12 **that same . . . in words**] i.e. that careful counting of the number of metrical feet, and measuring of short and long syllables, in each line of a poem. The sentence may refer to the Neoplatonic theory that the proportions of a poem (its **exquisite observing of number and measure**) correspond in some sense to the proportions of the world which God has created. See D. H. Craig, 'A Hybrid Growth: Sidney's Theory of Poetry in *An Apology for Poetry*', in Kinney 1988, 68.

13 **conceit**] mental conception; invention (in the rhetorical sense of the finding and elaboration of arguments or topics); see **88/4–9** note.

proper to] belonging exclusively to.

15–28 **And may . . . cleared by faith**] As Sidney points out, a number of **great learned men, both ancient and modern** (17–18) believed that David composed the Psalter by the direct inspiration of God. Among these were Jerome, Augustine, Isidore, Bede, and many other writers into the twelfth century; see Ringler's note to Rainolds 1940, 74. The humanists later followed Petrarch in asserting the poetic nature of the Psalms, which came to occupy a special position in the development of Renaissance literature (see below, 22–8 note). In France, translations of the Psalms (especially the version made by Clément Marot) had a profound influence on the work of the Pléiade (see Yates 1947, 44ff.).

19 **interpreted**] translated.

19–20 **songs . . . written in metre**] 'What else is a Psalm but a holy and spiritual kind of composition for singing?' Preface to Part III of Tremellius and Junius's Latin Bible (1607 ed.), fol. 106 (see **86/23–8** note). From early Christian times attempts had been made to analyse Hebrew poetry in terms of classical prosody. Josephus claimed that the songs of Moses were in heroic verse, and that David had composed several kinds of odes and hymns, some in trimeter, others in pentameter (*Antiquities of the Jews*, II, xvi, 4; IV, viii, 8; VII, xii, 3). Jerome thought he had found iambic, alcaic, and sapphic verses in the Psalms similar to those of Pindar and Horace (*Epistles*, LIII, ad Paulinum, in *PL* 22, col. 547). Lodge's *Defence of Poetry*, which repeats Jerome's observations, indicates how writers of the sixteenth century made use of these ideas (Smith 1904, I, 71). Compare Harington (Smith 1904, II, 207) and Puttenham 1936, 9, and see I. Barroway, *ELH* 2 (1935), 66–91. The metre of the psalms continued to be debated until the eighteenth century, when in his Oxford lectures on the *Sacred Poetry of the Hebrews* (1753) Bishop Lowth provided a new analysis which gave impetus to the late eighteenth-century cult of the sublime and the development of romantic poetic prose.

20 **hebricians**] the usual term for Hebrew scholars in the sixteenth century, probably in parallel with 'Grecians' for Greek scholars.

22 **merely**] exclusively.

22–8 **For what . . . cleared by faith**] Sidney's careful setting out of evidence to show that the Psalms are a poem suggests the importance he attaches to the point in the overall argument of the *Apology*. He has argued (1) from etymology (19), (2) from metrical form (20), and now proceeds to argue (3) from 'elocution' (manner of expression). He does so by marking the uses made of invocation (**awaking his musical instruments** (22–23), as in Ps. 57:9); of different voices or speakers (**changing of persons** (23), as in Ps. 2); and of *prosopopeias* (the attributing of speech to that which is not human, as in Ps. 19, or to an absent person, as in Ps. 22:8). A stylistic approach to the scriptures had been developed from one aspect of St Jerome's exegesis by many humanists, especially Erasmus. Tremellius and Junius frequently included literary and rhetorical notes in their Protestant edition of the Bible (see **86/23–8** note). Similarly in Sidney's circle Dudley Fenner, in *The Artes of Logike and Rhetorike* (1584), took most of his examples from Scripture. Sidney's account of the Psalms was remembered; see Henry Peacham, *The Compleat Gentleman* (1634), ed. Gordon (Oxford, 1906), 79–80. But the notion of the Psalms as the ideal poetry was widespread in the sixteenth and seventeenth centuries in England. See Hallett Smith, *HLQ* 9 (1945), 248–71; and Campbell 1959, chs V and VI.

23 **persons**] voices, personas.

prosopopeias] plural of 'prosopopeia' (see 22–8 note).

25 **poesy**] Ben Jonson defined this as the poet's 'skill, or craft of making' (*Discoveries*, Jonson 1988, 445). Sidney regularly gives this meaning to 'poesy' (compare **86/17, 30; 90/42**, etc.), which he carefully distinguishes from 'poetry', the product of this art (**81/30; 82/6, 41**, etc.).

26 **almost**] indeed; here used as intensive.

28 **him**] i.e. David.

30–3 **But they . . . Church of God**] The increased use of the Psalms in public worship was controversial, and was attacked both by radical Calvinists and by their opponents in the Church of England. On the one side, Richard Hooker rebutted the objections of the Puritan Thomas Cartwright to the prescribed use of the Psalter in churches (*Ecclesiastical Polity*, V, 37). On the other, after the publication of Sternhold and Hopkins's *Metrical Psalter* (1562) – which claimed that it was 'allowed to be sung in all churches of all the people together before and after evening prayer, and also before and after sermons' – some opponents of Calvinism objected to what they considered a dangerous popularization of liturgical psalmody. See Jeremy Collier, *Ecclesiastical History of Great Britain* (1708–14), part II, iv, 326, and Horton Davies, *Worship and Theology in England, I, From Cranmer to Hooker, 1534–1603* (Princeton, 1970), ch. 11.

30 **with quiet judgments**] i.e. without prejudice, objectively.

31 **working**] operation; the means by which poetry achieves its **end**.

35–7 **The Greeks . . . 'to make'**] Sidney is following Scaliger 1617, I, i. See 85/17–23 note, and compare Minturno 1725, preface.

36 *poiein*] (Greek) to make.

38   **have met with**] are in agreement with.

    a maker] Compare the beginning of Puttenham's *Arte*: 'A Poet is as much to say as a maker. And our English name well conformes with the Greeke word' (Puttenham 1936, 3). 'Maker' is common in fifteenth- and sixteenth-century. Northern English and Scots; a famous example is the poem 'Lament for the Makaris' by William Dunbar (1460?–1513?). To 'make' is used in the Middle Ages (and in the works of Spenser) for to 'write verse'. Compare Giraldi Cinthio, *Discorsi* (1554), 56 (Gilbert 1940, 270).

38–40   **which name . . . partial allegation**] I prefer to demonstrate the excellence of poetry by showing how it compares in its aims and range with other [arts and] sciences, rather than by making a simple assertion which, coming from me, would be taken to be prejudiced.

41–2   **the works of Nature**] things or events in the physical world (of which Nature is a personification), as opposed to the metaphysical or spiritual worlds. The meaning of 'nature' varies according to context.

41–85/1   **There is no art . . . set forth**] The idea that there is no art which is not a product of 'nature' comes from Aristotle. See *Physica*, II, 2, 194–22, and compare Plato, *Laws*, X, 889. Renaissance writers often invoke this idea; see Castelvetro 1576, 69: 'Art is not a thing different from nature, nor can it pass beyond the limits of nature, but intends to work to the same end as nature'. M.-A. Muret (see 108/36 note) in *Oratio*, xi (introducing the *Aeneid*), approaches poetry as Sidney does, arguing that 'no art is anything but a kind of imitation of nature, for there is no art that does not owe its seeds and principles to nature' (*Opera*, ed. Frotscher (Leipzig, 1834), II, 368). See also Hathaway 1962, 21. Consideration of the relationship between nature and art led to frequent debate on the hierarchy of the human arts. Coluccio Salutati (Salutati 1951, I, iii) discusses the relationship of poetry to the arts of the *trivium* and *quadrivium* (the two parts of the medieval university curriculum; see 85/9–10 note), urging that poetry is an art independent of other arts: 'the principles of all arts are linked with nature and all art imitates nature in such a way that invention is nothing else than a sort of subtle and keen perception of natural operations' (18); but 'the matter of poetry is not anything determinate as is treated in the *real* sciences, but is universal and wide-open, as subject only to the art of words' (20). Minturno begins *De poeta* with a comparison of the poet with the musician, geometer, astrologer, grammarian, orator, lawyer, and philosopher, and returns to these comparisons later (Minturno 1559, 87–100). The Florentine Benedetto Varchi (1503–66), in his *Lezioni della poesia* (2 vols, Trieste and Milan, 1858–9), discussing the branch of learning which best conveys and teaches spiritual perfection, runs through the claims of the speculative and moral philosopher, the lawyer, the rhetorician, the historian, and decides in favour of the poet, 'whom all arts serve' (ii, 576). Sidney is still following Scaliger's line of argument (Scaliger 1617, I, i, 3–6) (see 85/17–23 note).

42   **for his**] as its (i.e. the art's).

43   **actors**] stage performers. This is the first occurrence of the word in this sense cited by *OED*, although Marie Axton notes three earlier occurrences (Axton

1982, 21). The word may have been suggested by Scaliger's phrase (Scaliger 1617, I, i, 6; see below, 17–23 note).

p. 85/1 **Nature will have set forth**] i.e. Nature (as playwright) wishes the actors to perform on stage.

4 **diverse sorts of quantities**] different kinds of measurements.

musician in times] Editions from 1613 onwards read 'tunes' (compare 115/32 and Lyly 1916, 257 note); but 'times' is probably the correct reading. Late medieval musical theory was especially concerned with problems of measuring time; see G. Reese, *Music in the Middle Ages* (New York, 1940), 292–3. For the contrapuntal music of the sixteenth century, in which two or more melodies were set against each other, strict measurement of time was of course a practical necessity.

5 **agree**] go together.

5–6 **thereon hath his name**] gets his name from this (i.e. his dependence on Nature).

6 **standeth upon**] is concerned with.

6–7 **the natural virtues, vices, and passions**] Compare 87/37 note; 91/16. See Sidney's letter to his brother Robert: '"moral philosophy" . . . contains the true discerning of men's minds, both in virtues, passions and vices' (Duncan-Jones 1989, 285).

7–8 **'follow Nature . . . not err'**] Sidney is drawing on Cicero, *De officiis*, I, xxviii, 10. This precept from the Stoic school of philosophy (see 91/3 note) became a Renaissance commonplace. See Haydn 1950, 486ff.

8 **determined**] In legal discourse, 'to determine' is 'to come to a judicial decision'.

8–9 **historian**] This form (the earliest example in *OED* is from Elyot, *Governour*, 1531) was slow to supersede other forms such as 'historiographer' (compare 83/5), 'historician', 'historier'.

9–10 **grammarian . . . rhetorician . . . logician**] These are the scholars who teach or study the *trivium*, the traditional medieval curriculum leading to the B.A. The *quadrivium* was the curriculum leading to the M.A., composed of arithmetic, geometry, astronomy, and music. Together the *trivium* and the *quadrivium* made up the seven liberal arts. Grammar as a discipline was highly regarded by some of the early humanists, but by Sidney's time it was often dismissed as the obsession of pedants; see Rainolds 1940, 78 note. The relationship between logic and rhetoric, both in the Greek and Latin theorists and in the Renaissance, is complex. The most widespread generalization is that rhetoric is the theory of popular communication and logic the theory of learned communication. But Peter Ramus, in whose method of teaching logic Sidney had a lifelong interest (see 81/19 note), blurred the distinction between the two disciplines. Shepherd suggests that Sidney's wording here may reflect his interest in Ramist logic: 'Ramus intended to ground his method in nature; so Invention was taught before Judgment or

Disposition, thus inverting the order in which traditional Aristotelian logic had been taught. The Ramist order, which Sidney seems to accept for both logic and rhetoric, had, however, been the order in which rhetoric had traditionally been taught.' For an account of Ramist logic see Howell 1956, ch. 3.

11 **artificial rules**] general rules from which other verbal artificers or craftsmen may work.

12 **are compassed within the circle of a question**] are limited by the scope and purpose of the questions they answer. Compare the phrase in Sidney's letter to his brother Robert: 'not tied to the tenor of a question' (Duncan-Jones 1989, 292). In writing as a rhetorician or logician one chooses to be limited and circumscribed by the particular rhetorical purpose or logical issue involved. The arts are derived from nature; but in so deriving them one limits them in order to use them for particular kinds of verbal activity. Sidney seems to blur the traditional differences between logic and rhetoric deliberately. Thomas Wilson (following Cicero, *Topics*, XXI) distinguished between 'definite' questions which are 'comprehended within some end' (these are the special province of the rhetorician) and 'infinite' questions, the province of the logician, 'who talketh of things universally without respect of person, time, or place' (Wilson 1909, 2–3). But for Sidney here, as for the Ramists, all issues proceed from the particular (**are compassed within the circle of a question**), and so tend to be rhetorical in character and to pose, in Wilson's term, 'definite' questions. Now that Sidney and the Ramists have absorbed logic into rhetoric, Wilson's 'infinite' questions have to be dealt with by poetry.

13 **weigheth**] considers.

14 **metaphysic**] metaphysician. Pierre de la Primaudaye offers the same simple juxtaposition of physics and metaphysics: 'physike . . . is the studie of naturall things: metaphysike . . . of supernaturall things' (*The French Academie* (English trans., ed. of 1618), i, 72). Compare Bacon's use of the term 'metaphysics' throughout his writings; see *Novum Organum*, ed. Fowler (Oxford, 2nd ed., 1889), 64–8.

15 **the second and abstract notions**] 'Second notion' is a term in logic, defined by Sir William Hamilton (as quoted in *OED*) as follows: 'A first notion is the concept of a thing as it exists in itself . . . A second notion is the concept, not of an object as it is in reality, but of the mode under which it is thought by the mind.' (See also Hathaway 1962, 324–5, on Fracastorius's treatment of 'second intentions'.) Metaphysics is concerned with secondary qualities, which are not in the 'reality' of nature, and are thus entirely mental, and so beyond the physical world (that is, **supernatural**). But, Sidney adds, though metaphysics deals with concepts abstracted from reality, it is from **the depth of Nature** that this abstraction has to be made. The metaphysician is therefore ultimately dependent on nature, like the other practitioners of the liberal arts.

counted] regarded as.

15–16 **supernatural**] above or beyond the physical world (see 15 note).

16 **the depth of Nature**] See *OED* for the uses of the word 'depth' in traditional medieval logic (*s.* depth I. 6).

17–23 **the poet . . . his own wit**] The gist of Sidney's argument is taken from Scaliger 1617, I, i, 5–6. Sidney had clearly read this chapter with care. Parts of it are summarized here:

'Do not all learned men of the academy, law court, or theatre have one object, that is, persuasion? We agree that all discourse teaches. The end of teaching is knowledge (*scientia*). *Scientia* consists either in accepting inescapable conclusions or in recognising general notions. The end of persuasion is some mental or physical action. Fine speaking is only an instrument, a means, not an end. The end is persuasion to action. In deliberations and in judicial cases the speaker reacts to the audience. The opposite happens in demonstration: there the mind of the hearer depends upon the speaker. But in all forms of speaking (or writing), methods and issues overlap: all deal with human life, vices and virtues. In many ways the poet and the philosopher treat their material similarly. Both speak either in their own or in another's person. The philosopher has his interlocutors, the orator his prosopopeias [compare 84/23]; the orator sings somebody's praises and goes on to recount his life; the historian often adds eulogies to his narrative and intersperses it with his own judgments.

'Only poetry embraces all these activities, and as a result it is more outstanding than other arts because all other verbal arts reproduce things as they are, as a sort of picture for the ear [compare 86/19], but the poet produces another nature altogether [compare 85/18–19], and a variety of outcomes as a result, and in this process almost makes himself into another god. For in respect of the things that the Great Artificer established, all other arts and sciences which deal with them are actors or representatives [compare 84/43]. But the science of poetry presents more compellingly an actual appearance of what exists, and also of what does not exist. Indeed this art deals with things not as if it were narrating events from the outside as a reciter might do [compare 111/24–5], but rather as if it were establishing them in their actuality as another god might do. As a result the usual name, poet, seems to have been arrived at not by agreement among men, but rather by natural providence. For the learned Greeks most appropriately spoke of poetry as a sort of making. I wonder that our own ancestors were so perverse [compare 84/37–8], for the word "factor", which expresses the meaning, they preferred to reserve for oilmen and chandlers.'

On the emergence under Neoplatonic influence of the idea of the artist as an imitator of the creative processes of nature, see Panofsky 1968, 47ff., 63ff., 1115ff. But, as Panofsky pointed out later (*Renaissance and Renaissances in Western Art* (Stockholm, 1960), 188 note 3), there was a reluctance in the sixteenth century to claim for the artist anything like the creativity of God. Sidney makes no such claim. Indeed, he is more discreet than Scaliger, or Puttenham: 'if [poets] be able to deuise and make all these things of them selues, without any subiect of veritie . . . they be (by maner of speech) as creating gods' (Puttenham 1936, 4). On the development of the theory of poet as 'creator', see M. H. Abrams, *The Mirror and the Lamp* (New York, 1953), 272–4 and notes. Sidney's account of the 'other nature' is drawn from various sources. He draws on Scaliger, but may also owe a debt to the analysis of the mind given by Fracastorius (see 108/35 note) in his dialogue *Turrius, sive de intellectione*; see Hathaway 1962, ch. 23, 316–28 (from which the following summary is drawn). For Fracastorius, following Aristotle, knowledge derives from the senses. The mind forms images or 'appearances' of external things, and these 'appearances' have a sort of independent existence (compare 34–43 below). From these images the mind makes abstractions (i.e. **second and abstract notions,** 15) of things that cannot be sensed directly, so that a man 'can treat what is separated as if it were joined together, either in place or in subject or otherwise, whereby he makes chimeras and centaurs for himself, and gardens and palaces, and becomes a poet' (quoted Hathaway 1962, 322, from Fracastorius, *Opera omnia* (Venice, 1555), fol. 175v).

18–19 **doth grow . . . nature**] The exact meaning of this metaphor is a little obscure. All texts except Ponsonby have 'grow in effect another nature'. If 'grow into' is accepted then the poet seems to be cultivating himself in the hope of bearing the 'fruit' of virtuous action. If 'grow' is preferred then the poet would seem to be planting a new Nature like a garden in his poetry. But in either case, Sidney's drift is clear enough: that is, a poet's invention enables him to create an alternative world which may have little in common with the world we inhabit. Compare 103/31 note.

20–1 **Heroes, Demigods**] Many of the classical heroes had a god as one of their parents. By **Demigods** Sidney may mean those heroes (such as Hercules) who were granted divine status after death.

Cyclops] One-eyed flesh-eating giants, the most famous of whom was Polyphemus, blinded by the hero Ulysses. 'Cyclops' is now usually singular; Sidney is using the plural of the older form 'cyclop'. See Robertson 1973, 353/9 note.

Chimeras] The original Chimera was a monster with the head of a lion, the body of a goat, and the tail of a dragon. It was killed by the hero Bellerophon. Puttenham thought of '*Chimeres* & monsters' as products of the 'disordered' imagination (Puttenham 1936, 19).

Furies] Supernatural avengers of crime, especially crime against the ties of kinship.

22–3 **not enclosed within the narrow warrant of her gifts**] not dependent on her restricted patronage or authorization ('warrant').

23 **zodiac**] the perfect celestial circle which encloses the world and everything in it. On the zodiac as a symbol of perfection and inclusiveness, see D. J. Gordon in *England and the Mediterranean Tradition* (Oxford, 1945), 116. Sidney was no doubt aware that many Renaissance scholars wrote of God in creation working within the 'celestial zodiac'; see J. Seznec, *La survivance des dieux antiques* (London, 1940), 63ff. A figurative use of the zodiac was developed in the Latin poem (much used as a school text) *Zodiacus vitae* (1534) by Marcellus Palingenius (trans. Barnabe Googe, 1561).

wit] mind.

27 **brazen . . . golden**] In literary tradition the age of brass under the rule of Jove was considered the third age, between the age of silver and the present age of iron. See Ovid, *Metamorphoses*, I, 89ff. The golden age, under the rule of Saturn, was the first and best of all periods; but it was also the future age when humans would return to perfection and become immortal. Compare Virgil, *Eclogues*, IV. Thomas Chaloner uses the phrase 'golden worlde' in his translation of Erasmus's *Praise of Folly* (Erasmus 1965, 44); compare Sidney's allusion to the 'foolish world' which the historian is obliged to reproduce faithfully (94/1).

27 **the poets only**] only the poets.

28–9 **for whom . . . employed**] i.e. just as everything else was created for his use, so Nature seems to have employed her greatest skills in creating him. The idea that God's greatest skills were employed in creating mankind was based on the Bible (see Genesis 1:26ff. and Psalm 8:7–8), and was a favourite topic of Renaissance thinkers. See H. Baker, *The Dignity of Man* (Cambridge, Mass., 1947), esp. 235–40.

30 **know**] find out.

Theagenes] of Thessaly was the lover of Chariclea in the Greek prose romance *Aethiopica*, by the fourth-century bishop Heliodorus (see 87/32 note). The romance was highly thought of in the sixteenth century, and was translated into English by Thomas Underdowne in c. 1569. It was one of Sidney's models for *OA*. See Hoskins 1935, 41, and S. L. Woolf, *The Greek Romances in Elizabethan Prose Fiction* (New York, 1912), 307–8.

31 **Pylades**] the loyal friend of Orestes in Euripides's *Oresteia*, who helped Orestes to avenge the murder of his father Agamemnon, and who married Electra, Orestes's sister. The friendship between the two men became proverbial.

Orlando] Roland, the hero of medieval French romances about Charlemagne and his knights. The Italian form Orlando was made familiar to the sixteenth-century reader by a succession of heroic poems: *Morgante Maggiore* by Luigi Pulci (1432–84), *Orlando Inamorato* by Boiardo (1441–94), and *Orlando Furioso* by Ariosto (1474–1533). One of Sidney's admirers, Sir John Harington, published a translation of *Orlando Furioso* (1591) 'in English Heroicall verse'.

32 **Xenophon's Cyrus**] *Cyropaedia*, by the Athenian soldier, historian, and philosopher Xenophon (c. 444–350 B.C.), is a political treatise based on the fictionalized story of Cyrus the Great, founder of the Persian monarchy. It describes Cyrus as a man who 'excelled all men of his time in goodly personage, gentleness, prowess, liberalitie, wisedome and memorie' (Cooper's *Dictionary* (1565)), and was widely used in the education of sixteenth-century princes such as Edward VI and James VI of Scotland. Xenophon's *Cyropaedia* formed part of the curriculum of Shrewsbury school when Sidney was there. See Duncan-Jones 1991, 27. See also 87/31 note.

32–3 **Virgil's Aeneas**] For Scaliger, Virgil's epic poem the *Aeneid* was the supreme example of the poet's creation of 'another nature' (see above, 17–23 note, and

Scaliger 1617, esp. III, iv, 195). He saw the hero Aeneas as the perfect man (see III, xi, 207), as did many sixteenth-century readers.

33 **jestingly conceived**] taken as a joke.

34 **the one . . . the other**] Nature . . . the poet.

essential] real, as opposed to existing only in . . . fiction.

34–43 **any understanding . . . made him**] This passage is important for an understanding of Sidney's theory of poetry. It also reflects his poetic practice, according to John Hoskins, who says that his 'course was (besides reading Aristotle and Theophrastus) to imagine the thing present in his own brain that his pen might the better present it to you' (Hoskins 1935, 42). In many ways Sidney's theory resembles the Mannerist theory of painting. Whereas for the theorists 'of the Early and High Renaissance nature was the source from which all beauty was ultimately derived . . . for the Mannerists beauty was something which was directly infused into the mind of man from the mind of God, and existed there independent of any sense-impressions. The idea in the artist's mind was the source of all beauty in the works he created, and his ability to give a picture of the outside world was of no importance, except in so far as it helped him give visible expression to his idea . . . Lomazzo and Zuccaro both perfunctorily define painting as the imitation of nature, but . . . both had in mind more particularly the Scholastic idea that art works according to the same principles as nature . . . That is to say, they mean that both painting and nature are controlled by intellect – in the one case human and in the other divine intellect – that both obey certain laws of order . . . The emphasis is on the idea in the artist's mind, which is the proper object of imitation' (Blunt 1940, 140–1; see also Panofsky 1968, 35ff.). In the 1570s Sidney's interest in painting may have brought him into contact with painters developing Mannerism. He could have met the Mannerist painter and theorist Federico Zuccaro during his visit to England in 1575. See Roy C. Strong, 'Federigo Zuccaro's Visit to England in 1575', *JWCI* 22 (1959), 359–60. However, there were other intellectual forces at work in the sixteenth century which could have guided Sidney towards his theory of poetry, notably the work of the Florentine Neoplatonists. 'Each cause which operates by art or intelligence must first of all contain the form of that which it wishes to produce. This form is called by the Platonists the idea or exemplar . . . which is often more perfect and authentic than its realization' (Pico della Mirandola, *Commento*, ed. Garin (Florence, 1942), II, 6, 467–8). Similarly, Ficino in arguing that beauty is incorporeal shows that there is a close correspondence between the originating concept and the final form; see *Commentary on Symposium*, ed. Marcel (Paris, 1956), IV, 4, 173ff. Similar ideas were often expressed in the sixteenth century (compare Scaliger 1617, II, 1, 124–5; Fracastorius 1924 (see **86/44–87/4** note); and Paolo Beni, *In Aristotelis poeticam commentarii* (Padua, 1613), 57ff.), and in relation to writing poetry can be traced back through the Middle Ages to classical times; compare Geoffrey of Vinsauf, *Poetria nova* (*Arts poétiques du XII et du XIII siède*, ed. E. Faral (Paris, 1924), 43–57); Seneca, *Epistles*, 65. But any Florentine Neoplatonic thinking in Sidney was bound to be modified by his own English academic upbringing, which was in part at least Aristotelian, and by the influence of Protestantism, which laid a heavy emphasis on the personal mental act in theology and in worship and so could assimilate without strain elements of the Platonic theory of knowledge. The theology of Sidney's friend Philippe du Plessis Mornay is thoroughly platonized in the text which Sidney began to translate and which was published by Arthur Golding as *On the Treweness of the Christian Religion* (1587). Compare the following passage: 'For as the craftsman maketh his worke by the patterne which he had erst conceyued in his mynde, which patterne is his inward word: so God made the world and all that is therein' (Feuillerat 1912–26, III, 328). In many respects Sidney's thinking about poetry could coincide with rather than derive directly from Mannerist theories of painting. See D. H. Craig, 'A Hybrid Growth: Sidney's Theory of Poetry in *An Apology for Poetry*', in Kinney 1988, 63–7.

34–5 **any understanding**] i.e. anyone with any intelligence.

35 **standeth in**] depends on.

Idea] concept, mental picture. Used by Plato and his followers to mean a pattern or archetype of which individual things are imperfect copies. See above, 34–43 note.

fore-conceit] conception of a thing, existing in the mind before it has been given expression or artistic form. A phrase invented by Sidney.

37 **in such excellency**] as excellently.

38 **wholly imaginative**] existing only in the imagination; contrasting here with **substantially** (39–40). Compare the distinction Sidney makes between *eikastike* and *phantastike*, 104/19–20.

39 **by**] of.

build castles in the air] i.e. daydream.

39–40 **substantially it worketh**] it has a material effect.

41 **a particular excellency**] a single good thing.

43 **that maker**] the poet; in this case Xenophon, who (as sixteenth-century readers believed) wrote the *Cyropaedia* to teach kings their duties (see 85/32 note).

44 **balance**] compare.

p. 86/2 **the heavenly Maker**] God, who made Nature (the physical world), which is itself engaged in creating or making.

that maker] i.e. the poet (or alternatively, Nature).

2–3ff. **who having made man . . .**] Compare Genesis 1:26; Hebrews 2:7, and particularly Psalm 8.

4 **that second nature**] the physical world, which has been imperfect since the Fall of Adam. The 'first nature' was the perfect world as God created it before the Fall. Here again Sidney shares his ideas with the Mannerist painters, who held that man's artistic activity reproduces in miniature the creative process

of God. God produces nature, which in turn has a secondary creative power enabling it to produce **pleasant rivers, fruitful trees, sweet-smelling flowers** (85/25–6). But man with his intellect works in the same way as God worked in creating the world, although on an infinitely smaller scale. Poetry is the product of this Godlike intellectual activity in man. It shows us perfection, which God's original creation would have possessed. For Sidney, the fact that the **second nature** – that is, the world around us – is imperfect constitutes irrefutable evidence of the **fall of Adam** (7), which damaged the whole of creation.

4 **he**] man.

6 **her**] Nature's.

the incredulous of] those inclined not to believe in.

7 **erected wit**] intellect raised up by God to a likeness of his own. The erected wit is what sets man **beyond and over** the rest of God's creation (3). The phrase may also mean that the intellect is capable of raising or erecting itself above the fallen condition in which humanity finds itself.

7–8 **erected wit . . . infected will**] The emphasis in this passage on the corruption of both man and nature recalls the thinking of the Protestant theologian Calvin. Compare the following passages from Calvin's *Institutes*: 'For because formless ruins are seen everywhere, [Paul] says that everything in heaven and on earth strives after renewal. For since Adam by his fall brought into confusion the perfect order of nature . . . the creatures naturally long for the undamaged condition whence they have fallen' (III, xxv, 2). 'All parts of the soul were possessed by sin after Adam deserted the fountain of righteousness . . . the mind is given over to blindness and the heart to depravity . . . From this it follows that that part in which the excellence and nobility of the soul especially shine . . . needs to be healed and to put on a new nature as well' (II, i, 9). 'The will, because it is inseparable from man's nature, did not perish, but was so bound to wicked desires that it cannot strive after the right . . . man's mind, because of its dullness, cannot hold to the right path . . . Yet its efforts do not always become so worthless as to have no effect, especially when it turns its attention to things below. On the contrary, it is intelligent enough to taste something of things above . . . For when the mind is borne above the level of the present life, it is especially convinced of its own frailty' (II, ii, 12–13). Compare this with Sidney's **no small argument to the incredulous** (6). Calvin goes on to show that 'the knowledge of all that is most excellent in human life is said to be communicated to us through the Spirit of God . . . Some men excel in keenness; others are superior in judgment; still others have a readier wit to learn this or that art. In this variety God commends his grace to us . . . For why is one person more excellent than another? Is it not to display in common nature God's special grace, which, in passing many by, declares itself bound to none?' (II, 2, 13–17) This is perhaps what Sidney means when he says that the poet **with the force of a divine breath . . . bringeth things forth far surpassing** [nature's] **doings** (5–6): the divine breath is God's rather than the poet's.

8 **infected will**] corrupt desires.. The coupling of 'wit' with 'will' is commonplace in English writing before Sidney; see for instance the passage in

Ascham's *Schoolmaster* on 'Will' and 'Witte' in children (Ascham 1904, 200ff.).

10–11 **Thus much . . . learning]** This concludes Sidney's argument based on etymology which began at 83/34.

10 **given]** granted.

10–11 **with some probability of reason]** i.e. basing their arguments on probabilities (what was likely) rather than on 'scientific' proof. Ramist logicians held that all human knowledge was based on probabilities rather than certainties.

11 **name above all names]** Compare Philippians 2:9.

12 **ordinary]** straightforward, familiar.

opening] the opening presentation by the counsel for the defence; a legal term.

13 **palpable]** plain.

14 **description]** detailed account (a technical term from logic). Compare 100/24.

15–16 **principal commendation]** the highest praise.

17–20 **Poesy therefore . . . delight]** i.e. Poetry is the verbal representation (in memorable images) of ideas, in order to **teach and delight** (see *Misc. Prose*, 79.35–80.2 note). William Temple in his Ramist *Analysis* of Sidney's *Apology* (Temple 1984) states that this paragraph contains the whole issue (*tota controversia*) of the *Apology*. In this definition Sidney brings together many of the commonplaces of Renaissance literary theory. Aristotle writes in his *Poetics*, I, 1447a: 'Let us consider poetry itself . . . Epic poetry, tragedy, and comedy too, dithyrambic poetry, and most music on the flute and the lyre fall into the general class of invention', and Horace in his *Art* claims that poetry combines the functions of delighting and teaching its readers (*dulce et utile*). On Renaissance theories of imitation, see Greene 1982.

18 *mimesis]* (Greek) imitation.

19 **a speaking picture]** This saying was attributed by Plutarch to Simonides of Ceos (*fl.* 530 B.C.). Plutarch repeats it often in *Moralia*; see *On the Fame of the Athenians*, 3; *How to Tell a Flatterer from a Friend*, 15, and *How the Young Man Should Study Poetry*, 15: 'Realize not only that poetry is articulate painting and painting inarticulate poetry, but learn that we are not only pleased with seeing a beautiful thing but also with seeing a likeness'. See also *Ad Her.*, IV, xxviii, 39; Spingarn 1908, 270, note 1; Smith 1904, I, 342, and note, 386. But in organizing his definition of poetry Sidney follows Scaliger 1617, I, i, 2–6: 'What is called Poesy describes not only what exists, but also nonexistent things as if they existed, showing how they could or should exist. For the whole matter is comprehended in imitation. But imitation is only the means to the ultimate end, which is to teach with delight . . . Poetry and the other arts represent things as they are, as a picture to the ear.' Compare IV, i, 401: 'All discourse consists of idea, image, *mimesis*, just as all painting does: this is what Aristotle and Plato affirm.'

21ff. **three several kinds . . .]** three different kinds [of practitioners]. Sidney's classification of poets is based on Scaliger 1617, I, ii, 10–11 (see Spingarn 1908,

270). Sidney drew on this passage earlier in his argument: see **82/31–6** note. 'Classifying by antiquity there are three ages [of poetry]. First, the primitive, rude and uncultivated age of poetry of which memory leaves only a trace without a name, unless we count Apollo as its originator. Second, a venerable age, the source of Mystery and Theology: among the poets of which time are Orpheus, Musaeus, Linus . . . Of the third age Homer is author and father: Hesiod also belongs here, and others. But if records did not exist you would have thought Musaeus later than Homer, for he shows more cultivation and polish [compare **82/11ff.**] . . . A third kind of classification can be made according to poets' interests, from their subject matter . . . By means of analysis these can be reduced to three principal types. First, the theological poets [Scaliger draws on Boccaccio 1930, XIV, viii, which draws on Augustine, *City of God*, XVIII, 14], such as Orpheus and Amphion whose works were so divine that they are credited with infusing a soul into lifeless things [see **82/16** note]. Secondly, the philosophical poets, which are of two sorts – the natural philosophers, such as Empedocles, Nicander, Aratus, Lucretius, and the moral philosophers, again divisible into kinds – the political philosophers represented by Solon and Tyrtaeus, the poets of social economy by Hesiod, the general moralists by Phocylides, Theognis, Pythagoras [compare **82/31–6** note]. Thirdly, there are those of whom we are now going to speak.' The French poet Ronsard makes a similar threefold classification (*Oeuvres complètes*, ed. Laumonier (Paris, 1914), iii, 149–52; xiv, 5). A. C. Hamilton discusses the ways in which Sidney modifies Scaliger's classifications in 'Sidney's Idea of the "Right Poet"', *Comparative Literature* 9 (1957), 51–9. Wills follows Scaliger closely (Wills 1958, 60ff.). Both Scaliger and Wills make verse writing and didacticisim fundamental to poetry, and so do not need to define the 'right poet' very particularly according to subject matter. Sidney on the other hand has already committed himself to a theory of poetry as the imitation of ideals, and this he proceeds to show will serve to identify the 'right poet'. See **86/44ff.**

23–8 **Such were David . . . holy reverence**] Sidney adds these Scriptural examples to Scaliger's purely classical list. He draws here on the preface to Part 3 of the most highly regarded Protestant Latin translation of the Bible, *Testamenti Veteris Biblia Sacra*, etc., by Emanuel Tremellius and Franciscus Junius (1575–9; often reprinted). On fol. 117 of the 1607 edition, the translators explain that they have grouped certain books of the Bible together with the Psalms and given them the title of the 'Poetic' books because they are metrical, and not written in prose like the rest of the Scriptures (although fine passages are scattered through the prose books too, such as the **Hymns** of Moses (Exodus 15:1–9) and of Deborah (Judges 5)). Metrical writing, they add, is the best way to teach, delight, and move a reader. These books of sacred poetry comprise an attractive summary of the Law and the Prophets, set out succinctly, memorably, and effectively in figurative language and giving the same witness of God as the prose parts of the Bible: expressing the nature of Christ in part of Proverbs, the workings of Providence in Job, God's union with the Church in the Song of Songs, the vanity of human life in Ecclesiastes, and general morality in the second part of Proverbs.

25–6 **Emanuel Tremellius**] A Jew from Ferrara (1510–80), and a great Oriental scholar, he was converted to Protestantism by Peter Martyr, and lived at Oxford from the time of his conversion until the accession of the Catholic Mary I in 1553.

26 **Franciscus Junius**] the Elder (1545–1602): French Protestant theologian who worked with Tremellius at Heidelberg on their new Latin translation of the Bible from the original languages.

27 **the Holy Ghost**] caused the poetic books of the Bible to be written.

28 **a full wrong divinity**] i.e. in a religion other than Christianity.

29 **Homer in his hymns**] The so-called Homeric hymns are verse retellings of Greek legends whose authorship is unknown. They were translated by George Chapman in 1624 as *The Crowne of all Homers Workes*.

30–1 **St James's counsel**] James 5:13: 'Is any among you afflicted? let him pray. Is any merry? let him sing psalms.' On the appeal of psalm-singing see D. Stevens, *Music and Poetry in the Early Tudor Court* (London, 1961), 77ff.

36 **Tyrtaeus, Phocylides**] See 82/33, 34 notes.

Cato] This refers to the *Disticha moralia*, Latin translations of Greek couplets attributed to Cato, published by Erasmus in 1514 and widely used as a school textbook. For its use in the sixteenth century see Baldwin 1944, I, 595–606.

natural] concerned with the natural order.

Lucretius] Roman poet (95–52 B.C.), who wrote *De rerum naturae*, a philosophical poem dealing with the nature of the physical world. Lucretius was often grouped with Empedocles and Lucan by sixteenth-century critics, and was sometimes denied the title of poet. See note on Lucan, 38 below.

37 **Virgil's Georgics**] was a didactic poem on agriculture which continued to be highly regarded as a sou..._ of practical advice and information until well into the eighteenth century. For sixteenth-century opinions on the *Georgics* see Elyot 1883, I, 63, and Sir John Harington (Smith 1904, II, 206–7).

Manilius] a Roman poet in the time of Augustus, wrote *Astronomica*, an astrological poem in five books.

Pontanus] Giovanni Pontano (1426–1503), soldier, statesman, and scholar, viceroy to Ferdinand I, King of Naples, and tutor to his son Alfonso. His high reputation as a Latin poet is reflected in the fact that he is the only post-classical writer in Sidney's list of philosophical poets. Scaliger discusses his poem on the stars, *Urania*, in some detail (Scaliger 1617, VI, iv, 744–9).

38 **Lucan**] Roman poet (A.D. 39–65), who wrote the unfinished epic *Pharsalia* on the wars between Caesar and Pompey. In the sixteenth century a number of critics (including Ronsard and Castelvetro) disputed his claim to be a poet on the grounds that he was basically a historian. They were elaborating on a judgment which can be traced back through medieval scholars to Quintilian (*Institutes*, I, i, 90; see Herrick 1946, 37–8). Sidney refers to this debate when he observes **whether they properly be poets or no let grammarians dispute** (42–3), a sentence which seems to have been suggested by

Scaliger (Scaliger 1617, I, ii, 11): 'Surely the grammarians quibble in their usual fashion when they object that Lucan wrote history'. Compare Smith 1904, I, 336 and II, 196. The sixteenth-century dispute over the poetic status of Empedocles, Lucretius (see above, 36 note), and Lucan was central to the theoretical discussion of whether poetry was to be defined as the writing of verse or the creation of fictions. See Hathaway 1962, ch. 4, 65–80.

38 **who mislike**] whoever criticizes [philosophical poetry].

41 **fold**] linen cloth, used to wrap babies tightly – to swaddle them – thus restricting their movements.

41–2 **this second sort . . . invention**] Philosophical poetry, like historical poetry, is determined by its subject matter rather than by the imagination of the poet. Henri Estienne in the preface to *Poesis philosophica* distinguishes between poetry and philosophical writings in verse which are not really poems. Ben Jonson was giving judgment on the same grounds when he told William Drummond of Hawthornden that du Bartas was 'not . . . a poet but a verser, because he wrote not fiction' (Jonson 1988, 462). Castelvetro is rigorously exclusive in his definition of poetry: 'All works with subject-matter drawn from other arts and sciences are not strictly poetry. In these cases the poet is simply wrapping up other people's work in his own words' (Castelvetro 1576, 28–9). Sidney reverses the metaphor.

43 **grammarians**] Besides studying the relation between words in speech or writing, sixteenth-century grammarians were also concerned with etymology – hence their finicky preoccupation with the precise meaning of 'poet'. On the sixteenth-century view of grammarians as dull pedants, see 85/9–10 note.

44 **right poets . . . ariseth**] true poets, with whom this argument (the *Apology* as a whole) is chiefly concerned. These are the poets who fit Sidney's earlier description of the poet as **disdaining to be tied to any subjection, 85/17.**

44–87/4 **Betwixt whom . . . to see**] Sidney's distinction here between two different kinds of painters and poets is suggested by Aristotle in *Poetics*, ch. XV. See also chs II and XXV. Cicero reiterated the distinction in *Orator*, II, 8–9: 'Nothing can be formed by copying which cannot be made more beautiful than it is when merely sensed by eye or ear: it is achieved by the thought of the mind. So the statues of Phidias, which are of unsurpassed perfection. For in depicting Jove or Minerva the artist did not study one person for a likeness but let many beauties haunt his mind and derived a likeness by using them all.' This belief that particular beauties could be synthesized into a general ideal beauty (usually represented in Renaissance times by the story of the painter Zeuxis depicting Helen (or Venus); see Panofsky 1968, 15ff.) became central to most neo-classical theories of art. Fracastorius (see 108/35 note) develops an argument very similar to Sidney's in his dialogue on poetry, *Naugerius*. Other writers 'are like the painter who represents the features and other members of the body as they really are in the object; but the poet is like the painter who does not wish to represent this or that particular man as he is with his many defects, but who, having contemplated the universal and supremely beautiful idea of his creator, makes things as they ought to be'. These other writers 'imitate particulars, that is make use of the naked thing, but the poet does otherwise – he imitates the simple idea clothed in its beauty, which Aristotle calls the universal' (Fracastorius 1924, 60).

p. 87/1 **such a kind**] the same kind.

2 **meaner**] lesser.

5 **Lucretia**] The story of the Roman wife who killed herself after she had been raped by Sextus Tarquinius – as a result of which the Tarquins were driven from Rome and the Republic established – was retold many times; see Ian Donaldson, *The Rapes of Lucretia: A Myth and its Transformations* (Oxford, 1982). Augustine used it as the basis for a discussion of tragedy and suicide in his *City of God*, I, xviii. It was also a popular subject with Renaissance painters; see the lists in Pilger 1956, II, 386–90. Sidney may be recognizing an idea later adopted by the Mannerists, and articulated by the English painter Nicholas Hilliard in his *Arte of Limning*, that it is the painter's task to show how 'the minde (according to the diuerse affections . . . by reason of the apprehensions both sensible and imaginatiue) dooth diuersly change and alter the bodie with sensible alterations' (ed. P. Norman (Walpole Society, I, 1912), 23).

7ff. **For these third . . .**] Restates the assertions at 85/17ff., a development of Aristotle's discussion of the relation between imitation and verisimilitude (*Poetics*, chs VIII, IX, and XXV).

8 **most properly**] most fully.

9 **range**] echoes **ranging**, 85/23.

9–10 **reined with**] i.e. restrained by. The metaphor returns poetry to the context of horsemanship with which Sidney began his *Apology*.

11 **the first and most noble sort**] i.e. the divine poets discussed from 86/21 to 34.

12 **these**] i.e. the **right poets** who deserve the etymology of 'makers'. Compare 84/35–40.

waited on] honoured, distinguished.

13 **foredescribed**] discussed earlier.

14 **do merely make to imitate**] write exclusively with the intention of producing an imitation. The arrangement **make to imitate . . . imitate . . . to delight and teach . . . delight to move . . . teach, to make them know,** is an example of the rhetorical figure 'climax' (a series of words or sentences of increasing weight and in parallel construction), which Thomas Wilson called 'gradation', 'as though one should go vp a paire of stayres and not leaue till he come to the top' (Wilson 1909, 204). Compare 114/36–8.

15 **take . . . in hand**] undertake, put into practice.

18 **scope**] in archery, a mark for aiming at (see *OED s.v.* 1).

18–19 **want there not**] there is no lack of.

19 **bark**] a common Elizabethan metaphor for 'scoff'.

20   These] the **right poets.**

21–2   **Heroic, Lyric, Tragic . . .**] Sidney identifies eight genres. Sir John Harington
follows him (Smith 1904, II, 209), as does Francis Meres (Smith 1904, II, 319),
and Puttenham jumbles the same list (Puttenham 1936, 25–7). The history of
genre classification is complex; see Alastair Fowler, *Kinds of Literature: An
Introduction to the Theory of Genres and Modes* (Oxford, 1982). The eightfold
classification adopted by Sidney was apparently originated by an obscure
Roman rhetorician, Caesus Bassus, who was quoted in the popular com-
pendium on poetry (written before 1540) of L. G. Gyraldus, *Historia poet-
arum tam Graecorum quam Latinorum* (Basel, 1545), 87. The division is based
on Horace, *Art*, 73–85, who defined epic, elegy, iambic, comedy, tragedy, and
lyric in terms of their versification (for iambic, see below, 97/33 note). In lines
86–98 Horace showed how the different verse forms of comedy and tragedy
suited their different material. In *Satires*, I, x, and *Epistles*, II, ii, he gave further
hints for classifying poetry. Quintilian (*Institutes*, X, 1) dealt with the genres
of Latin poetry: heroic, elegy, satire, iambic, lyric, tragedy, and comedy; he
does not seem to acknowledge the Latin poets as writers of pastoral, or the
Greeks as writers of satire. Sidney's list is traditional. Though he classifies by
subject matter he retains elements of Horace's concern with versification;
hence the appearance of iambic as the name of a kind (see 97/33 note).
Sixteenth-century critics usually assemble their lists of genres from several
sources, such as Horace's account, and those of Aristotle (who divides poetry
into epic, tragedy, and comedy (*Poetics*, I)) and of the fourth-century grammarian Diomedes (who classified according to the speaker in the poetic
narrative; see Curtius 1953, 440ff.). The heterogeneity which resulted from
this eclecticism is particularly marked in Scaliger, who devotes most of book
I of his *Poetices*, in 57 chapters, to a bewildering number of kinds beginning
with pastoral (Scaliger 1617, ch. 4). Benedetto Varchi in his Florentine lectures arranged the eight genres (heroic, tragic, comic, lyric, elegiac, satiric,
pastoral, epigrammatic) in a descending order of importance (*Lezioni della
poesia*, II, 701). Sidney here does the same thing. In his detailed examination
of the genres (97/1ff.) he begins with pastoral, the 'lowest' (97/15), and
moves upwards to the 'Heroical . . . the best and most accomplished kind'
(99/37–8). His only innovation is the high place he gives to lyric, which he
sets above tragedy in the poetic hierarchy.

25   **numbrous**] metrical; a term perhaps coined by Sidney. On the evidence of
the *OED* it would seem that the words 'number', 'numbrous' and 'numerous' belonged to the critical vocabulary of the new English poetry associated
with Sidney and Spenser (see *OED* number, *sb.* 17; numbrous, 2; numerous,
5).

26–7   **but an ornament and no cause**] merely decorative, and not essential to.
Compare 39ff. below. Sidney's statement here follows from his insistence that
it is the matter of the imitation – the example offered to the reader – which
defines poetry. For the critical discussion on metre in Italy in the late sixteenth century, see Hathaway 1962, ch. 6, 87–117.

28   **versified**] wrote in verse.

NOTES TO PAGE 87 ♂♀ 149

28 **many versifiers**] See 86/41–2 note for the hesitation of some learned critics as to whether fact-tellers like Lucan and Empedocles could be called poets. Throughout medieval times verse was taken as the sure sign of poetry. But critics from classical times onwards distinguished good practitioners of the art from bad, and the bad were often denied the title of poet. See Horace, *Satires*, II, i, 28, and Quintilian, *Institutes*, X, i (with reference to Cornelius Severus). Scaliger, although he considers verse essential to poetry (see 101/26–7), discriminates between 'those who can attain but little glory, since they recount simple stories in verse and are called merely versifiers; and those who gain for themselves the help and patronage of the Muses by whose spirit they find out what escapes the others, and are called poets' (Scaliger 1617, I, ii, 6). Similarly, Elyot writes in *The Governour*: 'They that make verses, expressynge therby none other lernyngye but the craft of versifyeng, be nat of auncient writers named poetes, but onely called versifyers' (Elyot 1883, I, 120). Compare Puttenham 1936, 3.

29 **Xenophon**] see 85/32 note.

31 **as Cicero saith**] in *Epistles to his Brother Quintus*, I, i, viii, 19: 'The Cyrus by Xenophon is not drawn according to historical accuracy but in the likeness of a model ruler, in whom the writer associates supreme dignity with outstanding friendliness. With good cause our great Scipio Africanus never let the book out of his hands. In it nothing is omitted which has to do with the office of a loving and temperate ruler.' The *Cyropaedia* was admired for the same reasons in the Renaissance: see Castiglione 1928, Thomas Hoby's preface; Elyot 1883, I, 84 and II, 104; and 85/32 note.

absolute] perfect.

32 **heroical poem**] Spenser, in his letter to Raleigh about *The Faerie Queene*, assumes that *Cyropaedia* is a poem in prose (Spenser 1980, 737). Francis Meres extracts this passage on Xenophon and Heliodorus from the *Apology*, and adds: 'So Sir P. S. writ his immortal poem, *The Countess of Pembrooke's Arcadia* in Prose; and yet our rarest Poet' (Smith 1904, II, 315–16).

Heliodorus] See 85/30 note. Scaliger recommends the *Aethiopica* as a brilliantly constructed epic: 'I consider that this book should be very carefully read by the epic poet and that he should set it before him as his most excellent model' (Scaliger 1617, III, xcv, 332).

sugared] sweet (sugar was a rare and valuable commodity). A common epithet of praise in the sixteenth century as applied to speech and poetry.

33 **Theagenes and Chariclea**] see 85/30 note.

35 **a long gown maketh an advocate**] the robe of office makes the lawyer. The phrase may be a Protestant variation on the old proverb 'the cowl does not make the monk', but the change also invokes the form of the *Apology*, which is that of a legal speech.

37 **feigning notable images**] inventing of striking examples.

what else] whatever.

feigning . . . what else] C. M. Dowlin, 'PS's Two Definitions of Poetry', *MLQ* 3 (1942), 573–81, sees in this stress on the imitation of virtues and vices the influence of Plato, and quotes the *Republic*, 598D–E, 600E, 603B, etc. Aristotle, on the other hand, conceives of poetry as the imitation of action. But there seems no reason to look for a direct reading of Plato here, when in the sixteenth century Scaliger, among others, discussed the problem of 'whether a poet teaches morals or actions' (Scaliger 1617, VII, 832; see Hathaway 1962, ch. 5, 81–6). Scaliger argued that the poet depicts actions so that we may be stimulated to emulate the good actions and reject the bad. 'Action' is the mode of presenting what is to be taught; the moral 'attitude' (*affectus*) is what we are taught. In a story, the action described is an exemplification of the attitude we ought to acquire, or an instrument by means of which this attitude is to be acquired (this applies not only to tragedy but to all kinds of poetry). In life, on the other hand, 'action' is what we consider to be our final objective, and our 'attitude' is simply the condition in which we act. Sidney at 91/16 speaks again of the virtues and vices and passions of man as the subject of poetry; but he always assumes that poetry aims to do more than merely delineate moral attitudes – it aims to move men to action.

38   **note**] distinctive characteristic.

39   **senate**] law-making assembly.

40   **fittest raiment**] most appropiate clothing.

      matter . . . manner] subject-matter . . . style, technique.

      passed all in all] were superior to everyone else in every way. See *OED s.* all A.8.d.

41   **table talk**] informal conversation at mealtimes.

42   **chanceably**] at random.

      peizing] weighing, considering.

42–4   **peizing . . . subject**] i.e. carefully considering the proper position of every syllable in every word so as to convey accurately the moral value or social status of their chosen subject. This justification of verse, that it enables one to write with greater precision, control, and dignity, was to become a tenet of the neo-classical poets. Sidney's contemporary Vauquelin de la Fresnaye described verse as a means of clarifying thought and of making the structure of an argument more compact, although he used the examples of Heliodorus (see 85/30 note) and Montemayor to prove that verse was not essential to poetry (see *L'Art poétique*, publ. Pellissier, Paris, 1885, I, i, 87ff.). Compare Pope, preface to the *Essay on Man*.

p. 88/1   **weigh**] analyse.

      this latter sort] the third sort (see 86/44ff.).

1–2   **to weigh . . . his parts**] Here Sidney explains his procedure in the next stage of his argument, the Confirmation (see Introduction, p. 32). He announces that he will analyse the third sort of poetry by using two of the 'places' or headings from the art of logic, that is, (1) its **works** – the way it operates – and (2) its **parts** or constituent elements.

2 **his . . . his]** its . . . its.

3 **anatomies]** dissections.

4 **sentence]** In an earlier legal sense, 'the decision of the court', not merely the penalty imposed.

4–9 **This purifying . . . capable of]** This sentence introduces the most important passage in the *Apology* on the methods and aims of poetry (see *Misc. Prose*, 82.11–16 note, from which these observations are taken). The arguments are derived from the art of logic (for his interest in logic see **82/19** note). Every branch of learning, Sidney implies, must necessarily make use of the methods of logic, but only the art of poetry is capable of using these methods successfully; **learning**, which Sidney also calls the **purifying of wit** (that is, the refining of the intellect), was commonly divided into the three parts of logic. These three parts are here termed **conceit** (the ability to find ideas and arguments), **judgment** (the ability to put them in order) and **memory** (the ability to store them for future use). See below, 4 and 5 notes, for other meanings of these words. The triad of memory, judgment, and conceit occurs also in Spenser's House of Alma, *Faerie Queene*, II, ix, stanzas 49ff.; compare Wilson 1909, 31. Bacon writes: 'Intellectus or Understanding seems to be the generic term including Memory, Imagination, and Reason' (*Novum Organum*, ed. Fowler (Oxford, 2nd ed., 1889), 18). Bacon like Sidney relates the three divisions of the understanding (or wit) to the three parts of learning: 'The parts of human learning have reference to the three parts of man's understanding, which is the seat of learning: history to his memory, poesy to his imagination, and philosophy to his reason' (Bacon 1974, 67). On this division Bacon's whole scheme for the advancement of learning is based.

4 **wit]** understanding or intellect (compare **81/4**, **82/21**, **83/25**, **85/23**, etc.). Sidney often sets it against the 'will' or appetite (compare **86/7–8**).

  memory] Sidney lays unusual emphasis on the art of memory throughout the *Apology* – which is where he differs from the Ramists, who had no great interest in memory. See note on **102/4**; and *Misc. Prose*, 192.

  enabling] strengthening.

5 **judgment]** intellectual evaluation (compare **90/37**, 41, etc.).

  enlarging] meant 'liberating' as well as 'making larger'.

  conceit] the activity of the mind in forming notions or concepts about things; imagination (compare **84/13**, **90/34**, **93/2**, **95/6**, **99/27**). In other contexts the word could mean concept, the product of conception (compare **95/9**, **100/23–4**, **103/34**, **114/27**, **115/21**). For the full range of meaning in the sixteenth century see *OED s.* conceit, concept, conception; and see W. Rossky, 'Imagination in the English Renaissance: Psychology and Poetic', *Renaissance Studies* 5 (1958), 49–73.

6 **end]** purpose, goal.

7–8 **final end . . . perfection]** According to Plato, the aim of all learning is to achieve full knowledge by escaping from imprisonment in the flesh (*Phaedo*, 82–3; *Republic*, VII). Similarly for the twelfth-century theologian Hugh of St Victor (author of *Didascalion*) the supreme purpose of all human learning is to restore the integrity of human nature after the Fall; and for Dante, in his letter to Can Grande on the *Divine Comedy*, 'Briefly the end . . . is to rescue those who live in this life from their condition of misery and to guide them to the state of blessedness.' In this view of learning, as Erasmus observed in *The Praise of Folly* (Erasmus 1965, 126–8), Christians agreed with the Platonists. It became a cardinal principle with Renaissance writers; see Vives 1931, introduction, cliii–clvi; Bacon 1974, 3: 'the mind of man by nature knoweth all things, and hath but her own native and original notions (which by the strangeness and darkness of this tabernacle of the body are sequestered) again revived and restored'; Milton, *On Education*: 'The end then of learning is to repair the ruins of our first parents by regaining to know God aright, and out of that knowledge to love Him.' Many literary critics argued that the goal of poetry was 'beatitude': see Scaliger 1617, VII, ii, 830, and B. Varchi, *Lezioni della poesia*, II, 576. See also G. W. O'Brien, *Renaissance Poetics and the Problem of Power* (Chicago, 1956), 41ff.

8 **degenerate]** (as a result of the biblical Fall).

clayey lodgings] bodies (made of clay, according to Genesis).

9–16 **This . . . Mathematics]** Sidney may possibly be alluding to the account of the psychological origins of the different branches of learning given by the Spaniard Juan de Dios Huarte in his *Examen de ingenios* (1575; trans. R. Carew, 1594). Huarte divided the intellect into three parts, as Sidney does (see 4–9 note) – memory, judgment, and conceit – and went on to show how the dominance of one of these faculties in a man inclined him towards a particular branch of knowledge.

10 **formed impressions]** prejudices.

this felicity] i.e. the attainment of the highest possible perfection.

13 **persuading themselves to be]** convincing themselves that they would be.

the causes of things] See Erasmus 1965, 77, on philosophers who 'expounde the causes of thunder, of wyndes, of eclipses, and suche other inexplicable thynges, nothyng doubtyng, as if they had crepte into natures bosome, or were of counsaile with the Goddes'.

14 **natural and supernatural philosophers]** natural philosophers (roughly equivalent to modern scientists) and metaphysicians; see 85/14 note.

14–15 **admirable delight]** amazing pleasure.

15 **certainty of demonstration]** Mathematics is the one branch of learning which demonstrates certainties; all other branches, according to the Ramists, discover only what is probable (see 86/10–11 note).

16 **scope]** aim (compare 87/18 note).

18 **essence]** being. See 89/1 note.

balance] the heavier of two weights in a pair of weighing scales, as in the phrase 'balance of opinion'. **by the balance of** means 'on the evidence of'.

18–33 **But when . . . all the rest]** This passage recalls the influential treatise by Cornelius Agrippa, *De incertitudine et vanitate scientiarum et artium* (1530; trans. James Sanford, 1569, as *Of the Vanitie and Uncertaintie of Artes and Sciences*), which 'attacks the vanity of scientists who seem to affirm truths and fail to achieve self-knowledge' (*Misc. Prose*, 82.28–83.9 note).

19–20 **the astronomer . . . ditch]** Compare Sidney's *Astrophil and Stella*, 19:

> . . . like him that both
> Lookes to the skies, and in a ditch doth fall.
> (Ringler, 174, lines 10–11)

Plato tells the anecdote of the philosopher and astronomer Thales (see **82/32** note) falling into a well in *Theaetetus*, 174. The story was often repeated (compare Cicero, *De divinatione*, II, 30) as well as being applied to other philosophers. Erasmus applies it to Diogenes (*Apophthegmes*, I, 17), and Agrippa to Anaximenes as well as Thales (Agrippa 1569, fol. 43v). See Rainolds 1940, 83 note; and D. W. Robertson, *A Preface to Chaucer* (Princeton and Oxford, 1963), 273, for medieval allusions.

21 **mathematician . . . crooked heart]** Compare Seneca (*Epistles*, 88): 'You know what makes a straight line; what does that avail you if it does not teach you how to go straight in your life?', which is versified by Sidney's friend and biographer Fulke Greville in *A Treatie of Human Learning* (Greville 1938, I, 162). In Seneca's epistle the passage leads to the conclusion that all arts and their individual aims are subordinated to an 'architectonic' art, that is, the art which pursues the greatest common good (see A. E. Mallock, ' "Architectonic" Knowledge and Sidney's *Apologie*', *ELH* 20 (1953), 181–5; *Misc. Prose*, 82.28–83.9 note; and below, 23 and 25 notes). Seneca's epistle discusses the uncertain value of the liberal arts when divorced from the practice of virtue, which is one of the points that Sidney is making here (compare 31–3).

22 **opinions]** 'Opinion' was often used in the sixteenth century to mean personal prejudice, as opposed to 'judgment', which is founded on reason.

23 **serving sciences]** subordinate branches of learning. The phrase wittily plays on 'liberal arts', which derives from the Latin *liber*, free – the opposite of serving. Earlier Sidney has shown how the arts and sciences are limited in intellectual scope by reason of their dependence on particular aspects of nature (**84/41–85/16**). Here he shows their moral limitations, by arguing (as Seneca does in epistle 88; see above, 21 note) that they can only prepare the mind for virtue, they cannot give it. Sidney now follows the argument at the beginning of Aristotle's *Ethics* (I, 1–2). First Aristotle observes that all arts and sciences aim at some end or goal. 'Now since there are many actions, arts and sciences, it follows that there are many ends. Of medicine the end is health; of shipbuilding, a ship; of generalship, victory; of economy, wealth. But in those cases where several arts combine (as, for instance, under horsemanship is comprised the art of making bridles and all other horse furniture; and this and the whole art of war is comprised in generalship; and other arts combine together in the same way) – in all these, the ends of the chief arts [the architectonic arts; see 21 note] are more to be sought than the ends of the subordinate arts, because for the sake of the former, the latter are pursued . . . If therefore there is some end . . . which we seek for itself, and if we seek for other things on account of this . . . it is evident that this must be . . . the greatest good . . . This it would seem must be the end of that

which is the chief and master science of all [the architectonic art]; and this seems to be the political science, for it directs what arts should be cultivated by states, what individual people should learn . . . This end must be the highest good of man.' This doctrine of following a guiding principle in both thought and action, in **well-doing** as well as in **well-knowing** (27), was characteristic of Sidney, as Fulke Greville claimed when he wrote that Sidney devoted 'both his wit and understanding' to the task of making 'himself and others, not in words or opinion, but in life and action, good and great; in which architectonical art he was such a master, with so commanding and yet equal ways among men, that wheresoever he went, he was beloved and obeyed' (Greville 1986, 12). See also Rice 1958, 163ff. On the advocacy by Italian critics of poetry as an architectonic study serving the highest good of humanity, see Weinberg 1961, I, 28ff.

23 **private end**] particular purpose.

25 *architectonike*] (Greek) the master-art (or, as Sidney calls it, **mistress-knowledge** (24–5)) which draws together all the arts and sciences.

    stands] consists.

26 **in the ethic and politic consideration**] i.e. as a moral and social being.

27–31 **even as the saddler's . . . a soldier**] This passage counters Plato's argument in *Republic*, X, 600E, that every member of the ideal republic ought to practise a single craft for the good of the state, and that poets and painters, who are jacks of all trades and masters of none, have nothing to offer their fellow citizens except inadequate imitations of things (such as saddles) which have been better made by specialist craftsmen (such as saddlers). Sidney argues that poets serve the same purpose as saddlers, which is to promote **virtuous action** (31–2), but that they achieve this purpose more effectively than exponents of any other art or craft. His examples of the saddler, the horseman and the soldier once again remind the reader of the discussion of horsemanship which opens the *Apology*. See also 23 note above.

27 **next end . . . farther end**] immediate purpose . . . ultimate purpose.

29 **faculty**] discipline.

    the horseman's to soldiery] i.e. the horseman's objective is to serve the more important discipline of the soldier.

    soldiery] military science.

31 **ending end**] ultimate purpose.

34 **show we**] let us demonstrate.

36 **moral philosophers**] thinkers concerned with ethics. Sidney's '**speaking pictures**' (see 90/42) of the moral philosopher and the historian recall similar caricatures in Erasmus's *Praise of Folly* and Agrippa's *Of the Vanitie . . . of Artes and Sciences*. His use of technical terms from the arts of logic and rhetoric evokes both the endless splitting of hairs and the tedium of the philosopher's way of teaching (see *Misc. Prose*, 83/18 note).

38 **rudely clothed**] The excessive squalor and shabbiness cultivated by certain philosophical sects – notably the Cynics and Stoics (for the latter see below,

91/3 note) – was notorious. Compare Boccaccio 1930, 34. M.-A. Muret, *Oratio*, iv (*Opera*, I, 144), refuses to allow philosophy to come into disrepute because philosophers are said 'to live in filth and squalor, with patched clothes, always unwashed, always unshaved, always uncombed'.

39–40 **with books . . . names**] i.e. their books attack self-advertisement, yet advertise their authors. The sentence recalls Cicero, *Pro Archia poeta*, XI, 26: 'These same philosophers set their own names even upon the books in which they condemn the pursuit of glory.' Compare *Tusculan Disputations*, I, xv, 34.

40 **sophistically . . . subtlety**] using devious arguments to attack deviousness. In the sixteenth century 'subtlety' is often opposed to 'simplicity', which is defined by Elyot in the *Governour*: 'Trewely in euery couenaunt, bargayne, or promise aught to be a simplicitie, that is to saye, one playne vnderstandinge or meaning betwene the parties . . . And where any man of a couaytous or malicious minde will digresse purposely from that simplicitie . . . this in myne opinion is damnable fraude' (Elyot 1883, II, 220–1).

41–2 **casting largesse . . . of**] generously scattering.

42 **definitions**] According to Abraham Fraunce, 'that which declareth what a thing is' (*The Lawiers Logike* (1588), fol. 60r). See 89/1 note below, and compare 90/38, 95/13–14.

divisions, and distinctions] In logic, the parts and successive refinements of a definition. Thomas Wilson explains the relationship between definition and division: 'As a definition therefore doth declare what a thing is, so a deuision sheweth how many thinges are contained in the same' (*Rule of Reason*, fol. 14v). A distinction distinguishes between a thing and its non-essential qualities or properties – between a rose, for instance, and its redness (see Sister Miriam Joseph, *Shakespeare's Use of the Arts of Language* (Columbia, 1949), 314ff.).

42–3 **interrogative**] a rhetorical question which implies that the speaker expects his or her listeners either to agree or to disagree strongly (from Latin *interrogatio*).

44–89/7 **and teacheth it . . . societies**] Here Sidney goes through a simplified but traditional list of the parts or 'places' of logic in order to demonstrate how moral philosophy **teacheth what virtue is**: definition, causes and effects, opposites, agents, etc. (see below, notes on 89/1, 2, 3, and 4). Compare Wilson 1909, 23, 113, and Cicero, *Topics*, II–V. Aristotle in *Ethics* proceeded in this way: from the definition of virtue in book I, through the causes and instruments of virtue to the examination of social virtue in later books.

p. 89/1 **delivering forth his very being**] i.e. defining its essence. 'For Aristotle one defined a term by stating the *essence* of the object that it names (this statement is called the *definition*). The essence of a thing is that property which makes it the type of thing it is and not some other type of thing.' *The Encyclopedia of Philosophy*, ed. Paul Edwards (London and New York, 1967), V, 71.

2   **his enemy, vice**] This is definition by contrary – identifying the opposite of the thing being defined.

3   **his . . . servant, passion**] Passion here is virtue's instrument or agent: what virtue uses to manifest itself.

   cumbersome] obstructive, interfering.

4   **the generalities which containeth it**] the class or genus to which the subject under discussion belongs.

   containeth] The use of a singular verb with a plural noun is common in Elizabethan English.

   specialities] particulars; the different kinds of virtue which are identified by the process of 'division' (see 88/42 note).

6   **little world**] the microcosm. According to Elizabethan thinking, man is made in the contracted, and the physical universe in the expanded, image of God.

8ff.   **The historian**] Sidney reduces the historian to little more than an opinion-ated antiquarian. Complaints against the partisanship of local or national historians go back to ancient times. Compare Josephus, *Against Apion*, I, 3–5, on the contradictions, uncertainties, and prejudices of the Greek historians. Bitter political rivalries were also widespread among sixteenth-century historical writers. Defenders of history argued that even if histories did not always give the facts they could still give examples from which men could learn; compare Elyot 1883, II, 398ff. (quoted in 91/8ff. note); Amyot, preface to Plutarch's *Lives* (see 90/9–10 note); Montaigne, *Essays*, I, xx.

9   **authorizing himself . . . upon**] using as authoritative support.

11   **much ado**] considerable difficulty.

12   **accord**] reconcile.

   partiality] bias, prejudice.

12–14   **better . . . runneth**] Compare Descartes, *Discours de la méthode* (ed. T. V. Charpentier, Paris, 1881), 49, who is also discussing history: 'When one is too curious about things that took place in centuries gone by, one usually remains remarkably ignorant of what takes place in this.'

15   **novelties**] new things, news, gossip.

16   **a tyrant in table talk**] dominating the conversation at mealtimes.

   in a great chafe] in a rage.

18–19   ***testis . . . vetustatis***] Misquoted from Cicero's *De oratore*, II, ix, 36: 'History indeed is the witness of the ages, the light of truth, the life of memory, the governess [in the sense either of teacher or ruler] of life, the herald of antiquity.' The phrases were widely used. See Elyot 1883, I, 82; *Amiot to the Readers*, in North's *Plutarch*, I, 16; Fenton, *Certaine Tragicall Discourses* (1567; dedicated to Sidney's mother), introd. R. L. Douglas (London, 1898), I, 3. Jean Bodin discusses the phrase *magistra vitae* in the preface to his *Methodus ad facilem historiarum cognitionem* (1572).

19 **disputative**] 'academic' in the dismissive modern sense of 'slightly unreal'.

21 **Marathon**] where the Athenians defeated the Persian invaders in 490 B.C.

22 **Pharsalia**] or Pharsalos, where Caesar defeated Pompey in 48 B.C.

   Poitiers] where the Black Prince captured the French King John II in 1356.

   Agincourt] the site of Henry V's famous victory over the French in 1415.

23 **only**] alone.

24 **Old-aged experience**] the experience of old people or of ancient times.

   goeth beyond] can either mean 'is better than' or 'outmanoeuvres', 'defeats by strategy' (see *OED s.* beyond, B.2.d).

   fine-witted] subtle-minded; over-ingenious.

26–7 **the guide . . . the light**] Cook 1890 notes that the antithesis is sharpened if the Latin *dux* and *lux* are borne in mind.

28 **allege**] cite.

28–9 **conferring . . . by**] comparing . . . with. Ponsonby reads 'confirming'.

30 **the credit of**] their trust in.

   Brutus] This is the Marcus Brutus (85–42 B.C.) of Shakespeare's *Julius Caesar*, a committed republican who took part in the conspiracy to kill Caesar. Plutarch in his life of Brutus records that he spent his time before the battle of Pharsalia studying history.

   Alphonsus] Alfonso V of Aragon and I of Naples and Sicily reigned 1416–58. He was a great patron of the arts (see J. Burckhardt, *Civilization in the Renaissance of Italy*, III). The French historian Jacques Amyot (1513–93) describes how Alphonsus cured himself of sickness by having history read out to him: 'That Prince so greatly renowmed in Chronicles for his wisedome and goodnesse, . . . being sore sicke in the citie of Capua, when his Phisitions had spent all the cunning that they had to recouer him his health, and he saw that nothing prevailed: he determined with him selfe to take no mo medicines, but for his recreacion caused the storie of Quintus Curtius, concerning the deedes of Alexander the great, to be red before him: at the hearing whereof he tooke so wonderfull pleasure, that nature gathered strength by it, and ouercame the waywardness of his disease.' North 1895, I, 17–18. Sidney made extensive use of Amyot's discussion of history, which occurs in the preface to his translation of Plutarch's *Lives* (itself translated into English by Thomas North in 1579). See Elizabeth Story Donno, ' "Old Mouse-eaten Records: History in Sidney's *Apology*', in Kay 1987, 147–67.

31 **maketh a point**] comes to a full stop.

32 **the one . . . the other**] philosophy . . . history.

   precept] theoretical instruction.

33 **question**] proposition, motion in a debate. The *Apology* takes the form of an academic oration, but this paragraph more than any other recalls the actual circumstances of a university debate.

   standeth for] is posed to.

33–4 **the highest form**] the top class.

34 **moderator**] chair of an academic debate.

carry] win.

36 **serving sciences**] see 88/23 note.

37–8 **the poet . . . the historian and . . . the moral philosopher**] represent the three traditional disciplines in liberal studies. See Quintilian, *Institutes*, X, i. Amyot compares the three (see North 1895, I, 10–11, quoted in 90/9–10 note).

39–40 **For as for the divine . . . it is ever to be excepted**] Because as for theology . . . it must always be left out of consideration (that is, in disputes over which is the most valuable branch of learning. Sidney means that theology is so far superior to the other branches of learning that there can be no doubt of its pre-eminence). Sidney's position is like Bacon's, who rejected religious considerations in the study of the physical universe and insisted that reason should be used strictly for secular purposes. To do otherwise was to encourage fanciful philosophy as well as heresy; see *Novum Organum*, I, lxv and lxxxix. But he accepted that the study of physical nature could give humanity some faint idea of the nature of God; see *De augmentis scientiarum*, ch. III. Stephen Gosson, like Sidney, left religious considerations out of his *School of Abuse* 'because they [i.e. poets and corrupt dramatists] are not able to stand vppe in the sighte of God: and sithens they dare not abide the field, where the word of God dooth bidde them battayle, but runne to Antiquities . . . I haue giuen them a volley of prophane writers' (Gosson 1974, 99). Sidney's explanation for his omission of religious considerations from the *Apology* rebuts Gosson's claim that poets are moral cowards.

40 **scope**] aim, target (compare 87/18 note).

41–2 **passing . . . themselves**] being superior to all other disciplines in their own areas.

42 **And for the lawyer**] Sidney here explains why he has left the study of the law out of the competition between branches of learning which he has set up in this paragraph. His explanation resembles that of Amyot, who compares the usefulness of history and poetry (concluding, unlike Sidney, that history is the superior discipline), and goes on to say that history 'doth thinges with more grace and modestie than the ciuill lawes and ordinances doe: bicause it is more grace for a man to teach and instruct, than to chastise or punish' (North 1895, I, 11). Compare Boccaccio 1930, 21–32, and see Osgood's notes.

jus] the law (Latin).

43 **justice the chief of virtues**] This was Aristotle's opinion. Compare *Ethics*, V, 1: 'Justice is perfect virtue . . . In a proverb we say, "In justice all virtue is comprehended." And it is more than any other perfect virtue because it is the exercise of perfect virtue; and it is perfect because the possessor of it is able to exercise his virtue towards another person and not only in reference to himself.' The proverb quoted by Aristotle was adopted by Cicero (*De officiis*, II, xi, 38), and often repeated in political writing of the sixteenth

century. See Castiglione 1928, 272, and *Mirror for Magistrates*, ed. Campbell (1938), 65.

44 **rather *formidine poenae* than *virtutis amore*]** Through fear of punishment rather than love of virtue. From Horace, *Epistles*, I, xvi, 52–3: 'Oderunt peccare boni virtutis amore / Tu nihil admittes in te formidine poenae' (Good men hate to sin through love of virtue; but you will not allow yourself to sin from fear of punishment). Lodge uses this couplet in a similar way in his *Defence of Poetry* (Smith 1904, I, 81). The argument that virtue cannot be enforced through law appears frequently in sixteenth-century debates on religious freedom, such as Thomas Starkey's *Dialogue between Cardinal Pole and Thomas Lupset*, written c. 1536–8 (EETS, E.S. 12 (1871), 206); and the letter from the printer to the reader in Thomas Blennerhasset's *A Revelation of the True Minerva* (1582; Scholar's Facsimiles and Reprints, New York, 1941), which insists that 'the politike lawes of any common weale' cannot 'beate downe sinne' because 'the bodie cannot be brought to obey anie lawe except that the working of conscience bee the cause thereof'. Blennerhasset was a member of Sidney's circle.

to say righter] to speak more accurately.

p. 90/1 **he]** a man.

3 **him]** the lawyer.

3–4 **maketh him honourable]** gives him status.

to stand in rank with] to have the same status as.

these] the poet, the historian, and the moral philosopher.

5 **naughtiness]** wickedness.

6 **cabinet]** private chamber.

7 **manners]** morals.

8 **breed it]** cultivate it.

9–10 **The philosopher . . . example]** For these distinctions in the sixteenth century see Spingarn 1908, 20, and Smith, I, 389; but Sidney is adapting *Amiot to the Readers* on history. 'For it is a certaine rule and instruction, which by examples past, teacheth us to iudge of thinges present, and to foresee things to come: so as we may know what to like of, and what to follow, what to mislike, and what to eschew. It is a picture [compare 23] which (as it were in a table) setteth before our eies the things worthy of remembrance that haue bene done in olde time by mighty nations, noble kings and Princes, wise gouernors, valiant Captaines, and persones renowmed for some notable qualitie . . . These things it doth with much greater grace, efficacie, and speede, than the bookes of morall Philosophie doe: forasmuch as examples are of more force to moue and instruct, than are the arguments and proofes of reason, or their precise precepts, bicause examples be the very formes of our deedes, and accompanied with all circumstances. Whereas reasons and demonstrations are generall, and tend to the proofe of things, and to the beating of them into vnderstanding: and examples tende to the shewing of them in practise and execution bicause they doe not onely declare what is to be done, but also worke a desire to doe it, as well in respect of a certaine naturall inclination which all men haue to follow examples, as also for the beautie of vertue, which is of such power, that wheresoever she is seene, she maketh her selfe to be loved and liked' (see 94/44–95/3 note and 99/33ff.) (North 1895, I, 10–11). Sidney follows Amyot in arguing that the philosopher provides only precept, and the historian example, but both of them halt (11) – that is, walk on crutches – since they have only one leg each.

12 **thorny argument**] The humanists often called academic arguments or problems *spinosus*, thorny; and the literary critics of the sixteenth century often comment on the aridity of philosophical language compared with that of poetry. See Castelvetro 1576, 29; Daniello 1536, 19; Minturno 1559, 39; and Smith, I, 6 and 67.

the bare rule] the basic principle set down without supporting examples.

hard of utterance] obscurely expressed.

12–13 **misty to be conceived**] difficult to understand.

13–14 **wade in him**] i.e. immerse oneself in the study of philosophy.

15 **standeth so upon**] is so much concerned with.

17 **wanting**] lacking.

18–19 **particular truth . . . general reason**] compare 92/12ff. note.

20 **draweth no necessary consequence**] does not lead to any certain conclusions.

20–1 **less fruitful doctrine**] less effective teaching method.

24 **presupposeth**] imagines.

so as] so that.

25–6 **an image . . . description**] Sidney is making a distinction between different kinds of verbal composition similar to the distinction he made earlier between 'the meaner sort of painters' and the superior sort who have 'no law but wit' (see 87/1–4). Here he distinguishes logicians who supply 'accidental definitions' which merely assign the various inessential qualities and circumstances to things – **their shapes, colour, bigness, and particular marks** (30–1) – from writers who present the vivid 'conceit' or idea of a thing, the concentration of a thought into an image. Belief in the primacy of the sense of sight in learning processes was upheld by Plato (*Phaedrus*, 250d), Horace (*Art*, 180–2), and Cicero (*De oratore*, III, xl, 161), and was often reasserted in the sixteenth century. See Jean H. Hagstrum, *The Sister Arts* (Chicago, 1958), 68ff., and Robinson 1972. Compare Elyot 1883, I, 45: 'Finally euery thinge that portraiture may comprehende will be to him delectable to rede or here. And where the liuely sprite, and that whiche is called the grace of the thyng, is perfectly expressed, that thinge more persuadeth and stereth the beholder, and soner instructeth hym, than the declaration in writynge or speakynge doth the reder or hearer.'

27 **but a wordish description**] a merely verbal account.

28 **soul**] all the powers of the mind, intuitive and rational.

29 **outward things**] the physical world (as opposed to the mental or spiritual).

29–30 **an elephant or a rhinoceros**] These animals were traditionally believed to be enemies. Cooper in his *Dictionary* defines a rhinoceros as 'A beaste enemie to the Elephant, and hath an horne in his snout bending upward'. In 1515 the German artist Albrecht Dürer published a famous woodcut of a rhinoceros, the details of which he drew from travellers' tales and from his own imagination, and this woodcut – which Sidney may well have seen – remained the basis of representations of the animal into the eighteenth century. See F. J. Cole, 'The History of Albrecht Dürer's Rhinoceros in Zoological Literature', in *Science, Medicine, and History (Essays Written in Honour of Charles Singer)*, ed. E. Ashworth Underwood (London, 1953), I, 337–56. Sidney would also have been familiar with *imprese* or emblems, copied by his associate Abraham Fraunce from originals by Paolo Giovio, showing an elephant and a rhinoceros (see Duncan-Jones, 'Two Elizabethan Versions of Giovio's Treatise on *Imprese*', *English Studies* 55 (1971), 120–1).

30 **who**] whoever.

exquisitely] precisely.

31 **bigness**] size.

particular marks] distinguishing features.

31–2 **architecture**] architect, derived through French *architecteur* from Medieval Latin *architector*, see *OED s.* architector. Alternatively architecture may mean 'structure' (see *OED* architecture *s.* 3 and 5), in which case it is the same speaker (**who** at line 30) who describes both the animals and the palace.

34 **inward conceits**] imagination.

lively knowledge] knowledge derived – or seeming to be derived – from experience.

36–7 **grow . . . to**] develop.

37 **judicial**] rational.

so no doubt] This is the consequence clause required by the opening **For as in outward things** (29). The sense of the passage is: just as a picture is more effective than a verbal description, so the vivid examples offered by the poet are more effective than the theoretical principles laid down by the philosopher.

38 **virtues, vices**] compare 85/6–7.

replenisheth . . . poesy] i.e. Poetry brings the imagination and judgment into active play on matters which would otherwise lie inert in the memory. Compare 88/4–9 note.

40 **grounds**] basic principles.

42 **figured forth**] presented in visual form.

speaking picture] compare 86/19.

43 **Tully taketh much pains**] Here begins a section on the effectiveness of poetry in teaching its readers about virtue and vice: love of country, the nature of anger, etc.

Tully] Marcus Tullius Cicero (106–43 B.C.), the great Roman orator and statesman, whose prose style was admired to the point of adulation by many sixteenth-century latinists (see 114/1–6 note). His writings contain many examples of patriotism taken from Greek and Roman history; see for example *De officiis*, I, xxiv, 83–4; xlv, 159–60; III, xxiv, 93; xxv, 95; xxvii, 100; *De oratore*, I, xliv, 196–7; *De finibus*, III, 64.

p. 91/1 **Anchises**] the father of the hero Aeneas in Virgil's *Aeneid*. The episode referred to occurs in *Aeneid*, II, 634.

1–3 **Ulysses . . . Ithaca**] Ulysses stayed with the nymph Calypso in the island paradise of Ogygia for seven years, but longed to return to his homeland, Ithaca. His laments occur in Homer's *Odyssey*, V, 149ff. and 215.

3 **Anger . . . a short madness**] See Horace, *Epistles*, I, ii, 62, and Seneca, *De ira*, I, 1. A very familiar tag throughout the Middle Ages.

the Stoics] The Stoic school of philosophy was founded by Zeno at Athens, c. 315 B.C. Its tenets – especially those of the rejection of the outer world and the pursuit of inner virtue – were adopted by the Roman philosopher and playwright Seneca (c. 4 B.C.–A.D. 65) and by the philosopher-emperor Marcus Aurelius (161–80), both of whom were much admired in the sixteenth century.

4 **Sophocles . . . stage**] refers to the tragedy of *Ajax* by the Greek tragedian Sophocles (496–406 B.C.). This tells the story of Ajax after he has been driven mad with jealousy when the Greeks decide to award the arms of Achilles to Odysseus (Ulysses) instead of to him. In fact, Ajax's frenzied attack on sheep is reported rather than seen on stage (*Ajax*, 1061). Sidney may have known the play from Scaliger's translation of it into Latin (Duncan-Jones 1989, 222).

5–6 **Agamemnon and Menelaus**] brothers, the kings of Mycenae and Sparta respectively. Agamemon was the commander of the Greek forces in the Trojan War; Menelaus was the husband of Helen of Troy, over whom the war was fought.

6 **familiar**] intimate.

7 **the schoolmen**] scholastic philosophers of the Middle Ages; academics who taught in 'schools' or lecture-halls.

genus and difference] Two aspects of a thing's essence which were examined by logicians as part of the process of *definition* (see 88/42, 89/1 notes). 'The essence of a thing is that property which makes it the type of thing it is and not some other type of thing. The essence has two aspects: the *genus* is that which is predicable [i.e. can be said] . . . of other kinds of things as well, and the *differentia* is that which is possessed essentially only by things of one type . . . and not by things of any other type. Thus, in "Man is a rational animal" the genus is "animal", and the differentia is "rational" ' (*The Encyclopedia of Philosophy*, ed. Paul Edwards (London and New York, 1967), v, 71).

8ff. **wisdom and temperance in Ulysses and Diomedes, valour in Achilles . . .**] Lists of exemplary figures like this were common in sixteenth-century texts dealing with similar topics. Compare Castiglione 1928, 70: 'What minde is so fainte, so bashfull, and of so base a courage, that in reading the actes and greatnes of Cesar, Alexander, Scipio, Annibal, and so many other, is not incensed with a most fervent longing to be like them[?]' See also Elyot 1883, II, 398ff., in praise of history: 'Admytte that some histories be interlaced with leasynges [i.e. lies], why shulde we therefore neglecte them? sens the affaires there reported no thynge concerneth us, we beyng thereof no parteners, ne therby onely may receyue any damage. But if by redynge the sage counsayle of Nestor, the subtile persuasions of Ulisses, the compendious grauitie of Menelaus, the imperiall maiestye of Agamemnon, the prowesse of Achilles, and valiaunt courage of Hector, we may apprehende any thinge wherby our wittes may be amended and our personages be more apte to serue our publike weale and our prince; what forceth it though Homere write leasinges?' (With this passage compare Sidney's argument at 92/22ff.) Elyot takes his examples from Homer's epic on the Trojan war, the *Iliad*, while Sidney's examples are probably taken from post-homeric accounts of the Trojan war, although it is impossible to be certain which accounts he was using.

8 **Ulysses**] (Greek, Odysseus) fought on the Greek side in the Trojan war. He was famous for his **wisdom** and cunning. He conspired with **Diomedes** to steal the Palladium (a statue of Athene on which the luck of Troy was supposed to depend) from the besieged city.

Diomedes] one of the Greek heroes in the Trojan war. He showed **temperance** in refraining from punishing his wife for her unfaithfulness when he returned home.

9 **Achilles**] the greatest of the Greek heroes in the Trojan war, the protagonist of Homer's *Iliad*. He was regarded by many sixteenth-century readers as exemplary of virtue; George Chapman dedicated his translation of the *Seven Books of the Iliads* (1598) to the Earl of Essex as the 'most honoured now living instance of the Achillean virtues'.

Nisus and Euryalus] followers of the Trojan hero Aeneas, protagonist of Virgil's epic the *Aeneid*. They were close friends who died trying to defend each other during a sortie from the Trojan camp in Italy; see *Aeneid*, IX, 176ff., 433ff.

10 **an apparent shining**] a visible splendour.

11–13 **Oedipus . . . Agamemnon . . . Atreus . . . the two Theban brothers . . . Medea**] are all subjects of Greek tragedy, but were probably best known to Sidney and his readers from the tragedies of Seneca, translated into English between 1559 and 1567. (But Sidney may have known the Greek tragedy of **Medea** through a contemporary Latin translation; see below, 13 note.)

11 **Oedipus**] became king of Thebes, accidentally killed his father and married his mother, despite all his efforts to avoid this fate, which was prophesied by an oracle. On discovering his crimes he blinded himself and went into exile.

His story was dramatized by the Greek tragedian Sophocles in *Oedipus Tyrannus*, and by Seneca in *Oedipus*.

11 **Agamemnon**] (see above, 5–6 note) was the subject of tragedies by Aeschylus and Seneca. On returning home after the Trojan war he was given a hero's welcome, but was murdered soon afterwards by his wife Clytemnestra and her lover.

12 **Atreus**] Agamemnon's father, and subject like him to a curse placed by the gods on the descendants of Pelops. His wife Aethra slept with his brother Thyestes, for which Atreus served Thyestes's children to him at a banquet; hence Sidney's allusion to Atreus's **self-devouring cruelty**. The story is narrated in Aeschylus's *Agamemnon*, 1568ff., and in Seneca's tragedy of the same name.

13 **the two Theban brothers**] Eteocles and Polynices, the sons of Oedipus, succeeded to the throne of Thebes after Oedipus went into exile. They agreed to rule Thebes in alternate years, but Eteocles, who ruled first, refused to hand over the government to Polynices when his time was up. In response Polynices organized an expedition against Thebes, and the two brothers killed each other. The story is told in Aeschylus's tragedy *Seven against Thebes* and in Seneca's *Thebais*.

the sour-sweetness of revenge] 'Revenge is sweet' was a sixteenth-century commonplace (see Tilley, R 90). Sidney here transforms the saying into an oxymoron or condensed paradox. Compare 98/38.

Medea] on being deserted by Jason, whom she had helped to win the Golden Fleece from Colchis, avenged herself on him by killing their children and poisoning his new bride. The story was told by Euripides in his tragedy *Medea*, which was translated by George Buchanan (see 108/36–7 note) and published by Henri Estienne (see 82/31–6 note) in 1567. Seneca also wrote a *Medea*.

14 **the Terentian Gnatho**] Gnatho was a character in *The Eunuch*, a comedy by the Roman playwright Terence (c. 185–159 B.C.). His name became proverbial for a parasite or sycophantic hanger-on.

Pandar] Pandarus was the go-between who brought the lovers together in Chaucer's poem *Troilus and Criseyde* (the most celebrated of Chaucer's works in the sixteenth century). The word 'pandar', meaning 'go-between' or 'pimp' in Elizabethan English, derives from Chaucer's Pandarus.

15–16 **all virtues, vices, and passions**] compare 85/6–7 note.

16 **in their own natural seats**] i.e. in the parts of the body where, according to sixteenth-century anatomists, the humours which give rise to the **passions** are situated.

laid to the view] displayed, as a sixteenth-century anatomist displayed the parts of the body when performing a dissection.

17 **see through**] understand.

18 **determination**] conclusion reached after an academic debate.

19 **feigned**] fictional.

Cyrus in Xenophon] see 85/32 note.

20 Aeneas] see 85/32–3 note and 99/41–100/9.

21 the way of] the method used in.

Sir Thomas More's *Utopia*] The Latin text of *Utopia*, by Sir Thomas More (1478–1535), was first printed at Louvain in 1516. Ralph Robinson's translation appeared in 1551 and More's collected works in English and Latin in 1557 and 1563. More's text was widely held to depict an ideal commonwealth, and this view was reflected in some prefatory verses attached to Latin editions of *Utopia* from 1518 onwards, and included in Robinson's translation, which punningly converted Utopia, meaning 'no place', into Eutopia, meaning 'good place'. Both of Sidney's sixteenth-century editors print **Eutopia** here.

22–3 the fault of the man and not of the poet] Sidney's reservations about More's *Utopia* presumably derive from More's political and religious standpoint; he was executed by Henry VIII for opposing the reformation of the English church. In the dedication to his translation of *Utopia* Ralph Robinson makes a distinction similar to Sidney's between More's literary achievements and his personal shortcomings: 'it is much to be lamented of all . . . that a man of so incomparable wit, of so profound knowledge, of so absolute learning, and of so fine eloquence was yet nevertheless so much blinded, rather with obstinacy than with ignorance, that he could not or rather would not see the shining light of God's holy truth in certain principal points of Christian religion' (More 1985, 2). The Protestant historian Jean Bodin disapproved of the political doctrine underlying *Utopia*, and Sidney may have shared this disapproval. Chapter 6 of Bodin's *Methodus* (1572) begins with the complaint that the true nature of a commonwealth has never been investigated except by a few authors (and More is named), and these authors have been preoccupied with creating ideal commonwealths – fictions unfounded on rational experience. Bodin proceeds to refute what he sees as More's theory, that supreme authority in a commonwealth could be invested in more than one organ of state. Thomas Wilson praises More and his *Utopia* in somewhat ambiguous terms when he discusses 'feined narrations and wittie inuented matters' which can 'help wel to set forward a cause, and haue great grace in them . . . *Luciane* passeth in this point: and Sir Thomas More for his *Eutopia*, can soner be remembered of me, then worthely praised of any, according as the excellencie of his inuention in that behalfe doth most iustly require' (Wilson 1909, 199).

23 patterning] i.e. producing a blueprint for.

24 absolute] perfect.

26 regular] by rules.

30–1 *Mediocribus . . . columnae*] From Horace, *Art*, 372–3: 'But neither, men, nor gods, nor pillars meant, / Poets should ever be indifferent' (Jonson 1988, 368). That is, 'indifferent' or mediocre poetry is rejected by everyone, including the booksellers (whose wares were displayed in Rome on pillars).

34 Certainly, even our Saviour Christ] This introduces the supreme evidence that poetry can teach even the highest spiritual truths by means of examples.

That Christ's parables were poetic had been recognized by some medieval writers (see J. Pépin, *Mythe et allégorie* (Paris, 1958), 252–9) and was generally accepted during the Renaissance; see Boccaccio 1930, 49, and note, 166, citing Petrarch as well as Augustine; and Minturno 1725, Dedication. Bacon describes the parables as 'divine poetry' (Bacon 1974, 68).

35 **commonplaces**] 'A commonplace was a general argument, observation, or description a speaker could memorize for use on any number of possible occasions' (Lanham 1968, 110).

36 **Dives and Lazarus**] The story of the rich man (known as Dives from the Latin for 'rich man') who refuses to help the beggar Lazarus and is punished for it by being consigned to hell, is told in Luke 16:19–31.

37 **discourse**] narrative.

the lost child and the gracious father] The parable of the Prodigal Son – the young man who asks his father for his inheritance, spends it all and returns to his father to ask for help and forgiveness – is told in Luke 15:11–32. It was widely used by writers of poetry and prose fiction in Sidney's time; see Helgerson 1976. Sir John Harington follows this passage closely (Smith 1904, II, 205–6).

38 **through-searching**] all-seeing, penetrating; a term invented by Sidney.

estate] condition, status (an ironic comment on Dives's obsession with his 'estate' while he was alive).

39 **in Abraham's bosom**] i.e. in heaven.

constantly] continually, often.

40–1 **me seems**] it seems to me.

41 **prodigality**] wasteful extravagance.

41–2 **turned to envy a swine's dinner**] The prodigal son, who found employment as a swineherd after he had frittered away his inheritance, was reduced to such desperation during a famine that he longed to eat the food supplied to the pigs in his charge.

43 **historical acts**] actual events.

p. 92/3–4 **But the poet . . . right popular philosopher**] Compare the cancelled passage from *OA* quoted in 115/30–1 note, and Sir John Harington (Smith 1904, II, 199). Plutarch developed the idea of the poet as popular philosopher in *How the Young Man Should Study Poetry*. The idea was well known in the Middle Ages (see Curtius 1953, ch. 11, 203–13), and was a commonplace with sixteenth-century writers. Smith 1904, I, 389, quotes Minturno 1559, 38–40, beginning: 'Yet the people are to be taught and instructed in virtue, not by the precepts of the philosophers, but by examples of the poets, not historians . . . Poets should feign and set out such fables as will please people.' See also Clark 1922, 110–15.

5 **Aesop's tales**] Latin versions in verse or prose of the fables ascribed to the Greek slave Aesop (who was said to have lived in the sixth century B.C.)

remained the first reading books in children's formal education right through the Middle Ages, and indeed up to the nineteenth century in England. See Baldwin 1944, I, 607–40. Their moral usefulness, especially for those with little learning, was always recognized; see Quintilian, *Institutes*, V, xi, 1; Elyot 1883, I, 56. Richard Rainolde in *The Foundacion of Rhetorike* (1563) argues that Aesop's fables 'in effect containe the mightie volumes and bookes of all philosophers in morall preceptes, and the infinite volumes of lawes stablished' (sig. B1v).

5–6 **stealing under**] disguised beneath.

6 **formal tales of beasts**] tales ostensibly about animals. See *OED s.* formal, 2.c. Aesop's fables were not exclusively about animals (Rainolde describes the different sorts of fables in *The Foundacion of Rhetorike*, sig. A2v); but narratives in which animals acted and spoke like humans were often referred to as Aesop's fables.

more beastly than beasts] Compare 82/23–4 note and 83/9–10 note.

7 **hear . . . dumb speakers**] The wordplay is characteristic of Sidney. See 1/27, etc.

10 **images of true matters . . . not . . . fantastically or falsely . . . done**] Compare 104/19–20 note.

12ff. **Aristotle**] See *Poetics*, IX, 1451b: 'the poet's function is to describe, not the thing that has happened, but a kind of thing that might happen, i.e. what is possible as being probable or necessary. The distinction between historian and poet is not in the one writing prose and the other verse [compare 9/16] – you could put the work of Herodotus into verse, and it would still be a species of history. It consists really in this, that the one described the thing that has been, and the other a kind of thing that might be. Hence poetry is something more philosophic [*philosophoteron*, 13] and of graver import [*spoudaioteron*, 13] than history, since its statements are of the nature of universals [*katholou*, 15], whereas those of history are singulars or particulars [*kathekaston*, 16]. By a universal statement I mean one as to what such or such a kind of man will probably or necessarily say or do – which is the aim of poetry, though it affixes proper names to the characters; by a singular statement, one as to what, say, Alcibiades did or had done to him.' The meaning and implications of this passage were often discussed in Renaissance criticism. See Hathaway 1962, part 2, and 132–4 for bibliographical information.

12 **his discourse of poesy**] The *Poetics*, first printed in 1536, is a late work of Aristotle's which deals mainly with tragedy.

determineth] gives judgment on (compare 91/18).

13–16 *philosophoteron . . . spoudaioteron . . . katholou . . . kathekaston*] Sidney glosses these Greek terms accurately.

15–20 **His reason is . . . this or that**] See above, 12ff. note.

16 **the universal consideration**] things in general.

19 **imposed**] fictional.

Alcibiades] Athenian general (c. 450–404 B.C.), noted for changing sides for his personal advantage. He figures in two of Plato's dialogues.

20–1 **Thus far Aristotle . . . full of reason**] An acknowledgment of Sidney's debt to Aristotle's thinking on artistic matters (although it is not certain that Sidney knew the *Poetics* at first hand). Sidney's wording is by no means as respectful as that of Scaliger, who speaks of Aristotle as 'our director, the perpetual dictator of all good arts' (Scaliger 1617, VII, ii, 1, p. 858).

22ff. **For indeed, if the question . . .**] Sidney's argument goes: If history were to be equated with truthfulness, then it could be said to be superior to poetry; but two points must be considered. (1) Men require not simply a *statement* of truth; they need to *accept* truth to make it a basis for action. (2) In any case, history does not provide a statement of truth in relation to the whole structure of things; it can provide only isolated and often insignificant detail. Thus Sidney takes up a position against the new school of historians emerging at the end of the sixteenth century. Jean Bodin, for instance, asserted that history was basically *vera narratio*, a true narrative (*Methodus*, ch. I); this Sidney would deny. And Bodin's *Methodus* (Paris, 1566) rests on the fundamental assumption that much of human history has been influenced by things outside human control (that is, by climate, geography, etc.). Sidney rejects this as a form of determinism which gives 'that which we call fortune' (93/6–7) excessive power over human affairs.

24ff. **Vespasian's picture right . . .**] Compare Aristotle, *Poetics*, XV, 1454b, on the need for a portrait painter to improve on the appearance of his sitter. On Renaissance attitudes to this problem see Ronsselaer E. Lee, 'Ut pictura poesis: the Humanistic Theory of Painting', *Art Bulletin* 22 (1940), 197–269, esp. 203ff.; and Blunt 1940, 14ff. and 88ff. The Roman emperor Vespasian (9–79 A.D.) was said by the historian Suetonius to be unusually ugly (*Life of Vespasian*, 20) – which contrasted oddly with his discriminating patronage of the arts. Sidney could have seen pictures of him both in England and on the continent; see Duncan-Jones, 'Sidney and Titian', in *English Renaissance Studies: Presented to Helen Gardner* (Oxford, 1980), 9–10.

27 **as it should be, or as it was**] Compare Robortello's *De arte poetica*: 'The poet deals with things as they ought to be. Even if he narrates the fact he still presents it as it might or ought to happen. In inventing he must follow the law of possibility, or necessity, or probability. Thus Xenophon describing Cyrus depicted him not as he was, but as the best and noblest king can and ought to be' (Robortello 1548, 87). Both the idea and its illustration were very familiar in the sixteenth century (see Hathaway 1962, 145ff.), and Sidney is not necessarily drawing on Robortello here.

28 **doctrinable**] instructive.

the feigned Cyrus of Xenophon] See 85/32 note, and 27 note above.

28–9 **the true Cyrus in Justin**] Justin (second or third century A.D.) in his *Histories* abbreviated a lost history of the world, *Historiae Philippicae*, by the historian Trogus Pompeius, who lived during the reign of Augustus. Arthur Golding translated Justin's *Histories* into English in 1564. Justin's account of Cyrus occurs in book I, chs iv–viii. It is as unhistorical as Xenophon's.

29 **Aeneas in Virgil**] Aeneas is the hero of Virgil's *Aeneid*, a Trojan who escaped from the fall of Troy and established the dynasty which founded Rome. See 85/32–3 note.

the right Aeneas in Dares] Sidney here chooses to accept as authentic an account of the Trojan war which was attributed to a Trojan eyewitness, Dares the Phrygian (mentioned in Homer's *Iliad*, V, 9). This account was thought by medieval writers such as Chaucer to be more accurate than the versions of Homer or of Virgil. Most sixteenth-century writers, on the other hand, doubted its authenticity; see Vives 1931, 239. It gives a profoundly unflattering picture of Aeneas. Thomas Paynell translated it into English in 1553. Sidney of course improves his argument considerably by contrasting the noble fictions of Xenophon and Virgil with the bald narratives of the historians Justin and Dares.

30–1 **to fashion her countenance to the best grace**] to have the most graceful model for her face.

32 **Canidia**] Horace in *Epodes*, V, gives a horrific account of the attempts made by the witch Canidia to regain her lost beauty. Compare also *Satires*, I, viii, and *Epodes*, III, xvii.

Horace] Quintus Horacius Flaccus (65–8 B.C.), one of the most celebrated Roman poets. His *Ars poetica*, a poem on the art of poetry, was the most influential classical discussion of the subject in the Renaissance.

33 **ill-favoured**] ugly.

34–5 **If the poet . . . shunned**] Compare Wilson 1909, 197, where he is commending the usefulness of the poet's fables: 'If a man could speake against couetous caitiues, can he better shew what they are, then by setting forth the straunge plague of *Tantalus*, who is reported to be in Hell, hauing Water comming still to his chin, and yet neuer able to drinke: And an Apple hanging before his mouth, and yet neuer able to eate?' Horace, *Satires*, I, i, 18, also cites the mythical figure of Tantalus as a warning against covetousness.

34 **aright**] as he ought.

Tantalus] served up his son Pelops to the gods in a banquet. For this (or for stealing the nectar of the gods, or for revealing their secrets, depending what version you read) he was condemned to everlasting torment (see 34–5 note above).

Atreus] See 91/12 note. Atreus was the son of Pelops and grandson of Tantalus; all three committed crimes against the gods.

36 **where**] whereas. See also 95/42, 99/18, 106/30 and 36, and 112/14.

37–8 **cannot be liberal . . . of a perfect pattern**] has not the freedom to give an ideal example.

38 **Alexander**] the Great of Macedonia (356–323 B.C.) conquered large tracts of Europe and Asia. The Roman historian **Quintus Curtius** (first century A.D.) wrote a sensational life of Alexander purporting to show how power corrupted him.

Scipio] Africanus (234–183 B.C.), a Roman general who defeated one of Rome's most formidable enemies, Hannibal. He is the central heroic figure in Livy's *Histories*, XXI–XXXIX, but in his later years was accused of political corruption.

41 **Quintus Curtius]** See above, 38 note.

41ff. **And whereas a man may say]** Sir Walter Raleigh refers to Sidney's argument here on the nature of history in his *Historie of the World* (1652 edition) I/II, ch. 21, vi, 458–60.

41–2 **in universal consideration of doctrine]** i.e. as a teacher of things in general.

43–4 **doth warrant a man more in that]** serves as a better guarantee to a man for what.

44 **stand upon]** depends on.

p. 93/2 **a gross conceit]** an undiscriminating understanding. With his reference to the predictability of English weather (**it rained yesterday, therefore it should rain today**) Sidney has reduced the idea that history could serve as a means of predicting future events to an absurdity. But the intellectual problem of whether the course of future events may be extrapolated from the evidence of past ones was much debated in the sixteenth century, and became prominent in the thought of the seventeenth-century philosopher Francis Bacon. All argument by example, such as Sidney is considering, was traditionally thought of as induction – that is, 'a form of argument which leads the person with whom one is arguing to give assent to certain undisputed facts: through this assent it wins his approval of a doubtful proposition because this resembles the facts to which he has assented' (Lanham 1968, 42, quoting Cicero, *De inventione*, I, xxxi, 51). The 'undisputed facts' could be of two sorts: 'one consisting in the mention of actual facts [as in history], the other in the invention of facts [as in Aesop's fables]' (Aristotle, *Rhetoric*, II, 20, 1393a). Sidney sees that an induction from any single case has no logical validity; but an example has some pragmatic value in predicting what is to come. On poetry as proof, see Hathaway 1962, 147, and his note 6 for further references.

3 **informs a conjectural likelihood]** allows one to guess what is likely to happen.

3–4 **go by reason]** proceed logically.

4 **him]** the historian (the writer of **history**, 20).

frame] adjust, adapt.

7 **fortune]** Compare 38 below and 105/34.

9–10 **a feigned example . . . a true example]** Compare Aristotle on the two types of example, 2 note above. See also Fracastorius 1924, 68: 'But it makes no difference whether we see the emperor give such and such counsels for victory, or are shown them by the poet'.

10 **as for to move]** as far as arousing the emotions is concerned.

clear] perhaps means 'superior' (invented examples can be **tuned to the highest key of passion** while true examples cannot).

13 **Zopyrus**] The story is told by Justin (I, x), who derives it from Herodotus (*History*, III, 153–60).

15 **verifying**] proof.

16–17 **for his known valour so far credited**] i.e. his reputation for courage in battle made the Babylonians trust him so completely.

18 **Much like matter**] Much the same thing.

Livy] Titus Livius (59 B.C.–A.D. 17) was a Roman historian during the reign of Augustus, whose *Histories* of Rome survive largely in the form of epitomes or abstracts. The *Histories* served as a standard school text in the sixteenth century.

Tarquinius and his son] In his *Histories*, I, liii–iv, Livy tells how Sextus, son of Tarquin the Proud, last of the Roman kings (see 87/5 note), pretended to be a deserter from Rome to the Gabii, in order to deliver the town to his father.

20 **Abradatas**] In Xenophon's *Cyropaedia*, V–VII, Abradatas is king of Susa, husband of Panthea and ally of Cyrus, in whose cause he is killed. But Xenophon records no such **stratagem** involving Abradatas. Sidney has confused him with (1) Gadatas, who agrees to help Cyrus in a plot to seize an Assyrian fort (V, iii, 8–19), and (2) Araspas, who pretends to desert Cyrus in order to spy for him (VI, i, 39ff.).

occasion] opportunity.

21 **honest dissimulation**] justifiable (or even admirable) deceit.

25 **subject to**] inferior to.

faction] deed, course of action.

whatsoever action, or faction] Compare Sidney's discussion of history in his letter to his brother Robert: 'In that kind you have principally to note the examples of virtue or vice, with their good or evil successes; the establishment or ruins of great states, with their causes; the time and circumstances of the laws they write of; the enterings and endings of wars, and therein the stratagems against the enemy, and the discipline upon the soldier' (Duncan-Jones 1989, 292).

29 **from Dante's heaven to his hell**] This is one of the earliest references to the Italian poet Dante Alighieri in English literature. But there is no evidence that Sidney had actually read Dante's poetry, despite his later reference to the editor of Dante's *Divine Comedy*, Cristoforo Landino (see **116/34**). He could have derived all his references to Dante from a combination of hearsay and Landino's commentary on Virgil in his much-reprinted *Disputationes Camaldulenses* (1480). This phrase, for instance, recalls one from book IV of the *Disputationes*, which refers to Dante's poem as 'that journey in which he traverses the entire universe from the depths of Tartarus to the heights of heaven' (see T. Stahel, 'Cristoforo Landino's Allegorization of the *Aeneid*: Books III and IV of the *Camaldolese Disputations*', unpublished PhD dis-

sertation, Johns Hopkins University, 1968, 162–3). Sidney's claim that the subject matter of poetry is limitless would not have been accepted by all Renaissance critics; but compare Giraldi Cinthio (Gilbert 1940, 265): 'For there is nothing above the heavens or below, nor in the very gulf of the abyss, which is not ready to the hand and choice of the judicious poet'.

31–2 **I speak of the art, and not of the artificer**] Compare 91/32–3. For the phrase, compare Castiglione 1928, 79: 'but I speake of the arte, and not of the Artificers'. In the celebrated treatise on rhetoric *Rhetorica ad Herennium*, II, xxvii, 44, it is considered a fault in pleading to disparage an art or science because of the people who practise it – as in the case of those who blame rhetoric because of the blameworthy life of some orator.

33 **to**] as for.

33–4 **the praise of histories**] Elyot praises history in similar terms in the *Governour*, III, xxv, as does Amyot in his preface to the readers (North 1895, I, 10ff.), who asserts that historical examples show the beauty of virtue and that history 'also hath his maner of punishing the wicked'. Bacon elaborates on Sidney's distinction between poetry and history in the *Advancement of Learning*. Poesy 'is nothing else but feigned history . . . as well in prose as in verse', which gives 'some shadow of satisfaction to the mind of man in those points wherein the nature of things doth deny it . . . Therefore, because the acts or events of true history have not that magnitude which satisfieth the mind of man, poesy feigneth acts and events greater and more heroical. Because true history propoundeth the successes and issues of actions not so agreeable to the merits of virtue and vice, therefore poesy feigns them more just in retribution, and more according to revealed providence' (Bacon 1974, 80).

34 **in respect of**] with regard to.

    marking the success] noting the outcome (of events or actions).

37 **her**] i.e. virtue's.

39 **Ulysses in a storm**] in Homer's *Odyssey*, V.

40 **exercises**] opportunities to practise.

    magnanimity] noble conduct or state of mind.

42 **come to the stage**] come on stage, i.e. are represented on stage.

42–4 **as the tragedy writer answered . . . follow them**] The story is told by Plutarch in *How the Young Man Should Study Poetry*, 4: 'Euripides . . . said to those who railed at his Ixion as an impious and detestable character: "But I did not remove him from the stage until I had fastened him to the wheel"' (a form of torture). Renaissance critics usually claimed that rewards and punishments in plays had a moral purpose; see Doran 1954, ch. 5, 85–100.

44 **little animate**] hardly encourage.

p. 94/1 **captived to**] imprisoned by.

    a terror from] a dissuader from (by terrifying).

3 **Miltiades]** Athenian general who defeated the Persians at the battle of Marathon (see above, 89/21 note). He was later accused of treason by his own side after a failed expedition, and died in prison. Compare Cicero, *Republic*, I, iii, 5; Justin, II, 15; and *Mirror for Magistrates*, ed. Campbell (1938), 334.

Phocion] An Athenian general described by Plutarch as an 'excellent guardian of the virtues of justice and sobriety' who opposed the powerful statesman Demosthenes and was sentenced to death on a charge of treason in 318 B.C. The proceedings against Phocion, Plutarch writes in the *Life*, 'put the Greeks in mind of those against Socrates. The treatment of both was equally unjust.'

4 **Socrates]** The great philosopher (469–399 B.C.), whose life and ideas were interpreted in texts by Plato and Xenophon, was sentenced to death on a charge of introducing new gods and corrupting the young.

4–5 **the cruel Severus]** Lucius Septimius Severus, Roman Emperor 193–211, was a brilliant and ruthless general who successfully disposed of his rivals, Julianus in 193, Pescennius Niger in 194, and Clodius Albinus in 197 (see 84/2 and 5 notes). He died at York, aged sixty-six. In the sixteenth century a popular moralized life was written by Antonio de Guevara in *La década de los Césares* (1539) (trans. E. Hellowes, *Chronicles . . . of Tenne Emperours of Rome* (1577), 266–330).

5 **the excellent Severus]** Alexander Severus, Roman Emperor 222–35, was murdered in his thirtieth year by mutineers in his own army. In the sixteenth century Antonio de Guevara developed his reputation (see E. Hellowes, *Chronicles* (1577), 433–84), and he came to be seen by Elizabethan writers as a model ruler. Sir Thomas Elyot wrote a fictional biography of him, *The Image of Governance*, in 1540. See M. Lascelles, *RES* N.S. 2 (1951), 305–18.

6 **Sylla and Marius]** Lucius Sylla (138–78 B.C.) was a Roman dictator whose bitter struggles with Caius Marius (157–86 B.C.) and his faction filled Italy with terror for twenty years. Marius died of pleurisy during his seventh consulship. Sylla abdicated his dictatorship and died in retirement after writing his memoirs.

Pompey] the Great (106–48 B.C.), one of the most celebrated of Roman generals, was defeated by his rival Julius Caesar at Pharsalia in 48 B.C., fled to Egypt and was killed there.

Cicero] (see 90/43 note), who supported Pompey in his conflicts with Caesar, retired from public life after Pompey's defeat at Pharsalia, except for a brief period after Caesar's death. He was put to death by his political opponents in 43 B.C.

then] at the moment.

8 **Cato]** of Utica (95–46 B.C.), a man of unbending integrity, opposed the triumvirate of Caesar, Pompey, and Crassus, but later supported Pompey against Caesar. After Pharsalia he continued to resist until Caesar had subdued all Africa except Utica, where Cato committed suicide.

rebel Caesar] Julius Caesar (c. 102–44 B.C.), the great Roman general and politician, 'became technically a rebel against the Roman State when he crossed the Rubicon with his army on to territory immediately under the Senate's jurisdiction' towards the end of the wars between Caesar and Pompey (Watson 1997, 99 note).

his name] Caesar gave his name to future monarchs and emperors. In Sidney's time the Holy Roman Emperor was referred to as 'Caesar', Sidney's mission to the Emperor Rudolph II in 1577 being '*ad Caesarem*' (Duncan-Jones 1989, 225/557–9 note).

10 **who**] i.e. Caesar.

11 **his**] Sylla's. After the death of Sylla, Caesar as a young man supported the opponents of Sylla's policies (see Suetonius, *Julius Caesar*, 5). According to Sidney, this was Caesar's only honourable political act.

literas nescivit] (Latin) 'he was illiterate'. Suetonius, in *Julius Caesar*, 77, reports Caesar as saying *Sullam nescisse literas, qui dictaturam deposuerit*: 'Obviously, Sylla did not know even the alphabet of politics, since he let others do all the dictating' (the saying plays on 'dictatorship' and 'dictation'). Erasmus turns this quotation into a saying or apophthegm, and explains it, in *Apophthegmes*, II, 19.

12 **do well**] i.e. succeed as a dictator.

by] with reference to. Compare 14, 15.

13 **new punishments . . . for tyrants**] As in Homer's *Odyssey*, XI; Virgil's *Aeneid*, VI, 621; and Dante's *Inferno*, xii, 104.

14 *occidendos esse*] (Latin) [tyrants] must be killed. Tyranny was discussed by Cicero, *De officiis*, III, vi (compare *Pro Milone*, xxix, 80); Seneca, *De clementia*, I, xiff.; Dio Cassius, *Orationes*, VI and LXII; and Plutarch in *Moralia* (see for example his *Life of Publicola*, who gave his name to the Valerian Law by which it was made lawful to kill a man who should seek supreme power). But the first philosophical doctrine on tyrannicide was formulated by John of Salisbury (*Policraticus* (1159), VIII, 17ff.), according to whom 'it is just for public tyrants to be slain'. Compare Thomas Aquinas, *De regimine principum*, I, 3; 6; and 9ff. The morality of tyrannicide was vigorously debated in the sixteenth and seventeenth centuries, by, for example, Erasmus, John Knox, George Buchanan, and Milton. See J. W. Allen, *A History of Political Thought in the Sixteenth Century* (London, 1951); and with particular reference to drama, W. A. Armstrong, 'Doctrine of the Tyrant in the Renaissance', *RES* 22 (1946), 161–81. On Sidney's concern with tyranny and a subject's duty under it, see I. Ribner, 'Sir Philip Sidney on Civil Insurrection', *JHI* 13 (1952), 257–65.

15 **Cypselus**] ruled Corinth from c. 655 to c. 625 B.C. and founded the Cypselid dynasty of tyrants at Corinth.

16 **Periander**] son of Cypselus, ruled Corinth from c. 625 to c. 585 B.C. He was more of a tyrant than his father, but acquired an international reputation as a judge.

Phalaris] tyrant of Sicily in the sixth century B.C., roasted his victims in a bull made of brass and became a by-word for cruelty in a ruler.

Dionysius] I, tyrant of Syracuse in Sicily in the fourth century B.C., ruled for thirty-eight years. Sidney to prove his point has selected four tyrants who seemed successful in the eyes of historians. Herodotus specifically states that Cypselus 'died happy', while Periander, Phalaris, and Dionysius all became known as patrons of the arts.

17 **kennel]** pack of dogs.

speed] prosper.

18 **he]** i.e. poetry.

excelleth] is superior to.

19 **setting it forward]** spurring it on.

21 **laurel crown]** See 100/34 note.

22 **of]** over.

22–3 **howsoever . . . questionable]** however debatable this may be when it comes to teaching.

25–6 **his methodical proceeding]** the method by which he proceeds. 'Method' recalls the logical teachings of Ramus (see 81/19 note).

27 *philophilosophos]* (Greek) lover of philosophy. Possibly Sidney's own coinage.

28 **moving]** stirring the passions.

29–36 **And that moving . . . to consider]** Sidney like other Renaissance critics gives poetry three aims: to teach, to delight, and to move (or incite its readers to action). See Scaliger 1617, III, xcvi, 334; Minturno 1559, 102; and B. Varchi, *Lezioni della poesia*, II, 576. Varchi believes that the poet goes further than simply instructing his audience and giving them pleasure (Horace's *utile* and *dulce*; see 86/17–20 note). He also induces certain emotions in them which incite their minds to a degree of admiration (see 98/28–9 note) – in particular to an admiration which leads to active emulation. Poetry is therefore an art of persuasion, like rhetoric (see Rainolds 1940, 66 note). The triple aim of teaching, pleasing, and moving has been ascribed to rhetoric from ancient times; see Cicero, *De optime genere oratorum*, I, 3; *Orator*, XXI, 69; and *De oratore*, II, xxviii, 121. Quintilian held that rhetoric had this triple aim, while poetry was limited to delighting its audience. Augustine transferred the three aims from classical rhetoric to Christian preaching (*De doctrina christiana*, IV, 12). Rudolph Agricola (*De inventione dialectica* (Paris, 1529 ed.), II, iv, p. 167), argued that the three aims merge into a general persuasion; and he was followed by Ramus (e.g. in *Scholae Rhetoricae* (Basel, 1569), lecturing on Cicero's *Orator*), who specifically denied the triple aim to the orator. But Sidney here follows the Ciceronian tradition as it was represented by Thomas Wilson: 'Three thinges are required of an Orator. To teach. To delight. And to perswade' (Wilson 1909, 2). Wilson explains how delighting is involved in moving. 'Nothing is more needfull, then to quicken these heauie loden wittes of ours, and much to cherish these our lompish and vnweildie Natures, for except men finde delite, they will not long abide: delite them, and winne them: wearie them, and you lose them for euer. And that is the reason, that men commonly tarie the ende of a merie Play and cannot abide the halfe hearing of a sower checking Sermon. Therefore euen these auncient Preachers, must now and then play the fooles in the pulpit' (3). Wilson shows that it is mainly by amplification – the inventive elaboration of a given theme – that a writer effects this needful 'mouing of the affections [i.e. emotions]' (130ff.). Sidney applies traditional teachings on rhetoric to poetry.

30–1   **For who will be taught . . . to be taught?**] A common observation among humanist educational theorists. Roger Ascham's *Schoolmaster* opens with a lengthy discussion of the best method of moving children with desire to learn, based on the premise that 'yong children should rather be allured to learning by ientilnes and loue, than compelled to learning, by beating and feare' (Ascham 1904, 197).

31–2   **what so much good doth that teaching bring forth . . . as**] what good does teaching produce as great as.

34   **not *gnosis* but *praxis***] (Greek) not knowing but doing. From Aristotle's *Ethics*, I, iii.

34–6   **And how . . . to consider**] i.e. it is clear enough that nobody will ever do anything without being stimulated by the desire to do so.

37–8   **particularities**] minute details.

41   **painfulness**] painstaking care.

42–3   **passed half the hardness of the way**] i.e. got over half the difficulties of his journey.

44–95/3   **Nay truly . . . philosopher's book**] This passage articulates a Platonic idea well known to ancient writers (see Plutarch, *Life of Pericles*: 'The beauty of goodness has an attractive power; it kindles in us at once an active principle') and often repeated in the sixteenth century (see Castiglione 1928, 268: 'For in case good and ill were well knowne and perceived, every man woulde alwaies choose the good, and shunne the ill'; *Amiot to the Readers* in North 1895, I, 11; quoted in 90/9–10 note). In sixteenth-century England the confidence Sidney here expresses in the efficacy of the **inward light (95/2)** placed by God in the human mind is characteristic of Protestant thought. The sixteenth-century theologian Richard Hooker restates the belief (which had been developed by medieval theologians) in terms with which Sidney might have agreed: 'Law rational therefore, which Men commonly use to call the Law of Nature, meaning thereby the Law which human Nature knoweth itself in reason universally bound unto, which also for that cause may be termed, most fitly, the Law of Reason; this Law, I say, comprehendeth all those things which Men by the light of their natural understanding evidently know, or at leastwise may know, to be seeming or unseeming, virtuous or vicious, good or evil for them to do' (*Ecclesiastical Polity* (1593), I, 8).

p. 95/2   **inward light**] i.e. reason.

3   **seeing in Nature we know**] considering we know naturally.

5   **words of art**] technical terms.

5–6 **out of natural conceit**] i.e. by their own innate gifts of reason. Philosophy like other arts, as Sidney has noted at 85/5ff., is grounded in 'nature'.

7 *hoc opus, hic labor est*] (Latin) this is the task, this is the struggle (i.e. 'this is the hard part'). From Virgil, *Aeneid*, VI, 129.

8 **therein**] in that respect (that is, in its capacity to move).

I speak still of human] Sidney reminds us that he is leaving theology out of his argument; see 89/39–42.

10 **prospect into**] view of.

14 **blur the margent**] i.e. fill up the margins of a philosopher's text by surrounding it with commentaries – a practice followed in printed books as well as in the informal notes jotted by scholars.

15 **doubtfulness**] ambiguity. Compare Elyot 1883, II, 221, which warns against fraudulent men who twist covenants or bargains to their own ends by 'taking aduauntage of a sentence or worde, whiche mought be ambiguous or doubtefull, or in some thinge either superfluous or lackinge'.

16 **proportion**] correct relation to one another. See Puttenham 1936, 64: 'It is said by such as professe the Mathematicall sciences, that all things stand by proportion, and that without it nothing could stand to be good or beautiful'. Platonists argued that certain proportions or relations between the parts of a beautiful object or person awoke in the viewer's mind a recognition of the divine proportions by which the world was created. Pietro Bembo explains this in Castiglione 1928, 311ff.; and Puttenham argues that poetry, like music, reproduces the proportions of the original creation.

17–19 **and with a tale . . . chimney corner**] These illustrations of the attractive power of poetry were borrowed by Harington (Smith, II, 208); and compare Rosaline's description of Biron in Shakespeare, *Love's Labour's Lost*, II, i, 73–5, whose tongue utters 'such apt and gracious words / That agèd ears play truant at his tales, / And younger hearings are quite ravishèd'.

17 **forsooth**] truly.

19 **pretending no more, doth intend**] claiming to be nothing more than a story, yet has as its purpose.

21–2 **hiding them . . . pleasant taste**] The sugar-coating of a medicine was often used by critics to explain the way poetry works. See Gilbert 1940, Index, under *Poetry, a pleasant medicine* for many examples, and Smith, I, 390. The illustration goes back at least to Lucretius, *De rerum natura*, I, 936–50 and IV, 11–25, and was familiar in the Middle Ages. Cook quotes from the preface to part III, the Poetical Books, of Tremellius and Junius's Latin translation of the Bible (see 86/23–8 note), where the editors explain (fol. 105) how the Holy Ghost in these poetical books has sweetened God's teachings as experienced doctors sweeten medicine by smearing the lip of the cup with honey (Cook 1890, 90). Stephen Gosson, by contrast, argues that poets use sugar-coated words to conceal poison rather than medicine: 'The deceitfull Phisition giueth sweete Syrropes to make his poyson goe downe the smoother' (Gosson 1974, 77).

22 **aloes**] a plant whose bitter juice was used as a purgative.

23 **rhubarb**] the bitter, so-called Chinese rhubarb, one of the commonest of sixteenth-century purgatives. Sidney speaks of the corrective medicine of 'rubarbe wordes' in *Astrophil and Stella*, 14. See also Harington (Smith 1904, II, 208).

physic] medicine.

26 **Hercules**] the most famous of the Greek heroes, who undertook twelve labours, and was much admired by the Stoic school of philosophers (see above, **91**/3 note), who regarded him as the epitome of fortitude or courage in adversity. He was also traditionally regarded as a supreme orator who could draw audiences after him by the metaphorical golden chain of eloquence attached to his tongue; he is therefore associated with **wisdom** as well as with **valour** (27), and a good example of the persuasive powers of poetry. The knight Argalus in Sidney's *New Arcadia* is found by a messenger 'reading in a book the stories of Hercules' (*NA*, 371), whose influence perhaps stimulates him to challenge the renegade Amphialus to single combat.

Achilles] See **91**/9 note.

Cyrus] See **85**/32 note.

Aeneas] See **85**/32–3 and **92**/29 notes.

30–1 **That imitation ... of all other**] i.e. The kind of imitation practised by poets takes into account the nature of its readers, so that in delineating horrible things it does not produce horror, since its readers by their natures would be repulsed by horror.

30 **conveniency**] suitability. William Webbe (Smith 1904, I, 292) interprets Aristotle's term *to harmoston* as '*convenientiam*, fitness'. Compare also Horace, *Art*, 119.

31 **as Aristotle saith**] in *Poetics*, IV, 1448b: 'Imitation is natural to man from childhood ... It is also natural for all to delight in works of imitation ... This is proved by experience. The pictures of those very things which in themselves are disagreeable to look at when they are painted with utmost accuracy, we delight to gaze on, such for example, as those of vilest animals or of dead bodies.' Plutarch repeats this argument in *How the Young Man Should Study Poetry*. In *NA* Sidney repeatedly illustrates his remark in *Astrophil and Stella*, 34: 'Oh, cruell fights well pictured forth doe please'.

34 *Amadis de Gaule*] a medieval prose romance of Spanish origin, which was known throughout Europe in the French translation (1540) of Nicolas de Herberay des Essarts. It was one of the sources of *OA*; see Zandvoort 1929, 193–5.

wanteth much] comes far short.

36 **liberality**] generosity.

36–7 **Aeneas ... on his back**] In the *Aeneid*, II, 705–84, Virgil describes how Aeneas escaped from the destruction of Troy carrying his elderly father Anchises on his back.

38 **Turnus**] The tale of Turnus, king of the Rutuli, is told in the last six books of Virgil's *Aeneid*. Turnus is betrothed to Lavinia, Aeneas's destined bride, and is eventually killed by Aeneas.

40–1 *Fugientem . . . miserum est?*] Sidney is quoting from the speech of Turnus in *Aeneid*, XII, 645–6, in which he anticipates his own death. Thomas Twyne translated the words as follows in 1584 (Duncan-Jones 1989, 379): 'And shall this ground fainthearted dastard Turnus flying view? / Is it so vile a thing to die?'

43 **saving**] except when.

wrangling] squabbling.

43–96/1 **whether virtue be the chief or the only good**] This was a question often debated by the Stoics (compare Augustine, *City of God*, XIX, i). Cicero says in *De officiis*, II, x, 35, that he had often considered the question, and the second-century Neoplatonist philosopher Maximus Tyrius wrote a disputation about it. The discussion continued throughout the Middle Ages; see O. Lottin, *Psychologie et morale aux XIIe et XIIe siècles*, IV (Louvain and Gembloux, 1954), 549–663. In More's *Utopia* the Utopians 'reason of virtue and pleasure; but the chief and principal question is in what thing, be it one or more, the felicity of man consisteth' (More 1985, 84). See E. Surtz, *The Praise of Pleasure . . . in More's Utopia* (Cambridge, Mass., 1957), ch. 3.

p. 96/1 **whether the contemplative or the active life do excel**] This medieval question, derived from Aristotle's *Ethics*, I, 3, continued to be debated by generations of humanists. See Rice 1958, ch. 2, 30–57, and Yates 1947, 6ff.

2 **Plato**] See 82/38 note.

Boethius] Anicius Manlius Severinus Boethius (480–524) was a Christian philosopher who translated the logical treatises of Aristotle and who attempted to reconcile the philosophies of Aristotle and Plato. His most famous work was the *Consolation of Philosophy*, which was celebrated throughout the Middle Ages and remained highly esteemed in the sixteenth century – Elizabeth I herself translated it into English, as Chaucer had done before her. Boethius wrote it in prison, where he died shortly afterwards under torture.

Plato and Boethius well knew] that if they had failed to delight their readers, they would have remained very ineffectual philosophers. Plato uses poetic fables, as Sidney has already pointed out at 82/39ff.; while Boethius in his *Consolation of Philosophy* intersperses the prose arguments of mistress Philosophy on virtue, fate, and the nature of goodness, with passages in verse. Compare in particular *Consolation*, I, prose i.

3 **masking raiment**] costume for a masque – a form of entertainment popular at court and in aristocratic households (see 82/31 note). The masque often presented a story in verse, acted out by aristocrats as well as by professional players. Costumes were exotic and usually included a mask. Sidney may here be responding to Stephen Gosson's injunction to his readers in *The School of Abuse*: 'pul off the visard that Poets maske in, you shall disclose their reproch, bewray their vanitie, loth their wantonnesse, lament their follie' (Gosson 1974, 77).

4 **think virtue a school name**] i.e. consider virtue to be the obsession of academics, with no relevance outside the academy. Compare Horace, *Epistles*,
I, vi, 32; and *OA*, 20, where Pyrocles is defending himself against the accusations of his friend Musidorus: 'For, if we love virtue, in whom shall we
love it but in virtuous creatures? – Without your meaning be I should love
this word of virtue when I see it written in a book.' Compare also *NA*, 74,
and *OA*, 278–9, in which the corrupt nobleman Timautus is described as a
man of 'extreme ambition' who 'could be as evil as he listed, and listed as
much as any advancement might thereby be gotten. As for virtue, he counted
it but a school name.' On the advocacy of libertinism in Sidney's time, see
Haydn 1950, ch. 7, 380ff.; and compare Hooker's denunciation of 'their
brutishness which imagine that Religion and Virtue are only as the will
account of them' (*Ecclesiastical Polity*, I, 8).

5 *indulgere genio*] (Latin) to follow their natural inclinations. From Persius,
Satires, V, 151, where Luxuria urges men to get what they can out of life, since
it is all they have.

6 **they**] the philosopher's admonitions.

7 **good-fellow**] Sidney combines two contemporary meanings: (1) drinking
companion (2) thief (hence his reference to stealing, 8). Gosson refers to
poets as thieves (Gosson 1974, 130).

8 **steal**] move by imperceptible degrees – with a suggestion of 'steal' meaning
to obtain unlawfully.

8–9 **the form . . . love**] Compare 94/44ff.

10 **medicine of cherries**] A syrup of cherries was used for the treatment of
coughs and sore throats.

12 **as**] that.

13 **The one of Menenius Agrippa**] The story of how Menenius Agrippa, a
Roman consul in 503 B.C., persuaded the poorer classes of Rome – the ple-
beians – to return to the city after they had left to found a separate community was certainly **often remembered**. It is told by Livy, *Histories*, II, xxxii;
Plutarch, *Life of Coriolanus*; John of Salisbury, *Policraticus*, VI, xxiv; Boccaccio 1930, 50; Erasmus 1965, 34. Quintilian uses Aesop's fables and this
story of Menenius to illustrate the moving power of poetry (*Institutes*, V, xi,
1), and the story was included in J. Camerarius, *Fabellae Aesopicae*, a popular
school textbook. Richard Rainolde includes it in *The Foundacion of Rhetorike*
(1563), sig. B2v; so does Wilson in his *Rhetorique*, who compares the persuasiveness of such a 'merry' and 'foolish' tale with the ineffectiveness of 'the
quiddities of Duns Scotus', the medieval logician (Wilson 1909, 159). The
story is perhaps best known now from Shakespeare's *Coriolanus*, I, i, which
may owe something to Sidney's version; see Thaler 1947, 5–7.

14 **divided themselves from**] turned against.

15 **apparent show of utter ruin**] i.e. clear signs of impending disaster (to the
Roman state).

for that time] for that early period.

16   **upon trust of**] relying on.

16–17 **figurative speeches**] speeches making use of rhetorical figures, i.e. striking or unusual configurations of words or phrases such as were taught in schools and universities.

17   **farfetched**] Compare 113/38 note.

     maxims] precepts.

19   **geometry**] Plato, who regarded God as a geometer, based his idea of a liberal education on a study of proportion (see *Republic*, VII; and 95/16 note). It was often said that over the door of his Academy was written: 'Let no man enter here who knows no geometry', but the saying was of medieval origin. See Neal W. Gilbert, *Renaissance Concepts of Method* (New York, 1960), 88.

     conceived] understood.

     forsooth] indeed; so far from that being the case. Compare 101/16 note.

20   **homely**] plain, unpretentious.

     familiar] friendly.

24   **spender**] spendthrift, waster.

     tale] fiction.

     notorious] famous.

26   **applied by him**] to the current situation.

29   **The other . . . of Nathan**] The second story comes from the Bible, 2 Samuel 12. It tells of David's adultery with Bathsheba and his murder by proxy of her husband Uriah.

30   **confirm adultery**] i.e. strengthen his position as an adulterer.

31   **when he**] i.e. Nathan.

31–2 **his own shame**] i.e. David's.

32   **to call again so chosen a servant**] to recall to his duties a servant (i.e. David) who had been so carefully selected by God to serve Him.

33–4 **ungratefully**] unkindly.

35–6 **the second and instrumental cause**] is the parable itself. The first cause moving David to repentance would be the Holy Ghost, of which the parable was the instrument.

36   **glass**] mirror.

36–7 **that heavenly psalm of mercy**] Psalm 51, in which 'David prayeth for remission of sins, whereof he maketh a deep confession'.

40   **a conclusion**] A conclusion, that is, to the section of Sidney's *Apology* beginning at 88/4 which analyses poetry by its **works** (97/1) – its methods and aims.

42   **end**] aim, objective.

     most familiar to teach] most congenial in teaching.

p. 97/1   **decipher**] analyse.

   3   **narrowly**] closely, in detail.

  3–5   **as in a man . . . a blemish**] Cicero, in *De natura deorum*, I, xxix, 80–3, questions whether we are to conceive of the gods as having slight physical blemishes such as moles, and concludes that we are not. John Lyly, on the other hand, in *Euphues* (1578), points out that 'some men write and most men believe, that in all perfect shapes a blemish bringeth rather a liking every way to the eyes than a loathing any way to the mind' (Lyly 1916, 10).

   5   **defectious**] deficient.

   6   **species**] types (a term from logic).

   8   **whereupon is risen**] from which has emerged.

     tragi-comical] See 112/9 note.

   9   **mingled prose and verse**] On the mixture of prose and verse as a literary form see F. Dornseiff, *Zeitschrift für die alttestamentliche Wissenschaft* 11 (1934), 74. It was used in post-classical times by Petronius in his Latin 'novel' *Satyricon*, by Martianus Capella in *De nuptiis Mercurii et Philologiae*, by Boethius in *The Consolation of Philosophy* (see 96/2 note), in the twelfth century by Bernard Silvestris and Alan of Lille, and later by Dante, Giordano Bruno, and of course Sidney in *OA*.

     Sannazzaro] Jacopo Sannazzaro of Naples (1455–1530) was highly regarded as a poet in the sixteenth century. His Latin verse includes the *Piscatory Eclogues* (in which fishermen replace the traditional shepherds as speakers), which were much admired and imitated. Scaliger considered him 'in pastoral poetry the only poet worth reading after Virgil' (Scaliger 1617, VI, iv, 753); see 110/20–1 below. Besides some Italian verse Sannazzaro wrote a Latin religious epic, *De partu virginis*, and a pastoral romance in prose and verse, the *Arcadia*, finished in 1485. To this work Sidney refers here, and to it he owes more than just the title of his own *Arcadia*; see Zandvoort 1929, 189–91.

     Boethius] See 96/2 notes.

  10   **mingled matters heroical and pastoral**] As Sannazzaro did in *Arcadia*, Montemayor (imitating Sannazzaro) in *Diana* (c. 1559), and Tasso in *Gerusalemme liberata* (completed 1575), to which Spenser was indebted in the *Faerie Queene*.

10–11   **cometh all to one in this question**] i.e. makes no difference in this case.

  15   **misliked**] disapproved of.

15–16   **where the hedge is lowest . . .**] Compare Harington (Smith 1904, II, 195). For other instances of this proverb, see Tilley, H 364. Throughout the Middle Ages and beyond, pastoral verse was among the first poetry read by a schoolboy: especially the *Eclogues* of Virgil and those of the tenth-century poet Theodulus, and in Elizabethan times those of Mantuan (1448–1516). It was poetry **of the poor pipe** (16), that is, in 'low style' – the style considered suitable for the lower social classes; see Rubel 1941, ch. X. But in theory as well as in practice Sidney and many other Elizabethan poets of the 1580s found the conventions of pastoral useful as a means of contemplating the gap between the ideal, which poetry aims to bring into being, and the real, which is the material with which poetry must work.

16 **the poor pipe**] The pipe made of reeds or oat-straw represents the 'lowly' pastoral, just as the lyre represents the 'higher' forms of poetry (see previous note). Spenser, in *The Faerie Queene*, I, proem, expresses the transition from pastoral to epic in terms of musical instruments: 'I . . . am now enforst . . . For trumpets sterne to chaunge mine Oaten reeds'.

17 **Meliboeus**] In Virgil's *Eclogues*, I, the shepherd Meliboeus, who represents the people of Mantua, complains about the confiscation of his land and cattle – something that had happened to Virgil in 41 B.C.

18 **Tityrus**] Again in Virgil's *Eclogues*, I, the shepherd Tityrus speaks for Virgil when he rejoices in the freedom and security given him by his patron Octavianus (later Augustus) Caesar.

20–1 **pretty tales of wolves and sheep**] An example is the satire on the papal court in Mantuan, *Eclogues*, IX, which was imitated by Spenser in the September Eclogue of *The Shepheardes Calender*:

> Sike as the shepheards, sike bene her sheepe,
> For they nill listen to the shepheards voyce . . .
> They wander at wil, and stray at pleasure . . .
> And bene of ravenous Wolves yrent,
> All for they nould be buxome and bent [i.e. obedient].
> (Spenser 1989, 157)

Compare Spenser's May Eclogue, 123ff. A contrast between wrong-doing and patience is brought out better in the tales of the Sheep and the Dog, the Wolf and the Wether, and the Wolf and the Lamb in the *Fables* of the great fifteenth-century Scottish poet Robert Henryson, an English version of which appeared in London in 1577. Sidney refers to an 'old tale' about 'wolves that mean to destroy the flock' in his *Defence of Leicester* (*Misc. Prose*, 130/7–9, and see note). The pastoral as Sidney and Spenser practised it drew not only upon the classical tradition of Theocritus and Virgil, which was vigorously developed by neo-Latin poets in the fifteenth and sixteenth centuries (see W. L. Grant, *Renaissance Studies* 4 (1957), 71–100), but also upon a native, quasirustic tradition of complaint literature (see J. Peter, *Complaint and Satire in Early English Literature* (Oxford, 1956), ch. 3, 40–59).

21 **the whole considerations**] i.e. every aspect.

22 **contention for trifles**] competition for trivial prizes. In Virgil's *Eclogues*, III, the shepherds Menalcas and Damoetas stake a calf against a set of beech-wood bowls in a singing match. Similar singing matches occur in Virgil's *Eclogues*, VII, between Corydon and Thyrsis; in *OA*, First and Second Eclogues (52ff. and 124ff.) – especially the latter, where the competition between Nico and Pas has a dog and cat as its prizes; and in Spenser's August Eclogue in *The Shepheardes Calender*, where the stakes are a lamb and a cup. See Ringler 1962, 362 note.

23–7 **Alexander and Darius . . . *nobis***] This passage juxtaposes the wars of Alexander the Great (who defeated Darius, king of Persia, in 330 B.C.) and the singing match between Thyrsis and Corydon in Virgil's *Eclogues*, VII (see

26–7 note below), illustrates how pastoral may act as political commentary: from the perspective of later times both contests look equally **trifling** (22–3).

24 **cock of this world's dunghill**] For this common expression, see Tilley, C 486.

25 **afterlivers**] those who live after; a word coined by Sidney. Compare Robertson 1973, 110/4.

26–7 *Haec memini . . . nobis*] From Virgil, *Eclogues*, VII:

These rhymes I did to memory commend,
When vanquish'd Thyrsis did in vain contend;
Since when, 'tis Corydon among the swains;
Young Corydon without a rival reigns.
(Dryden's translation)

28 **the lamenting Elegiac**] Sidney here gives a rather narrow description of elegy (which Cooper, in his *Dictionary*, defined simply as 'lamentable verses'). Puttenham gives a more comprehensive account, suggesting that the subject matter of elegy was either 'the perplexities of loue' or death (Puttenham 1936, 25, 48ff., 56ff.). Scaliger discusses the whole range of elegiac poetry (Scaliger 1617, I, 1, 117–18). Sidney here plays down the importance of the love-elegy, which had gained prominence in Latin through Propertius, Tibullus, and Ovid. To some educationalists and moralists of the sixteenth century this kind of poetry was highly suspect; see 103/44 note. Although Sidney seems to glance at the love-elegy when he describes the poet's representation of the **passions of woefulness** (32–3), he implies that elegiac verse is primarily reflective, moralizing verse such as was particularly associated with the distinctive elegiac verse form in Latin literature.

30 **Heraclitus**] of Ephesus, a philosopher who flourished about 500 B.C., was said to have been always weeping for **the wretchedness of the world**.

31 **who**] the elegiac poet.

32 **painting out**] depicting.

33 **the . . . Iambic**] From Greek *iambos*, a satirical poem with a characteristic metre based on the rhythms of speech. Sidney makes the same distinction between **Iambic** and **Satiric** as Scaliger makes (Scaliger 1617, I, xii, 44), who distinguishes the direct, personal, abusive attacks of Juvenal and Persius, 'more aptly called iambus', from the indirect attacks of satire proper, as exemplified by the satires of Horace.

33–4 **rubs the galled mind**] A gall is a sore made by chafing; as used in this phrase, see Tilley, G 12. Compare Gosson's attack on playwrights who 'by the priuie entries of the eare, slip downe into the hart, and with gunshotte of affection gaule the minde, where reason and vertue should rule the roste' (Gosson 1974, 89).

34 **making shame . . . villainy**] i.e. making the obvious shame experienced by those who are the targets of their attacks act as a public proclamation of their wrong-doing.

35 **naughtiness**] wickedness.

36 *Omne . . . amico*] an adaptation of a couplet from the *Satires* of the Roman poet Aulus Persius Flaccus (34–62), known as Persius: 'Omne vafer vitium

ridenti Flaccus amico / tangit, et admissus circum praecordia ludit' (*Satires*, I, 116–17) (Flaccus (Horace) the rascal, probes every fault of his friend while making him laugh; and once inside he plays with the secrets of his heart). Gosson quotes the same lines as part of the playwrights' defence against the charges he brings against them (Gosson 1974, 88).

37 **sportingly**] playfully.

37–9 **laugh at folly . . . folly**] This recalls Chaloner's preface to his translation of Erasmus's *Praise of Folly*: 'what excuse [Erasmus] maketh, the same I requyre maie serue for me: that thynges spoken foolisshely, by Folie, maie be euin so taken, and not wrested to any bitter sence or ernest applicacion. For surely if the crabbedst men that be, are wont to take a fooles woordes as in sporte, for feare lest others myght recken they would not wynche [wince] without a galled backe: Than how muche more is a domme [dumb] booke written generally to be borne withall? namely where the title pretendeth no grauitee, but rather a toye to stirre laughter, without offence in the boke, if the reader bringe none offence with hym. For than truely he maie chaunce to see his owne image more liuely described than in any peincted table. But if that waies he mislike the deformitee of his countrefaicte, let hym muche more mislyke to be suche one in deede' (Erasmus 1962, 4).

40 *circum . . . ludit*] Persius's words quoted in 36 note above.

41 **headaches**] a rare anticipation of the modern figurative use.

a passionate life] a life dominated by the emotions.

p. 98/1 *Est . . . aequus*] Even in [the squalid and unpleasantly situated town of] Ulubrae [we will find happiness] if we keep a serene mind. From Horace, *Epistles*, I, xi, 30, substituting *nos* (we) for *te* (you).

2–3 **the Comic . . . odious**] Many Renaissance writers observe that in the first period of Greek comedy the dramatists were always looking for laughs and were licentious rather than critical. Scaliger 1617, I, vii, 26–7, and Boccaccio 1930, 70, 72, 93, condemn these early dramatists for presenting filthy characters on the stage and encouraging lascivious men to commit crimes. In England, Richard Edwards in the prologue to his comedy *Damon and Pithias* (1571) announces his intention to break away from the offensive preoccupation of earlier comedies with 'young desires', and George Gascoigne's tragicomedy *The Glass of Government* (1575) sets itself up in opposition to the scurrilous subject matter of the Roman comedy-writer Terence (Gascoigne 1910, II, 6). Like other Elizabethans, Sidney applies the age-old condemnation of comedy to his own time and place, and in doing so makes a gesture of assent to Gosson's attack on the scurrility of contemporary drama in *The School of Abuse*. The word **abuse** in line 4 may echo the title of Gosson's attack. On the mounting opposition to the new playhouses outside London during the 1570s among the authorities, see W. Ringler, *Stephen Gosson* (Princeton, 1942), ch. 4, 53–82.

2 **naughty**] evil.

2–3 **stage-keepers**] Here this probably means men who own or run theatres, although 'stage-keeper' could also mean a theatrical employee who kept the stage in order.

3–4 **To the argument . . . after**] See 103/44ff.

3 **abuse**] misuse, corrupt practice.

4–5 **Comedy . . . life**] a more precise variation on the usual Renaissance definition of comedy as 'an imitation of life, the mirror of custom and the image of truth' (see Smith, I, 369), usually ascribed to Cicero. Compare also Aristotle, *Poetics*, 5, 1449a; 'Comedy is an imitation of those who are worse than we are but not in every sort of evil, but only in that baseness of which the ridiculous is one form'. Sixteenth-century theorists usually extend Aristotle's account, as Sidney does, by giving comedy a didactic function: comedy teaches men virtue by deriding and censuring their foolishness. See Doran 1954, 105ff. and notes.

8 **oblique . . . right**] refers to angles; **odd . . . even** to numbers. Hooker (*Ecclesiastical Polity*, I, 8), commending a maxim of Aristotle, *De anima*, 1, agrees that 'he that knoweth what is straight, doth even therby discern what is crooked . . . Goodness in actions is like unto straightness.' This idea that good must be known through the discernment of evil runs through Protestant thought in the sixteenth and seventeenth centuries and forms the basis of Milton's thinking on Christian liberty, famously articulated in his treatise on censorship, *Areopagitica*. See Cook 1890, 94–5 note.

10–11 **the filthiness of evil . . . the beauty of virtue**] Sidney may be recalling Elyot's commendation of history, which, he claims, teaches 'the beautie of vertue and the deformitie and lothelynes of vice' (Elyot 1883, II, 401). Earlier in the *Governour* Elyot's line of argument in defence of comedies anticipates Sidney's here: 'Comedies, whiche they [i.e. the critics of poetry] suppose to be a doctrinall of rybaudrie, they be vndoutedly a picture or as it were a mirrour of man's life, wherin iuell is nat taught but discouered; to the intent that men beholdynge the promptnes of youth unto vice, the snares of harlotts and baudes laide for yonge myndes, the disceipte of seruantes, the chaunces of fortune contrary to mennes expectation, they being therof warned may prepare them selfe to resist or preuente occasion. Semblably remembring the wisedomes, advertisements, counsailes, dissuasion from vice, and other profitable sentences, most eloquently and familiarely shewed in those comedies, vndoubtedly there shall be not litle frute out of them gathered' (Elyot 1883, I, 124–5).

10 **foil**] Something that sets off the beauty of something else – usually a jewel – by contrast.

13 **niggardly**] tight-fisted, miserly.

Demea] the miserly father in the comedy *Adelphi* by Terence (see 91/14 note). Terence's comedies were widely used for teaching purposes in the sixteenth century, often in bowdlerized forms, and were sometimes acted by schoolboys.

14 **Davus**] a tricky servant in Terence's *Andria*.

Gnatho] the sycophant in Terence's *Eunuch*. See 91/14 note.

vainglorious] boastful.

Thraso] the loudmouthed soldier in *The Eunuch*. His name, like Gnatho's, had become a common noun by the sixteenth century; see *OED* under Gnatho, Thraso. Critics often drew attention to the representative quality of characters in classical comedy. Minturno writes, for instance, in *L'arte poetica*: 'Terence illustrates . . . in Demea, harshness and avarice . . . in Davus, clever service' (Minturno 1725, 39). See also Ascham 1904, 208, on the role of servants in Terence and Plautus and on the contemporary English stage. Scaliger's *Poetices* deals with the various types of dramatic *personae* and shows how they work (*persona* originally meant mask, and in Roman plays standard masks were worn by each character type) (Scaliger 1617, I, xiii, 44ff.). A proper performance of a classical comedy requires that each *persona*, or character type, should be an animated fiction on the stage. Since the distinguishing marks of any person are to be found in his or her physical appearance, behaviour, and social position, the audience's attention must be drawn to these marks when presenting the *persona*. Guided by the traditional rhetorical teaching on the delineation of character, Scaliger deals with the social position, the profession, function, age, and sex of the *persona*; then with his or her name, physical appearance, manners, sayings, deeds, and feelings. He describes the distinctions in dress to be observed. All these marks are 'the badges (*insignia*) of the *personae*' (48). Compare 16 below.

16 signifying badge] distinguishing mark (see previous note). The characters should be made recognizable for what they are when they appear on stage (e.g. a miser, a young lover) by the way they dress, their behaviour, etc. On these aspects of dramatic presentation in England see T. W. Craik, *The Tudor Interlude* (Leicester, 1958), particularly chs III and IV. By Sidney's time the need for decorum in characterization – the need for a character to speak, dress, and act in a manner suitable to her or his social rank – was well established. Richard Edwards, in the prologue to his comedy *Damon and Pithias* (1571), urges the dramatist to 'frame each person so / That by his common talke you may his nature rightly know'; and Thomas Whetstone in the prologue to *Promos and Cassandra* (1578) demands a strict decorum in presenting 'graue olde men', 'yonge men', 'strumpets', etc.

comedian] writer of comedies, or comic actor.

17–18 as I said before] See 4ff. above.

20 *in pistrinum*] (Latin) condemned to hard labour. A *pistrinum* was a pounding mill usually operated by horses and donkeys, in which, in Roman society, slaves were sometimes set to work as punishment.

20–1 the sack . . . measure] i.e. viewers of comedy may find it easier to recognize other people's faults than their own. Sidney perhaps associates a mill (*pistrinum*) with sacks (through such proverbial expressions as 'more sacks to the mill'), and here alludes to the Aesopic fable of the man with two sacks, one filled with his neighbours' faults which is always visible to him, the other filled with his own faults, which he carries behind his back and so cannot see. On the popularity of this fable, see Baldwin 1944, II, 504–6.

21 **dance the same measure**] dance to the same tune.

whereto] to which.

25 **Tragedy**] Like other Renaissance critics, Sidney here insists that tragedy is exclusively concerned with the aristocracy; see Hall 1945, 37ff., 174ff. According to Scaliger (Scaliger 1617, III, xcvi, 332), tragedy differs from epic in that it only rarely admits people of low rank into the action. 'Tragic matters are grand and terrible: the commands of kings, slaughters, despairs, executions, exiles, bereavements, parricides, incests, conflagrations, battles, blindings, weepings, lamentations, conquests, funerals, epitaphs and memorials' (333). Tragedy deals with the public words, actions and images of men and women of noble birth. This idea of tragedy came to incorporate a dreadful warning directed towards people of the same rank as its protagonists; see Gilbert 1940, 218, note 10. Thus a major function of tragedy is to make **kings fear to be tyrants** (27); compare Elyot 1883, I, 71: a man shall 'in redyng tragoedies execrate and abhorre the intollerable life of tyrantes'.

25–6 **openeth . . . tissue**] Compare Horace, *Epistles*, I, xvi, 39–45: 'Whom doth false honour please and lying infamy terrify, whom but the villain, who is diseased with vice? . . . All the family and his neighbours see this man to be polluted within, though seemingly fair of skin.' Stephen Gosson claims that in writing the *School of Abuse* he is engaged in the curative act here described by Sidney: 'Though my skill in Physicke bee small, I haue some experience in these maladyes, which I thrust out with my penne too euery mans viewe, yeelding the ranke fleshe to the Chirurgions knife' (Gosson 1974, 73).

28 **affects**] emotions (from Latin *affectus*).

28–9 **admiration and commiseration**] amazement and pity. Compare 112/5. This is Sidney's version of Aristotle's analysis of the effects of tragedy (*Poetics*, VI): 'Tragedy is an imitation of an action . . . exciting pity and terror' and bringing about the catharsis (purgation) of such emotions – that is, cleansing the body of them, as a purgative cleanses a diseased body of its impurities. Like other Renaissance critics, Sidney reproduces only part of Aristotle's discussion of tragedy, which was endlessly discussed. For a full account of this discussion among the Italian critics at the end of the sixteenth century, see Hathaway 1962, part 3, 205–300. Scaliger quotes Aristotle's definition of tragedy and then prunes it to: 'Tragedy is an imitation through actions of an illustrious fortune, with an unhappy outcome, composed in dignified verse' (Scaliger 1617, I, vi, 26). Castelvetro speaks of tragedy's efficacy in producing fear and pity (like Sidney he inverts Aristotle's 'pity and terror') in the mind of the spectator (Castelvetro 1576, XII, 268). The catharsis or purgation is a general moral after-effect, the delight we derive from tragedy arises from the recognition that justice has been done, and its usefulness lies in fortifying the mind against the assaults of passion. Minturno believes that a cleansing from moral faults is effected directly by the contemplation of horrible things (Minturno 1725, 76–7). We are constrained to virtue by fear that these things might happen to us; our pleasure arises from being done good to. Sidney here is being as moralistic as Minturno. He inverts the order of Aristotle's 'pity and terror' and replaces 'terror' with 'admiration'. On admiration as a critical term see Gilbert 1940, appendix, 459. For Sidney, admiration seems to be a kind of emotional shock, the amazement felt by the audience when confonted with an exceptionally heroic order of behaviour. By replacing Aristotle's 'terror' with admiration, Sidney avoids the difficulty of having to explain how the contemplation of horror can ever be an instructive or delightful process. The tragic effect produces a moral effect. The shock, followed by reflection, teaches the spectator certain moral lessons about the instability of worldly success (29ff.). Sidney plays down the sensationalism of some of the Italian critics and accentuates the rational usefulness of tragedy.

31–2 *Qui sceptra . . . redit*] 'The tyrant who rules harshly fears those who fear him; terror returns to its agent' (Duncan-Jones 1989, 230/750–1 note). From Seneca's *Oedipus*, III, 705–6 (with the order of *saevus duro* reversed). Sidney used this couplet as a basis for a love epigram in *Certain Sonnets* 14: 'Faire seeke not to be feard, most lovely beloved by thy servants, / For true it is, that they feare many whom many feare' (Ringler 1962, 143). He also quotes the couplet in his letter to Elizabeth I against her marriage to the Duc d'Alencon (*Misc. Prose*, 56/12).

33 **Plutarch**] (c. 46–120) a Greek biographer and moral philosopher, one of the most highly regarded of classical authors during the Renaissance. His series of *Parallel Lives*, each of which compares the life of an eminent Greek historical figure with that of an eminent Roman, was translated by Thomas North in 1579. His *Moralia* is a collection of treatises or essays on a wide variety of topics.

yieldeth a notable testimony] i.e. gives an example worth noting.

34 **Alexander Pheraeus**] Plutarch tells the story of the tyrant Alexander of Pherae (d. 358 B.C.) in *On the Fortune or Virtue of Alexander*, II, 1, and more fully in the *Life of Pelopidas* who was killed by this Alexander in 364 B.C. The tyrant, says Plutarch, paid so 'little regard to reason or justice that he buried some persons alive, and dressed others in the skins of bears and wild boars and then by way of diversion baited them with dogs or despatched them with darts; that having summoned the people of Meliboea and Scotusa . . . he surrounded them . . . and . . . put them to the sword . . . ; that he consecrated the spear with which he slew his uncle . . . and offered sacrifice to it as to a god . . . Yet upon seeing a tragedian act the *Troades* of Euripides, he went hastily out of the theatre . . . for . . . he was ashamed that his citizens should see him, who never pitied those he put to death, weep at the sufferings of Hecuba and Andromache.' M.-A. Muret in his oration on the *Aeneid* (*Opera* (Leipzig, 1834), II, 370) also uses this story to show how poetry can affect people's conduct; and compare *Hamlet*, 2. 2. 566–9.

36 **so as**] so that.

38 **sweet violence**] Aristotle uses the Greek word *hedas*, 'sweet', several times in discussing tragedy. Sidney himself is fond of oxymorons like this; see e.g. 81/23.

39 **it was that**] it was because.

p. 99/1 **Lyric**] lyric poet. Sidney presents the traditional, learned conception of lyric poetry which can be illustrated from Scaliger 1617, I, xliv, 105ff.: 'Next after the majesty of the heroic comes the noble lyric poetry'. Such poems were sung to the accompaniment of the lyre; hence the name lyric. 'There are many types'; those which sing 'the cares of love'; those 'in praise of heroes or of places or of mighty deeds'; 'hymns of praise in which thanks are given to the immortal gods for victory'; 'hymns recited at the altars to the gods, pieces compounded of the praise of brave men . . . and pieces made up of common maxims and proverbs and of all sorts of exhortation to virtuous living.' Sidney concentrates on the lyric as a song of praise; it is in this capacity that Gosson is prepared to recognize the value of poetry when performed at banquets (Gosson 1974, 82).

lyre] ancient U-shaped stringed instrument, usually used to accompany songs.

2 **well-accorded**] in perfect harmony, in tune.

3 **natural problems**] A problem in logic was a question proposed for discussion in an academic context. These could be solved only through analysis; thus here 'problems' are set against 'precepts', or straightforward moral instructions. Sidney demonstrates how lyric poets deal with 'problems' in *Astrophil and Stella* 58; and see Ringler's note on 'problemes' in *Astrophil and Stella* 3 (Ringler 1962, 460). Many short sixteenth-century poems – such as those in *Tottel's Miscellany* (1557) – are made up of statements of moral precepts and expositions of problems of natural philosophy.

4 **lauds**] praises.

5 **barbarousness**] lack of literary culture. Ascham in *The Schoolmaster* uses the term to refer to rhyme ('that barbarous and rude Ryming', 'the barbarous bringing in of Rymes', Ascham 1904, 289 and 293), and tells us that Cicero applied it to 'poore England', whose inhabitants he accused of 'mere barbariousnes' (292–3).

6 **the old song of Percy and Douglas**] Presumably this is some version of the ballad of Chevy Chase, which describes the fatal encounter between the Earls of Percy and Douglas on the English/Scottish border. In 1711 the essayist Joseph Addison could still call this 'the favourite Ballad of the people of England'.

that I found not] without finding.

8 **crowder**] player on a 'crowd' or Welsh fiddle. Blind minstrels were often associated with the recitation of heroic tales in late medieval times; an example is Blind Harry, the reputed author of *Wallace*. Puttenham refers to 'blind harpers', 'their matters being for the most part stories of old time, as the tale of Sir *Topas*, the reportes of *Beuis* of *Southampton*, *Guy* of *Warwicke*, *Adam Bell*, and *Clymme* of the *Clough* & such other old Romances or historicall rimes, made purposely for recreation of the common people at Christmasse diners & brideales' (Puttenham 1936, 83). In the accounts kept by Thomas Marshall of Sidney's expenses while still a boy, for September 1566, an entry reads: 'Item, given by Mr Philip's commandment to a blind harper who is Sir William Holles' man of Nottinghamshire: 12d.' (Duncan-Jones 1991, 38).

rude] crude.

8–9 **which, being so evil apparelled . . . eloquence of Pindar?**] This passage might be read as a refutation of Stephen Gosson's objection to contemporary innovations in music (Gosson 1974, 82–5). Gosson argues that modern elaborations on the simplicity of ancient melodies encourage sexual licence: 'When the Sicilians . . . forsooke the playnsong that they had learned of their auncestours in the Mountaynes . . . they founde out such descant in Sybaris instrumentes, that by daunsing and skipping they fel into lewdnesse of life' (85). Sidney, by contrast, here considers the movement from 'rude style' to 'gorgeous eloquence' to be desirable – although not unproblematically so (see his admission at 15–23 below that Pindar did not always use his 'gorgeous eloquence' for the best purposes).

9 **that uncivil age**] the medieval period, when the events described in the 'old song of Percy and Douglas' took place.

10 **Pindar**] Perhaps the greatest of the Greek lyric poets, born at Thebes c. 522 B.C. Horace (*Carmina*, IV, ii) lists the kinds of lyric which Pindar composed: hymns to the gods, praise of heroes, *epinicia* celebrating the achievements of the Olympic champions, and funeral songs. Only the *epinicia* survive. Pindar was little known at first hand in England until the late sixteenth century (see R. Shafer, *The English Ode to 1660* (Princeton, 1918), 74) but Sidney may well have known Henri Estienne's edition of his works (Paris, 1560).

In Hungary] Sidney spent some weeks there in mid-1573 (see Duncan-Jones 1991, 65). Hungary experienced a remarkable resurgence of national culture in reaction to its defeat at Mohacs (1526) by the Ottoman Turks, against whom for centuries the old kingdom of Hungary had stood as Christendom's eastern defence.

10–13 **In Hungary . . . brave courage**] Gosson's *School of Abuse* describes the 'right vse of auncient Poetrie' as being 'too haue the notable exploytes of woorthy Captaines . . . song to the Instrument at solemne feastes, that the sounde of the one might draw the hearers from kissing the cupp too often; the sense of the other put them in minde of things past, and chaulk out the way to do the like' (Gosson 1974, 82). Like Sidney, Gosson cites the '*Lacedaemonians*' or Spartans as devotees of this practice (see below, lines 13ff.).

12 **soldierlike**] soldierly. Sidney hoped to test his own soldiership against the Turks in Hungary, perhaps (Duncan-Jones suggests) 'under the leadership of the famous Hungarian general and military theorist Lazarus Schwendi' (Duncan-Jones 1991, 65; and see note).

13 **The incomparable Lacedemonians**] Sidney like other Protestant humanists admired the discipline and efficiency of the Lacedemonians or Spartans. Plutarch describes their songs as follows: 'Their songs had a spirit which could rouse the soul, and impel it in an enthusiastic manner to action . . . There were three choirs in their festivals corresponding with the three ages of man. The old men began, "Once we were valiant youth"; the young men answered, "If you will, behold us now"; and the boys concluded, "Soon we will be more valiant still" . . . And the king always offered sacrifice to the muses before a battle . . . It was at once a solemn and dreadful sight to see

them measuring their steps to the sound of music and without the least dis-
order in their ranks or tumult of spirits, moving forward cheerfully and com-
posedly with harmony to battle' (*Life of Lycurgus*, 21. Compare also *The
Ancient Customs of the Spartans*, 14, and *On Praising Oneself Inoffensively*, 15).

14 **field**] battlefield.

16 **lusty men**] men in their prime.

18–19 **victories of small moment**] the victories of champions at the Olympic
games.

19 **sport**] entertainment.

20 **fault . . . poetry**] Compare 93/31–2.

22 **toys**] trivial things.

Philip of Macedon] (c. 382–336 B.C.), the conqueror of Athens and father
of Alexander the Great.

23 **Olympus**] a mountain on the summit of which the Greek gods were supposed to live. Many sixteenth-century writers thought that the Olympic
games were held on Mount Olympus, when in fact they took place at a religious site called Olympia. Cooper made this mistake in his *Dictionary*, as
did Spenser in the *Faerie Queene*, III, vii, 41. See D. T. Starnes and E. W.
Talbert, *Classical Myth and Legend in Renaissance Dictionaries* (Chapel Hill,
1955), 107.

his three fearful felicities] Plutarch (*Life of Alexander*, 3) records that Philip
of Macedon 'had just taken the city of Potidae and three messengers arrived
the same day with extraordinary tidings. The first informed him that
Parmenio had gained a great battle against the Illyrians; the second, that his
racehorse had won the prize at the Olympic games; and the third, that [his
wife] Olympias was brought to bed of Alexander.' The story was told by
Erasmus, *Apophthegmes*, II, 2, trans. Udall (1542), 182. The **felicities** are
fearful presumably in the sense that such a run of good luck was thought to
arouse the displeasure of the gods.

24 **Pindar often did**] awake the thoughts of his readers (24–5).

26 **rests**] remains.

the Heroical] Nearly all Renaissance critics agree that heroic or epic poetry
is the greatest of all forms of writing (Castelvetro is an exception in prefer-
ring drama). See Hall 1945, 46ff. and 190ff. For Scaliger, the epic is pre-
eminent because it is the most comprehensive poetic form (Scaliger 1617, I,
iii, 13). Minturno too concludes after some discussion that the epic is the
greatest of all genres (Minturno 1559, 105). For Sidney the epic presents the
most fully worked-out 'example' for its readers to follow, a perfect portrayal
of the human ideal in action.

27 **backbiters**] detractors, slanderers.

conceit] in this case, 'delusion'.

28 **Achilles**] the hero both of Homer's *Iliad* and of the *Achilleid*, an incomplete
epic poem by the Neapolitan poet Publius Statius (c. 40–c. 96).

Cyrus] the subject of Xenophon's *Cyropaedia*, which Sidney considers an epic in prose.

29 **Aeneas**] the protagonist of Virgil's *Aeneid*.

Turnus] Aeneas's antagonist in the same poem.

Tydeus] one of the seven heroes who took part in the war against Thebes in Statius's epic the *Thebaid*. Sidney's friend Cesare Pavese wrote an introduction and notes to an Italian translation of the *Thebaid* (Venice, 1570) which Sidney may have seen (Duncan-Jones 1991, 80).

Rinaldo] a knight in Ariosto's *Orlando furioso*, and the hero of Torquato Tasso's *Rinaldo* and *Gerusalemme liberata*.

31 **magnanimity**] generosity of mind.

32 **misty fearfulness and foggy desires**] Sidney suggests here that emotions cloud the intellect; an idea that was developed by Bacon in *Novum Organum*, aphorism xlixff. Compare 90/12–13, 103/11–12, and 110/13.

the saying of Plato and Tully] The saying comes from Plato's *Phaedrus*, 250D, which is referred to by Cicero in *De finibus bonorum et malorum*, II, xvi, 52, and *De officiis*, I, v, 14. Sidney obviously found the saying memorable; compare *Astrophil and Stella* 25 (Ringler 1962, 177): 'That Vertue, if it once met with our eyes, / Strange flames of *Love* it in our soules would raise'. Compare also 94/44ff.

33 **who**] whoever.

34 **this man**] the epic poet (the 'who' of line 32).

35 **holiday**] festive.

deign not to disdain] a wordplay for emphasis.

37 **to the maintaining**] in support of.

40 **worthies**] heroes.

41 **Aeneas**] On the idealising of Aeneas in the sixteenth century, see 85/32–3 note. Passages which expatiate on Aeneas's virtues, as Sidney does here, are common. Boccaccio writes in *De genealogia deorum*: 'Re-read those lines in the *Aeneid* where Aeneas exhorts his friends to endure patiently their labours to the last. How fine was the ardour of his wish to die a fair death from his wounds to save his country. How noble his devotion to his father when he bore him to safety on his shoulders through the midst of the enemy . . . What strength of character in spurning and breaking the chains of an obstreperous passion. What justice and generosity . . . among friends and strangers at the games' (Boccaccio 1930, 74–5). Pontanus (*De sermone*, ed. S. Lupi and A. Risicato (Lucca, 1954), II, v, 61–2) writes: 'Indeed what is there in the way of piety, religion, endurance, courage, and again what in respect of the uncertainty of human affairs and the changes of fortune, which Virgil neglects in his treatment of Aeneas? So that even for those who have departed this life, one may learn in full what rewards there are and to whom they were properly meted out, and the same with punishments. And Horace said about Homer . . .' (quoting the couplet from which Sidney quotes at

100/9). Compare also Montaigne, *Essays*, II, xxxvi, who attaches the same quotation from Horace to a commendation of Homer and Virgil. There is a lengthy eulogy of Aeneas in Scaliger 1617, III, xi, 207ff., proclaiming his excellence in thought and action, 'in war and peace', 'as a ruler', in his piety (209), in his fortitude (213), etc., but this offers no close verbal parallel with Sidney here.

42 **tablet]** notebook or small picture.

44 **religious ceremonies]** statues of household gods.

44–100/1 **to leave Dido]** Dido, Queen of Carthage, gave hospitality to Aeneas and his followers, and Dido and Aeneas became lovers. But Jupiter sent the messenger-god Mercury to command Aeneas to leave Carthage and sail to Italy, where he was to found the Roman state. He obeyed, and Dido killed herself. This passage answers Gosson's insinuation that Virgil abused his art in describing 'the lust of Dido' (Gosson 1974, 76); and compare Ascham's disapproval of Virgil's 'choice of examples for Imitation' when writing the Dido episode (Ascham 1904, 272).

p. 100/2 **craved other]** demanded the opposite.

6 **government]** behaviour.

7 **prejudicating humour]** an inclination to be prejudiced.

in excellency fruitful] i.e. producing excellent effects.

9 *melius . . . Crantore]* The quotation comes from the opening of Horace's *Epistles*, I, ii, addressed to Lollius:

> Trojani belli scriptorem, maxime Lolli, . . .
> Dum tu declamas Romae, Praeneste relegi.
> Qui, quid sit pulchrum, quid turpe; quid utile, quid non,
> Planius, ac melius Chrysippo et Crantore dicit.

(While you were speaking in public at Rome, Lollius the firstborn, I have been reading at Praeneste the author of the Trojan War over again. He shows what is becoming, what is dishonourable; what is profitable, and what is not, much more openly and satisfactorily than Chrysippus and Crantor.) Chrysippus of Soli (c. 280–204 B.C.) was the most eminent of the early Stoic philosophers after Zeno. Crantor (*fl.* 300 B.C.) was the first of the commentators on the philosophical texts of Plato.

11–12 **who often are sick, but . . . cannot tell where]** Gosson treats poetry and drama as diseases, but himself admits that diagnosis of these diseases is problematic: 'the Anatomy of man [is] set out by experience: But the abuses of plaies cannot be showen, because they passe the degree of the instrument' (Gosson 1974, 95). Compare 102/24.

11 **in faith]** honestly.

12 **his]** its; but 'him' (13) transforms Poetry into a person, as happens with abstract nouns elsewhere in the *Apology* (see for instance 98/4–5, where

Comedy is referred to as **he**, and in the passage below, 15–35, in which **Poetry** (15) again becomes **him** (20)).

13 **the sum that contains him**] i.e. the whole discipline.

13–14 **the particularities descending from him**] the elements of which poetry is composed.

14 **fast**] firm.

carping] fault-finding.

15–35 **Since then . . . triumph**] This is a careful summary of the *Apology* up to this point, in which each clause can be referred back to particular stages of Sidney's argument.

15–16 **of most fatherly antiquity**] the original parent.

16 **as from whence**] since it is the art from which.

21 **retain themselves within their subject**] are limited by their subject-matter.

23 **stuff**] cloth (out of which clothes are made).

23–4 **doth not . . . conceit**] i.e. does not derive an idea from the material he is concerned with, but invents material for himself to suit the idea he wishes to put across. **matter** in this case seems to mean physical material – the actual events studied by the historians, the physical world on which philosophers base their observations – as opposed to intellectual material or **conceit**.

24 **his description**] the analysis of him.

end] purpose, objective.

31–2 **the flowers of it**] its attractive verbal techniques. Christ used these in parables such as those of Dives and Lazarus and the Prodigal Son, 91/34–43.

32 **kinds**] genres.

32–3 **in their united forms . . . severed dissections**] when seen as a whole, and when their component parts are examined separately like the parts of a dissected body. 'Dissection' was a new word in sixteenth-century English; the more usual term was 'anatomy'.

34 **the laurel crown**] In 1341 the Italian poet Petrarch was awarded a laurel crown such as victorious generals had been presented with in ancient Rome. Similar coronations of poets with laurel became common in fifteenth- and sixteenth-century Italy; see J. Burckhardt, *Civilisation of the Renaissance in Italy* (London, 1960), III, 4, pp. 123–4, and E. H. Wilkins, 'The Coronation of Petrarch', *Speculum* 18 (1943), 155–97. On the significance of the laurel crown in early modern England, see Richard Helgerson, *Self-crowned Laureates* (Berkeley, Los Angeles and London, 1983), ch. 1.

35 **of**] above.

36 **But because we have ears**] Here Sidney begins his rebuttal of charges against poetry.

37 **to weigh greatly**] heavy (in a pair of weighing scales).

39-40 **yielding**] admitting.

41 *mysomousoi*] Muse-haters (Sidney's invention). This interjection of invented Greek words is typical of Erasmus, especially in *The Praise of Folly*, and anticipates Sidney's discussion of Erasmus as a 'playing wit', 101/7ff.

42 **seek a praise**] look for approval.

p. 101/1 **quips and scoffs**] clever remarks and jeers.

2 **carping**] See 100/14 note.

spleen] an abdominal organ thought to be the seat of ill-tempered laughter.

3 **stay**] hold back.

a through-beholding] a thorough consideration of.

4 **full of very idle easiness**] i.e. pointless and glib. Boccaccio attacks as detractors of poetry those 'garrulous and detestably arrogant' writers who 'condemn everything that the best man can do', and who 'seem to cheapen and vilify [poetry] . . . by obscene raillery' (Boccaccio 1930, 18-19).

5-6 **an itching tongue may rub itself upon it**] inverts Sidney's description of satirical iambic poetry **which rubs the galled mind** (97/33-4) – here it is the galled mind that is doing the rubbing.

7 **playing wit**] playful cleverness. Pontanus in *De sermone* and Castiglione in the *Courtier* gave elaborate treatment to the art of conversation, and carefully distinguished *asteimus*, **playing wit**, from *sarcasmus*, sarcasm (Castiglione 1928, 133-79). Stefano Guazzo, in his *Civile Conversation* (Brescia, 1574; trans. George Pettie, 1581), has a lengthy discussion of 'the slaunderous, who with the falseness of their tongues, seeke to blemishe the brightnesse of others names' (Pettie's translation, introd. Sir Edward Sullivan (2 vols, London, 1925), I, 65-77). Conversation or writing which ridiculed people or texts to the point of unwearied frivolousness (as, for example, in texts by the Italian satirist Pietro Aretino (1492-1556) and many of his countrymen; see J. Burckhardt, *Civilisation of the Renaissance in Italy* (London, 1960), II, 3), as well as the more weighty humanist literature of sustained paradox (to which More, Erasmus, and Rabelais contributed), could bring embarrassment to the speaker or writer, as Sidney suggests. The eminent Elizabethan schoolmaster Richard Mulcaster explains: 'If anie kinde of writer for vaunt, not for want of wit, or vpon som particular cause else, do practis his pen or whet his tung against the good in learning, as Lucian doth in most places of hole works, as Agrippa doth in his vane book of vanities in science, theie cannot wound learning, tho theie strike at the warts which be in som professors' (Mulcaster 1925, 50). Mulcaster goes on to show that 'euen if the good qualitie transubstantiate the euill' yet 'such fellowes bewrie [betray] their own folie, euen in jeast to turn their heles against their own helps, & by their fond doing to stir som fond heads, to mislike that in earnest, which theie ment but in jeast' (51).

7-9 **the discretion . . . plague**] These are 'three examples of the mock-encomium, a favourite humanist genre with which the *Apology* itself has some kinship'

(Duncan-Jones 1989, 233/853–5 note). Cornelius Agrippa (see 15 below) praised **the discretion of an ass** in the last chapter of his satire on the arts of learning, *The Vanitie . . . of Artes and Sciences*. Erasmus, in the *Praise of Folly*, recalls that the second-century poet Favorinus wrote in praise of a 'feuer quartane' (Erasmus 1965, 9); and Thomas Wilson refers to Favorinus's 'triuial cause' (Wilson 1909, 8 and 14). Francesco Berni (c. 1496–1535) wrote comic poems in praise of debt and plague (*Il primo libro dell'opere burlesche* (Florence, 1558), 9–18, 80–7).

10 **turn**] reverse, invert.

11 *Ut . . . mali*] The verse is adapted from Ovid's *Ars amatoria*, II, 661–2: 'Dic habilem, quaecumque brevis, quae turgida, plenam: / Et lateat vitium proximitate boni' (Call the meagre pretty, and the excessive well-rounded, so that any fault may be concealed by being associated with a virtue).

15 **Agrippa**] Henricus Cornelius Agrippa of Nettesheim (1486–1535), a celebrated exponent of the so-called occult philosophy, or art of magic. He served as secretary to the Holy Roman Emperor Maximilian I, studied at various universities, and held in European courts a variety of appointments which brought him little personal profit but fame and many quarrels. Among other works he published *De occulta philosophia* (1531–3) and the text to which Sidney refers here, *De incertitudine et vanitate scientiarum et artium* (Antwerp, 1530; trans. as *Of the Vanitie and Uncertaintie of Artes and Sciences* by J. Sanford, 1569), a satire on contemporary aspirations to learning (see **88/18–33** note). On Sidney's use of this work in the *Apology*, see A. C. Hamilton, 'Sidney and Agrippa', *RES* N.S. 7 (1956), 151–7.

13 **Erasmus . . . commending of folly**] Erasmus's *Praise of Folly* (1509; trans. Thomas Chaloner, 1549) was the most celebrated sixteenth-century example of the 'mock encomium' (see 7–9 note). Chaloner said of it: 'by the judgement of many learned men, [Erasmus] neuer shewed more arte, nor witte, in any the grauest boke he wrote, than in this . . . Whiche the reader hauyng any considerance, shall soone espie, how in euery mattier, yea almost every clause, is hidden besides the myrth, some deaper sence and purpose' (Erasmus 1965, 5).

15 **railers**] witty users of abusive language.

another foundation] a different, deeper purpose – that is, Erasmus praised folly and Agrippa abused the study of the arts in order to teach their readers. See 13 note. James Sanford explains in his translation of Agrippa, 'although this Authoure sharply inueigheth against them . . . yet his intent is, not to deface the worthinesse of Artes and Sciences, but to reproue and detecte theire euil vses, and declare the excellencie of his wit in disprouinge them, for a shewe of Learning' (Agrippa 1569, sig. *3r).

16 **Marry**] an exclamation, originally 'Mary' (the mother of God). Sidney uses this type of exclamation when he wishes to add a note of amused surprise or contempt; compare **109/31**, and '**forsooth**', **96/19**.

pleasant] witty.

17 **correct . . . the noun**] This is particularly bad grammatical practice when

correcting a sentence in an inflected language such as Latin, when the case of the noun helps to explain the sense of the verb.

18 **confirm**] firmly establish.

19 **scoffing cometh not of wisdom**] Compare Proverbs 14:6 ('A scorner seeketh wisdom, and findeth it not').

20–1 **good fools**] wags, comedians. On this use of 'good', see *OED s.v. adj.* 7.c.

21 **humorous**] peevish, irritable.

24 **versing**] writing in metre. Agrippa attacks **rhyming and versing** in *Of the Vanitie . . . of Artes*: Poetry was devised, he says, 'to no other ende, but to please the eares of foolishe men, with wanton Rithmes [i.e. rhymes], with measures [i.e. metres], and weightinesse of sillables, and with a vaine iarringe of wordes, and to deceiue mens mindes with the delectation of fables, and with fardels of lies' (Agrippa 1569, D3r).

It is already said] See 87/26–7 note.

26 **presuppose**] assuming.

27 **Scaliger**] See 108/35 note. Scaliger asserts that historically the poet gets his name not from inventing fables but from composing verses (Scaliger 1617, I, ii, 6), which in II, 124ff., he treats as essential to poetry.

28 *oratio . . . ratio*] (Latin) speech . . . reason.

28–9 *oratio . . . mortality*] An educational axiom in the sixteenth-century for which plenty of support could be found in the classical and Christian traditions. Among the Greeks, see in particular Isocrates, *Nicocles*, 6–10, and *Antidosis*, 253. Cicero discusses the basis of human society in *De officiis*, I, xvi, 50, and concludes that it is founded on the 'bond of reason and speech', since this is what distinguishes human beings from beasts. Compare Cicero, *De inventione*, I, iv, and *De oratore*, I, viii; Quintilian, *Institutes*, II, xvi; Augustine, *De doctrina christiana*, I, xxii. Pontanus, *De sermone*, begins: 'Nature gave man reason which perfected him in his animal condition, and also speech; with this intention: that under the guidance of his intellect he should be as like as possible to the angels'. See also Baldwin 1944, II, 272.

29 **mortality**] humanity.

31 **his forcible quality**] its accent and pitch; that is, the emphasis given to each of its syllables.

32 **his best measured quantity**] the length of its vowels, carefully measured. Scaliger argues that verse has a natural music (Scaliger 1617, I, ii, 6). Each fraction of human utterance is marked by both quality and quantity. Quality depends on the sharpness or weight of sound. Quantity concerns the passage of time: it relates to the time, the rhythm, and the movement of sounds. See also 115/26 note.

33 **without, perchance**] unless, perhaps.

number] groups of metrical feet.

measure] rhythm or metre (for both these terms, see 84/12 note).

order, proportion] Like **measure**, these words can be applied either to the organization of a poem in verse, or to the patterns of music, or to the moral condition of a society. If these four aspects of verse were dismissed as trivial it would therefore reflect badly on society in our time.

35 **Music . . . senses**] The humanists took up the ideas of the ancient Greeks about the effects of music on its hearers. Plato (*Laws*, II, 667–70) and Aristotle (*Politics*, 8, 5) taught that music could present to the mind through the sense of hearing a direct imitation of anger, courage, temperance, etc., and so reproduce these qualities in the listener. The belief became an Elizabethan commonplace, comprehensively set out by Richard Hooker in *Ecclesiastical Polity*, V, 38, where he considers 'the admirable facility which Musick hath to express and represent to the Mind, more inwardly than any other sensible mean, the very standing, rising and falling, the very steps and inflections every way, the turns and varieties of all Passions, whereunto the Mind is subject . . . so, although we lay altogether aside the consideration of ditty or matter, the very Harmony of sounds being framed in due sort, and carried from the ear to the spiritual faculties of our Souls, is by a native puissance and efficacy greatly available'. Compare also E.K.'s gloss on the October Eclogue, 27, in Spenser's *Shepheardes Calender* (Spenser 1989, 178).

Gosson links poetry with music, particularly piping, in *The School of Abuse*, and holds that both have been devoted to trivial uses in the Elizabethan period (Gosson 1974, 79–85). Sidney's discussion of the relation between the two arts may be a response to Gosson's attack on contemporary practices in both.

37 **memory . . . knowledge**] A common phrase; compare Tilley, M 870. Thomas Wilson gives a systematic anatomy of the mind in his *Rhetorique* (Wilson 1909, 209). At the front of the brain is the common sense, which receives impressions from the senses of hearing, sight, touch, etc.; these impressions are then analysed and sorted by the understanding, which is located in the middle part of the brain, and stored in 'the memorie called the Threasure of the minde', which 'lieth in the hinder part'.

40 **knitting up of the memory**] i.e. connecting of one memory to another so that each can be conveniently located ('knit' means 'knot').

42 **great affinity to**] close relationship with.

43 **accuseth itself**] calls attention to itself; i.e. a missing word makes itself obvious by the effect it has on the **whole work.**

p. 102/4 **the art of memory**] Memory had been the fourth of the five branches of study in the traditional art of rhetoric, but in the later Middle Ages it came to be developed as a separate subject, notably by members of the Dominican and Franciscan orders, including the Franciscan philosopher Ramon Lull (c. 1235–1316), who produced a 'logical algebra' of mnemonics later known as 'Lully's art'. Interest in the art of memory reached its height in the fifteenth- and sixteenth-centuries. In England, William Fulwood's *Castel of Memorie* (1562) rapidly went through three editions, the third of which was dedicated to Sidney's uncle the Earl of Leicester. Sidney's Italian acquaintance the ex-Dominican Giordano Bruno (1548–1600) published a new art of memory, *De umbris idearum* (Paris, 1582), and included sections on memory in several of his works. Most Renaissance scholars paid serious attention to the art. The basis of it remained, as in rhetoric, a doctrine of 'places', as Sidney explains from 5ff. In order to memorize his arguments and their proper order, an orator was taught to visualize, say, a room he knew well, in which certain features of the room were associated with stages of the argument, and certain objects or images were mentally positioned in relation to these features as a means of recalling specific points. Wilson 1909, 213, explains how to arrange images appropriately in the 'places' of memory: 'A place is called any roome, apt to receiue images'. The notion of the trained memory as a storehouse of images is said to have originated with the poet Simonides of Ceos (see 106/34 note), and was developed in discussions of rhetoric (see Cicero, *De oratore*, II, lxxxvi; *Ad Herennium*, III, xvi–xxiv; Quintilian, *Institutes*, XI, ii, 18–22). Sidney argues that with verse the positioning and relationship of words to one another have the same mnemonic effect as a system of 'places'. Harington (Smith 1904, II, 206) follows and simplifies this passage in the *Apology*. See Yates 1969.

6 **that**] presumably, the ability to furnish the memory with 'places'.

7 **seat**] position.

9 **scholar**] schoolboy.

10 **Cato**] See 86/36 note.

12 *Percontatorem . . . est*] Horace, *Epistles*, I, xviii, which is quoted and translated by Bacon: 'an inquisitive man is a prattler' (Bacon 1974, 30).

13 *Dum . . . sumus*] Ovid, *Remedium amoris*, 686: 'While each pleases himself, we are a gullible set'.

14 **delivery**] communication, teaching.

16 **Physic**] medicine.

16–17 **the rules . . . verses**] Compare Harington (Smith 1904, II, 207). Acting on the principle that verse helps the memory, medieval and Renaissance teachers versified many branches of knowledge. The most widely used Latin grammar of the late Middle Ages was the verse *Doctrinale* of Alexander of Villedieu (born c. 1170). In 1570 William Buckley of Cambridge produced his *Arithmetica memorativa* in Latin verse. Many medical treatises in English verse as well as in Latin on disease and physiology survive from the fifteenth-century and earlier, and some twelfth-century Latin verses on the art of preserving health, ascribed to the medical school of Salerno, were familiar to Elizabethan men of letters; see Puttenham 1936, 12; Smith 1904, II, 361.

18 **the only handle of**] i.e. the best way of getting a grip on; compare 100/14.

20–1 **most important imputations laid to . . . poets**] The charges against poets had come down from ancient times. Most of them had been gathered together and answered by Boccaccio in *De genealogia deorum* (Boccaccio 1930, 17–96). The young Erasmus wrote an oration on the subject (see A. Hyma, *The Youth of Erasmus* (University of Michigan, 1930), 239–331), in which he distinguishes three hostile factions: (1) the ignorant who despise all writing as 'poetry' and

who wish to destroy the whole republic of letters; (2) those who wish literary studies to be strictly monitored because they consider poetry to be a waste
of time which could be better employed; (3) those who require all writing to
be of one approved modern kind and who despise the classics. Elyot finds it
necessary to rebut charges that poetry is useless, unworthy of the attention
of great captains and kings, and detrimental to the reader's morals, since it
contains 'nothyng but baudry . . . and vnprofitable leasinges [lies]' (Elyot
1883, I, x–xiii). Vives noted that 'Poetry is openly hated by certain people;
there has been a long and varied dispute on the matter' (Vives 1931, 121). The
arguments of Erasmus, Elyot and Vives are pedagogical: they are opposing
theories of education which dismiss poetry as non-vocational and time-
wasting. This constitutes the first charge against poetry dealt with in the
Apology. The second is that poetry propagates intellectual untruths (see note
on 42ff. below). This is the charge brought against poetry by Cornelius
Agrippa (Agrippa 1569, ch. 4, fol. 11r–13v). The third objection is social: that
poetry, especially in popular stage comedies, affronts public morality. This
objection had been officially upheld by the church throughout the Middle
Ages (see E. K. Chambers, *The Medieval Stage* (Oxford, 1903), I, 9ff. and 31ff.,
and II, 290ff.), and was reasserted in the sixteenth-century by many of the
stricter moralists both in the reformed and unreformed churches (see also
98/2–3 note). The best-known statement of this opposition on social grounds
in England was Gosson's *The School of Abuse* (1579), to which Thomas Lodge
wrote an answer (Smith 1904, I, 61–86).

A full, succinct account of most of the charges brought against poetry in
Elizabethan times, together with a rebuttal of them all, is given in Wills 1958,
92–126, drawing (as Fowler indicates, 25ff.) chiefly on Lodovick Vives's *De
causis corruptarum artium*, II. Poetry is said to be worthless because in cater-
ing solely for men's pleasure it implies that men are no better than beasts. It
deals in lies and blasphemies, whitewashes bullies and criminals, and encourages sexual profligacy and other crimes. Eratosthenes, Plato, and Aristotle
called it a pack of lies. When the poets Lucan and Virgil tell the truth they
are no longer considered to be writing poetry (compare 86/38 note above).
On the stage poetry has always been a source of licentiousness and shame.
The scandalous nature of love poetry need not be gone into. Plato banished
poets from his ideal state. If poetry were a good thing, poets would be good
men, but many of them are notorious drunkards. Finally, Democritus and
others have shown that in order to be a poet one has to be insane. Compare
Atkins 1940, 104–5.

Sidney's list of charges and his responses to them are drawn from several
sources. On specific points it is possible that he recalled passages from Elyot
(see 103/21 and 44 notes) and Agrippa (see 101/15 note above). It is worth
mentioning that Harington (Smith 1904, II, 199), who follows Sidney closely
in his account of poetry, names Agrippa as the accuser and confronts his
arguments directly.

20 to] against.

24 **nurse of abuse**] This is the charge most fully elaborated by Gosson in the
School of Abuse. **abuse** means 'corruption'.

25 **a siren's sweetness**] The sirens of Greek mythology, who were encountered by Ulysses in the *Odyssey*, XII, lured sailors to their death with the sweetness of their singing. In classical times they were usually represented as birds with the heads of women, but later they were often confused with mermaids (who had the bodies of beautiful women and fishes' tails) and apparently also with serpents; see Florence McCulloch, *Medieval Latin and French Bestiaries* (University of North Carolina, 1960), 166–70, and on the allegorization of these sirens, D. W. Robertson, *A Preface to Chaucer* (Princeton, 1963), 142–4. Agrippa speaks of 'a certayne venemous sweetnesse' of 'the Mermaides' who 'with voyces, gestures, and lasciuious soundes, doe destroye and corrupt mens myndes' (Agrippa 1569, fol. 29v). Compare also Gosson 1974, 77 ('The *Syrens* song is the Saylers wracke'), and Ascham 1904, 226, who attacks 'the *Siren* songes of *Italie*', and describes the way in which Italian customs and Italian books in translation are capable of transforming an Englishman into a 'meruelous monster' (228).

the serpent's tale] The pun on 'tail' is obvious. Sidney may here be combining the sirens, who were part woman and part bird, with Renaissance pictures of the serpent which tempted Eve, in which the serpent has the face of a woman (a famous example is Michelangelo's painting of the Fall in the Sistine chapel). The sexual element in the Fall (evoked by the phrase **sinful fancy**, 25–6) is often emphasized in such pictures (see Catherine Belsey, 'Cleopatra's Seduction', in *Alternative Shakespeares*, vol. 2, ed. Terence Hawkes (London and New York, 1996), 55–6).

26 **to ear**] to plough. Compare Chaucer's *Knight's Tale*: 'I have, God woot, a large feeld to ere' (*Works*, ed. F. N. Robinson (Oxford, 1957), 26), which refers to the length of the story to be told.

27–8 **before poets did soften us**] See 105/1–4 note.

29 **manlike**] manly.

30–2 **they cry out . . . commonwealth**] Detractors give tongue like a pack of hounds when they make the point that Plato banished poets from his ideal commonwealth, as if they had become wiser than Plato himself. 'Tales of Robin Hood' became a catchphrase for extravagant boasts, as in the sixteenth-century couplet: 'Many men speke of Robyn Hode & of his Bow / Which never shot therewith, I trow'; see Tilley, R 148.

31–2 **Plato . . . commonwealth**] See 106/21 note. For the phrase, compare Gosson's *Schoole*: 'No merueyle though *Plato* shut them out of his Schoole, and banished them quite from his common wealth' (Gosson 1974, 77).

32 **this is much**] i.e. this is serious.

33 **to the first**] That poetry is time-wasting; see above, 20–1 note. Thomas North's preface to his translation of Guevara's *The Fauored Courtier* (*The Dial of Princes*, 1568 ed., sig. S3r) pronounces that 'the reading of ylle and vayn bookes [including voluptuous books, interludes and comedies] can not bee called a pastime, but aptly a very losse of tyme'; and George Gascoigne confesses that 'I finde my self giltie of much time mispent . . . in penning and endightyng sundrie toyes and trifles' (Gascoigne 1910, II, 211). See also Boccaccio 1930, 21–32.

34 *petere principium*] (Latin) beg the question: that is, the statement is based on a premise which is not proven (i.e. that poetry is a waste of time).

41 **out of earth**] from the earth. The phrase reminds Sidney's readers that he is not dealing with knowledge from heaven – that is, with religious matters. Compare 12/17–20 and 89/39–42 and 95/8–9.

42 **the second . . . they should be . . . liars**] Here **should** denotes a reported statement (see Abbott 1870, § 328). Cornelius Agrippa had made his primary charge against poetry that it 'doeth deserue to bee called the principall Author of lyes' (Agrippa 1569, ch. 4, fol. 11r); but the charge was ancient. The saying that poets are liars was attributed to Solon (see **82/34** note) by Aristotle in *Metaphysics*, I, 2, 983a. Xenophanes of Colophon (c. 530 B.C.), himself a poet, attacked Homer and Hesiod for falsehood. Pindar felt the need to defend himself as a truthteller in his First Olympian Ode. By Plato's time the debate was a thoroughly familiar one. The old charge was sharply reiterated by Eratosthenes of Cyrene (276–196 B.C.) and refuted as fiercely by Strabo (c. 54 B.C.–A.D. 24); see **82/8–10** note. The argument went on throughout the Middle Ages. John of Salisbury (*Entheticus*, 183ff.) and other twelfth-century writers argue that the lies of the poet serve truth by using words figuratively (see Curtius 1953, 206); Thomas Aquinas on the other hand returns to the old charge 'that Poets lie in many things, as the proverb says' (see Curtius 1953, 218). A qualified opposition to poetry remained characteristic of medieval scholasticism and was perpetuated, as many other scholastic notions were, by sixteenth- and seventeenth-century radical Protestants (see **103/44** note). From the earliest days of Christianity there had been a steady current of opposition to the religious falsehoods of pagan poets. Many (but not all) humanists of the fifteenth- and sixteenth-centuries denied the charge. Boccaccio gave a general defence in *De genealogia deorum* (Boccaccio 1930, 62–9). He makes use of Augustine's *De mendacio*, which identified the varieties of the lie, and shows that as poetry does not claim to convey literal truth it cannot reasonably be charged with not providing it. Coluccio Salutati also deals with the question and justifies poetry (Salutati 1951, I, 65ff.). Pontanus (*De sermone*, II, ch. v, pp. 61–3) indicates the different sorts of lie and carefully exculpates poetic fictions.

Sidney is therefore dealing with a familiar theme. He counters the old charge with a re-statement (as he says, paradoxically phrased) of Aristotle's discussion of the position taken by Plato. Plato had attacked poetry as an imitation twice removed from the truth (*Republic*, X) – not so much a lie as an enfeeblement of truth. Aristotle distinguished between the 'real', which belongs to the realm of the intellect, and the 'actual', which deals with matters of sense and experience, and so was able to offer a definition of imitation which relates it with the 'real': 'if it be objected that the description is not true to fact, the poet may perhaps reply, "But the objects are as they ought to be"' (*Poetics*, XXV, 1460B), and what 'they ought to be' is what they 'really' are. Sidney's answer to the charge that poets are liars is similarly contained in his understanding of poetry as 'imitation', which is basically Aristotelian.

p. 103/2 **though he would**] even if he wished.

3–5 **The astronomer**] Compare Agrippa 1569, ch. 30, fol. 44v: astronomers 'doe no lesse differ touching the greatnesse and distaunce of the Sunne, the Mone and other Starres, neither is there among them any constancie of opinion nor veritie of celestial things'.

4 **escape**] avoid [being a liar].

5 **physicians**] According to Cornelius Agrippa: 'when the common people will shewe any that lyeth shamefully, they say to hym: Thou lyest like a Phisition' (Agrippa 1569, fol. 144r). 'Well neere alwaies there is more daunger in the Phisition, and his medicine, than in the sicknesse itself' (fol. 142).

aver] state as a fact.

6 **Charon**] in Greek mythology, the ferryman who rowed the dead across the river Styx to the underworld. Compare *NA*, 343: 'many of those first over-thrown had the comfort to see the murtherers overrun them to Charon's ferry'.

8 **affirm**] assert.

8–9 **the poet ... nothing affirms**] In Minturno 1559, 68, Syncerus, the spokesman for Platonism, asks similarly: 'How can he deceive, who himself invents everything?' But this type of justification for the poet was implicit in the old distinction between *fabula ficta*, fiction, 'which contains [from a legal point of view] nothing true, nor anything resembling the truth' (*Ad Herennium*, I, viii, 13), and *historia*, history, which is the record of things actually done. Compare Isidore of Seville, *Etymologies*, II, xli (*PL* 82, col. 122). Augustine (*Confessions*, III, vi) saw the problem clearly, and was troubled that the fables of the poets, which claimed to be nothing more than fiction, should nevertheless have the power to absorb him so completely: 'Verses and poems I can turn to true food, and "Medea flying" though I did sing, I affirmed it not; though I heard it sung, I believed it not'. Harington (Smith 1904, II, 201) follows Sidney's argument here closely.

10 **artists**] those skilled in the 'liberal arts'; men of learning.

10–11 **especially the historian**] The historian is still Sidney's chief opponent. Compare Agrippa 1569, sig. E2r: 'Historiographers doo so mutch disagree emonge themselves, and doo write so variable and diuers thinges of one matter, that it is impossible, but that a number of them shoulde be verie Liers'. He goes on to show their methods of lying.

13–14 **circles about your imagination**] To draw a circle on the ground was to define the area within which the magic was operative. For a detailed description of such a circle, see Marlowe, *Doctor Faustus* (c. 1592; ed. Roma Gill, London and New York, 1965), I, iii, 9–13. But compare Sidney's allusion to the 'sweet charming force' of poetry, 104/28.

14 **conjure you**] means both 'cast a spell on you' and 'appeal to you in all seriousness' (compare 116/20).

15 **authorities of**] supporting evidence from.

entry opening words.

16 **inspire into**] literally, 'breathe [invention] into'.

good invention] worthy theme.

19 **without**] unless.

20 **before-alleged**] referred to earlier in Sidney's argument (see **96/29–37**).

durst scarce say] would hardly dare to say.

21 **none so simple would say**] nobody would be so naive as to say.

Aesop] See **92/5** note. Compare Elyot 1883, II, 400: 'I suppose no man thinketh that Esope wrote gospelles, yet who doughteth but that in his fables the foxe, the hare, and the wolfe, though they never spake, do teache many good wysedomes'.

24–5 *Thebes* . . . **old door**] Labelled doors were used to indicate the locality of the action in court and university plays in Sidney's time; see Allardyce Nicoll, *The Development of the Theatre* (3rd rev. ed., London, 1948), 119–20.

25–6 **arrive . . . to**] learn to.

27 **what . . . what**] i.e. of what . . . of what. See *OED s.* what, *rel. pron.* C. I, 7.c.

28 **give the lie to**] denounce as lies.

affirmatively] literally.

29–30 **as in History . . . falsehood**] just as they come to history looking for truth and leave it weighed down with lies.

31ff. **use the narration**] Recalls the conclusion of Plutarch's *On Listening to Lectures*: 'Let the listener make his memory a guide to invention: looking on the discourse of others only as a kind of first principle or seed'.

31 **imaginative ground-plot**] In the sixteenth century the term 'ground-plot' is used to mean a plot of land ripe for development, either as a garden or for building. Thomas Hill uses the term in his discussion of the invention of gardens in *The Gardener's Labyrinth* (1577), ed. Richard Mabey (Oxford, 1987), 23: '*Pliny* . . . reporteth, that a Garden plot in the ancient time at *Rome*, was none other, then a smal and simple inclosure of ground, which through the labour and diligence of the Husbandman, yielded a commodity and yearly revenue unto him. But after years (that man more esteemed of himself, and sought an easier life) devised and framed this ground plot for the mind, as for pleasure and delight'. In the *Arcadia* Sidney seems at one point to use 'ground-plot' to mean land fit for human habitation: 'wretched Gynecia, where canst thou find any small ground-plot for hope to dwell upon?' (*OA*, 81). Elsewhere he uses it figuratively: 'But as a painter doth at the first but show a rude proportion of the thing he imitates, which after with more curious hand he draws to the representing each lineament, so had her thoughts (beating about it continually) received into them a ground plot of her device, although she had not in each part shaped it according to a full determination' (*OA*, 189). Here the 'ground plot' sounds like a plan or sketch for something that has yet to be made – whether a picture, a

building or a garden. But it may still be associated in Sidney's mind with the cultivation of the soil; on the following page Cleophila is 'still expecting the *fruit* of the happy and hoped-for invention' (190, my emphasis).

If Sidney is using 'ground-plot' in the *Apology* to mean 'ground suitable for cultivation', he may be suggesting that the reader use poetry as the soil in which to cultivate 'profitable' ideas; that is, ideas which will be of value in producing the 'fruit' (94/34) of earthly learning, 'virtuous action' (88/31–2). Compare Plutarch's reference to the discourse of others as a 'first principle or seed', 31ff. note above; the quotations from Plutarch's *On the Education of Children* at 109/40 and 42–3 notes; and Olney's reference to the 'perpetual spring of ever-growing invention' in his epistle *To the Reader* (printed at the beginning of these Notes, p. 118). See also Spenser's account of the 'noursery / Of vertue', *Faerie Queene*, VI, Proem, st. 3.

33 **hereto**] to this.

34 **argueth a conceit of**] implies that the poets are thinking of.

36 **'John a Stile' and 'John a Noakes'**] John (who lives) at the stile and John (who lives) at the oaks; fictitious names used in legal arguments and debates, equivalent to 'John Doe' and 'Richard Roe', still used in American law.

38 **lively**] lifelike.

42 **bishop**] The word 'bishop', which belonged to the European tradition of names given to chess-pieces, seems to have replaced the Middle English word 'alfin' as the name for this piece as a result of new developments in the game of chess in the sixteenth-century. See H. R. Murray, *History of Chess* (rev. ed., Oxford, 1963), 424.

44 **Their third is**] The third argument against poetry is that it is a school of corruption (**abuse**); see 102/20–1 note. Here Sidney restricts himself to a rebuttal of the charges that poetry encourages (1) sexual immorality (103/44–104/44), and (2) 'effeminacy' – that it weakens men by luring them away from the traditionally masculine arts of war (105/1–106/14). Both were charges often seriously made by humanists in sixteenth-century England. Juan Vives acknowledges the corrupting power of erotic poetry and the need for selective reading (Vives 1931, 126ff.). Similarly Elyot, though denying that poetry is 'nothing but bawdry and unprofitable leasings', urges the wise reader in entering the garden of the Muses to trample the nettles of immorality under his feet (Elyot 1883, I, 123); a warning which was often repeated by English poets in the 1570s. Elyot's anxiety about the corrupting effects of erotic poetry went further in his *Defence of Good Women* (1540); see G. B. Pace, 'Elyot against Poetry', *MLN* 56 (1937), 597–9. See also the attack on the 'Trim songes of loue' which address themselves to 'Venus that same strompet vyle' in *The Court of Virtue* (1565), by the Protestant surgeon John Hall (Hall 1961, 15–16).

In the last quarter of the sixteenth century, during the Counter-Reformation, the scruples of both Catholics and Protestants multiplied. Weinberg 1961, I, 8, 297–348, gives an account of the swing towards a purified Christian poetic among the Italian theorists. An English Catholic rejection of erotic poetry is offered by Robert Southwell in his dedications to

Saint Peter's Complaint (1595) and *Mary Magdalen's Tears* (1591). On the Protestant reaction (of which the so-called 'Puritan' attack on the stage is only one aspect) see Sasek 1961, esp. chs 4 and 7. In general most English Protestants thought poetry of value when it promoted civic virtues, militant patriotism, or respect for religion, and this is the position Sidney takes here. In 1582 the Privy Council attempted to replace 'such lascivious poets as are commonly read . . . in . . . grammar-schooles' by poetic texts 'heroicall and of good instruction' (see Warton's *History of English Poetry*, sect. liii).

p. 104/2–4 **Comedies . . . the Lyric . . . the Elegiac**] In dealing with these earlier (97/28ff., **99/1ff.**) Sidney had kept discreetly silent about their association with love.

4 **Elegiac**] elegiac poet.
want] lack.

4–5 **even to the Heroical**] even as far as the epic. Harington (Smith 1904, II, 209) quotes this passage from the *Apology*. The Italian epic poets of the sixteenth century fused the martial themes of classical epic with the love interest of medieval romance (compare Tasso, *Gerusalemme liberata*, I, ii–iii). Often the heroic itself in the late sixteenth century is defined in terms of the infinite sufferings of love. Giordano Bruno in *Gli heroici furori* (1585), dedication (addressed to Sidney), writes of 'Love having taken to itself wings and become heroical'.

5ff. **Alas, Love . . .**] Boccaccio, answering the same charge that poetry corrupts, likewise breaks off to exclaim: 'Worthy indeed is their homage to Love, whose power overcame first Phoebus, then Hercules – each victorious against monsters' (Boccaccio 1930, 77). Compare also Spenser, *Shepheardes Calender*, October Eclogue, 85–114, and *OA*, 20. Rhetorically, an apostrophe or exclamation is useful, as Quintilian (*Institutes*, IX, ii) observes, in raising the emotional tone. Sidney of course cannot exonerate poetry as he himself practised it from the charge of being preoccupied with love. Instead he launches into a passage full of elaborate rhetorical figures (reminiscent of many passages in the two *Arcadias*), with the wordplay of **defend** and **offend** (6); the succession of **grant . . . grant . . . grant** (8–12; a recognised figure of 'admittance' or 'paramologia'; see Puttenham 1936, 227–8); the antithesis of **beastly fault . . . only man, and no beast**, 8–9; and the paregmena (use of the same word in various cases) **beastly . . . beast, lovely . . . Love, grant . . . granted.** In these ways he gives impetus to a vulnerable argument, and yet by humour and irony saves this elaborate construction (5–17) from sounding pompous.

8 **love of beauty**] Compare *NA*, 106: 'O Zelmane, who will resist [Love] must either have no wit, or put out his eyes. Can any man resist his creation? Certainly, by love we are made, and to love we are made. Beasts only cannot discern beauty; and let them be in the roll of beasts that do not honour it.' The general idea that only man discerns beauty, which is both the cause and the product of love, is a Renaissance commonplace.

11–12 **spent a good deal of their lamp-oil**] Ronald Levao suggests that this is an unkind dig at the philosophers' sexual impotence: 'spend' in Elizabethan

English could mean 'ejaculate', but the philosophers have spent only lamp-oil in love's service. See Levao, 'Sidney's Feigned Apology', in Kay 1987, 133.

13 **they will have**] they wish to be.

15 **sentence**] i.e. legal judgment, verdict.

16–17 **Poetry . . . Poetry**] Compare *OA*, 20: 'Those troublesome effects you say it breeds be not the fault of love, but of him that loves'.

wit] mind, intellect.

19–20 **eikastike**] imitative; **phantastike** dreamlike, imaginary (here in a derogatory sense). The terms are presumably Greek feminine adjectives agreeing with '**Poesy**' (18). Sidney may owe his discussion of them to a similar discussion by Jean de Serres or Serranus (c. 1540–98) in the preface to his Latin translation of Plato's *Ion* (see S. K. Heninger, 'Sidney and Serranus' *Plato*', in Kinney 1988, 27–44). Plato made the distinction in the *Sophist* (235) between the art of representing and the art of suggesting an appearance (the 'phantastic'), and concludes (266ff.) that this art of the phantastic is worthless and possibly harmful. See Hathaway 1962, 14–16, for the development among sixteenth-century Italian critics of this distinction, which was also appropriated by the French Pléiade. Ronsard, *Abrégé de l'art poétique françois*, defines 'invention' as the natural faculty of an imagination conceiving ideas and the forms of everything that can be imagined, earthly and heavenly, living and inanimate, in order to represent, describe, and imitate them; but by the invention is not meant fantastic and melancholic imaginings. The fullest use of the distinction was made by Jacopo Mazzoni in the dispute in Italy during the 1580s over the poetic stature of Dante; see Weinberg 1961, II, 636–46, 877–83. Sidney's use of the distinction reinforces his earlier distinction between daydreams, which are **wholly imaginative**, and poetry, whose fictions are based on 'real' ideas – ideas of things as they ought to be and could be in reality – which may be put into practice **to make many Cyruses** (85/38–43). Compare this passage with Puttenham's discussion of the good and bad forms of 'phantasie' (Puttenham 1936, 18–20).

20 **fancy**] the mental apprehension of an object perceived by the senses; also the faculty of forming mental representations of things not present to the senses.

21–2 **some excellent perspective**] On the increasing excitement – and anxiety – in late sixteenth-century England over the power of perspective to create illusions, see Gent 1981, 23–5.

22–3 **fit for building and fortification**] Early theorists of the Renaissance regarded painting as an activity combining practical observation with artistic representation: 'Painting is a science because of its foundation on mathematical perspective and on the study of nature', according to Anthony Blunt (Blunt 1940, 26). Hence the painter's concern with mathematics, perspective, and proportions, as well as with domestic, civic, and military design. The great German painter Albrecht Dürer wrote a series of practical treatises at the end of his life on the scientific aspects of the painter's craft: *Instruction in Measuration with Compass and Triangle* (1525), *The Theory of Fortification* (1527), and *Four Books on Human Proportion* (1528).

23–4 **Abraham . . . Isaac**] In Genesis 22:1–13, Abraham is commanded by God to sacrifice his son Isaac as a test of his obedience. Abraham prepares to obey, but at the last moment God expresses his satisfaction with this proof of Abraham's loyalty and permits him to sacrifice a ram instead. The sacrifice of Isaac was a common theme in medieval and Renaissance painting, and Théodore de Bèze (see 108/34 note) wrote an influential play about it in French, *Abraham sacrifiant* (1550, trans. Arthur Golding 1577). For other six-teenth-century versions of the story see Leah Scragg, *Shakespeare's Alternative Tales* (London and New York, 1996), ch. 4, esp. 82–7.

24 **Judith killing Holofernes**] The story is told in the book of Judith, which was omitted along with the rest of the apocrypha from Protestant editions of the Bible. Judith cut off the head of Holofernes, an enemy of the Jews, with the help of an assistant. She was frequently represented in the Renaissance; see the list of paintings in Pilger 1956, I, 191–6. Salluste du Bartas wrote a poem on the subject, *La Judit* (1574).

David fighting with Goliath] In 1 Samuel 17, the young shepherd David is selected by God as the Jewish champion in the war against the Philistines, and kills the Philistine giant Goliath with a stone flung from a sling. For Renaissance paintings see Pilger 1956, I, 138–9. Sidney's insistence on a careful choice of subject and his condemnation of erotic themes are in line with the artistic developments of the Italian Counter-Reformation; see Blunt 1940, ch. viii, 103–36. But Boccaccio, in condemning artists who abuse their art by their licentiousness, makes a similar reference to painting (Boccaccio 1930, 38).

25 **ill-pleased**] pleased by evil sights.

wanton] erotic.

26 **better hidden matters**] matters better hidden.

26–7 **shall the abuse . . . odious**] This question is also answered in the negative by Isocrates (*Nicocles*, 4) and by Aristotle (*Rhetoric*, I, i). Quintilian (*Institutes*, II, xvi) denies that because rhetoric can be put to wrong uses it is necessarily bad. 'For if this line of argument were followed, neither generals, nor magistrates, nor medicines, nor wisdom itself were praiseworthy . . . The sword is not made simply for the soldier – a thief can use the same weapon.' 34–44 below expands Quintilian's argument.

27 **yield**] admit.

28 **charming**] bewitching; influencing by magic (compare 82/21). Stephen Gosson claims that poets 'bewitch the reader with bawdie charmes' (Gosson 1974, 126).

30 **concluding**] finally proving.

31 **contrariwise**] on the contrary.

it is a good reason] it is good logic (to say that . . .).

31–3 **whatsoever . . . most good**] Castiglione argues the same thing in the *Courtier* when confuting the opinion of old men who consider the present to be worse than the past: 'Therefore when our olde men prayse the Courtes of times past because there were not in them so vitious men, as some that are in ours, they do not know that there were not also in them so vertuous men, as some that are in ours. The which is no wonder, for no ill is so evil, as that which ariseth of the corrupt seede of goodnesse. And therefore where nature nowe bringeth forth much better wittes than she did tho [then], even as they that be given to goodnesse doe much better than did those of their time, so also they that bee given to ill doe much worse' (Castiglione 1928, 90).

32–3   **upon . . . title**] everything derives its **title** (the name appropriate to its status) from its proper use.

34   **rampire**] defence.

34–6   **the skill of Physic . . . the most violent destroyer?**] A sixteenth-century commonplace. Compare Stephen Gosson, *An Apologie of the Schoole of Abuse* (1579): 'When we accuse the Phisition for killing his patient, we finde no faulte with the Arte it selfe, but with him that hath abused the same' (Gosson 1974, 125).

36   **even and right**] terms from carpentry: literally, make level and straight (that is, fair and just), as opposed to **crooked**. Compare 88/21.

41–2   **With a sword . . . country**] For the dual uses of the sword for purposes of offence and defence, fidelity and treachery, see Maslen 1997, 117–18, 134–5, 153–4, and 156. Sidney's choice of analogy may have been prompted by the joint attack on the misuses of logic and fencing in Gosson's *School of Abuse* (Gosson 1974, 102ff.), which is followed by an acknowledgement that both words and swords are necessary for the defence of a nation (106 and 109).

43   **fathers of lies**] Gosson uses this phrase in *The School of Abuse* (see Gosson 1974, 78). Compare Sidney's own phrase at 102/23, **the mother of lies** (which Agrippa also uses, Agrippa 1569, sig. D4v).

p. 105/1–4   **before poets . . . fit to be done**] The charge that poetry (and other forms of learning) produces and was the product of effeminacy – in other words, that it had a debilitating effect on the 'masculine' virtues – was an ancient one. See 106/3 and 107/8–11 notes, and compare Cicero, *Tusculan Disputations*, II, ii, 27. Gosson argues that Elizabethan poetry has feminized the nation in *The School of Abuse*: 'Consider with thy selfe (gentle Reader) the olde discipline of Englande, mark what we were before, & what we are now: Leaue *Rome* a while, and cast thine eye back to thy Predecessors, and tell mee howe wonderfully wee have beene chaunged, since we were schooled with these abuses' (Gosson 1974, 90–1). See also 25 note below.

1   **in price**] valued.

4   **Sphinx**] In Greek mythology the sphinx was a monster with a woman's bust and the body of a lion who asked riddles of passers-by. When the hero Oedipus answered her riddle she killed herself. For Oedipus see 91/11–13 note.

5   **hath the precedence of**] goes back further than.

6   **in our plainest homeliness**] at our most primitive.

Albion] According to medieval historians the island of Britain was called Albion before the Trojan conqueror Brutus renamed it after himself. Thomas Cooper in his *Dictionary* suggests that earlier Greek adventurers 'wondering and rejoycing at their good arriual nameth this Ile in Greek Olbion . . . *happie*, Felix'.

8 **chainshot**] cannonballs linked by a chain, designed to cause widespread damage among footsoldiers and cavalry.

8–9 **bookishness**] 'Bookish' was already a disparaging term in the sixteenth century.

9–15 **certain Goths . . . countries**] The story is told in the continuation of Dio Cassius, *Roman Histories*, LIV, 17, which sets it during the siege of Athens by the Goths in A.D. 267. It also appears in Montaigne's *Essays*, I, xxiv, *Of Pedantisme*.

10 **spoil**] plunder.

11 **hangman**] villain, rogue. See Ringler 1962, 22 and note.

belike] no doubt.

execute the fruits of their wits] put into practice the ideas of those.

16 **the ordinary doctrine of ignorance**] is that all reading is a waste of time (**ordinary doctrine** means 'common teaching'). 'These persones that so moche contemne lernyng' are considered by Elyot in the *Governour* (Elyot 1883, I, 98ff); and see J. H. Hexter, 'The Education of the Aristocracy in the Renaissance', in *Reappraisals in History* (London, 1961), 45–70. The foolish shepherd Dametas expresses the 'ordinary doctrine' in *NA*, 126.

18 **but Poetry**] excluding poetry.

20 **all government of action**] all control over one's own and other people's actions.

23 *jubeo . . . libenter*] From Horace's *Satires*, I, i, 53: 'iubeas miserum esse libenter' which Sidney adapts to mean 'I willingly tell him to remain a fool'.

25 **Poetry is the companion of the camps**] The idea that the profession of arms was perfectly compatible with the art of letters had been current among many writers in the Middle Ages, and was developed by sixteenth-century educationalists such as Sir Thomas Elyot and Roger Ascham. A number of writers of the 1570s presented themselves as equally dedicated to the arts of war and of poetry: among them the soldier-poets George Gascoigne and George Whetstone, as well as Sidney himself. See Smith 1904, I, 395. The close alliance between Mars, god of war, and the Muses, patrons of learning, was a favourite Renaissance topic. Scaliger (*Oratio* ii (Toulouse, 1621), 16) writes: 'The most honourable business of war, which raises men to the rank of gods, ought not to remove anyone from literary glory, since letters are often received and cherished in the bosom of armies'. George Buchanan in the preface to *Jephthes* (1566) speaks of the close agreement between military matters and literary studies and of a sort of secret sympathy between them (compare also Buchanan's account of James I of Scotland, quoted in **108/33** note). M.-A. Muret in *Oratio* xxiii (*Opera*, I, 275), compares the arts of letters and arms at length.

camps] military encampments.

25–6 **Orlando Furioso**] The title of Ariosto's epic poem, first published in 1516 and in its final form in 1532. See 85/31 note.

26 **honest King Arthur**] sounds a little condescending: 'good old King Arthur'. Arthurian stories remained very popular in the sixteenth century, but were dismissed by the learned as hopelessly old-fashioned (see Wilson 1909, 145), or as dangerous to their readers (see Hall 1945, 203–7). Ascham in *The Schoolmaster* famously wrote of Malory's *Morte Darthur* that the 'whole pleasure' of the book depended on 'open mans slaughter, and bold bawdrye' (Ascham 1904, 231). 'This is good stuffe,' he went on, 'for wise men to laughe at, or honest men to take pleasure at . . . What toyes, the dayly readyng of such a booke, may worke in the will of a yong ientleman, or a yong mayde, that liueth welthelie and idlelie, wise men can iudge, and honest men do pitie'. Sidney's phrase here may recall Ascham's frequent use of the term 'honest'.

27 **the quiddity of *ens* and *prima materia***] Terms from scholastic philosophy: **quiddity**, the essential nature, that which makes a thing what it is; *ens*, being, existence; *prima materia*, first matter, the mere possibility of being. Defenders of poetry often made scornful remarks about philosophical jargon; compare Lodge (Smith 1904, I, 67), who castigates 'your dunce Doctors in their reasons *de ente, et non ente*'. This passage of the *Apology* recalls Erasmus's witty suggestion in the *Praise of Folly* that contemporary armies could be replaced by theologians (whose jargon he also mocks) in the war against pagans and heretics: 'haue ye any painem, or heretike, that will not geue place and yelde straight to so many fine fine argumentes of our maister doctors? Vnlesse he were . . . fensed with lyke armour? . . . And surely in my iudgement christen princes shoulde doe politikely, in stede of grosse Lans-knightes [mercenary footsoldiers] . . . to arme, and sende foorth all these brauling Dunsmen, and stubborn Occanistes, and inuincible Albertistes, together with the whole rablement of Sophistrers, against the Turkes and Sarasins' (Erasmus 1965, 82).

corslet] body-armour.

28 **even Turks and Tartars**] For the Turkish respect for poetry, see 83/18–19. In the *Travels* of Sir John Maundeville, the great chan of Tartary – which is one of the most warlike nations on earth – is a notable patron of 'minstrels' of all nations.

31 **if to a slight conjecture a conjecture may be opposed**] i.e. since the charge that poetry effeminates its male readers is pure hypothesis, a hypothesis may be used to answer it.

31–2 **as by him . . . knowledge**] See 82/5–22.

32 **motions of**] incitements to.

33–4 **Alexander's example . . . footstool**] Plutarch wrote two tracts *On the Fortune or the Virtue of Alexander* in which he showed that personal qualities rather than luck (**Fortune**) accounted for the achievements of Alexander the Great.

35 **though Plutarch did not]** even if Plutarch had not done so.

the phoenix] Only one of these mythological birds was supposed to exist at a time. The phoenix was said to be the most splendid bird in the world.

36–7 **This Alexander . . . with him]** Plutarch describes Alexander's education in his *Life of Alexander*, 7–8. He gained from Aristotle 'not only moral and political knowledge, but was also instructed in those more secret and profound branches of science. When Alexander was in Asia he wrote home to Aristotle chiding the philosopher for having published openly this sublimer knowledge and adding: "I had rather excel the bulk of mankind in the superior parts of learning than in the extent of power and dominion". Alexander loved polite learning too, and his natural curiosity made him a man of extensive reading. The *Iliad* he thought as well as called, a portable treasure of military knowledge; and he had a copy corrected by Aristotle which is called "the casket copy". Onesicritus informs us that he used to lay it under his pillow with his sword.' Alexander's admiration for Homer (noted also in Cicero, *Pro Archia poeta*, X) is very frequently mentioned in Renaissance defences of literature: Elyot 1883, I, 59; Lodge (Smith 1904, I, 64); see Smith's note, I, 364; Rainolds 1940, 85 note; E. K.'s gloss to Spenser's *Shepheardes Calender*, October Eclogue; Wills 1958, 78, and Fowler's Introduction, 28.

37–8 **Callisthenes]** was a nephew and pupil of Aristotle who joined Alexander's Asian campaign of 330–327 B.C. as its official historian, expressed his disapproval of Alexander's absolutism, and was put to death for plotting against him. The story of his downfall is told in Plutarch's *Life of Alexander*; see also Justin, *History*, XII, vi; Cicero, *Pro Rabiro Postumo*, IX, 23; and Elyot 1883, II, 57.

38 **indeed]** in fact.

39–40 **the chief thing . . . alive]** Plutarch tells this anecdote in his *Life of Alexander* and in *How a Man May Become Aware of His Progress in Virtue*, 16; and Cicero told it in *Pro Archia poeta*, X, 24. It was often repeated in the sixteenth century, e.g. by Erasmus, *Apophthegmes*, 36 (trans. Udall, p. 223), Montaigne, *Essays*, II, xxxvi, E. K. in his gloss to Spenser's *Shepheardes Calender*, October Eclogue.

42 **Cato misliked Fulvius]** M. Fulvius Nobilior, who became a Roman consul in 189 B.C., defeated the Aetolians in Greece. In this campaign he was accompanied by the poet Ennius (239–169 B.C.), a Calabrian by birth who became a Roman citizen and acquired the reputation of being the father of Roman poetry. In *Pro Archia poeta* Cicero recalls the encouragement Fulvius gave to Ennius; and the story of Cato's dislike of him was often repeated. See Cicero, *Tusculan Disputations*, I, i, 3; Agrippa 1569, ch. 4, fol. 12v; Gosson 1974, 78; and E.K.'s gloss to the October Eclogue in Spenser's *Shepheardes Calender*.

carrying] taking.

p. 106/2 **Cato Uticensis]** See **94/8** note. Sidney is distinguishing this later member of the famous Roman family from the Cato contemporary with Fulvius (see next note). Cato of Utica was celebrated in European literature as a model of republican virtue, for example by Cicero in *Cato*, by Lucan in *Pharsalia*, by Sallust in *Catiline*, 54, and by Dante in *Purgatory*, i.

reverenced] revered.

3 **the former**] the earlier of the two famous Catos. Cato the censor (234–149 B.C.) was the great-grandfather of Cato of Utica, famous for his strict morality and his fierce opposition to what he considered the debilitating effect of Greek culture on the Romans: 'yet [according to Plutarch, *Life of Cato the Censor*] it is said that he learned Greek very late in life'. During his censorship in Rome (at that time the highest civic office in Rome) he made a point of showing his contempt for philosophy and luxury and of never sacrificing to the Graces (see 4 note). He mocked the slow teaching methods used in the school of the orator Isocrates by remarking that Isocrates's scholars grew old in learning their art, as if they intended to practise it after their death (compare 6, **Pluto**, as god of the dead). Sidney's reference to his late interest in Greek may be a response to Stephen Gosson's allusion to C. Marius, who 'chalengeth praise vnto him selfe, in that hee neuer learned the Greeke tongue, neither ment to be instructed in it hereafter, either that he thought it too farre a iorney to fetche learning beyond the fielde, or because he doubted the abuses of those Schooles, where Poets were euer the head Maisters' (Gosson 1974, 80).

4 **the graces**] In Greek mythology the Graces (usually three in number) were the goddesses of loveliness and grace.

4–5 **cried out upon**] denounced.

5 **four score**] eighty.

6 **Pluto**] In Greek mythology, the god who ruled over the ghosts of the dead in his underground kingdom.

7 **carried**] taken.

8 **unmustered**] unenlisted.

9–10 **Scipio Nasica . . . best Roman**] Livy (*Histories*, XXIX, 14) tells how when, acting on the words of an oracle, the Senate in 204 B.C. required a special envoy, they chose Scipio Nasica – a soldier who had fought with distinction in Spain – because 'they judged him to be the best of all the good men in the whole state'.

10–11 **the other Scipio brothers**] The brothers P. Cornelius Scipio Africanus (236–183 B.C.) (see 92/38 note) and L. Cornelius Scipio Asiaticus were cousins of Scipio Nasica. P. Scipio acquired his surname Africanus by the defeat of Hannibal at Zama in 202 B.C. L. Scipio was called Asiaticus after his victory over Hannibal's ally Antiochus at Mount Sipylus in 190 B.C. Cicero, *Pro Archia poeta*, IX, 22, mentions that the poet Ennius was buried in the vault of the Scipios. Boccaccio in *De genealogia deorum*, XIV, v, xix, repeats the story, and so do many other writers; see Wills 1958, 80; and Rainolds 1940, 86 note.

13–14 **So as . . . validity**] So that, since Cato objected to the poet Ennius not for being a poet but for illegally accompanying the army as a civilian; and since Cato's objections were overturned by greater authorities than himself; it is therefore inappropriate for the poet-haters to invoke his authority in support of their case.

15–17 **Plato . . . most worthy of reverence]** There is plenty of evidence in the *Apology* (e.g. 82/29ff., 107/32ff.) for Sidney's admiration of Plato. See Irene Samuel, 'The Influence of Plato on Sir Philip Sidney's *Defence of Poesy*', *MLQ* 1 (1940), 383–91.

17–18 **of all philosophers . . . the most poetical]** Compare 82/39ff. and 96/2–3.

18 **the fountain]** the spring. This may refer to the spring on mount Helicon in Greece, which was sacred to the Muses, or simply to poetry as the source for many of Plato's techniques and as the original teacher of the knowledge he seeks. Compare 109/18 note, and Elyot's praise of 'noble Homer' (Elyot 1883, I, 58ff.) 'from whom as from a fountaine proceded all eloquence and lernyng' – which draws on Ovid's *Amores*, III, ix, 25.

21 **a philosopher . . . a natural enemy of poets]** Compare 88/36ff. Plato (*Republic*, X) testifies to this enmity: 'With reason we then dismissed it from our Republic [II, III] . . . And let us add, lest we be accused of a kind of barbarousness and rusticity, that there is an old variance between philosophy and poetry.' On the history of this opposition see Stanley Rosen, *The Quarrel between Philosophy and Poetry: Studies in Ancient Thought* (New York and London, 1988), and Curtius 1953, ch. 11, 203–13.

23–4 **putting it in method]** i.e. making a methodical theory out of it.

24 **school-art]** academic discipline.

25 **spurn at]** kick (like a horse).

26 **ungrateful prentices]** who use the skills taught them by the tradesmen to whom they are bound as apprentices to set up rival businesses of their own. Sidney may here be remembering Gosson's attack on the tendency among modern poets and musicians to 'despise the good rules of their ancient masters and run to the shop of their owne deuises, defacing olde stampes, forging newe Printes, and coining strange precepts' (Gosson 1974, 85). If so, Sidney implies that Gosson, who cites the ancient philosophers in his attack on poetry, is merely envious of the 'force of delight' wielded by true poets which is 'barred' to him as a mere controversialist.

29–30 **for Homer seven cities strave]** The story of the seven Greek cities which competed for the honour of having been Homer's birthplace originated in a group of epigrams in the *Greek Anthology*, XVI, 295–9, was repeated by Cicero in *Pro Archia poeta*, VIII, 19, and became a Renaissance commonplace. See Landino, Preface to Dante, sig. 2B3v; Boccaccio 1930, 90; Salutati 1951, I, 4; Wills 1958, 78; Montaigne, *Essays*, II, xxxvi; and Rainolds 1940, 87 note. The seven cities are Smyrna, Rhodes, Colophon, Salamis, Chios, Argos, and Athens.

30–1 **many cities banished philosophers]** Empedocles, for instance, was denied entry to Acragas, and Damon, Anaxagoras, and Protagoras were banished from Athens.

31–3 **For only repeating . . . Syracusans**] Plutarch tells the story in his *Life of Nicias*, who led the Athenians in their defeat by the Syracusans. Some of the Athenians owed their lives to their knowledge of the plays of Euripides, since 'Of all the Grecians his was the Muse with whom the Sicilians were most in love. From every stranger that landed in their island they gleaned every small specimen or portion of his work, and communicated it with pleasure to each other. It is said on this occasion a number of Athenians upon their return home went to Euripides, and thanked him in the most respectful manner for their obligations to his pen.'

34 **philosophers unworthy to live**] Socrates was the most famous of these; but Prodicus of Ceos was also sometimes said to have been put to death with Socrates.

Simonides] of Ceos (c. 555–468 B.C.), the first of the great lyric poets of Greece, lived for a time in Sicily, where the tyrant Hieron I of Syracuse was his patron. In 476 Simonides brought about a reconciliation between Hieron and his brother Theron. Several of the odes of **Pindar** (see **99**/10 note) celebrate Hieron's achievements. Landino mentions the moderating influence of these two poets on the tyranny of Hieron in his preface to Dante's *Divine Comedy*, sig. 2B3v.

36 **Dionysius**] of Syracuse, 405–367 B.C. (see **94**/16 note), is said to have given Plato to the Spartan ambassador, who sold him as a slave. Cicero alludes to the story in *Pro Rabiro Postumo*, IX, 23.

37 **who should do thus**] that is, whoever used arguments like these against the philosophers.

38 **cavillation**] petty fault-finding.

39–41 **read *Phaedrus* . . . abominable filthiness**] Sidney may be alluding to Scaliger's *Poetices*: 'Plato should look to himself and see how many foolish, filthy stories he brings in. How frequently does he insinuate opinions which stink with the vice of the Greeks. Certainly it would be praiseworthy never to have read the *Symposium*, the *Phaedrus*, and other enormities' (Scaliger 1617, I, ii, 10). Both of these dialogues celebrate the love of men for boys. And in Plutarch's *Dialogue on Love*, 4, Protogenes asserts that 'there is only one genuine Love, the love of boys' (Duncan-Jones 1989, 239/1096 note).

43 **thence**] from that place.

43–4 **alloweth community of women**] See Plato, *Republic*, V, in which Socrates argues that the state itself should have the function of a family, and that neither women nor children should be identified as the property of individual men.

44–107/1 **grew not for effeminate wantonness**] i.e. was not imposed to combat sexual libertinism.

p. 107/2 **listed**] liked.

I honour philosophical instructions] Sidney organizes his defence against Plato's charge skilfully. So far he has not confronted the charge at all, and has relied on counter-attacking philosophy. He now goes on to accept that philosophy, although attacked by St Paul, can be a worthwhile study; but then, he argues, why shouldn't poetry also be worthwhile, even if it has been attacked by Plato – who is, after all, a less eminent authority than St Paul.

5–6 **(who yet . . . prophet)]** omitted in Ponsonby.

5 **allegeth]** alludes to.

5–6 **twice two poets]** St Paul's phrase 'For in him we live, and move, and have our being' (Acts 17:28) closely resembles verses in (1) the astronomical poem *Phenomena* by the third-century Greek poet Aratus, and (2) the *Hymn to Zeus* by the Stoic philosopher Cleanthes (c. 330–c. 231 B.C.). The third poet referred to by Paul is the semi-legendary figure Epimenides of Crete (sixth century B.C.), in Titus 1:12: 'One of themselves, a prophet of their own, said, Cretans are always liars, evil beasts, gluttons'. The fourth poet is the Greek comic dramatist Menander (c. 342–292 B.C.), whose play *Thais* supplies Paul with the saying 'Evil communications corrupt good manners' (1 Corinthians 15:33). St Paul's uses of the Greek poets had been noted by Jerome in his commentaries (see *PL*, 26, col. 606), and by Boccaccio (Boccaccio 1930, 86). Protestant educationalists relied heavily on these passages to justify the Christian use of pagan learning; see Sasek 1961, 8off.

6–7 **setteth a watchword upon]** i.e. utters a warning against (a watchword is a 'cautionary word or speech'). The reference is to Colossians 2:8: 'Beware lest any man spoil you through philosophy and vain deceit'.

7–8 **So doth Plato . . . Poetry]** i.e. Plato warns against the abuse of poetry, not against poetry as such.

8–11 **Plato found fault . . . such opinions]** Here Sidney deals with what he considers the main charge made by Plato against the poets. It is in fact only one of the charges Plato makes against poetry (in *Republic*, II). His other objections were: that it encourages drunkenness, effeminacy and idleness by its seductive use of sound and rhythm; that the imitation it practises is at two removes from the truth (*Republic*, X); and that it stimulates unruly passions in its recipients. On these grounds, Plato argues, poets should be banished from the ideal commonwealth – apart from those who write the praises of the gods and heroes. In answering only the first of Plato's charges Sidney follows the common line of medieval discussion which tested the claims (and usually found them wanting by Christian standards) of the poet-theologians of antiquity; see Curtius 1953, 215–21. Josephus, in *Against Apion*, II, 36–7, explains that the expulsion of the poets from Plato's commonwealth was to prevent the supplanting of true notions of God with false ones; compare also Augustine, *City of God*, XVIII, xii–xviii. Agrippa 1569, fol. 11r–12r, attacks the poets' lies about divinity and recalls their expulsion by Plato. Renaissance apologists for poetry, however, put forward a different set of arguments. Salutati in *De laboribus Herculis* makes a defence that poets did not invent the stories of the gods, and that philosophers and theologians were as much to blame (Salutati 1951, I, ch. 12, 62). See Weinberg 1961, I, 254, for an anticipation of Sidney's argument in Francesco Patrizi, *De institutione reipublica* (1534); and compare Vives 1931, 127, where he argues, like Sidney, 'that if these tales could formerly injure students, they can do so no longer, for we know that those gods were bad and wicked beings who deserved ruin not heaven'.

9 **light tales**] sexually *risqué* stories. Stephen Gosson's *Apologie of the Schoole of Abuse* (1579), dedicated, like the *School of Abuse*, to Sidney, includes an extended attack on the sexual antics of the pagan gods as 'horrible . . . blasphemies' promoted by poets (Gosson 1974, 125–7).

10 **unspotted essence**] unsullied being (God).

13 **the very religion**] the actual religion.

14 **stood upon**] was based on.

many-fashioned] of many different kinds; with a punning suggestion that the pagan gods were 'fashioned' or made by the ancient Greeks.

15 **followed according to their nature of imitation**] i.e. the poets reproduced the fantasies and illusions of others, since it is their nature to imitate.

15–16 **Who list**] whoever wishes.

16–17 **Plutarch . . . providence**] Sidney refers to three essays in the *Moralia*: *Isis and Osiris*; *The Obsolescence of Oracles*; and *On the Delays of the Divine Vengeance*.

16 **Isis and Osiris**] were gods of the ancient Egyptians, whose cult spread to Greece and Rome.

19 **the light of Christ**] i.e. the Gospels.

21 **atheism**] a new word in late sixteenth-century English. Ascham speaks of atheism in *The Schoolmaster* as a dangerous modern trend (Ascham 1904, 233); and Lyly's *Euphues* includes a dialogue with an atheist (Lyly 1916, 147ff.).

22 **justly construe**] i.e. interpret for the best.

23–4 ***Qua authoritate . . . exigendos***] Scaliger refers to Plato, 'whose authority certain barbarous and uncouth men seek to use in order to expel poets from the republic' (Scaliger 1617, I, ii, 10) Scaliger goes on: 'Even if he condemns some of the [poets'] books, we need not go without the rest, for they are very often adduced by Plato himself in support of his arguments'.

26 **without further law**] without more ado. Sidney here seems to be using 'law' in the sense of 'allowance given to certain runners at the start of a race'; see *OED* s. law. 20.

29 **Ion**] One of the shorter Platonic dialogues which explores the nature of poetic inspiration. The dialogue was often invoked by sixteenth-century defenders of poetry without acknowledgement of its anti-poetic stance. See Landino, Preface to Dante's *Divine Comedy* (see 116/4–5 note), Francesco Patrizi and other writers of Platonized poetics (see Weinberg 1961, I, ch. 7, 250–96), and Minturno 1559, 74–6.

33–4 **under whose lion's skin . . .**] Refers to Aesop's fable of the ass who dressed himself in a lion's skin and passed for a lion until he was unmasked by a stranger who had seen real lions. Erasmus mentions this fable with relation to foolish philosophers or 'foolelosophers' who 'take vpon theim most sem-

blant of wysedome, and walke lyke Asses in Lyons skynnes . . . yet on some
syde their longe eares pearyng foorth, dooe discouer them to come of Midas
progenie' (Erasmus 1965, 10; and compare 71). Gosson too alludes to the
fable with reference to philosophy (Gosson 1974, 78); and see Agrippa's
chapter on asses (101/7–9 note).

36–7 **he attributeth unto Poesy . . . divine force**] In 'the afore-named dialogue',
Ion, Socrates discusses poetry with a degree of irony: 'For the authors of those
great poems which we admire, do not attain to excellence through the rules
of any art, but they utter their beautiful melodies of verse in a state of inspiration, and, as it were, possessed by a spirit not their own . . . like the Cory-
bantes, who lose all control over their reason in the enthusiasm of the sacred
dance . . . For a poet is indeed a thing ethereally light, winged and sacred,
nor can he compose anything worth calling poetry until he becomes inspired
and as it were, mad, or whilst any reason remains in him . . . Every rhap-
sodist or poet . . . is excellent in proportion to the extent of his participation
in the divine influence . . . And thus it appears to me that the god proves
beyond a doubt, that these transcendent poems are not human as the work
of men, but divine as coming from the god. Poets then are the interpreters
of the divinities – each being possessed by some one deity; and to make this
apparent the god designedly inspires the worst poets with the sublimest
verse.' Sidney denies that the poet receives 'a very inspiring of a divine force'.
He thinks of poetry as a human activity aiming at excellence through following 'rules of art' and the use of reason, and he restricts divine inspiration
to the composition of the Scriptures. His attitude was somewhat unusual in
the sixteenth century, when the notion of the 'divine fury' of the poet was
widespread. On the development of the notion, see Curtius 1953, 473–5;
Weinberg 1961, I, chs 7 and 8; Hathaway 1962, Part 5, and particularly ch.
34, 437–59, for rejection of the theory on rational grounds; and for some
account of the notion in England, see F. L. Schoell, *Études sur l'humanisme
continentale en Angleterre à la fin de la Renaissance* (Paris, 1926), and Wills
1958, 72ff., 124ff., and Fowler's Introduction, 29–34.

37 **very**] true.

39 **the honours have**] Omission of a relative ('which' after 'honours') is common
Elizabethan practice. See Abbott 1870, § 244.

40 **them**] the poets.

41 **Alexanders, Caesars, Scipios**] See 105/36–7; 106/10–13; and 108/29ff.
Compare Harington's phrase, 'so many Alexanders, Caesars, Scipios' (Smith
1904, II, 195).

42 **Laelius . . . the Roman Socrates**] See Cicero, *De amicitia*, VI, and *De officiis*,
I, xxvi, 90: 'It is a fine thing to keep an unruffled temper, unchanging behaviour, and the same outward appearance in every condition of life: these qualities, history tells us, were as characteristic of Gaius Laelius as they were of
Socrates'. Laelius (born c. 186 B.C.) was a close friend of Scipio Africanus
the younger, a prominent member of the philosophical Scipionic circle, and
a great patron of literature. He is introduced as interlocutor into several of

Cicero's dialogues, notably *De amicitia* and *De republica*. Cicero tells us (*Letters to Atticus*, VII, 3, 10) that the plays of Terence were believed by many to have been written by Laelius, either wholly or in part. Terence hints at his collaboration with Laelius in the Prologues to *Heautontimorumenos* (*The Self-tormentor*) and *The Brothers*. Compare Vives 1931, 136, and Ascham 1904, 288.

44 **Socrates . . . wise man**] See Plato, *Apology*, 21, where Socrates says: 'Chairephon made a pilgrimage to Delphi . . . He actually asked if there was any man wiser than I. And the priestess [of Apollo] answered, No.' Sidney refers again to Socrates as 'the wight most wise / By *Phebus*' doome' in *Astrophil and Stella* 25 (Ringler 1962, 177).

p. 108/1 **old time**] old age.

1–2 **putting Aesop's fables into verses**] In Plato's dialogue *Phaedo*, 60, Cebes asks Socrates why, since he has come to prison, he has 'put into verse those fables of Aesop and the Hymn to Apollo'. Socrates replies that he was urged to do so by his *daimon* (an intermediary between gods and mortals) in a recurrent dream. Plutarch tells the story in the *Moralia* (*How the Young Man Should Study Poetry*, 2), Ascham refers to it in *The Schoolmaster* (Ascham 1904, 253), and Harington mentions it in his preface to *Orlando Furioso* (Smith 1904, II, 204).

5 **Plutarch . . . gathered of them**] See *How the Young Man Should Study Poetry* in Plutarch's *Moralia*. As Sidney points out (6ff.), Plutarch quotes poetry frequently throughout the *Moralia* and the *Lives*.

7 **guards**] borders, decorative trimmings.

10 **what dispraise may set upon it**] i.e. whatever attempts may be made to discredit poetry.

12–21 **So that . . . springs of Poesy**] This passage summarizes the second part of the *Apology*, the Refutation (see Introduction, p. 32).

13 **low-creeping**] i.e. petty – with a possible reference to the serpent which tempted Eve, and which was condemned by God to creep on the ground and be trodden underfoot by Eve's descendants (Genesis 3:14–15). Compare 'earth-creeping', 117/4, and Horace's phrase 'serpit humi' ('Creeps on the ground'; *Art*, 28).

17 **engarland**] crown with a garland of laurel leaves. The word is apparently Sidney's invention; he uses it again in *Astrophil and Stella*, 56.

18 **laureate, as . . . triumphant captains**] Compare 100/34, and see note there.

19 **the price they ought to be had in**] i.e. their value.

19–20 **ill-favouring**] infectious; refers to the early modern belief that foul air can infect water with contagious diseases such as the plague.

22 **career**] 'Race course, or running track in the tiltyard; Sidney is imagining himself either on horseback, or as himself a horse' (Duncan-Jones 1989, 384).

24–5   **so hard a stepmother**] Stepmothers were widely believed to be cruel to their stepchildren. See *Astrophil and Stella*, 1: 'Invention, Nature's child, fled step-dame Studie's blowes' (Ringler 1962, 165).

25   **to pass all other**] to be better than anyone else.

26   **all**] everything they do.

26–7   **makers of themselves . . . others**] creators of their own work, not dependent on the work of others.

28   *Musa . . . laeso?*] Virgil, *Aeneid*, I, 12: 'O Muse! the causes and the crimes relate; / What goddess was provok'd, and whence her hate' (Dryden's translation). Virgil had in mind the hostility of the goddess Juno to Aeneas, which plagues him throughout the *Aeneid*.

29–39   **Sweet Poesy . . . builded upon virtue**] Like Sidney, Cicero defended poetry by listing the eminent men who had cultivated it (*Pro Archia*, viiff.). Many Renaissance writers use this method to defend poetry; see e.g. Boccaccio 1930, 138–40). Elyot's *Governour* gives an account of great rulers of antiquity down to Charlemagne who cherished the arts (Elyot 1883, I, 99ff.); Thomas Drant in the Dedication to his translation of Horace's *Art of Poetry* (1567) mentions among other patrons Pietro Bembo and Francis I of France. See also Wills 1958, 78ff.; E. K.'s Gloss on October in the *Shepheardes Calender*; Webbe (Smith 1904, I, 233); Meres, copying from Sidney (Smith 1904, II, 322); and Puttenham 1936, 16ff. Puttenham concludes: 'Since therefore so many noble Emperours, Kings and Princes haue bene studious of Poesie and other ciuill arts, & not ashamed to bewray their skils in the same, let none other meaner person despise learning' (22). See also Rainolds 1940, 85 note; and Bacon 1974, 44–54.

30   **David**] Compare 84/15ff. and 86/23ff.

   Adrian] the Roman Emperor Hadrian (117–38). Elyot praises his learning in the *Governour* (Elyot 1883, I, 108); and E. Hellowes, *Chronicles . . . of tenne Emperours of Rome* (1577), 75, recalls that he 'compounded certaine workes in Heroicall metre'.

   Sophocles] the Athenian tragic dramatist who (495–406 B.C.), was appointed in 440 as one of the ten generals in the war against Samos.

31   **Germanicus**] (15 B.C.–A.D. 19), nephew and adopted son of the Emperor Tiberius: a successful general and also, by reputation, a fine poet. Elyot observes that he was considered 'equall to the moost noble poetes of his time' (Elyot 1883, I, 109–10).

32   **Robert, king of Sicily**] Robert II of Anjou (1309–43): a lover of fine literature and the patron of Petrarch (see 100/34 note). He was eulogized by Boccaccio, *De genealogia deorum*, XLV, ix and xxii.

32–3   **King Francis of France**] Francis I (1494–1547): an active and strongly nation-alist king, whose military and cultural exploits in Italy brought the Renaissance to France. He was a liberal patron of the arts, encouraging, among others, Rabelais, Erasmus, Budé, the publishing family of the Estiennes, Marot, and Leonardo da Vinci. Ascham praises him in *The Schoolmaster*

(Ascham 1904, 213) in a passage castigating the English nobility for their contempt for learning.

33 **King James of Scotland**] Which King James Sidney had in mind is uncertain. The other exemplary figures in this list of the patrons and practitioners of poetry are introduced in pairs. Did Sidney add this example to the list as an afterthought – perhaps while revising the text of the *Apology* – as a compliment to James VI of Scotland? James VI (b. 1566) was no more than sixteen when Sidney wrote the *Apology*; but Sidney refers to his tutor, George Buchanan, at lines 36–7, and may have had access to some of James's verses, which were published in 1584 as *Essayes of a Prentis*. James later contributed a sonnet to the Cambridge collection of elegies on Sidney (*Academiae Cantabrigiensis lachrymae* (1587), sig. K1r), which may suggest that James and Sidney were aware of one another's literary interests. See Duncan-Jones 1989, 384–5.

Sidney may also have had in mind the earlier James I of Scotland (1394–1437). George Buchanan, *Rerum Scoticarum historia* (Edinburgh, 1582), X, xxxviii, describes how James I founded and maintained several schools, and how he 'not only cherished learned men but was himself present at many of their disputations: and whenever he had freedom from affairs of state he loved to listen to literary talk; and earnestly laboured to counteract the false opinion of well-born minds that letters draw men away from public affairs to ease and idleness, and soften warlike minds and break up and weaken all their noble impulses'. James I was for nearly twenty years a prisoner in England and is usually regarded as the author of *The Kingis Quhair*, a stanzaic poem in the courtly Chaucerian style. His tragedy is told in the *Mirror for Magistrates* (ed. Campbell (1938), 154–60).

Bembus] Pietro Bembo (1470–1547): priest, humanist, and courtier at the courts of the Estes, the Montefeltros, and the Medicis; secretary to Pope Leo X; and cardinal (1539). He 'wrote poems and prose, including a defence of the Tuscan language analagous to Sidney's defence of English here' (Duncan-Jones 1989, 385), and was a key figure in Castiglione's *Courtier*.

34 **Bibbiena**] Bernardo Dovizi, Cardinal Bibbiena (1470–1520): humanist scholar in the service of the Medicis, secretary to Lorenzo the Magnificent, general and diplomat, he was made cardinal in 1513. He wrote a five-act comedy, *La calandra*, in the style of Plautus, and was represented as speaking on the subject of comedy in the second book of Castiglione's *Courtier*. Gabriel Harvey urged Spenser to imitate him (see Smith, I, 116).

Beza] Théodore de Bèze (1519–1605), a Burgundian and a celebrated poet, was educated at Orléans and Paris, became professor of Greek at Lausanne, and published the tragedy *Abraham sacrifiant* and an edition of the New Testament. Sidney made use of his commentary on the psalms in his translation of them. Beza was a close associate of Calvin, and after Calvin's death in 1564 (and therefore at the time when the *Apology* was written) was the leader of the Calvinists at Geneva.

35 **Melanchthon**] Philip Melanchthon (1497–1560), German reformer and humanist. He was educated by his uncle, the Biblical scholar Reuchlin, and at several German universities; became professor of Greek at Wittenberg, where he was Luther's chief associate in the reformation movement; and was

one of the most influential Renaissance educationalists. For several years he lived with Hubert Languet, Sidney's teacher and correspondent. He was commended as a poet by Scaliger (Scaliger 1617, VI, iv, 736).

Fracastorius] Girolamo Fracastoro (1483–1553), a humanist and natural philosopher who studied at Padua under Pomponazzo, and became a professor of logic, a musician, a physician and a poet. His medical poem *Syphilis* was praised by Scaliger (Scaliger 1617, VI, v, 753–8). Sidney probably knew his two dialogues on the mind, *Naugerius* and *Turrius*, which were published in 1555. The dialogues are products of the influential mid-century neo-Aristotelian school of Padua (see Hathaway 1962, 306ff.), where Sidney studied for several months in 1574–5.

Scaliger] Julius Caesar Scaliger (1484–1558): a brilliant scholar whose *Poetices libri septem* (1561), which Sidney knew well, is the most learned and comprehensive of all sixteenth-century treatises on poetry (see Weinberg 1961, II, 743–50). Scaliger claimed to have come from a noble Italian family. He settled at Agen in France in his fortieth year, and wrote a good deal of poetry as well as several works on natural philosophy.

36 Pontanus] Giovanni Pontano (1426–1503), scholar, soldier, diplomat at the court of Naples and president of the Academy there, was one of the great Latin poets of the Renaissance (see Scaliger 1617, VI, iv, 744–9). His astronomical poem *Urania* was particularly highly regarded, but he also wrote history and treatises on philosophy and politics.

Muretus] Marc-Antoine Muret (1526–85): French humanist and colleague of George Buchanan at Paris in 1544. He edited many Latin poets, and much of his other writing is in the form of elegant academic lectures.

36–7 George Buchanan] (1506–82): Scottish poet and pedagogue, probably the greatest of the British humanists. Most of his early manhood was spent in France. He became a Protestant in 1563, and was tutor to the young king James VI. He wrote outstanding Latin poetry – lyric, satire, and drama (see 113/7) – as well as a famous translation of the Psalms into Latin verse. He also wrote a much-read history of Scotland, and *De jure regni apud Scotos*, a treatise influential in the development of the idea of British political liberty. He was in England on several occasions, and was on friendly terms with Roger Ascham, Walter Haddon, and Anthony Cooke (tutor to Edward VI).

38 Hospital of France] Michel de l'Hôpital (1503–73), the Chancellor of France, contributed to the reform of the French administration and attempted to promote religious toleration. He was a patron of literature and wrote poems himself.

41 poetize] write poetry; apparently Sidney's invention, adopted by other Elizabethan writers.

42 hard welcome] hostile reception.

p. 109/1 decketh] decorates.

1–2 decketh our soil with fewer laurels] i.e. gives us fewer eminent poets (and military triumphs). But the phrase may not be wholly metaphorical. Nowadays the true laurel (*laurus nobilis*, the bays traditionally awarded to poets) is not very common in England. The name 'laurel' is now applied to the common or cherry laurel (*laurus cesarus*) which seems to have been introduced into western Europe from Turkey by Sidney's friend and correspondent Charles de l'Écluse. There is no evidence to suggest that the true laurel was more plentiful in England before Sidney's time, although it seems to have suffered from periodic blight. See Shakespeare, *Richard II*, II, iv, 8, drawing on the second edition of Holinshed's *Chronicles* (1586–7); and John Evelyn, *Sylva*, ed. A. Hunter (York, 1776), I, 396.

2 **heretofore**] before now.

3–4 **when the trumpet . . . loudest**] i.e. when Mars, the Roman god of war, summoned Englishmen to heroic action. Sidney may be referring to the French wars which culminated in Henry V's victories; see 89/22 and note.

4–5 **overfaint quietness**] inactivity produced by cowardice. Sidney's attitude to the relative peace enjoyed by England in the first half of Elizabeth's reign is very different from that of John Lyly, who describes the 'twenty and odd years with continual peace' as a 'marvel' accomplished by Elizabeth's virginity (Lyly 1916, 439). Stephen Gosson in *The School of Abuse* warns against allowing the 'fruites of peace' enjoyed by the English under Elizabeth to seduce them into cowardice and complacency (Gosson 1974, 95ff.).

5 **strew the house**] i.e. prepare a welcome. Paul Hentzner, who visited England in 1598, reported that the royal presence chamber at Greenwich palace was strewn with hay 'after the English fashion' (*Travels in England* (1598), quoted from *Life in Shakespeare's England*, ed. John Dover Wilson (Harmondsworth, 1944), 244).

6 **mountebanks at Venice**] The eloquent stallholders of Venice seem to have made a strong impression on English travellers. Shuckburgh quotes from *Coryat's Crudities* (1611): 'Truly I often wondered at many of these natural orators. For they would tell their tales with such admirable volubility and plausible grace, even extempore, and seasoned with singular variety of elegant jests and witty conceits, that they did often strike great admiration into strangers that never heard them before' (Shuckburgh 1891, 142). Erasmus's *Praise of Folly* compares friar preachers to 'these Ceretans [mountebanks], suche as in Italie are wont in markette places standyng on stalles . . . to preache vnto the people in commendacion of some pardone, feigned medecines, or suche lyke toyes of theyr owne inuencion, to gette money withall, and bleare the simples eies' (Erasmus 1965, 91–2). Ben Jonson's Volpone disguises himself as a mountebank in *Volpone*, II, i. See also Lea 1934, II, 358–62.

6–11 **Truly even that . . . pain of a pen**] An ambiguous sentence. One reading might be: 'The lack of good poets in England during this period of inactivity can be taken both as a compliment to poetry, which would rather deal with military ventures overseas than with peaceful domestic affairs, and as a reason for the poets' poor reputation among the English, who are at present too lazy to be bothered with either reading or writing poetry.' E.K. in the gloss to *The Shepheardes Calender* observes that Spenser 'sheweth the cause of contempt of Poetry to be idlenesse and basenesse of mynd' (Spenser 1989, 181). Both Sidney and his uncle Leicester favoured a militant foreign policy for England in the 1580s.

7–9 **Venus . . . Mars . . . Vulcan**] The story of how Vulcan, the god of smiths and the husband of Venus, made a net to catch Venus and Mars in the act of adultery is told by Homer, *Odyssey*, VIII, 266–367, and by Ovid, *Metamorphoses*, book IV. It is also cited by Plato, *Republic* III, as an example of the poets' tendency to debase the gods.

11 **base men with servile wits**] In *Astrophil and Stella*, 3 and 15, Sidney suggests as he does here that contemporary English poetry is dominated by plagiarists ('servile wits'). The phrase also implies that Elizabethan poets who print their work are glorified domestic servants who will write anything for money. Stephen Gosson went still further, comparing contemporary poets to vagabonds: 'We haue infinite Poets, and Pipers, and suche peeuishe cattel among us in Englande, that liue by merrie begging, mainteyned by almes, and priuily encroch vppon euerie mans purse' (Gosson 1974, 84).

13 **Epaminondas**] a Theban general (d. 363 B.C.), who helped to make Thebes the most powerful state in Greece. Sidney has in mind the account in Plutarch, *Precepts of Statecraft*, 15: 'Epaminondas being appointed *telearch* by the Thebans through envy and contempt, did not reject it, but said that the office does not make the man, but the man the office. He brought the office of *telearch* into great and venerable repute, which was before nothing but a kind of duty of carrying off the refuse from the narrow streets and lanes of the city and of maintaining the gutters.' Compare Gosson 1974, 103.

15 **no more but**] by merely.

16 **disgracefulness . . . Poesy**] a possible echo of Ascham's *The Schoolmaster*. In modern England, Ascham complains, if a young man show signs of modesty his courtly contemporaries 'say, he is rude, and hath no grace, so vngraciouslie do som gracelesse men, misuse the faire and godlie word grace' (Ascham 1904, 206–7).

16–23 **For now . . . order**] For a conjectural interpretation of this difficult passage see 23 note below.

18 **without any commission**] without authority (perhaps with a punning allusion to the High Commission of the Church of England, the body responsible for censoring printed texts).

post] hurry, gallop.

Helicon] Like many medieval and Renaissance poets (Dante and Spenser among them), Sidney writes as if Helicon itself were the well or stream of the Muses; but strictly speaking it is the range of mountains in Boeotia on which the Muses' fountain Hippocrene was located. And Sidney exploits further associations. The fountain sprang from the hoof-print of the legendary flying horse, Pegasus, and in medieval verse (compare Dante, *Paradise*, xviii, 82) Pegasus becomes the favourite steed of the Muses and the poet's own mount in his poetic flights. Sidney's **bastard poets** are mounted on vastly inferior horses (compare **Pacolet's horse**, 111/28).

19 **post-horses**] horses used in relay and ridden to exhaustion.

20 **they**] poets 'made . . . of better clay' (see 21 note below); that is, the better poets, as opposed to the 'bastard poets' of line 17.

21 *Queis . . . Titan*] 'for whom the Titan [Prometheus] made entrails of better clay' (adapted from Juvenal, *Satires*, XIV, 33–5). In Greek legend, Prometheus made the first man and woman from clay, which he animated with fire stolen from the gods.

23 **knights of the same order**] A puzzling phrase. Why should the **base men** who publish their poetry be described, even ironically, as **knights**? The phrase may refer to 'knights of the post': gentlemen or tradesmen down on their luck who hung about court-rooms offering to go bail for people in custody, in return for payment. Giving false witness was another of their functions. See R. B. McKerrow (ed.), *The Works of Thomas Nashe* (London, 1908), IV, 94. Sidney has described the 'bastard poets' of his time as 'posting' over Helicon (see lines 17–19 above), which may have suggested 'knights of the post' to him. He may here imply that such men commit perjury when they call themselves poets, and that gifted and well-born amateur poets refuse to publish for fear of being thought to share their willingness to do anything for money. He may also suggest that the trade of the 'bastard poets' is lying – in contrast to the true poet who 'never lieth' (109/9).

   Alternatively, it is possible that the whole passage from 16 to 23 is a reference to one of the most famous poets of Sidney's time, George Gascoigne. In 1575 Gascoigne's poetry collection *The Posies* was withdrawn from circulation by the Elizabethan censors; this would explain Sidney's phrase **without any commission** (see 18 note). In *The Posies* Gascoigne printed a series of verses composed on horseback – hence Sidney's allusion to the 'bastard poets' as horsemen. Gascoigne follows the series with a boastful account of the speed with which he composed them: 'And thus an ende of these five Theames, admounting to the number of .CCLVIII. verses. Devised riding by the way, writing none of them untill he came at the ende of his Journey, the which was no longer than one day in ryding, one daye in tarying with his friend, and the thirde in returning to Greyes Inne: and therefore called Gascoignes memories' (Gascoigne 1907–10, I, 70). One of the 'Theames', a sequence of sonnets which might be expected to catch Sidney's eye, begins 'In haste post haste' (Gascoigne 1907–10, I, 66–8); hence the reference to the poets who **post over the banks of Helicon**. Finally, Gascoigne alludes to himself as the Green Knight in several autobiographical poems in *The Posies* (see Gascoigne 1907–10, I, 367–82). Thus poets who wished to distinguish themselves from a poet whose work had been banned by the High Commission might well choose not to publish so as to avoid being **accounted knights of the same order** as the Green Knight, Gascoigne.

24–5 **admitted into the company**] The phrase, together with the term **dignity** (24), suggests the admission of a new member into one of the City Gilds such as the Stationers' Company of London (incorporated in 1557). See Philip Gaskell, *A New Introduction to Bibliography* (Oxford, 1972), 174–5.

25 **paper-blurrers**] rapid scribblers who produce blots as they write. Compare Erasmus 1965, 74, commenting on those who set up as authors: 'These men, as generally they are muche bounden unto me, so in especiall are suche of theim, as dooe blotte theyr papers with merest trifles'.

very] actual.

26 **want of desert**] worthlessness.

26–7 **in despite of Pallas**] despite our lack of learning (Pallas or Minerva was the classical goddess of wisdom). A translation of the familiar Latin tag *invita Minerva*. Compare Horace, *Art*, 385.

28 **mended**] corrected, improved.

29 **so have I neglected the means to come by it**] Needless to say, this is not true. Sidney's poems are the products of careful experimentation and meticulous craftsmanship.

30 **overmastered**] conquered (as Sidney's payment of **tribute** suggests).

32 **look themselves**] examine themselves.

32–3 **unflattering glass of reason**] The idea of the contrast between the flattering mirror, which shows things better than they are, and the honest mirror, which shows things as they are indeed, was a common one in Sidney's time. George Gascoigne used it as the central metaphor for his satire *The Steele Glas* (1576) (Gascoigne 1907–10, II).

33 **if they be inclinable unto it**] (to see) whether they have a gift for writing poetry.

34 **drawn by the ears**] dragged along roughly (as in handling animals).

35 **ancient-learned**] learned writers of ancient times.

35–6 **divine gift**] According to such learned writers as Cicero, Horace, and Plutarch (see J. F. D'Alton, *Roman Literary Theory and Criticism* (London, 1931), 472–5), and in the Renaissance, poetry was the gift of the gods. This was a belief held by many followers of Plato. Sidney, on the other hand, denies that poetry is given by direct inspiration from God (see 107/36–8) or that it is the product of a 'divine frenzy'. He thinks of it instead as the product of a natural 'inclination' (33; compare Horace, *Art*, 294–8), of a certain inborn attitude of mind, or of what scholastics and some Renaissance critics, following Aristotle, would call a 'habit of the practical intellect' (see Weinberg 1961, I, 7, 10, 495–6). It is only in this sense that poetry for Sidney is a 'divine' (because natural) gift. Poetry does not come simply from acquiring the 'art' – from possessing a knowledge of the rules; a 'poetic nature' is prerequisite; only then can the art be learned. An influential group of Italian writers in the late sixteenth century took the same position (see Hathaway 1962, 437ff.). In Tomitano's words: 'We men cannot alter Nature . . . as a work that belongs to God . . . but we can often correct or amend it' (quoted in Hathaway 1962, 441). Sir John Harington throws light on this passage in the *Apology* when he reproves Puttenham for labouring 'to proue, or rather to make Poetry an art'. What Puttenham does succeed in proving by printing his own bad verses, Harington claims, is 'that which M. *Sidney* and all the learneder sort that have written of it do pronounce, namely that it is a gift and not an art', something that Puttenham plainly lacks (Smith 1904, II, 196–7).

37 **genius**] In the Renaissance, the genius was the guardian spirit of the individual soul which guided a man's inclinations or abilities in a certain direction.

38–9 *orator fit, poeta nascitur*] (Latin) An orator is made, a poet born. A common saying but apparently not of classical origin. See Smith 1904, I, 397 note. W. Ringler, *JHI* 2 (1941), 497–504, shows that the phrase appears as early as a third-century commentary on Horace's *Art* but came into popular use after it was used by Polydore Vergil in *De rerum inventoribus* (1499) and by Badius Ascensius in the Preface to his edition of Terence (1502).

39–40 **Yet confess I . . . to guide him**] Compare Gosson 1974, 88: 'in all our recreations we shoulde haue an instructer at our elbowes to feede the soule'.

40 **manured**] worked at, cultivated. Compare Plutarch, *The Education of Children*, 4, on the subject of natural gifts: 'Man's ground is naturally good . . . and experience tells us that if it be well manured it will be quickly capable of bearing excellent fruit' (compare 42–3 note below). Scaliger develops the theme in his poem 'Ingenium paratur agro' (*Poemata*, 1591, II, 187).

Daedalus] a great craftsman and originator of the arts in classical mythology who created the Cretan labyrinth and was then kept prisoner in it by the tyrant Minos. He escaped from captivity with his son Icarus by making wings out of feathers held together with wax. Before flying to freedom he advised Icarus not to fly too close to the sun lest its heat melt the wax and his wings fall apart. Icarus ignored his father's advice and perished as a result. Here 'Daedalus' is used allegorically to mean instructions for perfecting an art or craft. Horace's *Carmina*, IV, ii, begins: 'Whoever seeks to rival Pindar must fly on waxen wings made with Daedalean art'; compare Pindar, *First Olympian Ode*, 105. According to Natalis Comes, *Mythologia* (Geneva ed., 1636, 29), who lists under 'Daedalus' all the great craftsmen of antiquity, Minerva the goddess of learning herself was educated by a Daedalean nurse 'who taught her in her tender years all the most ingenious arts'.

41 **both in this and in other**] both in poetry and in other arts.

42 **due commendation**] praise which has been earned.

42–3 **Art, Imitation, and Exercise**] The learning process, especially in rhetoric, was taken to consist of three parts. The analysis goes back to Greek education. Plato, for instance, writes in *Phaedrus*, 269D: 'If you are endowed by nature with a genius for speaking you will become a distinguished speaker if you add theory and practice' to your natural aptitude. See P. Shorey, *Transactions of the American Philological Association*, 40 (1909), 185–201. Cicero in *De inventione*, I, i, 2, discusses whether eloquence depends chiefly on study, art, and exercise or on innate gifts, and finds (like Sidney) that the original gift is necessary, but that it must be trained and perfected by application. But all learning processes were considered essentially similar. Plutarch in *The Education of Children*, 4, observes that as in arts and sciences so also in teach-

NOTES TO PAGES 109–10 </> 229

ing virtue three things are necessary: nature, reason or learning, use. 'And as in husbandry it is first necessary for the soil to be fertile, next the husband-man skilful, and lastly the seed good; so here nature resembles the soil, the teacher the husbandman, the precepts the seed' (compare 40 above). The teachers of rhetoric usually took innate ability (*ingenium*) for granted, and split off imitation as part of the theoretical training necessary; see R. McKeon, 'Literary Criticism and the Concept of Imitation in Antiquity', *MPh* 34 (1936), 1–35, especially 27ff. Thus *Ad Herennium*, I, ii, 3 (which can speak for countless manuals on rhetoric in medieval and Renaissance times): skill in speaking 'we can acquire by three means, by Art, Imitation and Exer-cise. Art is a set of rules that provide a definite method and manner of speak-ing. Imitation stimulates us to achieve effects in speaking by careful and conscious following of certain models. Exercise is constant practice and ex-perience in speaking.' On the triad in later teaching, see Crane 1937, 83ff.

Later the rhetoricans' triad is applied to other activities: Ascham in *The Schoolmaster* applies the method to the teaching of grammar, in *Toxophilus* to archery. Sidney's discussion of the failure of English poets to follow the method recalls *The Schoolmaster*, which complains that the introduction of rhyme into England was a result of poor imitative practice – it was 'receyued into England by men of excellent wit in deede, but of small learninge' – and includes as examples of these witty writers 'Chauser, Th. Norton, of Bristow' (co-author of *Gorboduc*) and 'my L. of Surrey' (Ascham 1904, 289).

43 **these, neither . . . nor**] neither with these . . . nor with these. The suggestion that contemporary English poets ignore the theories and examples which would help them cultivate their natural gifts is embodied in E.K.'s comments on George Gascoigne in the November eclogue of *The Shepheards Calender*: 'Ma. George Gaskin a wittie gentleman, and the very chefe of our late rymers, who and if some partes of learning wanted not (albee it is well known he altogyther wanted not learning) no doubt would have attayned to the excellencye of those famous Poets. For gifts of wit and naturall prompt-nesse appeare in hym aboundantly' (Spenser 1989, 197).

artificial rules] rules on which an art is based.

imitative patterns] models to be imitated.

we] i.e. 'the paper-blurrers' (25).

p. 110/1 **cumber**] encumber.

2 **fore-backwardly**] back to front.

2–4 **for where . . . begotten by knowledge**] i.e. we do not exercise our minds in the active discovery of truth, but instead we fall back on the familiar prod-ucts of other people's analysis, with the result that we reproduce *phantastike* (104/20) representations of things that have no real existence – 'matter which never was begotten by knowledge'.

4–5 **matter . . . matter**] The distinction between *res* (matter) and *verba* (words), made by Roman grammarians, was introduced rather loosely into the lit-erary theory of Horace (*Art*, 38–72, 310), and developed in various ways by

Renaissance critics. See Weinberg 1961, II, Index, s. Res: Verba; and A. C. Howell, '*Res et Verba*: Words and Things', *ELH* 13 (1946), 131–42.

6 *quodlibet*] (Latin) 'anything we like'; any question or thesis proposed as a topic for scholastic debate. Sidney is reasserting that contemporary poets take up any theme that comes to hand and assume that if they spin it out in verses it will turn into a poem.

8 *Quicquid . . . erit*] Adapted from Ovid's *Tristia*, IV, x, 26: 'Et quod conabar dicere, versus erat' ('And whatever I tried to say turned into verse').

9 **marshalling . . . rank**] i.e. arranging it in a precise order, as a general organizes his troops before battle.

11 *Troilus and Criseyde*] Up to 1700 *Troilus and Criseyde* was by far the most popular of Chaucer's poems. See Caroline F. E. Spurgeon, *Five Hundred Years of Chaucer Criticism and Allusion* (Cambridge, 1925), I, lxxvi–lxxvii.

12–13 **in that misty time**] Refers either to the mists of superstition, when England was in the grip of Catholicism (compare 84/27–8, 'the eyes of the mind, only cleared by faith'), or to the lack of rules or good examples in medieval English poetry, which meant that poets worked as if in a mist. Both meanings may be intended.

13 **in this clear age**] Again, this may refer either to the religious or the intellectual clarity available to the inhabitants of post-Reformation England.

14 **wants**] faults. Sidney may be referring to the supposed irregularity of Chaucer's metre. Changes in the English language meant that sixteenth-century readers did not understand the principles on which this metre was based.

15 **the *Mirror of Magistrates***] a collection of narrative poems on the misfortunes of great men and women in English history, conceived by the printer-poet William Baldwin as a continuation of John Lydgate's fifteenth-century poem *The Fall of Princes*. It is a work of 'parts', since the narratives are written by several poets in a variety of styles. Publication of the first edition was delayed on the orders of the Lord Chancellor Stephen Gardiner in c. 1554. The *Mirror* was first published in 1559 and went on being reprinted with additions until well into the seventeenth century. See *Mirror for Magistrates*, ed. Campbell (1938), introduction.

meetly] aptly.

16 **the Earl of Surrey's lyrics**] A number of poems by Henry Howard, Earl of Surrey (c. 1517–47) were printed in Richard Tottel's *Songes and Sonettes* (1557). Some of his contemporaries saw Sidney as Surrey's poetic heir (see Duncan-Jones 1989, 386).

17 **The *Shepherd's Calendar***] Spenser published *The Shepheardes Calender* in 1579 under the pseudonym Immerito ('unworthy'), and dedicated it to 'the noble and vertuous Gentleman, most worthy of all titles both of learning and chevalerie, Maister Philip Sidney'.

18 **eclogues**] pastoral poems, usually in dialogue form.

19 **old rustic language**] archaic country dialect. In the 1580s most English

writers no longer favoured the use of archaic diction which had been popular
earlier: see Rubel 1941, 105 and 113. Sidney is not being quite fair to Spenser;
both Theocritus and Virgil did in fact use rural dialects in their Eclogues, as
Vives points out (Vives 1931, 137). Virgil in his Eclogues, says Vives, 'was
striving to catch the charm of the country dialect, in which kind of effort
Theocritus allowed himself considerable indulgence'. Sidney too used the
'old rustic language' in his pastoral *Ister Bank*; see Ringler 1962, 66, and notes,
413. Castiglione's *Courtier* contains an extended debate on the desirability of
using archaic language in written texts (Castiglione 1928, 49–63), during
which the point is made that 'those words that are no more in use in Florence, doe still continue among the men of the Countrie' (54).

20 **allow**] approve of.

20–1 **Theocritus . . . Virgil . . . Sannazzaro**] Sidney cites the authority of the three
outstanding pastoral poets: in Greek, Theocritus, the Sicilian poet of the
third century B.C.; in Latin, Virgil as author of the *Eclogues*; in neo-Latin,
Jacopo Sannazzaro (1455–1530) (see 97/9 note), whose *Piscatory Eclogues*
were highly regarded for several centuries. Independently of Sidney, Webbe
measures Spenser's achievement in the *Shepheardes Calender* similarly against
Theocritus in Greek, Virgil in Latin, but against Calpurnius and Mantuan
in neo-Latin (Smith 1904, I, 262).

23 **let but most of the verses be put in prose**] This is an exercise called
'metaphrasis' (see Ascham 1904, 253–8), recommended as useful to poets
and other writers by Erasmus in his treatise *De copia* (1514): 'It will be of
enormous value to take apart the fabric of poetry and reweave it as prose,
and, vice versa, to bind the freer language of prose under the rules of metre'
(Erasmus 1978, 303) But Sidney's point is, of course, that turning bad verse
into prose exposes its irrationality. See also Plato, *Republic*, X, 601.

25 **ordering**] planning.

26–7 **a confused mass . . . barely accompanied with reason**] Compare George
Gascoigne, *Certain Notes of Instruction* (Smith 1904, I, 51–2): 'I would exhorte
you also to beware of rime without reason; my meaning is hereby that your
rime leade you not from your first Inuention, for many wryters, when they
haue layed the platforme of their inuention, are yet drawen sometimes (by
ryme) to forget it or at least to alter it, as when they cannot readily finde out
a worde whiche maye rime to the first (and yet continue their determinate
Inuention) they do then eyther botche it vp [i.e. patch it] with a worde that
will ryme (howe small reason soeuer it carie with it), or els they alter their
first worde and so percase decline or trouble their former Inuention: . . .
rather searche the bottome of your braynes for apte wordes than chaunge
good reason for rumbling rime.' Gabriel Harvey noted at the end of this
paragraph in his copy of Gascoigne's text: 'A pithie rule in Sir Philips *Apologie for Poetrie*. The Inuention must guide and rule the Elocution: *non contra*
[not the other way round]' (Smith 1904, I, 360).

26 **tingling**] tinkling. This is apparently the earliest use (deriving from Tyndale's
translation of 1 Corinthians 13:1) of this derogatory adjective applied (as
became common later) to rhyme.

29 **honest civility**] decent behaviour.

30 *Gorboduc*] was a political tragedy written jointly by Thomas Sackville, first
    Lord Buckhurst (1536–1608), one of the principal contributors to the *Mirror
    for Magistrates*, and Thomas Norton (1532–84), a lawyer, whose translation
    of Calvin's *Institutes* was first published in 1559. *Gorboduc* was acted at Court
    in 1561 by the gentlemen of the Inner Temple. The text was printed in a
    pirated edition in 1565, and in an authorized edition, under the title *The
    Tragedy of Ferrex and Porrex*, in 1571. It describes the disasters that befell
    Britain in ancient times as a result of King Gorboduc's decision to divide the
    kingdom between his two heirs. The moral of the fable was that Elizabeth I
    should either name her successor or give birth to one.

31–2 **climbing to the height of Seneca's style**] Sidney's comparison of *Gorboduc*
    with the works of Seneca was very high praise (despite his incorporation into
    this phrase of a well-worn pun on 'stile' – a set of steps for getting over a
    fence or wall). During the Renaissance, the tragedies of L. Annaeus Seneca
    (c. 5 B.C.–A.D. 65), the Stoic philosopher and tutor of Nero, were more
    highly regarded than those of the Greek tragedians. Giraldi Cinthio, for
    instance, claims that he 'surpasses in prudence, gravity, decorum, majesty,
    and skill in the use of sentences [adages] all the Greeks who ever wrote'. Most
    Renaissance critics looked to tragedy as Sidney does for 'stately speeches',
    'well-sounding phrases', 'high style' (i.e. the sort of style which is suitable for
    use by rulers, or to refer to great events), and 'notable morality' (i.e. morals
    which are worth remembering). It is not essential, Scaliger observes (Scaliger
    1617, III, xcvi, 333), for a tragedy to have an unhappy ending, so long as the
    action is grim (*atrox*). A 'notable morality' is most important, and there are
    two ways of achieving it: first, by using *sententiae* (moral maxims); and sec-
    ondly, by vigorous sustained metaphor (334). Trissino (Gilbert 1940, 223) also
    emphasized the importance of *sententiae* in tragedy. See W. Clemen, *English
    Tragedy before Shakespeare* (London, 1961), 69–70.

33 **very**] true.

34 **defectious**] competed with 'defective' in the late sixteenth century. Compare
    97/5.

    circumstances] In rhetoric and logic, this is the term for the adjuncts of any
    action – time, place, manner, cause, etc. – which provide the means by which
    a case can be built up on 'circumstantial' evidence. See *Ad Herennium*, II,
    iv, 6–7. On the doctrine of circumstances taught in Elizabethan schools,
    see Baldwin 1944, II, 311–18. Ancient rhetorical teaching here contributed a
    good deal to neo-classical theories of the dramatic unities. In rhetoric the
    circumstances were to be exploited selectively to make the case presented
    as coherent, credible, and persuasive as possible. Renaissance critics believed
    that the same care was necessary to establish a dramatic illusion. It was an
    unacceptable strain on credibility if a stage, obviously one place, should be
    used as if it were many places. In the same way it was reasonable to observe
    Aristotle's precept (38–9) in *Poetics*, V, 1449b: 'Tragedy attempts to keep
    within a single revolution of the sun, or to exceed it but little, but the epic
    is indefinite in time and thus unlike tragedy'.

36 **faulty . . . time**] See 34 note above.

38   **uttermost**] most.

38–9 **Aristotle's precept**] See 34 note above.

39–40 **many days, and many places**] *Gorboduc* moves from the abdication of the king to the later rivalry between his two sons and a long period of civil war; and the action takes place in several courts.

40   **inartificially**] inartistically. This is an early use of a term adapted from rhetorical theory; compare 114/15. According to Scaliger, the story of a play must be set out to conform as far as possible with reality (Scaliger 1617, III, xcvi, 334ff.). For tragedy is designed not simply to excite admiration or amazement, but to teach, to move, and to delight. We are delighted by jokes in a comedy; and in serious matters we are delighted by accuracy and appropriateness, for most men hate lies. For this reason, battles at Thebes got through in two hours do not please, and no sensible poet arranges that someone shall make a journey from Delphi to Athens, or from Athens to Thebes, in a moment of time; as in Aeschylus, when Agamemnon is killed and buried so quickly that an actor has scarcely time to draw breath. Nor is it satisfactory if Hercules has to throw Lichas into the sea, for that cannot be represented without a break in the action. The plot should be succinct and yet be made as varied and multiplex as possible. For instance, in the story of Hecuba in Thrace and Polydorus, since dead men cannot be introduced, use ghosts to tell the action. So likewise in the story of Ceyx and Halcyon. If you were to make a tragedy out of this, don't start with the departure of Ceyx, for, since the performance can take only six or eight hours at the most, it is not realistic to have a storm spring up on stage, and the ship wrecked in the middle of the sea out of sight of land. Use a chorus and messengers. Again in *Poetices*, VI, iii, 708, Scaliger raises similar objections against the Greek dramatists who move Theseus and his army from Athens to Thebes, have them fight a battle, and a messenger report back, all within a few hours. Similar cavils, accompanying stricter requirements, increase during the second half of the sixteenth century; see Spingarn 1908, 91ff. George Whetstone in the Dedication to *Promos and Cassandra* (1578) castigates the typical English dramatist of the time: he 'is most vaine, indiscreete and out of order: he fyrst groundes his worke on impossibilities; then in three howers ronnes he throwe the worlde, marryes, gets Children, makes Children men, men to conquer kingdomes, murder Monsters, and bringeth Gods from Heauen, and fetcheth Diuels from Hel' (Smith 1904, I, 59). And see 112/2 note.

43   **under-kingdoms**] subsidiary states.

p. III/1 **conceived**] understood.

4–5 **Upon . . . that**] immediately.

7   **two armies . . . four swords**] Compare Shakespeare, *Henry V*, IV, *Chorus*:

> our scene must to the battle fly,
> Where O for pity, we shall much disgrace,
> With four or five most vile and ragged foils,
> Right ill-disposed in brawl ridiculous,
> The name of Agincourt.

Jonson in the Prologue to *Every Man in His Humour*, proclaiming his general assent to Sidney's teaching, scorns

> To make a child now swaddled to shoot up . . .
> Past three score years; or with three rusty swords . . .
> Fight over York and Lancaster's long jars.

Such contentions make the point not that a confusion of times and places is intrinsically wrong but that by refusing to stick to one place and one span of time a poet is making things much harder for himself and his audience, and that he is likely to impair the coherence and thus the effectiveness of his presentation. Shakespeare uses this argument in the Choruses of *Henry V* to justify his flouting of it.

8 **pitched field**] field of battle.

10 **princes**] The word 'prince' could apply to both men and women.

traverses] misfortunes, hardships.

12–13 **how absurd it is in sense, even sense may imagine**] The sentence plays on two meanings of 'sense': 'reason' and 'the senses'. It means something like: 'even our own senses of sight and hearing will demonstrate to us the irrationality of such a production'.

13 **Art**] literary and dramatic theory.

14–15 **the ordinary players in Italy**] K. M. Lea suggests that Sidney may well have seen troupes of Italian actors in Venice in 1574 (Lea 1934, I, 262). Although many of their plays had extravagant storylines, an increasing use was being made at this time of standardized sets for comedy, tragedy, tragi-comedy, and pastoral; see *ibid.*, I, 326–7. Architectural theory developing from Vitruvius (first century A.D.), *De architectura* (printed 1486), encouraged the use of a fixed scene and consequently of an almost unbroken action on the stage; see Allardyce Nicholl, *The Development of the Theatre* (3rd ed., London, 1948), 81ff.

15–16 **some bring in . . . Eunuchus in Terence**] Perhaps a reference to the discussion of the unities in Castelvetro 1576, 60, where he deals with Terence and Plautus. But Sidney is confusing the *Eunuch* with *Heautontimorumenos* (*The Self-tormentor*; see 107/42 note). In the *Eunuch*, probably the most popular of Terence's plays, the action seems to be completed in one day, for the lover Phaedria, who intends to go off into the country for three days, returns in a matter of hours. But *The Self-tormentor* clearly occupies more than one day. As Scaliger observed: 'Half the story happens one evening; the second half takes place in the morning' (Scaliger 1617, VI, iii, 709). Scaliger probably, and later critics certainly, believed that the play had been produced in two parts on successive days; see Cook 1890, 119–20 notes, and Smith 1904, I, 400. It is interesting to note that an English play of Sidney's time that discusses the unities of time and place in its prologue, George Whetstone's *Promos and Cassandra* (1578) (see 110/40 note), is written in two parts.

16–17 **far short of twenty years**] i.e. Terence's play may deal with events that span two days, but this is very much less than the twenty years it would take for a child to grow up and be ready to get another child (10–12).

18 **Plautus hath in one place done amiss**] Compare Scaliger 1617, VI, iii, 708: 'I can never approve that in the *Captives*, Philocrates goes away and Philopolemus comes back from Aulis to Aetolia in a very short time'.

21–2 **tragedy is tied to the laws of Poesy, and not of History**] Compare Spenser's Letter to Raleigh on *The Faerie Queene*: 'For the Methode of a Poet historical is not such, as of an Historiographer' (Spenser 1980, 738). Sidney is reasserting the Aristotelian theory (see *Poetics*, IX, 1451b) of the independence of the poet, as against the doctrine put forward by Castelvetro that 'it is fitting that the plot of a tragedy and of an epic should accept such actual events as are common to it and to the truth of history; ... the plots should be composed of happenings that can be called historical, although Aristotle had a different opinion' (Castelvetro 1576, 188). Scaliger in his account of tragedy (Scaliger 1617, III, xcvi, 333–4) seems to incline to Sidney's position, and suggests that although history should not be distorted (and some of the ancients were guilty in this respect) the writer of tragedy should be free to interpret actions poetically to bring out their moral lesson.

23–4 **to frame the history to the most tragical conveniency**] i.e. to adapt the historical narrative to the requirements of tragedy.

25 **the difference betwixt reporting and representing**] Here Sidney neatly summarizes Scaliger's argument, referred to above (110/40 note). Castelvetro elaborates on the distinction between reporting (narrative) and representing (drama): 'Dramatic presentation . . . is different from narrative, first in that it uses words and things instead of the original words and things, while narrative uses only words in the place of things, and indirect discourse in place of direct discourse. Secondly, the dramatic method is less ample with respect to places and times' (Castelvetro 1576, 56ff.). In addition, the narrative method relates things that are visible and invisible, audible and not audible, and the dramatic represents only things that are visible and audible. And narrative does not stir the emotions so much as drama does.

26–7 **Peru . . . Calicut**] Sidney refers to places in the extreme West and East of the known world. Peru was conquered by the Spaniard Francisco Pizarro (1478–1541), and Calicut (Calcutta, now called Kozhikode) was the first port on the south-east coast of India reached by the Portuguese explorer Vasco da Gama (c. 1460–1524) in 1498. Calicut remained one of the chief ports for trade between Europe and India during the sixteenth century.

28 **Pacolet's horse**] is the flying horse of the enchanter Pacolet in the late-medieval romance *Valentine and Orson*, printed at Lyon in 1489, and translated into English by Henry Watson in c. 1550. The tale was popular in England from the sixteenth to the eighteenth century.

29 *nuncius*] (Latin) messenger. Most Renaissance critics explain the function of the messenger as enabling the playwright to avoid depicting excessive violence on stage; but Castelvetro also recommends it as a way to avoid awkward improbabilities (Castelvetro 1576, 56ff.). See Gilbert 1940, 309ff., and compare Scaliger quoted in 110/40 note.

31–2 **as Horace saith**] In *Art*, 147, Horace condemns the dull cyclic poets and shows that the good epic poet does not start at the very beginning (*ab ovo*, 'from the egg'), but like Homer goes to the critical moment and starts *in medias res*, in the middle of the action. The openings of the classical epic poets had been analysed and European practice codified in twelfth-century poetic theory, but the particular importance in drama of beginning *in medias res* was not much discussed before the sixteenth century. Scaliger in a chapter of rules for poets (Scaliger 1617, III, xcv, 331) gives as the first law: 'Never begin with the egg', and notices that both Virgil and Lucan obey this law. In the next chapter, on Tragedy and Comedy, he recommends restricting the action of a play to a single place and time (see 110/40 note). In III, xcvi, 334–5, he insists: 'The argument of a play should be very succinct, and yet the plot full of variety and interwoven strands. For example: Hecuba in Thrace is forbidden to return by Achilles. Polydorus is already slain . . . Since the dead cannot be introduced on stage, their likenesses either as images or ghosts may be used: thus with Polydorus.' Sidney follows Scaliger, but fills out his account from personal knowledge of Euripides's tragedy *Hecuba*, by drawing on the opening speech of the play ('for safety's sake, with great riches' (34–5) and 'to make the treasure his own' (37) seem to be taken from this speech). See Myrick 1935, 105–7, for a discussion of Sidney's knowledge of Euripides.

38 **sleight**] trick.

42 **where doth Euripides?**] 'begin' is understood.

44 **This need no further to be enlarged**] This argument need not be taken any further.

p. 112/2 **mingling kings and clowns**] Compare George Whetstone, Dedication to *Promos and Cassandra* (continuing the passage quoted in 110/40): 'And (that which is worst) their ground is not so vnperfect as their workinge indiscreete: not waying, so the people laugh, though they laugh them (for theyr follyes) to scorne. Manye tymes (to make mirthe) they make a Clowne companion with a Kinge; in theyr graue Counsels they allow the aduise of fooles; yea, they vse one order of speach for all persons: a gross Indecorum, for a Crowe wyl yll counterfet the Nightingale's sweete voice; even so affected speeche doth misbecome a Clowne' (Smith 1904, I, 59–60). Sidney's phrases were remembered; compare *The Pilgrimage to Parnassus* (c. 1598–9), ed. J. B. Leishman (London, 1949), 129, lines 664–6: 'Dost thou know a playe cannot be without a clowne? Clownes have been thrust into playes by head and shoulders, ever since Kemp could make a scurvey face.'

clowns] peasants, country-dwellers.

3 **carrieth**] demands.

thrust in . . . by head and shoulders] i.e. shove in any old how.

5 **admiration and commiseration**] These are the effects of tragedy (see 98/28–9 note), while **the right sportfulness** (compare 98/4ff.) is the aim of comedy.

6 **Apuleius**] (second century A.D.): Latin philosopher, author of the *Metamorphoses, or Golden Ass* (trans. W. Adlington, 1566), from which Sidney took hints for the *Old Arcadia*. The *Golden Ass* tells of the misfortunes of Lucius,

who gets accidentally turned into an ass, and is full of stories, ranging from the comic to the tragicomic – the most famous of which is the romance of Cupid and Psyche. The work is therefore a mixture of genres, and released from observing the unity of epic. The *Golden Ass* is prose fiction, not drama, and therefore a strange example for Sidney to use at this point in his argument. Gosson, however, refers to 'the *Golden Ass*' as having been 'throughly ransackt, to furnish the Playe houses in London' (Gosson 1974, 169), and mentions '*Cupid* and *Psyche* plaid at *Paules*'. Chambers (*The Elizabethan Stage*, II, 15) notes a performance of this play on 26 December 1581. Perhaps Sidney had it in mind when he mentioned Apuleius here.

9   **Plautus . . . *Amphitrio*]** In the Prologue to *Amphitryon* Plautus spoke of his play as a tragi-comedy, thinking of it apparently as a mixture of the serious and the humorous, which introduces both the gods of tragedy and the slave, the typical character of comedy. Scaliger explains Plautus's intention in Scaliger 1617, I, vii, 31. Sixteenth-century discussions of tragi-comedy invariably start from a consideration of this play; see Doran 1954, 190ff.

10   **daintily]** sparingly, fastidiously (compare 114/19).

    hornpipes] vigorous dances.

13   **doltishness]** stupidity.

15   **tract]** course.

16   **well-raised]** exalted, kept at a high level.

17   **comedians]** writers of comedy.

112/17–113/11   **But our comedians . . . teaching delightfulness]** The basis of Renaissance discussion on the nature of the comic is Cicero, *De oratore*, II, lviii–lxx, 235–80, following Aristotle, *Ethics*, IV, 8. For Cicero, comedy is based on ridicule; ridicule is provoked by an exhibition of some shame or deformity (but the shame or deformity must not be to excess); and the comic effect may be produced either by action or by wordplay. Cicero, urging moderation in all things, objected to scurrility or obscenity as a source of the ridiculous; but the line of decency was difficult to draw, and some classical and medieval writers of comedy (against whom Boccaccio campaigned; see Boccaccio 1930, 182 note, and compare 98/2–3 note) were often scurrilous and obscene. Ridicule continued to be considered the basis of comedy and the source of laughter in the Renaissance. A fresh account of the verbal aspects of the comic is given by G. Pontanus, *De sermone* (1499), book IV. Castiglione in *The Courtier*, book II, follows Pontanus, but the courtly context of his discussion gives a more general and social emphasis to his treatment of the comic. Castelvetro presented a full literary analysis in *Poetica d'Aristotele* (Castelvetro 1576, 92ff.). Comedy is based on human shame or deformity, either of the mind or of the body. If of the mind, it rises from folly, not vice; if of the body, it can be evoked only if the shame or deformity is not painful or harmful. The chief sources of comedy are deception and ignorance; see Charlton 1913, 134–6. Sidney's formulation of a distinction between laughter and delight in comedy is a modification of the theory

238 ↂ NOTES TO PAGE 112

of laughter set out by G. Trissino in *Poetica*, part VI (1563). Trissino claims to give a philosophical account of comedy, not an oratorical account such as that of Cicero; but he still relies heavily on Cicero's *De oratore*. The ridiculous, according to Trissino following Aristotle, is a mild form of the ugly, and the source of the ridiculous is ugliness and deformity. It is evident that laughter springs from the pleasure of the senses, or from the memory or anticipation of such pleasure. Such pleasure does not come from every object that causes delight, but merely from those objects that have some share of ugliness; for if a man see a beautiful woman or a splendid jewel he does not laugh, nor does he laugh on hearing music in his praise, nor in reacting with his senses to things that are pleasant and grateful to the touch, the taste, or the smell. These together with the pleasure evoke 'admiration' not laughter. But if the object presented to the sense has some mixture of ugliness, then it moves laughter, as an ugly and distorted face does, an inept movement, a silly word, a mispronunciation, a rough hand, a wine of unpleasant taste. Those things especially cause laughter from which better results were expected. The pleasure in the ridiculous comes to us because man is by nature envious and malicious, as is clearly seen in little children, for almost all of them are envious and always delight to hurt. Man never naturally delights in the good of others except through accident, that is, through some good which he hopes to acquire for himself. Hence if anyone sees someone find money, he does not laugh or take pleasure, but rather is envious, but if he sees someone fall into the mud, he laughs, because the harm which does not befall us is always, as Lucretius says, pleasant to observe in others. For if we ourselves suffer, the sight of the same sort of suffering in others does not make us laugh. One hunchback does not laugh at another hunchback. If the evils we see in others are deadly or very painful, as are wounds and fevers, they do not move laughter, but rather pity, because we feel that similar evils will come to us. As man is composed of mind and body, so ugliness in him is double, of the mind as well as of the body, and the special deformities of the mind are ignorance, imprudence, credulity, and the like; and so in jokes we laugh especially when we see such things in persons who are thought to be substantial and of good intelligence (adapted from Gilbert 1940, 227–9). More briefly, but following Cicero more closely, Thomas Wilson suggests the same sort of doctrine: 'An occasion of laughter . . . is the fondnes [i.e. folly], the filthines, the deformitie, and all such euill behauiour, as we see to be in other. For we laugh alwaies at these things which either onely or chiefly touch handsomely and wittily, some especiall fault or fond behauiour in some one body or some one thing' (Wilson 1909, 135–6).

Sidney avoids Trissino's cynicism, which makes envy the force behind laughter, and seeks an inner, mental sanction for comedy. He also suggests, unlike Trissino, that we might derive delight from recognizing under the guise of fiction behaviour which we ourselves have indulged in: characters who perform on stage what **we play naturally** (113/10). The true delight of comedy lies in our recognition of its remarkable conformity with nature.

20–1 **in themselves they have, as it were, a kind of contrariety**] i.e. laughter and delight may be seen more or less as opposites.

22 **conveniency to ourselves**] fitting our own natures.

31 **go down the hill against the bias**] As in the game of bowls, when the slope of the ground counteracts the expected swerve given to the bowl by its bias.

32 **for the respect of them**] for their sake.

35 **Alexander's picture**] Plutarch gives an account of the portraits of Alexander in his *Life of Alexander*, 4. The portrait by Apelles was the most famous.

36 **twenty mad antics**] refers to the 'antique' or grotesque style of decoration popular in Elizabethan times. The style is described by Henry Peacham as follows: 'an vnnatural or vnorderly composition for delight sake, of men, beasts, birds, fishes, flowers &c. without (as wee say) Rime or reason, for the greater variety you shew in your inuention, the more you please' (*The Art of Drawing* (1606)). See Croft-Murray 1962–70, I, 26–7, from which this citation is taken, and Duncan-Jones 1989, 388.

36–8 **Hercules . . . at Omphale's commandment**] After completing his Twelve Labours, the Greek hero Hercules was for a time infatuated with Omphale, Queen of Lydia. In the *Moralia* Plutarch refers to comic pictures of him in women's clothes (*Whether an Old Man Should Engage in Public Affairs*, 4), and paintings like the one Sidney describes were fairly common in the Northern Renaissance (see Duncan-Jones 1989, 388). For a list of paintings on this subject, see Pilger 1956, II, 112–16.

41 **all the end of the comical part**] the whole aim of comedy.

44 **forbidden plainly by Aristotle**] in *Poetics*, V, as quoted in the note on **98/4–5** above. Probably Sidney also remembered the fuller discussion of the proper sources of humour in Aristotle's *Ethics*, IV, 8, 1128a – the discussion on which the Ciceronian and Renaissance accounts of comedy were based (see **112/17–113/11** note).

p. 113/2–7 **For what is it . . . homines facit**] Sidney seems to disapprove of using 'Fortune's slaves' as comic butts: people who by birth cannot help being what they are, whether poor or foreign. Comedy should instead exploit acquired characteristics. This seems to exclude the mockery of 'deformed creatures' such as Trissino's 'hunchbacks' from the province of 'right comedy'.

6–7 **Nil habet . . . homines facit**] Juvenal, *Satires*, III, 152–3: 'Poverty contains no sharper misery than that it makes men ridiculous'.

8–9 **But rather . . . traveller**] Sidney describes characters who turn up regularly in Renaissance drama, rather than types from Roman comedy.

8 **busy**] impertinent, obtrusive (compare Robertson 1973, 77/29).

heartless] cowardly.

Thraso] is the boastful soldier in Terence's *Eunuch* (see **98/14** note). He had a large sixteenth-century progeny, including the hero of Nicholas Udall's *Ralph Roister Doister* (c. 1553).

9 **a self-wise-seeming schoolmaster**] a teacher who thinks himself wise. Sidney introduces such a schoolmaster into his masque *The Lady of May*. See also Lea 1934, I, 39.

an awry-transformed traveller] a traveller who has been altered for the worse by his travels. This was another familiar figure in sixteenth-century literature: Roger Ascham describes at length the fate of Englishmen who have travelled to Italy and have returned 'worse transformed, than euer was any in *Circes* Court' (Ascham 1904, 226; see 223–36). Sidney observes in a letter to his brother Robert: 'I think ere it be long . . . we travellers shall be made sport of in comedies' (Duncan-Jones 1989, 285).

10 **walk in stage names**] given fictional names; presented as fictions.

naturally] in real life.

11 **as in the other**] i.e. in tragedy. The complimentary reference to George Buchanan as a model for the writer of tragedies has something of the appearance of an afterthought (compare 108/36–7 note).

14 **they**] i.e. tragedy and comedy.

17 **honesty**] chastity.

18 **that lyrical kind**] Apart from the writers of the Pléiade in France, most Renaissance critics dealing with poetry in the vernacular tended to follow Horace and Aristotle, who ignore the lyric. Although Sidney both in practice and in theory (see 87/21–2 note and 99/1ff.) respected the genre, he restricts himself here to the conventional characterization of the lyric as a song in praise of God or of a mistress. See Tuve 1947, 84ff. (compare 99/1ff. note). Sidney arranges his arguments with his usual skill, commending and defending the lyric by assuming that it could and perhaps should be dedicated to the praise of 'the immortal beauty, the immortal goodness of . . . God', and finding fault with the technique of the contemporary English lyric by limiting his examination of it to secular love poetry.

23–5 **of which . . . new-budding occasions**] i.e. we could turn our attention to any aspect of God's beauty and goodness and still find new subject matter for our poetry.

25–6 **the banner of unresistible love**] Compare Song of Solomon 2:4.

27 **so coldly they apply fiery speeches**] This is a witty allusion to the oxymoron 'icy fire', much used by imitators of Petrarch. Sidney uses it here to attack those who give the impression of having 'read lovers' writings' rather than experienced love for themselves. Compare Sidney's refusal to make use of other people's writing in *Astrophil and Stella*, I.

28 **swelling**] grandiose, bombastic (with a possible pun on another sense of 'swelling': 'pregnant').

28–9 **hang together**] are connected (Sidney is speaking ironically).

29 **me**] In the Penshurst MS 'me' reads 'my father'.

29–30 **at north-west and by south**] Compare *Hamlet*, II, ii, 362–3.

32 **betrayed**] conveyed to the reader.

forcibleness or *energia*] The first known use in English of a form of the word 'energy', coming in through Latin rhetoric by a Renaissance modification of the sense given it by Aristotle (*Rhetoric*, III, ii, 1411b). According to Scaliger, there are four poetic virtues: wisdom, variety, *efficacia*, and sweetness. *Efficacia* he deals with in ch. xxvi, 266ff.; it is his term for what the Greeks call *energeia*. It is the power of presenting the subject matter clearly, and refers not to the words used in presenting the subject but to the vivid mental apprehension of things themselves. An excess or a deficiency of *energeia* is a fault: an excess is affectation in straining to produce an effect, or to write on a subject, which is beyond one's powers (compare 37 note); while a deficiency produces the languidness characteristic of modern poets. Virgil in particular strikes a happy mean. So for Sidney the **forcibleness or *energia*** is the intellectual clarity with which a poet apprehends the fore-conceit or Idea (85/35), and makes his readers apprehend it. Compare 85/34–43 note; and Ringler 1962, 459 note.

35 **for the outside of it, which is words**] The idea that words are a form of clothing for pre-existent subject matter is common in sixteenth-century writings on language; see e.g. Erasmus's *De copia*: 'Style is to thought as clothes are to the body. Just as dress and outward appearance can enhance or disfigure the beauty and dignity of the body, so words can enhance or disfigure thought' (Erasmus 1978, 306).

36 **diction**] choice of words. This is the first known use of the word in this sense, which during the eighteenth century was to become one of the technical terms of literary criticism.

honey-flowing matron] A 'matron' is a mother, and 'honey-flowing' suggests that her breasts are lactating. Again, the metaphor is a common one in sixteenth-century references to eloquence.

37 **a courtesan-like painted affectation**] All these terms became commonplace in criticism. Compare Harvey 1913, 189; *Hamlet*, III, i, 51–3; *Paradise Regained*, IV, 343–5; Fulke Greville, *A Treatie of Human Learning*, in Greville 1938, I, 181, where wanton rhetoric 'staines the Matrone with the Harlot's weed'. 'Painted' became a stock epithet for a deceiving rhetoric; see Baldwin 1944, II, 414–15. Sidney probably uses 'affectation' in the technical sense in which Scaliger uses it (see 32 note). Quintilian, in *Institutes*, VIII, gives a detailed discussion of *cacozelia*, or vicious affectation, as a fault in all styles of writing: it includes all that is turgid, trivial, over-ripe, redundant, far-fetched (*arcessia*), extravagant, etc. See the discussion of '*Cacozelia* or Fonde affectation' in Puttenham 1936, 210.

38–41 **far-fetched words ... winter-starved**] This passage closely resembles *Astrophil and Stella*, 15:

> You that do search for everie purling spring,
>   Which from the ribs of old *Parnassus* flowes,
>   And everie floure, not sweet perhaps, which growes
> Neare therabout, into your Poesie wring;
> You that do Dictionarie's methode bring
>   Into your rimes, running in ratling rowes ...
>   You take wrong waies, those far-fet helpes be such,
>   As do bewray a want of inward tuch.
>   (Ringler 1962, 172; and see notes, 466)

38 far-fetched] unfamiliar. In its common sixteenth-century form, 'farfet', this
is one of Sidney's favourite words; compare 96/17. Puttenham lists 'the figure
Metalepsis, which I call the *farfet*, as when we had rather fetch a word a great
way off then to vse one nerer hand to expresse the matter aswel & plainer'
(Puttenham 1936, 183); and Erasmus's Folly mocks the practice of contemporary rhetoricians who 'mingle their writinges with wordes sought out of
strange langages', 'farre fetched vocables', and 'disused woordes of anti-
quitee' (Erasmus 1965, 11). On Elizabethan attitudes to exotic borrowing in
vocabulary, see Jones 1953, ch. IV, 94–141. Concern for the vernacular language in which the Scriptures would be fully intelligible to all English readers
led most influential writers to castigate affectation and excessive borrowing.
Arthur Golding, who claimed to have completed Sidney's translation of *The
Trewenesse of Christian Religion*, set out in his dedication to Leicester what
may have been Sidney's own principles. 'If any words or phrases shall seeme
straunge (as in some places perchaunce they may) I doubt not but your Lord-
ship will impute it to the rarenesse and profoundnesse of the matters there
handled, not accustomed to be treated in our language . . . Great care hath
been taken, by forming and deryuing of fit names and termes, out of the
fountaynes of our own tongue, though not altogether most vsuall, yet alwaies
conceyuable and easie to be vnderstood; rather than by vsurping the Latin
termes, or by borrowing the words of any forreine language, least the matters
. . . might haue bene made more obscure to the vnlearned, by setting them
downe in terms vtterly vnknowne unto them.' Compare Jones 1953, 122–3,
and note 49. As Sidney also disapproved of archaic and dialect words (see
110/19 note), his respect for 'the fountaynes of our own tongue' would lead
him to advocate the forming of compound words (see 115/23–4 note) if
enrichment of the vocabulary was required.

38–9 monsters . . . strangers . . . poor Englishman] Sidney's vocabulary here
seems to echo Roger Ascham's description of the 'plaine English man' who
returns from Italy transformed into a stranger ('a right *Italian*') and a 'meruelous monster' (Ascham 1904, 225 and 228).

39–40 coursing of a letter] excessive use of alliteration ('coursing' means 'hunting';
a commoner phrase for alliteration was 'hunting the letter'). Compare Epistle
Dedicatory to *The Shepheards Calender*: 'I scorne and spue out the rakehellye
route of our ragged rymers (for so themselves use to hunt the letter)'. In 1560
Thomas Wilson found fault that some 'vse ouermuch repetition of some one
letter' (Wilson 1909, 167), and by the 1580s heavy initial alliteration was no
longer much practised except for comic effects. Compare Puttenham 1936,
174; Mulcaster, 1925, 286, who allows 'the figure of like letter' if it is not over-
done; and Campion in 1602 (Smith 1904, II, 330). Sidney and Spenser use
alliteration constantly, unobtrusively, and cleverly, often to reinforce syntax.

41 figures and flowers] Compare Puttenham 1936, 138, on 'figures and figuratiue
speaches, which be the flowers as it were and coulours that a Poet setteth
vpon his language by arte'.

winter-starved] damaged by frost. 'Winter-starved' occurs again with
'flowers' in *Astrophil and Stella*, Ninth Song (Ringler 1962, 222).

p. 114/1–6 **Truly I could wish . . . make them wholly theirs]** This articulates Sidney's attitude to sixteenth-century Ciceronianism: the practice of using Cicero as a stylistic model for both poetry and prose (see 90/43). He rejected the slavish imitation of Cicero practised in the mid-century, when, in the words of Francis Bacon, 'Car of Cambridge and Ascham [did] with their lectures and writings almost deify Cicero and Demosthenes, and allure all young men that were studious unto that delicate and polished kind of learning' (Bacon 1974, 26). On this movement see Harvey 1945, Introduction, 14–30. Like Cicero himself and Gabriel Harvey, Sidney believed wisdom and eloquence more valuable than eloquence alone. As he wrote in a letter to his brother Robert, 'so you can speak and write Latin not barbarously, I never require great study in Ciceronianism, the chief abuse of Oxford. *Qui dum verba sectantur, res ipsas negligunt* [who, while they follow the words, neglect the subject matter]' (Duncan-Jones 1989, 293).

3–4 **imitators of Tully and Demosthenes]** In a well-known passage of the *Institutes* (X, i), Quintilian reported that Livy in a letter to his son advised him to take Demosthenes and Cicero (Tully) as models. Many Renaissance critics repeated Livy's advice.

4–5 **Nizolian paper-books]** Commonplace books of phrases from the classics, named after Marius Nizolius, an Italian scholar (born 1498), whose *Thesaurus Ciceronianus* (1535) long retained its usefulness as a Latin phrase-book; see Q. Breen, *Renaissance Studies*, 1 (1953), 48–58. Sidney's friend Henri Estienne wrote an attack on the 'Nizolian' method, *Nizoliodidascalus* (1578) (see Duncan-Jones 1989, 388). On the practice of filling notebooks with choice phrases employed by Elizabethan scholars, see Crane 1937, ch. 2, 33–48.

5 **translation]** transformation. 'Translation' had many meanings in the 16th c.; it could mean, for instance, translation from one language to another (its modern sense); the transference of subject-matter from one stylistic form to another (see 110/23 note); and the metamorphosis of a thing or person from one shape to another.

6 **devour them whole, and make them wholly theirs]** The analogy between reading and eating was a favourite with the early humanists. It derives from Seneca's Epistle 84: 'We also, I say, ought to copy these bees, and sift whatever we have gathered from a varied course of reading, for such things are better preserved if they are kept separate; then, by applying the supervising care with which our nature has endowed us, – in other words, our natural gifts, – we should so blend those flavors into one delicious compound that, even though it betrays its origin, yet it nevertheless is clearly a different thing from that whence it came. This is what we see nature doing in our own bodies without any labor on our part; the food we have eaten, as long as it retains its original quality and floats in our stomachs as an undiluted mass, is a burden; but it passes into tissue and blood only when it has been changed from its original form. So it is with the food which nourishes our higher nature, – we should see to it that whatever we have absorbed should not be allowed to remain unchanged, or it will merely enter the memory and not the reasoning power.' Quoted in Greene 1982, 74. See also Bacon's essay 'Of Studies' (1625).

6–7 **now they cast . . . to the table**] Compare Ralph Lever, *The Arte of Reason* (1573), sig. Iv: 'As for Ciceronians and sugar tongued fellows which labour more for finenes of speach than for knowledge of good matter, they ofte speak much to small purpose, and shaking forth a number of choice wordes and picked sentences, they hinder good learning, with their fond chatte'. Ascham uses a metaphor similar to Sidney's when he recommends that the writer whose style is 'ouer rancke and lustie' should practise the art of the *epitome* or summary, 'as certaine wise men do, that be ouer fat and fleshie: who leauing their owne full and plentifull table, go to soiorne abrode from home for a while, at the temperate diet of some sober man: and so by litle and litle, cut away the grosnesse that is in them . . . *Tullie* himselfe had the same fulnes in him: and therefore went to *Rodes* to cut it away . . . in binding him selfe to translate . . . *Demosthenes* and *Aeschines* orations' (Ascham 1904, 262–3). Sidney later implies that Demosthenes acts as a corrective for Ciceronian 'fulnes' (**I would but invoke Demosthenes' soul,** 19).

7–9 **those Indians . . . nose and lips**] Compare Richard Eden's *Decades of the Newe Worlde* (1555), fol. 209r: 'Bisyde these also, they weare certeyne ringes of golde at theyr eares and nostrelles which they bore ful of holes on both sides, so that the ringes hange vppon theyr lyppes'. This occurs in the middle of a description of the elaborate jewellery worn by men and women in the West Indies.

8 **earrings**] In Elizabethan and Stuart England, as now, these were worn by both sexes.

11 **Tully . . . Catiline**] Catiline's conspiracy – an attempted revolution – took place in Rome during the civil wars between Caesar and Pompey, while Cicero (Tully) was consul. Cicero's speeches against him led to the expulsion of Catiline from the city. His fellow conspirators were executed and Catiline was later killed in battle.

12–13 ***Vivit. . . . venit***] Thomas Wilson translates this Latin phrase in the course of defining **that figure of repetition,** *geminatio verborum*: 'Doublettes as when we rehearse one and the same worde twise together . . . Tullie against Catiline, enueighing sore against his traterous attempts, saieth after a longe rehearsed matter, and yet notwithstanding al this notorious wickednesse: The man liueth still, lieueth? Naie Marie, he cometh into the counsaile house, which is more' (Wilson 1909, 200–1). Sidney quotes from memory this same famous opening to Cicero's *In Catilinam*, I.

13 **well-grounded**] fully justified.

15 **artificially**] by art.

choler] anger.

16 **hale**] drag.

17 **familiar epistle**] informal letter, defined by Angel Day, *The English Secretorie* (1586), as 'the familiar and mutuall talke of one absent friend to another' (1595 ed., 8). Cicero's letters to his friends were collected as *Epistolae familiares*.

too too] a common mannerism for emphasis in prose and poetry, especially, according to *OED*, between 1540 and 1660. Here used as a comic example of 'doubling' (14). The phrase occurs only in Olney.

too too much choler to be choleric] i.e. when any show of anger would be wholly inappropriate (after all, a 'familiar epistle' is a letter to a friend). Duncan-Jones sees a pun on 'colour', or rhetorical figure (Duncan-Jones 1989, 389).

18   **store of**] many.

similiter cadences] a partial anglicizing of the Latin *similiter cadentia*, similar endings; more commonly known by the Greek term *homoioteleuton* (see Lanham 1968). Sidney is referring to the use of rhyme, assonance, and other figures of repetition by public speakers. Gabriel Harvey remarked that *similiter cadentia* were 'somewhat overmuch affected of M. Ascham in our vulgare Tongue' (Harvey 1913, 115). An account of 'Like ending and like falling' was given by Wilson: 'Then the sentences are said to end like, when those wordes doe ende in like sillables which do lacke cases. Thou liues wickedly, thou speakest naughtely . . . Sentences also are said to fall alike when diuers wordes in one sentence ende in like cases, and that in rime. By great trauaile is gotten much auaile' (Wilson 1909, 202). Wilson is one of the first to object to excessive use of these devices, especially in preaching, and he goes on: 'Diuers in this our time delite much in this kinde of writing, which beeing measurably vsed, deliteth much the hearers, otherwise it offendeth, and wearieth mens eares with satietie. S. Augustine had a goodly gifte in this behalfe, and yet some thinkes he forgot measure, and vsed ouermuch this kinde of figure. Notwithstanding, the people were such where he liued, that they tooke much delite in rimed sentences, and in Orations made ballade wise.' Earlier, in dealing with composition, he remarked (166ff.): 'Some end their sentences all alike, making their talke rather to appear rimed Meeter, then to seeme plaine speeche, the which as it much deliteth being measurably vsed, so it much offendeth when no meane is regarded. I heard a preacher deliting much in this kind of composition . . . Some not best disposed, wished the Preacher a Lute, that with his rimed sermon he might vse some pleasant melody, and so the people might take pleasure diuers waies, and dance if they list' (compare 40ff. below). A tradition of highly ornamented prose for sermons persisted throughout the medieval period and into the seventeenth century; see Lyly 1916, Introduction, xliff. See also Erasmus's detailed attack on the rhetorical excesses of 'frier preachers' who 'counterfeicte the Rhetoriciens in their sermons', Erasmus 1965, 88–92.

doth sound with] is appropriate to.

19   **daintiness**] fastidiousness (compare Robertson 1973, 178/25).

20–2   **the sophister . . . for his labour**] With Sidney's account here of a superficial logician, compare Thomas More, *Confutation of Tyndale* (1532), in *Works* (1559), 475: 'For lyke wyse as though a sophyster woulde with a fonde argumente, proue vnto a symple soule, that two egges wer thre, because that there is one, and there be twayne, and one and twayne make three; the simple vnlearned man, though he lacke learnyng to foyle his fond argument, hathe

246 CURRENT NOTES TO PAGE 114

yet wit ynough to laugh therat, and to eate two egges himself, and byd the sophyster take and eate the thyrde.' It is not certain that Sidney took this anecdote from More, for stories involving this simple fallacy were told in schools for generations.

23 **opinion**] of reputation for.

23–4 **seeming fineness**] superficial skill.

25–33 **Now, for similitudes . . . not to be satisfied**] This passage has usually been taken to be an assault on the so-called Euphuists: practitioners of a highly wrought style, Euphuism, which made extensive use of transverse alliteration, assonance, antithesis, and (what Sidney is attacking here) references to exotic bits of natural history (see 26 note below). For accounts of the characteristics of this style, see Lyly 1916, Introduction, and Jonas Barish, 'The Prose Style of John Lyly', *ELH* 23 (1956), 14–35. Although John Lyly's prose fiction *Euphues: The Anatomy of Wyt* (1578) gave its name to the style, Lyly did not invent it; instead he polished and gave a personal stamp to a form of Ciceronianism practised at Oxford in the 1570s. See W. Ringler, 'The Immediate Source of Euphuism', *PMLA* 53 (1938) 678–9. Stephen Gosson was a Euphuist (see Gosson 1974, 41–3), and this passage might refer to his style as well as to Lyly's. Gosson uses **stories of beasts, fowls, and fishes** on pp. 95, 99, 100, 112–13, and elsewhere.

Sidney objects to Euphuism on logical grounds The end of discourse should be effective persuasion, not **seeming fineness** (23–4). Ornamentation for its own sake, in particular the excessive use of **similitude** or simile (compare also Hoskins 1935, 16), does not reinforce argument. Sidney could have learned as much from the discussion of simile in Aristotle's *Rhetoric*, III.

26 **herbarists**] authors of works on the properties of herbs. Characteristic of Euphuistic prose is its witty references to exotic flora and fauna drawn from handbooks on natural history, in particular the works of Pliny and Erasmus. Many of the plants, animals and stones it refers to are obviously invented. Compare also *Astrophil and Stella*, 3.

rifled up] searched out and stolen from.

27 **to wait . . . conceits**] to serve (i.e. to illustrate) any of our ideas.

27, 31, 32 **conceits . . . memory . . . judgment**] Compare 88/4–9 note.

28 **similitude**] simile.

29 **contrary disputer**] opponent in a dispute.

31 **over-swaying**] distracting (with an excess of irrelevant material).

32 **any whit**] at all.

34 **Antonius and Crassus**] introduced as speakers in Cicero's three dialogues *De oratore*. Marcus Antonius (143–87 B.C.), the grandfather of the Mark Antony portrayed in Shakespeare's *Julius Caesar*, was renowned as a public speaker. He held a succession of offices of state and was killed at Rome in the civil wars between Marius and Sylla. L. Licinius Crassus, a statesman who died in 91 B.C., was regarded by his contemporaries as the greatest of Roman

orators. In the second book of *De oratore* Cicero compares these two orators. 'I used to think that Crassus never acquired more learning than was to be obtained by an elementary education; and that Antonius had no learning of any sort at all.' But in fact 'the one thought to appear a more reasonable man if he despised the Greeks, and the other if he appeared completely unlearned'. See also Castiglione 1928, 46: 'And I remember that I have redde in my dayes, that there were some most excellent Orators, which among other their cares, enforced themselves to make everie man believe, that they had no sight in letters, and dissembling their cunning, made semblant their Orations to be made verie simply, and rather as nature and truth ledde them, than studie and arte, the which if it had beene openly knowne, would have put a doubt in the peoples minde, for feare least hee beguiled them.'

36   **not to set by it**] not to think much of it.

   sensibleness] clarity.

37   **credit**] trust. The establishment of an orator's credentials and of a sympathetic rapport with the audience (*ethos*) was considered in rhetoric to be the essential basis for successful persuasion. See Aristotle, *Rhetoric*, II, 1ff., and Cicero, *De oratore*, II, xlv, 189ff.

39   **tracks**] features, attractions (see OED *s.v.* and *s.* tract, *sb.*³). This occurs in Olney; other texts read 'knacks', i.e. tricks.

39–40   **generally**] frequently.

40   **dance to his own music**] Compare Wilson 1909, 167, cited above 18 note.

41   **curiously**] elaborately, affectedly. Castiglione advises the ideal courtier to 'eschue as much as a man may, and as a sharpe and daungerous rocke, too much curiousnesse' (affectation) (Castiglione 1928, 46).

42–4   **I have found . . . professors of learning**] This passage summarizes Sidney's position on how writers should display their learning; and a similar position was taken throughout the seventeenth-century by many gentlemanly amateur poets. It derives from Castiglione's influential discussion of *sprezzatura*, translated by Thomas Hoby as 'Recklesnesse', 'a certaine disgracing to cover arte withall'; see Castiglione 1928, 45–9. Puttenham takes a position slightly different from Sidney's (Puttenham 1936, 253): 'we doe allow our Courtly Poet to be a dissembler only in the subtilties of his arte: that is, when he is most artificiall, so to disguise and cloake it as it may not appeare, nor seeme to proceede from him by any studie or trade of rules, but to be his naturall: nor so euidently to be descried, as euery ladde that reades him shall say he is a good scholler, but will rather haue him to know his arte well, and little to vse it'. The eloquence of Puttenham's courtier poet is 'artificiall' – that is, learned from the rules of art as they are taught in books and schools; while the eloquence of Sidney's has been acquired empirically and can thus be considered more 'naturall'. This is the distinction Harington made; see 109/35–6 note.

43   **smally**] little.

43–4   **professors of**] claimants to.

p. 115/2 art] the rules or skills of rhetoric taught in schools.

3 **to show art, and not to hide art**] recalls *ars est celare artem* (it is art to hide art), a phrase of post-classical origin.

5 **pounded**] placed in a pound or enclosure for stray animals. Sidney may still be thinking of himself as a horse (see Duncan-Jones 1989, 389, and compare 108/22 note).

6–7 **in this wordish consideration**] i.e. in matters of diction and style.

8 **which is not**] which is not to presume.

11 **bend**] turn.

12–25 **our language . . . a language**] Sidney denies the force of what had been common allegations against English: (1) that it was not a 'pure' language; (2) that it was a language which had no rules. See Jones 1953, especially chs IV–VI.

13 **occasion**] opportunity.

14 **a mingled language**] See Sir John Cheke's letter of 1557 (Castiglione 1928, 7–8): 'I am of this opinion that our own tung shold be written cleane and pure, unmixt and unmangeled with borowing of other tunges, wherin if we take not heed by tijm, ever borowing and never payeng, she shall be fain to keep her house as bankrupt'. Compare E.K.'s complaint in the preface to *The Shepheardes Calender* that 'they have made our English tongue, a gallimaufray or hodgepodge of al other speches' (Spenser 1989, 16). Many scholars resisted the infiltration of English with borrowed words from other languages; Sidney, on the other hand, believes that such borrowings have enriched the English tongue. In this he shares the opinion of Count Lewis in the *Courtier*, who considers borrowings in Italian to be necessary if it is to become 'commune, plentifull, and variable, and (as it were) like a delicious garden full of sundrie flowers and fruites' (Castiglione 1928, 58).

15 **best of both the other**] Since Sidney sets English against Latin and Greek in line 24, he probably intends them here too. It is against these two languages that Drayton in his *Elegy: to Henry Reynolds* claims that Sidney set up English in successful rivalry.

15–16 **it wanteth grammar . . . it wanteth not grammar**] it lacks grammar . . . it does not need grammar, with a play on 'wanteth'. Linguistic interest in English in the first part of the sixteenth century was largely restricted to the enriching of the vocabulary in order to bring it up to the level of the classical languages. Grammar was studied only in relation to Latin. But after Sir John Cheke's time a new interest in English spelling and pronunciation, which culminated in Richard Mulcaster's *Elementarie which entreateth of the right writing of our English tung* (1582), led on to a consideration of English grammar. In 1580 William Bullokar promised a 'ruled Grammar for Inglish' and fulfilled the promise in 1586. The first systematic grammar was the work of a Ramist, Paul Greaves, *Grammatica Anglicana* (1594). But in the 1580s poetic theory and practice were closely bound up with linguistic issues, as Gabriel Harvey explains in a letter to Spenser: 'There is no one more regular and justifiable direction, eyther for the assured and infallible Certaintie of our English Artificiall Prosodye particularly, or generally to bring our Language into Arte and to frame a Grammer or Rhetorike thereof, than first of all vniuersally to agree vpon one and the same ortographie, in all pointes conformable and proportionate to our common natural prosodye' (Smith 1904, I, 102).

19 **the Tower of Babylon's curse**] Babylon the capital of Chaldea was thought to have been built on the site of the Tower of Babel (Genesis 10: 10). The tower was built at a time when all the people of the earth spoke the same language, and it was intended to reach as far as heaven. 'And the Lord said, Behold, the people is one, and they have all one language; and this they begin to do: and now nothing will be restrained from them, which they have imagined to do. Go to, let us go down, and there confound their language, that they may not understand one another's speech. So the Lord scattered them abroad from thence upon the face of the earth: and they left off to build the city' (Genesis 11: 6–8). The tower is often invoked in Renaissance discussions of language.

20 **that a man should be put to school to learn his mother-tongue**] It was at least a generation after Sidney's time before there was any demand among educationalists for English composition to be taught in schools. Richard Carew (1555–1620), who admired Sidney and was at Oxford with him, wrote an account of *The Excellency of the English Tongue* (see Smith 1904, II, 285–94) which was included in William Camden's *Remains concerning Britain* (1614 ed.). He took up many of Sidney's points, praising English for its lack of 'those declensions, flexions, and variations, which are incydent to many other tongues, but a few articles gouerne all our verbes, and Nownes, and so wee neede a very shorte grammar', and claiming that the language is easy to learn (Smith 1904, II, 288). Compare also Agrippa 1569, sig. C3v: 'Grammar dothe of righte boaste her selfe to be the arte of speakinge, but falsely, sithe that we learne it much better of our mothers, and of nourises, then of the Grammarians.'

21–2 **uttering . . . the end of speech**] An Elizabethan commonplace. Compare Wilson 1909, 2; Harvey 1913, 115; and Ralph Lever, *The Arte of Reason* (1573), Forespeach (Introduction), in which Lever vigorously proclaims the resources of English for intellectual purposes.

23–4 **compositions . . . together**] compound words. Sidney was much praised for his use of compounds by his successors. Joseph Hall, *Virgidemiarum* (1598), VI, 255–8, claims that Philisides (Sidney's pen-name for himself in the *Arcadia*) imported this 'new elegance' from France, and that it had been overused by later poets. On Sidney's use of compounds in poetry see Ringler 1962, Introduction, liii, and Rubel 1941, 204. On Sidney's compounds in the *Apology*, see Cook 1890, 130 note. In addition to his inventions in Greek (94/27 and 100/41), some compounds are adapted from classical languages: 'death-bringing' (86/33) from Latin *mortifer*; 'earth-creeping' (117/4), 'low-creeping' (108/13) from Greek *hamaitupes*; 'honey-flowing' (113/36) from Latin *mellifluus*. Others are Sidney's own invention: 'paper-blurrers' (109/25); 'poet-whippers' (100/10); and 'afterlivers' (97/25). W. L. Renwick, *MLR* 17 (1922), 1–16, argues that in their use of compounds as in other features of style the English New Poets of the 1580s were imitating the practice of the French Pléiade. But the most likely French influence is that of du Bartas, whose *Sepmaine sainte* Sidney translated, and whose idiosyncratic practice in compounding words is discussed in *Works of Guillaume de Salluste Sieur du Bartas*, ed. U. T. Holmes, J. C. Lyons and R. W. Linker (Chapel Hill, 1935), I, 173–8.

26 **of versifying there are two sorts**] The two ways of making verse referred to here are known as the 'accentual' and the 'quantitative'. In accentual metre (the most common form in English from Chaucer's time to our own), the syllables in each line are counted and the heavy or light accent or stress of the syllables are played off against one another. Quantitative metre (the form used by ancient Greek and Latin poets) is based on the quantity or length of each syllable – the time it takes to say aloud. Short and long syllables are arranged in formal patterns which vary according to the sort of poem you are writing. See Philip Hobsbaum, *Metre, Rhythm and Verse Form* (London, 1996), chs 1 and 6.

In the sixteenth century quantitative metre was commonly referred to as 'verse' (28) and accentual metre as 'rhythm' or 'rhyme' (30 and **116/1**); compare **102/2**. In medieval Latin the terms *rithmi* and *rithmici versus* were used to denote the more popular accentual verse in contrast to the more learned quantitative verse. Common use of similar sound endings in *rithmi* led to the use of 'rime' (later 'rhyme') as the general term for compositions with this feature. In the sixteenth century 'verse' continues to be contrasted with 'rhyme'; compare the juxtaposition of these terms in texts by Gascoigne, Spenser, Stanyhurst, and Harvey (Smith 1904, I, 50, 89, 140, and 360).

27 **quantity**] See above, 26 note.

28 **number**] the number of syllables in a line (and of lines in a stanza); see Robertson 1973, 89/25.

29 **accent**] stress (see 26 note).

30 **Whether**] which.

30–1 **Whether of these be the most excellent**] Argument over which of the two metres (the accentual or the quantitative) was better for English poetry was intense in the second half of the sixteenth century. For a full discussion of the debate and of Sidney's role in it, see Attridge 1974; and on the place of the debate in the formation of English national identity, see Helgerson 1992, 25–40. Two manuscripts of the *Old Arcadia* include a discussion on metre between two shepherds, Dicus and Lalus, 'Dicus liking the measured, and Lalus the rhyming', which may have formed the basis for this passage in the *Apology* (Robertson 1973, 89–90). Dicus argues that since the chief beauty of poetry lies in its musical quality, quantitative metre is best (compare **more fit for music**, 31–2), because it closely resembles music in its attention to the timing of each syllable, word and phrase. When verse is set to music the two artforms perfectly complement one another, 'so that either by the time [of the music] a poet should straight know how every word should be measured unto it, or by the verse as soon find out the full quantity of the music. Besides that it hath in itself a kind . . . of secret music, since by the measure one may perceive some verses running with a high note [i.e. with resonant phrases] fit for great matters, some with a light foot [i.e. at a rapid pace] fit for no greater than amorous conceits.' Lalus retorts that Dicus 'did much abuse the dignity of poetry to apply it [i.e. to enslave it] to music, since rather music is a servant to poetry, for by the one the ear only, by the other the mind, was pleased'. If music does not respond well to the carefully counted syllables of accentual verse, 'it is the musician's fault and not the poet's, since the poet is to look but to beautify his words to the most delight, which no doubt is more had by the rhyme, especially to common ears to which the poet doth most direct his studies, and therefore is called the popular philosopher' (compare 92/4). This passage, as well as the *Apology* here, confirms Sidney's serious interest in naturalizing classical metres, an interest which was ascribed to him by Spenser (Smith 1904, I, 89).

32 **both words and time**] 'words' refers to verse, and 'time' to music. Both quantitative verse and music are concerned with measuring the time taken to utter each syllable or to sing each note. Ponsonby has 'tune' for 'time' but the speech of Dicus in *OA* suggests that 'time' is the correct reading. See 30–1 note, and compare 85/4 note.

32–3 **more fit lively to express divers passions**] better suited to expressing a variety of emotions vividly – as if they were being lived. Compare 101/35 note. Puttenham too seems to have valued the poet's ability to alter the mood of his listeners: an adept use of metre 'doth alter the nature of the Poesie, and make it either lighter or grauer, or more merry, or mournfull, and many wayes passionate to the eare and hart of the hearer, seeming for this point that our maker by his measures and concordes [i.e. metres and rhymes] of sundry proportions doth counterfait the harmonicall tunes of the vocall and instrumentall Musickes' (Puttenham 1936, 84). Puttenham is talking about the placing of lines of different metres within a stanza, Sidney about the placing of words within a line.

33 **the low or lofty sound**] It is hard to know precisely what Sidney means here. Does he mean 'soft or loud', 'sweet or majestic' (see 36–7), or 'merry, or mournfull' (Puttenham's phrase; see 32–3 note above)? He could be suggesting that verse is able to replicate the intonation patterns of spoken English. According to rhetorical teaching on the art of delivering an oration, volume, tone, and pitch were to be modulated according to the nature of the discourse; see *Ad Herennium*, III, xi, 19–xiv, 25. Perhaps Sidney believed that each syllable of each written word could be given a definite tonal value equivalent to the varied tones of speech, just as contemporary proponents of quantitative verse believed that it would be possible to establish the precise length of each syllable in English (see 33–4 note below).

33–4 **well-weighed syllable**] Many Elizabethan discussions of quantitative verse degenerate into an ineffectual attempt to establish the length of syllables in English words. Thus every syllable in Elizabethan quantitative verse could be said to have been 'well-weighed' (carefully measured or considered). Compare 101/30–2.

34 **The latter**] i.e. modern rhymed verse.

35 **in fine**] to conclude.

37ff.   **Truly the English**] This is one of the most emphatic statements of the new-found confidence with which Sidney's generation viewed their native language. 'The suddenness with which writers began to recognise the eloquent nature of the mother tongue enables us to date the turning point not earlier than 1575 nor later than 1580' (Jones 1953, 211).

37   **vulgar**] modern, vernacular.

38–116/14   **for, for the ancient . . . too much enlarged**] This passage seems to be based on Sidney's rules for scansion (derived apparently from the Rules of Archdeacon Drant (see Smith 1904, I, 89ff.)), which were written in the margin of one of the manuscripts of the *Old Arcadia* (*OA*, 71–2). The fourth rule reads: 'Because our tongue being full of consonants and monosyllables, the vowel slides away quicklier than in Greek or Latin, which be full of vowels and long words. Yet are such vowels long as the pronunciation makes long.' And the fifth: 'Elisions, when one vowel meets with another, used indifferently as the advantage of the verse best serves . . . and like scope doth Petrarch take to himself sometimes to use'.

39   **elisions**] shortening words by conflating syllables. This happens when a word ending in a vowel is followed by a word beginning with a vowel.

  Dutch] German. On Sidney's difficulty with German see his letter to Languet, February 1574: 'Of the German language . . . I absolutely despair. It has a sort of harshness' (Feuillerat 1912–26, III, 84).

40   **sweet sliding**] i.e. smooth progress.

42   *antepenultima*] (Latin) last but two. The term is also used by Puttenham (Puttenham 1936, 71, 115, etc.) and by seventeenth-century prosodists.

44   **dactyls**] A 'dactyl' is a stressed followed by two unstressed beats (as in 'particle').

p. 116/1   **rhyme**] modern accentual verse. Compare 115/26 note.

3   **absolutely**] well.

  caesura] Sidney adapts the classical term to the requirements of English. In Latin the caesura refers to the division of a metrical foot and in particular to the division of a foot in the middle of a line. Sidney regards it as the 'breathing place' or natural pause in an English long line. Gascoigne leaves the use of the caesura 'at discretion of the wryter' (Smith 1904, I, 54), while Puttenham thinks that 'in euery long verse the *Cesure* ought to be kept precisely' – that is, after the fourth syllable (Puttenham 1936, 75).

6   **masculine**] Sidney's use of the term as applied to rhyme ending in stressed syllables ('due: true') is the first recorded use in English; similarly with **female** (7) (or feminine) as applied to two-syllabled rhyme between words ending in unstressed syllables ('father: rather'). W. Ringler maintains that Sidney reintroduced feminine rhyme into English verse (Ringler 1962, Introduction, lvi).

8   *sdrucciola*] slippery (Italian): rhymes in which there are several unstressed

syllables after the last stressed syllable. The Italian term had a limited currency in seventeenth-century English discussions of prosody; see *OED s. v.*

12 **motion: potion**] In Sidney's time these words had three syllables (mo-ti-on).

15–117/12 **So that . . . epitaph**] The conclusion of Sidney's *Apology* falls into three parts, as was usually recommended for the conclusion of an oration (see *Ad Herennium*, II, xxx, 47–xxxi, 50). The parts are: (1) a summing-up, 15–20; (2) an amplification invoking authorities, 20–37; (3) an emotional appeal to the self-interest of the audience, 38 to the end.

17 **blames**] charges.

18–19 **poet-apes**] crude imitators of poets (apes were supposed to be addicted to copying humans). Compare 'Pindare's Apes' in *Astrophil and Stella*, 3, which refers to the imitation of Pindar and other Greek poets practised by the Pléiade. The metaphor of the 'poet-ape' derives from Latin school verse of the late medieval period; see Curtius 1953, Excursus XIX, 538–40.

20 **I conjure you**] I appeal to you (**in the name of the Nine Muses**, 21–2). The word 'conjure' may also contain a comic suggestion that Sidney is casting a magic spell on his readers (compare 103/5 notes).

23 **next inheritors to fools**] may refer to the common sixteenth-century practice of paying money to obtain the legal guardianship of the mentally ill, with the aim of getting control of their inheritance.

25 **the ancient treasurers of . . . divinity**] i.e. those who kept the ancient gods alive in people's memories. Compare Aristotle, *Metaphysics*, III, iv, 12. His authority was often invoked on this point; see Boccaccio 1930, XIV, viii, and 163 note.

26 **Bembus**] See 108/33 note. Compare the first chapters of *Le prose* by Pietro Bembo.

27 **Scaliger**] See 108/35 note. His recurrent theme in *Poetices libri septem* is the wisdom to be derived from the *Aeneid*; but the reference here is precise. 'Certainly you cannot become a better man, or a man better adapted to society from the precepts of any philosopher than you can by reading Virgil' (Scaliger 1617, III, xix, 238).

29 **Clauserus, the translator of Cornutus**] L. Annaeus Cornutus (first century A.D.), a Stoic philosopher and teacher, taught the poets Persius and Lucan. Most of his written work is lost. Conrad Clauser, a German humanist, published a translation, with commentary, of his *De natura deorum gentilium* (Basel, 1543). Sidney draws here on Clauser's prefatory letter to his kinsman, Christoph Clauser. 'Who were these first philosophers? Hesiod and Homer, from whom all human philosophy took its beginning, through whom the Holy Name was pleased to reveal it: these presented the precepts of philosophy to us under the veil of fables. Do you seek dialectic, or logic, and all the arts of discourse? You will discover it in the fables of the poets. Do you seek physics or natural philosophy? . . . Do you seek ethics, all the divisions of moral philosophy? You will discover them amply set out in the fables of the poets.'

30 **fables**] fictions.

31 *quid non?*] (Latin) what not?

32–3 **mysteries . . . written darkly**] In some medieval and Renaissance thought about the nature of verbal composition a certain degree of 'darkness' or obscurity was seen as essential to the greatest poetry; see H. J. Chaytor, *From Script to Print* (Cambridge, 1945), 68ff.; Boccaccio 1930, 157 note; and Rainolds 1940, 74 note. Sidney invokes this ancient belief to claim his audience's indulgence towards his presentation of his own theory of poetry, which is quite different.

34–5 **Landino . . . a divine fury**] Sidney again makes use of a theory which he has earlier rejected (see 107/36–7 note). Cristoforo Landino (1424–98) was one of the most influential Florentine humanists of the Medici court, tutor to Lorenzo the Magnificent, author of *Disputationes Camaldulenses* and Latin poems, translator of Pliny, and commentator on Virgil, Horace, and Dante. He discusses 'divine fury' in his edition of Dante's *Divine Comedy* (Florence, 1481), Prologue (vii), and in the *Disputationes*, book III, in a passage which Sidney seems to echo several times in the *Apology*: 'Whom sooner than Plato should I believe that poetry is of the gods rather than men? For he says in the *Ion* that it is not given us by human means but creeps into our minds by a divine madness. Moreover, in the book entitled *Phaedrus*, when he had done explaining the three other kinds of divine madness, then he declares – if I am not mistaken – that there is a fourth which is to be understood as poetical. He tells us that, while they had their abode in the heavens, our souls shared in that harmony which exists in God's eternal mind and which is produced by the motions of the heavens. Yes – even weighed down by desire for perishable things and so fallen into this lower world, locked in our bodies, hampered by our earthly joints and our decaying limbs – they remain just capable of registering in the ear those human symphonies which, far as they are from the heavenly harmony, are still its likenesses and images. They lead us to an unacknowledged recollection of heavenly things, inflame us with the burning desire to fly back to our former homeland, and so we come to know that true music of which they are the shadowy resemblance. So far as we may in the filthy dungeon of the flesh, we endeavour to echo that music in our own – not with the tuning of voices, as common and frivolous musicians do . . . but rather as those do that with graver judgment imitate the divine harmony, and in choicest song express our deepest thoughts, and moved by the divine madness reveal things so wonderful, inspired so far beyond merely human capacity, that when the madness ebbs, they wonder at themselves and are dumbstruck. These do not merely flatter the ear, they soothe the soul with sweet nectar and divine ambrosia. These then are our godlike poets, the holy priesthood of the Muses' (*Disputationes Camaldulenses*, ed. Peter Lohe (Florence, 1980), III/18–112/18, trans. R. M. Cummings). For Landino's influence on Renaissance literary theory, see A. Chastel, *Marcel Ficin et l'art* (Geneva and Lille, 1954), 25 and notes.

35 **divine fury**] madness inspired by the gods. See Plato, *Ion*, 534.

36 **make you immortal**] From ancient times poets had promised eternal fame to their subjects; see Curtius 1953, excursus IX, 476–7. Renaissance poets

became more insistent; see Clements 1942, ch. 3, 84–121. Erasmus in *The Praise of Folly* remarked that it was the characteristic foolishness of poets to make this promise: 'it is a wonderous thyng to see, how . . . they wene to be made immortall, and Gods peres, promisyng others also like immortalitee therby' (Erasmus 1965, 73).

38–41 **Thus doing . . . superlatives**] This passage resembles Erasmus's account of the pride taken by 'paper-blurrers' in seeing their books in 'euery bokebynders shoppe', in reading 'theyr names, surnames, and bynames' on the title-pages, and in furnishing their texts with 'epistles, with verses, and with mattiers of praise, sent from fooles, to fooles: and from asses, to asses' (Erasmus 1965, 75).

38 **in the printers' shops**] This is not exactly desirable, considering Sidney's attitude to contemporary poets who appeared in print (compare 109/11–23).

39 **of kin to many a poetical preface**] i.e. like your relations, many dedicatory poems will carry your name.

40 **most fair, most rich, most wise**] phrases such as were addressed to many a dedicatee in a 'poetical preface'.

  dwell upon] i.e. spend your life surrounded by.

41 **superlatives**] In his *Certayne Notes of Instruction Concerning the Making of Verse or Ryme in English* (1575) George Gascoigne states that in praising his mistress 'I would . . . finde some supernaturall cause wherby my penne might walke in the superlatiue degree' (Smith 1904, I, 48).

  libertino patre natus] son of a freedman (i.e. a slave who has been freed). Horace applies this phrase to himself in *Satires*, I, vi, 6.

42 *Herculea proles*] offspring of Hercules.

43 *Si quid mea carmina possunt*] Virgil, *Aeneid*, IX, 446: 'If my verses can achieve anything'.

p. 117/1 **Dante's Beatrix, or Virgil's Anchises**] In Dante's *Divine Comedy* Beatrice inhabits Paradise; in the *Aeneid* Aeneas meets his dead father Anchises in the Elysian fields, the place where those favoured by the gods live in perpetual happiness. Landino (*Disputationes Camaldulenses*, book IV) points out that Dante took the *Aeneid* as his model.

2 **fie of**] shame on.

3 **cataract of Nilus**] Compare Cicero, *Somnium Scipionis* (a text which, with the commentary by Macrobius, was held in immense prestige in the Middle Ages), V, 13: 'Filled with the sound of the music of the spheres, men's ears are deafened. No sense in man is duller than hearing, just as those people who dwell near the place where the Nile falls down from the great mountains to the regions called Catadupa, have no sense of hearing on account of noise.' Compare also Seneca, *Naturales quaestiones*, IV, ii, 5.

  planet-like music] refers to the notion of Pythagoras, often appropriated by Renaissance writers, that the movement of the stars and planets produces heavenly music which can only be faintly heard on earth by the best of earth's inhabitants. See Cicero, *Somnium Scipionis*, V, and Landino, *Disputationes Camaldulenses*, quoted above, 34–5 note. Gosson's attack on poetry also attacks the innovations of contemporary music and urges musicians 'If you will bee good Scholers, and profite well in the Arte of Musicke . . . looke vp to heauen: the order of the Spheres, the vnfallible motion of the Planets' (Gosson 1974, 83). Sidney is implying that poet-haters like Gosson are tone-deaf.

5 **rustical disdain**] i.e. the contempt felt by country-dwellers for what they do not understand. The peasant Dametas in the two *Arcadias* is full of it.

6 **mome**] fool. In fairly common use in the sixteenth-century, the term may be derived from the proper noun '**Momus**', who is the son of Night in Greek myth and the personification of bad-tempered criticism. Cornelius Agrippa suspects that for his attacks on the arts 'the peeuishe Poets will put me in theyr verses for Momus' (Agrippa 1569, sig. A1v).

7 **Midas**] king of Phrygia, acted as judge in a musical contest between Apollo and Pan, and awarded the prize to Pan. As punishment for his poor taste Apollo changed his ears to those of an ass. See Ovid, *Metamorphoses*, XI, 146ff.

8 **Bubonax**] Sidney's conflation of two names, Hipponax and Bupalus. The unusual ugliness of Hipponax (c. 500 B.C.), a satiric poet from Ephesus, was portrayed by two sculptors, Bupalus and Athenis. Hipponax's counter-attack in verse was said to have driven the sculptors to suicide. See Pliny, *Natural History*, XXXVI, 12.

8–9 **rhymed to death . . . in Ireland**] The Irish were said to be able to kill men or animals with their poetry, and Sidney's own father had been threatened with death by Irish bards (see Duncan-Jones 1989, 390–1, and Duncan-Jones 1991, 110). Reginald Scot in *The Discoverie of Witchcraft* (1584), III, 15, reported that the Irish 'will not stick to affirm that they can rime either man or beast to death'. See also Shakespeare, *As You Like It*, III, ii, 185; Ben Jonson's Apologetic Preface to *Poetaster*, and Campion (Smith 1904, II, 330).

11–12 **when you die . . . epitaph**] In *The Pilgrimage to Parnassus* (ed. Leishman), V, 533–4, Philomusus borrows this threat to the despiser of poetry: 'Noe Epitaph adorne his baser hearse / That in his lifetime cares not for a verse'.

INDEX

Abondio, Antonio 49
Abradatas 61, 63, 93/20, 171
Abraham 49, 91/39, 104/23, 166, 209
Achilles 53, 72, 91/9, 95/26, 99/28,
    105/41, 162–3, 178, 192
Adam 43, 86/7, 141–2
Ad Herennium see Rhetorica ad
    Herennium
Adrian *see* Hadrian
Aeneas 26, 53, 58–9, 67, 72, 85,
    91/20, 92/29–35, 95/26–37,
    99/29–100/6, 103/42, 139–40,
    162–3, 165, 168, 178, 193–4
Aeschylus 164, 233
Aesculapius 119
Aesop, fables of 92/5–7, 103/21–3,
    108/1, 123, 166–7, 170, 180, 187,
    205, 218–20
Agamemnon 91/5–11, 139, 162–4
Agricola, Rudolph 175
Agrippa, Henry Cornelius 37
    Vanitie of the Artes and Sciences
    34–5, 101/12–16, 123, 131, 152–4,
    196–204 *passim*, 213, 219, 249,
    256
Agrippa, Menenius 96/13–29, 180,
    217
Ajax 91/4–6, 162
Alan of Lille 182
Albinus, Clodius 84/3–6, 131, 173
Albion 105/6, 211
Alcibiades 92/19, 167
Alençon-Anjou, Francis, duke of 3,
    7, 12–14, 71, 189

Alexander of Villedieu 200
Alexander Pheraeus 98/34–8, 189
Alexander the Great 6, 27, 48, 55,
    65, 72, 92/38, 97/23, 105/33–41,
    107/41, 112/35, 157, 169, 183, 192,
    212–13, 219, 239
Alfonso V of Aragon 89/30, 157
Amadis de Gaule 20n, 95/34, 178
Amphion 41, 45, 82/22, 86/29,
    124–5, 144
Amyot, Jean 37, 156–60, 172, 176
Anaxagoras 215
Anaximenes 153
Anchises 58, 91/1, 95/37, 99/43,
    117/2, 162
Antonius, Marcus 114/34, 246–7
Apelles 239
Apollo 44, 83/4, 107/44, 124, 127–8,
    131, 144, 256
Apuleius, Lucius 11, 112/6, 236–7
Aquinas, Thomas 174, 203
Araspas 171
Aratus 126, 144, 217
Aretino, Pietro 196
Ariosto, Lodovico, *Orlando Furioso*
    37, 85/31, 99/29, 105/25–6, 139,
    193, 212; *see also* Harington,
    John
Aristotle 34, 37, 55, 75, 94/34,
    105/36, 116/25, 121–3, 127, 134,
    138, 140, 186, 199, 201, 203, 213,
    227, 253
    Art of Poetry (*Poetics*) 86/17–18,
    92/12–21, 95/31–3, 108/4,

Severus, Lucius Septimius 94/4–5, 131, 173
Shakespeare, William
  As You Like It 256
  Coriolanus 180
  Hamlet 189, 240–1
  Henry V 121, 233–4
  Julius Caesar 157
  King Lear 69
  Love's Labour's Lost 177
  Richard II 224
  Venus and Adonis 121
Sibyl 84/11, 131
Sidney, Henry (Sidney's father) 5, 7, 129–30
Sidney, Mary (Sidney's mother) 5
Sidney, Mary (Sidney's sister) see Pembroke
Sidney, Philip
  Arcadia, New 9–10, 29, 37, 128, 149, 178, 180, 204, 207, 211, 256
  Arcadia, Old 8, 29–31, 40–1, 49, 73, 121, 128, 131, 166, 178–83 passim, 205–8, 236, 250–2, 256
  Astrophil and Stella 5, 6, 29–30, 121, 125, 153, 178, 190, 193, 220–1, 225, 240–2, 246, 253
  Certain Sonnets 121, 189
  Defence of Leicester 7, 9, 14–16, 183
  Discourse on Irish Affairs 7
  Lady of May 239
  letters 12–14, 59, 120, 129–30, 135–6, 171, 189, 240, 243, 252
Sidney, Robert 59, 120, 129, 135–6, 171, 240, 243
Silvestris, Bernard 182
Simonides 106/34, 143, 200, 216
sirens 102/25, 202
Socrates 47–8, 94/4, 107/44–108/2, 173, 216, 219–20
Solomon, Song of 19, 86/23, 144
Solon 82/34–8, 126–7, 144
Sophocles 91/4–7, 108/30, 162, 164, 221
Sortes Virgilianae 83/44, 131
Southwell, Robert 206–7

Spenser, Edmund 25–6, 69, 134, 148–9, 222, 225, 248, 250–1
  Faerie Queene 151, 182–3, 192, 206, 235
  Shepheardes Calender 2–3, 15, 20, 25–6, 35, 49, 110/17–21, 122, 128, 183, 199, 207, 213, 221, 224–5, 229–31, 242, 248
  View . . . of Ireland 129
Sphinx 105/4, 210
Starkey, Thomas 159
Statius, Publius 192–3
Strabo 123, 203
Stubbes, Philip 3
Suetonius 168, 174
Surrey, Henry Howard, earl of 14–15, 69, 110/16–17, 229–30
Sylla, Lucius 94/6 and 10, 173–4, 246

Tantalus 26, 92/34, 169
Tarquinius, Sextus 51, 93/18, 147, 171
Tarquin the Proud 93/18, 171
Tasso, Torquato 182, 193, 207
Temple, William 4, 8, 120, 143
Terence 98/13–14, 185–7, 220
  Eunuch 91/14, 111/15–18, 164, 187, 234, 239
  Heautontimorumenos 107/42–3, 220, 234
Tertullian 16, 45
Thales 82/32, 126, 153
Theagenes 85/30, 87/33, 139
theatre 13, 16–33 passim, 61–73 passim, 98, 110–13, 91/4–7, 93/41–4, 103/23–5, 110/28–113/17, 126, 185–9, 192, 205–7, 223, 232–40
Theban brothers (Eteocles and Polynices) 91/13, 163–4
Theocritus 110/20, 183, 231
Theognis 126, 144
Theophrastus 140
Thraso 98/14, 113/8, 187, 239
Thyestes 164
Tibullus, Albius 184
Titian 168